ADAPTING BUILDINGS AND CITIES FOR CLIMATE CHANGE

A 21st Century Survival Guide

Second Edition

Sue Roaf

David Crichton and Fergus Nicol

AMSTERDAM • BOSTON • HEIDELBERG • LONDON • NEW YORK • OXFORD
PARIS • SAN DIEGO • SAN FRANCISCO • SINGAPORE • SYDNEY • TOKYO

Architectural Press is an imprint of Elsevier

ELSEVIER

Architectural
Press

Architectural Press is an imprint of Elsevier
Linacre House, Jordan Hill, Oxford OX2 8DP, UK
30 Corporate Drive, Suite 400, Burlington, MA 01803, USA

First edition 2005
Second edition 2009

Notices

Knowledge and best practice in this field are constantly changing. As new research and experience broaden
our understanding, changes in research methods, professional practices, or medical treatment may become
necessary.

Practitioners and researchers must always rely on their own experience and knowledge in evaluating and using
any information, methods, compounds, or experiments described herein. In using such information or methods
they should be mindful of their own safety and the safety of others, including parties for whom they have a
professional responsibility.

To the fullest extent of the law, neither the Publisher nor the authors, contributors, or editors, assume any liability
for any injury and/or damage to persons or property as a matter of products liability, negligence or otherwise,
or from any use or operation of any methods, products, instructions, or ideas contained in the material herein.

British Library Cataloguing in Publication Data
Roaf, Susan.
  Adapting buildings and cities for climate change. – 2nd
  ed.
    1. Architecture and climate. 2. Architecture–Environmental
    aspects. 3. Architecture and energy conservation.
    4. Ecological houses. 5. Dwellings–Energy conservation.
    6. Construction industry–Appropriate technology.
    I. Title
    720.4'7-dc22

Library of Congress Control Number: 2009928670

ISBN: 978-1-85617-720-7

For information on all Architectural Press publications
visit our website at www.architecturalpress.com

Typeset by Macmillan Publishing Solutions
www.macmillansolutions.com

Printed and bound in Italy
09 10 11 12 13   10 9 8 7 6 5 4 3 2 1

CONTENTS

PREFACE TO THE SECOND EDITION

Much has changed since I wrote the preface to the first edition of this book in 2004. The possibilities we wrote of then have begun to manifest themselves as realities in the forms of floods, fires, famines and economic meltdown. The simple question I asked then, however, about why are we doing it all wrong, has not been answered.

What has really surprised me has been the rate of the changes we see happening all around us. In 2003 the best science told us that the summer Arctic ice would be gone by 2070 and we were shocked. We were recently told that it may be gone in less than a decade. Reports are out that suggest that fundamental resources like Lake Mead in Nevada, the body of water in a hot desert that provides the water and energy for Las Vegas, may be gone within decades. We were told in 2003 that we must not exceed 550 ppm of carbon dioxide (CO_2) in our atmosphere if we want to comfortably survive, now that figure has fallen to 350 ppm, well below current levels.

Today we look around and see a world divided between those who are unrestrained in their energy profligacy, building irresponsible cities where cities should never be, vying to see who can build the tallest building in the world and literally unconnected to the fact that they are contributing to the destruction of our common future. Do they really think that in 10 years' time anyone will want to own or occupy such buildings that are even now environmental pariahs? Are such people so out of touch with reality?

On the one hand, we see the growing generation of climate change refugees, from Myanmar and the Maldives to Hull and Tewkesbury, people who have lost their homes, their livelihoods and all too often their loved ones. Many different groups are now deeply affected by the 'Perfect Storm' we are entering, from those driven from their lands by heat and drought to investors who have been landed with a generation of buildings they can no longer afford to cool in a warming world, or are able to sell.

On the other hand, we see ordinary people and communities stepping up to take the lead, where so many of our so called 'leaders' have failed us, and new paradigms of how buildings and communities can be resourced and organized to protect the quality of life of those in them. We are on the threshold of a new and truly twenty-first century language of low-carbon and resilient buildings informed and born of the Global Commons.

The final conclusion of our book is pretty stark. We have been told by the science that we only have a few years to reduce our carbon emissions to levels that will prevent climate chaos, to

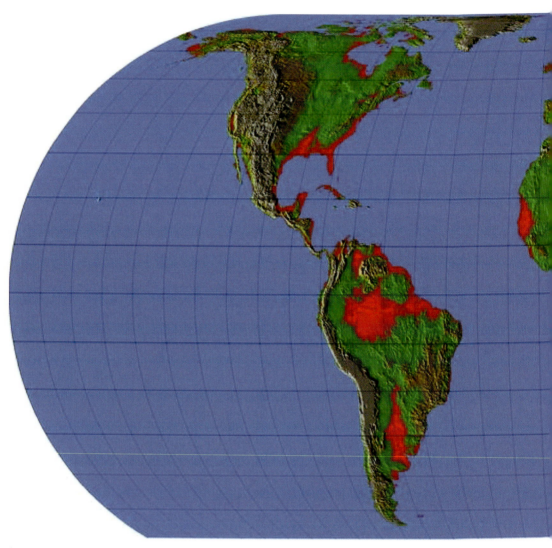

1.
Map of the world showing in red those areas that would be inundated if all the ice caps melted, causing a rise in global sea levels of up to 100 m.
Source: Laurence Williams (2002) *An End to Global Warming*. Pergamon. Reproduced with permission.

effectively mitigate. We believe that in the face of rapid and catastrophic change the more pressing challenge is to develop the processes by which we can adapt to at least three degrees of climate change in the coming handful of decades. All around us now is evidence that many are not taking the scale of task ahead seriously. There is no doubt that much can be achieved with new approaches to design, and technological fixes, but it is ultimately only with a fundamental re-ordering of our priorities, our aspirations and our societies that we will create a social, economic and physical environment in which *Homo sapiens* can hope to survive, en masse, safely, through to the end of this century.

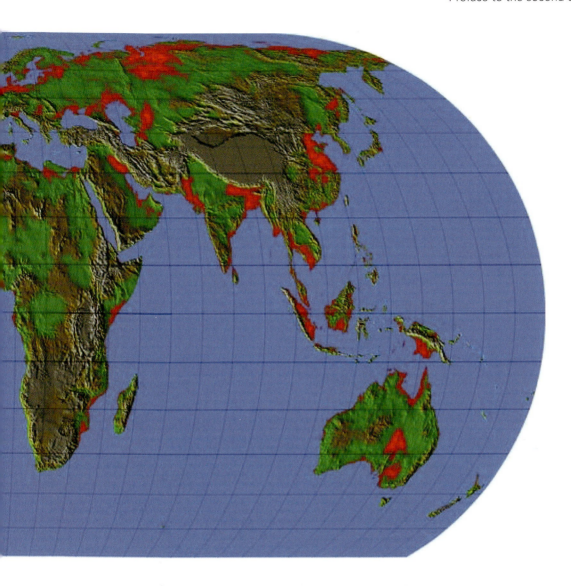

This may be a pretty tall order but with the pace of environmental change in the world around us speeding up, perhaps we will find the will and the way, together, to adapt our buildings and cities, economies and societies in time, because we certainly cannot do it alone.

Sue Roaf
April 2009

ACKNOWLEDGEMENTS TO THE SECOND EDITION

David Crichton, Fergus Nicol and Sue Roaf would like to thank the following people for their help in putting the second edition of this book together: Janet Rudge and Sari Kovats for Chapter 8; Aubrey Meyer, Fiona Mullins and Peter Reid for their help with the text; and all those who otherwise helped with it in thought, word or deed.

For the illustrations: UKCIP, Laurence Williams, Adrian Arbib, Aubrey Meyer, Claire Palmer, Mary Hancock, Charles Knevitt, Louis Hellman and Bill Bordass, to name a few.

At Architectural Press thanks go to Hannah Shakespeare and Mike Travers.

It should be noted that the views expressed in this book are solely those of the authors.

ABOUT THE AUTHORS

Sue Roaf

Sue Roaf is Professor of Architectural Engineering at Heriot Watt University, Edinburgh, and Visiting Professor at the Open University. With degrees from Manchester University, The Architectural Association and Oxford Polytechnic, she has worked widely on ecobuilding design, carbon accounting, adapting buildings and cities for climate change, traditional technologies, and sustainable and low-carbon buildings. She co-designed and owns the Oxford Ecohouse, the first building in the UK with a photovoltaic roof, and does much to promote resilient low-impact and low-carbon architecture through the research, teaching, publishing and conferences she organizes on Solar Cities, Carbon Counting, Architectural Education, Thermal Comfort and Post Occupancy Evaluation. Her PhD was on the Windcatchers of Yazd and she spent 10 years in Iran and Iraq as an architect, archaeologist, anthropologist, lecturer and landscape architect. She has two sons, Christopher and Richard. She has written and edited 10 books, including *Ecohouse: A Design Guide*; *Closing the Loop: Benchmarks for Sustainable Buildings*; and *The Ice-Houses of Britain*. She lecturers widely to audiences around the world.

Fergus Nicol

In the 1960s and early 1970s Fergus Nicol researched building physics and human thermal comfort at the Building Research Establishment and the Human Physiology Unit of the Medical Research Council. He also taught in the Schools of Architecture at the University of Science and Technology in Kumasi Ghana and the Architectural Association in London. After a period managing a bookshop he returned to teaching and research in 1992.

Fergus is best known for his work in the science of human thermal comfort, where he has developed, with Professor Michael Humphreys, the 'adaptive' approach to thermal comfort. He has run a number of projects over the last 15 years funded by the EPSRC and other funding agencies and a major EU project, Smart Controls and Thermal Comfort (SCATS). He is a professor at London Metropolitan University, where he is deputy director of the Low Energy Architecture Research Unit (LEARN). He is an affiliated Professor at Heriot Watt University and Emeritus Professor at Oxford Brookes University.

Fergus is a member of UK and European consultative committees on comfort issues. He is helping CIBSE to write the new edition of their Guide A and is an active member of their

Overheating Task Force. He was responsible for the international conference *Air Conditioning and the Low-Carbon Cooling Challenge* in Windsor, UK, in July 2008, attended by many international experts in thermal comfort and thermal comfort standards. He is convenor of the Network for Comfort and Energy Use in Buildings, which boasts nearly 300 members from all over the world and in a wide variety of academic disciplines, consultancies and government bodies.

David Crichton

David is an economist with 30 years' experience in the insurance industry. He has held senior underwriting and claims management positions in both property and casualty business, and has won a number of insurance industry awards, including the first AIRMIC risk management prize awarded to an insurance practitioner. He is a freelance consultant and researcher on climate change impacts and insurance. He has authored a number of books, reports and papers on insurance and climate change.

David has advised governments and insurers in four continents, and has worked for the Association of British Insurers, the CII, the DTI, EU, NATO, NOAA, OECD, various branches of the United Nations, and WWF. He has also been a member of several academic or research boards in the UK. He is a Visiting Professor at the Benfield UCL Hazard Research Centre at University College London This is the leading academic hazard research centre in Europe, specializing in natural disasters and insurance (http://www.benfieldhrc.org/). He is also Visiting Professor at Middlesex University Flood Hazard Research Centre, an Honorary Research Fellow at the University of Dundee, a Fellow of the Chartered Insurance Institute and a Chartered Insurance Practitioner. He is a member of the UK Advisory Committee on Natural Disaster Reduction, part of the United Nations ISDR initiative.

Janet Rudge

Janet Rudge is currently the Energy Officer for Ealing Borough Council, specializing in programmes for the Fuel Poor. She is a registered architect and has worked in both public and private offices. Since 1992 she has researched and taught Environmental and Energy Studies at the University of East London and the Low Energy Architecture Research Unit (LEARN) at London Metropolitan University. She has also worked helping to establish the Network for Comfort and Energy Use in Buildings. Her own research has concentrated on fuel poverty and health, with publications including papers in, for example, the *International Journal of Biometeorology*, *Journal of Public Health* and *Energy and Buildings*. She co-edited, with Fergus Nicol, *Cutting the Cost of Cold: Affordable Warmth for Healthier Homes*, a multidisciplinary reference source on the health impact of cold homes. Dr Rudge is currently an invited lead expert on cold homes for a World Health Organization European project to assess the burden of disease of inadequate housing.

Sari Kovats

Sari Kovats is a lecturer in Environmental Epidemiology at the London School of Hygiene and Tropical Medicine. Her areas of interest are in health issues related to climate change, and she has published widely on the health impacts of heatwaves and associated public health responses, the role of temperature in the transmission of food-borne and water-borne disease, the association between temperature and rainfall and mortality in cities and the health impacts of flooding. She was a Lead Author in the Fourth Assessment Report of the Intergovernmental Panel on Climate Change.

2.
Social equality is an essential ingredient for secure communities in changing times: San Paolo, Brazil.
Source: Photobucket.com

PREFACE TO THE FIRST EDITION

This is a book I have been thinking about writing for over 25 years. Every study I have worked on, in those intervening years, has been a stepping-stone towards this publication on the future of architecture. That journey started in the far distant past, in the ancient villages and cities of Iraq, the cradle of civilization where, through seven years of excavation, we touched the lives of those people who ate from the pots, played with the toys, drove the chariots and built the buildings that we uncovered, not decades or centuries, but millennia ago, on the once fertile plains, once again scarred by war. The path to this book passed through nomad tents on tribal roads, and across vast deserts where families, using little more energy than twigs to cook on, lived in comfort, and in some cases luxury, in the extreme climates of what we would see only as barren lands.

Climate in those regions, on the fringes of agriculture, has always been about survival, but the study that first alerted me to the scale of the potential impacts of climate change on our lives in the more temperate lands was one, not on buildings in hot deserts, but on the ice-houses of Britain. Writing on their history in the 1980s, it became obvious that this ancient technology, forgotten behind the miracle of refrigeration, had become climatically obsolete as the world warmed, and that even very small changes in global temperatures, fractions of a degree, could be responsible for the demise of a great international industry, if those changes cross a critical thermal threshold, such as the temperature at which ice melts.

Figure 1 shows how central to our very survival the simple substance ice is, and what a key role it is playing in the re-ordering of global climates, oceans and landscapes.

By the late 1980s the growing global problems of ozone depletion and climate change were beginning to be talked of more often. My concern was growing at the unfairness of the reality – that people in the developing countries are already dying in large numbers because of climate change, whilst it is those in the West who are generating the carbon dioxide emissions that are warming the world.

The desire to show that it need not be like this led to the building of the first photovoltaic home in Oxford, in which my family still comfortably resides. This simple building emits only a few hundred kilograms of CO_2 a year instead of five or six thousand and is *more* comfortable than a highly polluting one. We cut down our greenhouse gas emissions to less than 10% of typical emissions with no loss of quality of life. So why isn't everyone doing it? Why are architects building 'glass houses' and windowless plywood 'blobs' instead of the types of solid, resilient, buildings that offer us some hope for survival in the coming decades?

It beats me! But what I do know is that the road that many of us have followed from the Energy Crisis of the 1970s through the growing issues of climate change, fossil fuel depletion and sustainability has led us towards a present, and a future, that is very different from anything that has been before. One can see why many people want to avoid thinking about it – a future where the issue is increasingly not about comfortable concepts like 'sustainability', but about the harsher realities of designing for 'survival'.

If only the global community had acted more firmly in the 1970s when they saw the challenges ahead perhaps we would not now be facing the predicaments around us! The unavoidable truth is that it has been left to our generation alone, of all those that have come before, to face the awesome challenge of redesigning the world to accommodate the new forces of the late fossil fuel age, of dark cities, a world of slowing economic growth, of climate change and an exploding global population.

It is the scale of the catastrophic changing of circumstances around us that makes it difficult to grasp at any heart to the problem. We are still only equipped with the old ways of thinking, that showed us an illusion of a clear path ahead. But many of us who, for years, have been watching, and working so diligently to get a handle on controlling the impacts of late-twentieth-century development have been surprised by how wrong we got it. We have only been scratching the surface of the problem. In what we once saw as the manageable game of sustainable development, our eyes have been so far off the ball that what follows in this book may be unbelievable, or unpalatable, to many readers. Very few people – remarkable among them being my co-authors David Crichton and Fergus Nicol and the pioneering thinker Edward Mazria[1] – have been able to see beyond the 'business as usual' carrot that draws us, blinkered, on our way.

Few have questioned the horizons, or understood that what we once saw as a single, efficient, road forward to a clean, bright, future has now widened out into a quagmire of complex interrelated forces that urgently require us to think outside the envelope of our own buildings, and above all, to open windows, to embrace a new age of architecture, planning and politics of development. We *can* make a difference, we *can* leave a world fit for our children and grandchildren, but the task is urgent and the task is huge.

Can it be that for decades we have been looking for the warnings in all the wrong places? Because the one thing that is increasingly clear is that the writing is now on the landscape, and the wall.

Sue Roaf

NOTE

1 See <http://www.metropolismag.com/html/content_1003/glo/index.html>.

ACKNOWLEDGEMENTS TO THE FIRST EDITION

My heartfelt thanks go to my co-authors David Crichton and Fergus Nicol, both of them visionaries in their fields. Also to those who have so generously contributed to the contents of the book – Janet Rudge, Sari Kovats, Fiona Mullins, Aubrey Meyer, Colin Campbell – and all of those who have helped in preparing the contents of this book through thought, word or deed.

For wonderful illustrations I would like to thank: UKCIP, Laurence Williams, Richenda Connell, Jacquelyn Harman, Adrian Arbib, Mark Lynas, Paul Eugene Camp, Aubrey Meyer, Claire Palmer, Fergus Nicol, Jane Matthews, Gavin Kenny, Mary Hancock, David Crichton, Edward Mazria, Rob Wilby, Isaac Meir, Charles Knevitt, Bryan Lynas, Tim Helweg, Rodrigo Leal, John Mardaljevic, Bill Hughes, Colin Campbell, Louis Hellman, Steve Sharples, Cliff Wassman, Janet Rudge, Sari Kovats, Russell C. Schnell, Mark Watham, Alex Hollingsworth, Rosanna Salbashian, Bill Bordass, Catherine Streater, David Infield, Emma Perry and Frances Bergmann.

For helping to make the book happen at Architectural Press I thank: Alison Yates, Catharine Steers, Elaine Leek and Margaret Denley.

We are deeply grateful to the following sponsors for making it possible to have this book in colour – their support has meant a great deal to us. Thank you:

The Ecology Building Society
Friends of the Earth

It should be noted that the particular views expressed in this book are solely those of the authors.

1 CLIMATE CHANGE: THE BATTLE BEGINS

WAR IS ALREADY UPON US

The war against climate change pitches mankind against a global threat that vastly eclipses that of terrorism,[1] in battles that have already claimed the lives of hundreds of thousands of ordinary men and women from every continent. Climate change has led us into an era in which war and conflict are endemic,[2] the widespread extinction of species approaches catastrophic proportions,[3] and whole regions and countries will be lost beneath the swelling seas and the expanding deserts of a rapidly warming world. And the really bad news is that 'the world has only one generation, perhaps two, to save itself'.[4]

We all instinctively know, already, that the climate is changing, from the small noticed things like the unseasonable patterns of the flowering of plants, the falling of snow and the growing in strength of the wind and the rain. With this knowledge comes a growing apprehension of danger. Deep down, in quiet moments, we ask ourselves questions that a year or two ago were unthinkable:

- What will I do when the lights do go out?
- Will the house flood next year?
- Will my home get so hot this summer that I won't be able to stay in it?
- How long could I survive in this building without air conditioning?
- Where will we go?
- Will we survive?

This book is written to enable you, the reader, to get a clearer view of the ways in which the climate is changing and how these changes will affect *your* life tomorrow and the day after, in the buildings, settlements and regions in which you live and work. Only by emotionally registering, by consciously taking on board, the scale of the impending global disaster ahead will any of us find the strength to act in time to avert the worst of its impacts.

But not only do we have to act fast, we also have to act *together*. Actions will only be effective if we all act together because each of us is 'involved' in the fate of all mankind through the common air that we breathe and the climate we occupy.

As you will see throughout this book, people can apparently be 'familiar' with the excellent science of climate change, and 'know' intellectually the problems that exists, but still fail to engage

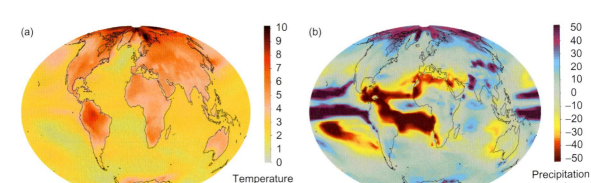

1.1.
Scientists have established that climate change is really happening and can, to an extent, model future climates. Here we see the change in the annual average (a) temperature and (b) precipitation, predicted for the 2080s period, relative to 1961–1990, for one climate model, the HadCM3 ensemble-average under an A2 forcing scenario.
Source: UKCIP02 Scientific Report,[5] p. 19.

with them, or act upon that knowledge. We know now that many of the gases we emit from the burning of fossil fuels are altering the climate. Every schoolchild learns, or should learn, how these gases are building up in the upper atmosphere to form an increasingly dense layer that allows solar radiation into the Earth's atmosphere, but as this layer gets denser, it prevents more and more heat from radiating back out into space, so warming the lower atmosphere and changing our climate.[6]

The evidence for climate change is growing more alarming each year. The exceptionally hot summers such as those of 2003 and 2005 warned experts that the pace of this warming is faster than previously envisaged in their worst case scenarios.[7] Yet rather than acting to reduce emissions, many apparently well-meaning and well-informed people appear to act wilfully to make the situation worse in communal acts of 'denial', and nowhere more so than in the built environment. Buildings are responsible for producing over half of all climate change emissions, but year on year, 'modern' buildings become more and more energy profligate and damaging to all our children's future. Climate change is personal. 'They' are harming 'our' grandchildren.

In London, for instance, where more is known about the urban impacts of climate change than for almost any other city in the world, the Greater London Authority and the then Deputy Prime Minister heavily promoted the huge developments of the Thames Gateway area. Situated to the east of the capital on the coastal flood plains of the Thames Estuary this area has periodically flooded throughout history, well before rising sea levels and stronger storm surges increased the risk of loss of life and property to the seas here. Leading architects have even suggested that proposed settlement densities are too low, even when they must 'know' of the risks of putting buildings and people in such locations. Are such architects going to live there themselves? Are they ignorant or simply cynically exploiting a business opportunity? How much do such architects and developers really 'know'?

Former US President George W. Bush had repeatedly refused to acknowledge that climate change is happening at all, to the extent that by the end of 2003 there were 12 US states suing the US Environmental Protection Agency because of the failure of the US Government to take action against climate change. And yet the US administration knows of the dangers of climate

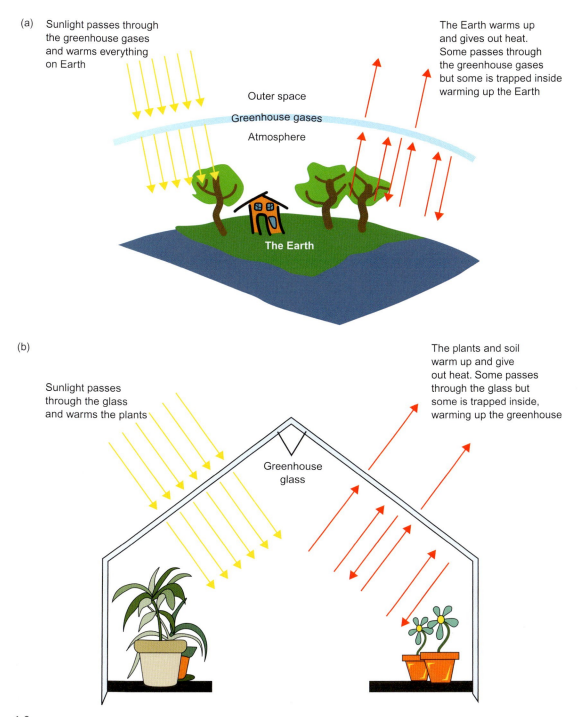

(a)   Sunlight passes through the greenhouse gases and warms everything on Earth

The Earth warms up and gives out heat. Some passes through the greenhouse gases but some is trapped inside warming up the Earth

Outer space

Greenhouse gases

Atmosphere

The Earth

(b)

Sunlight passes through the glass and warms the plants

The plants and soil warm up and give out heat. Some passes through the glass but some is trapped inside, warming up the greenhouse

Greenhouse glass

1.2.
The basics of climate change are taught in all British schools and such images of how the greenhouse effect (b) works in relation to the global atmosphere (a) are very familiar to children by the age or 7 or 8.
Source: http://www.defra.gov.uk/environment/climatechange/schools/12-16/info/cause.htm.

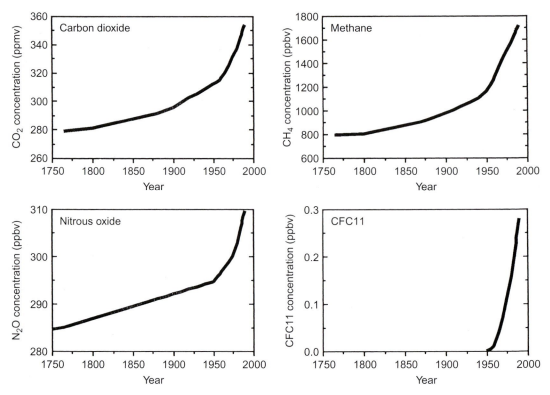

1.3.
In the middle of the twentieth century more and more of the world's rapidly growing population bought cars and heated and cooled their buildings, resulting in a rapid increase in concentrations (parts per million/billion by volume) of the major greenhouse gases in the global atmosphere: carbon dioxide (CO_2), nitrous oxide (N_2O), methane (CH_4) and CFC11.
Source: Houghton J.T., Jenkins, G.J., Ephraums, J.J. (eds) (1990) *Climate Change: The IPCC Scientific Assessment.* Cambridge: Cambridge University Press, p. xvi.

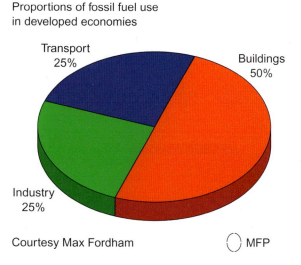

Proportions of fossil fuel use
in developed economies

Transport
25%

Buildings
50%

Industry
25%

Courtesy Max Fordham   ◯ MFP

1.4.
Graph showing the relatively large impacts of buildings in the developed world in terms of their emissions of climate change greenhouse gases.
Source: Max Fordham and Partners.

change to their own homeland because a Pentagon Report in 2003 told them of the endemic war and conflict the world would face as a result of it.[2] Bush changed his mind on this issue in 2007 when he publicly admitted that climate change was happening and yet his administration continued to obstruct action to mitigate and adapt to the changing climate. His successor Barak Obama had swiftly passed a radical Climate Change Bill through Congress in June 2009.

The Australian government continues to be oblivious to the pleas for shelter of the islanders of Tuvalu, where the whole island is more frequently being covered completely by the rising sea every year; and, with impending disaster so close to their own doorsteps, the Australians are refusing not only to give the islanders a refuge but also to consider cutbacks in their own greenhouse gas emissions, on this, the most vulnerable continent on the planet to the impacts of the warming climate. But, perhaps it is too difficult to connect the idea of gas emissions to environmental impacts in remote islands, and it could be understandable that the Australian people feel no sense of responsibility for the plight of the people of Tuvalu, despite the fact that the government of Australia has now begun to take on board the severity of the impacts of climate change as a result of an entrenched drought in parts of the country and the recent report to government of Ross Garnaut on their dire social and economic implications for Australia. But how much do the Australian people 'know' about the plight of their own sunburnt country in a changing climate? Drought is teaching them rapidly now.

Should the word 'know' here be replaced, perhaps, with 'care'?

No wonder that so many people today feel that 'it's a mad world', but why? Surely we are a rational species? Perhaps it all has to do with the actual process of changing, the extent and speed of the required changes, and the costs and risks of acting, or not acting, to make those changes happen.

J.K. Galbraith noted in 1958 that 'conventional wisdom' generally makes people indisposed to change their minds and reminds readers of John Maynard Keynes' famous words:[8]

Conventional wisdom protects the continuity in social thought and action. But there are also grave drawbacks and even dangers in a system of thought which by its very nature and design avoids accommodation to circumstances until change is dramatically forced upon it ... the rule of ideas is only powerful in a world that does not change. Ideas are inherently conservative. They yield not to attack of other ideas but to the massive onslaught of circumstances with which they cannot contend.

We are faced now with the massive onslaught of the circumstances of climate change. This book describes some of those circumstances in relation to buildings, settlements and lifestyles of this, and future decades. As you read on it will become clearer how very difficult, if not impossible, we will find it to contend with the impacts of climate change, to meet head on the challenges of changing 'social thought and action', and to redirect the supertanker of conventional wisdom.

That is why you, the reader, are important, and why this book has been written to make you 'disposed to change your mind', and in turn change the minds of those in your circle of influence, and those in theirs, and so on until the ripple grows to be a tidal wave of change in the attitudes of our society. And though none of us wants it, and we may wish that we lived in different times, it is the responsibility of each and every one of our generation, and ours alone in the whole history of humankind, to take up arms in this battle for our very survival.

But why has it taken us so long to act? The Climate War is already upon us. How did it come to this?

THE ENEMY WAS SIGHTED LONG AGO

The possibility that the climate could be changing was first identified as far back as the 1960s, and the battle against climate change, and its main contributory gas, carbon dioxide (CO_2), began.

Physical measurements of global CO_2 emissions have been taken since the 1950s.[9] The Mauna Loa atmospheric CO_2 measurements constitute the longest continuous record of atmospheric CO_2 concentrations available in the world. The clear upland atmosphere of the Mauna Loa volcano on the Pacific island of Hawaii is one of the most favourable locations on the planet for measuring undisturbed air because possible local influences of vegetation or human activities on atmospheric CO_2 concentrations are minimal and any influences from volcanic vents may be excluded from the records.

The methods and equipment used to obtain these measurements have remained essentially unchanged during the 50-year monitoring programme. Because of the favourable site location, continuous monitoring, and careful selection and scrutiny of the data, the Mauna Loa record is considered to be a precise record and a reliable indicator of the regional trend in the concentrations of atmospheric CO_2 in the middle layers of the troposphere. The record shows an 18% increase in the mean annual concentration, from 316 parts per million by volume (ppmv) of dry air in 1959 to 373 ppmv in 2002 and 389 in 2009. The 1997–98 increase in the annual growth rate of 2.87 ppmv was the largest single yearly jump since the Mauna Loa record began in 1958.

Such data are used to inform and validate the computer models of the climate[10] which have been used to depict and predict former, current and future climates right down to a resolution of fifty, and now even five, kilometre squares.[11] Such models have provided sufficiently credible evidence, where, for instance, predicted temperatures resemble closely temperatures experienced, for the virtually universal consensus amongst internationally respected scientists and meteorologists that increasing atmospheric concentrations of CO_2, and other gases, with significant absorptivity in the far infrared, 'the greenhouse gases', have already led to significant changes in the climate of the world with far-reaching implications for everyone on this planet.[12]

It was the scientists who charted, and modelled, the first manifestations of the enemy that threatens our species, but issues such as the changing climate, the loss of biodiversity, terrestrial and atmospheric pollution, and resource depletion, are only the standards of the enemy, caught flying in the wind. What the intellectuals, economists and politicians did was to identify the real enemy in our ecosystem – ourselves.

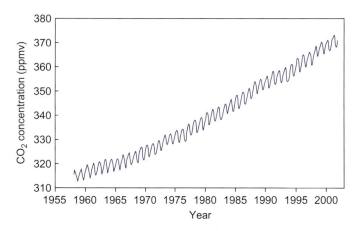

1.5.
The Mauna Loa carbon dioxide record, 1958–2002.
Source: Climate Monitoring and Diagnostics Laboratory of the US National Oceanic and Atmospheric Administration, Mauna Loa, Hawaii.

THE WARNING IS SOUNDED

The global environmental trumpet was sounded for the first time, warning of the enormity of the problems we face, at the first general meeting of the Club of Rome in 1970. The meeting was convened to discuss the state of the world and the development of a computer model of world *problematique*, to include issues with global dimensions such as population, resources and environment.[13]

In 1970 and 1971, the first large-scale modelling studies of global environmental conditions were actually created, both prepared as input to the 1972 United Nations (UN) Conference on the Human Environment, and both noting the possibility of 'inadvertent climate modification'. The Study of Critical Environmental Problems (SCEP) focused on pollution-induced 'changes in climate, ocean ecology, or in large terrestrial ecosystems'. It cited the global climate models as 'indispensable' in the study of possible anthropogenic climate change.

In 1971 the influential *Study of Man's Impact on the Climate* (SMIC)[14] also endorsed the climate models. Both SCEP and SMIC recommended a major initiative in global data collection, new international measurement standards for environmental data, and the integration of existing programs to form a global monitoring network. These reports are widely cited as the originators of public policy interest in anthropogenic climate change and all these early studies predict 'overshoot and collapse'.

By the time that Edward Goldsmith and four colleagues published their seminal book *A Blueprint for Survival*[15] in 1972, climate change had been woven into the fabric of wider environmental concerns, even by non-experts in the climate field, such as these authors. The book contained a general plea for the application of ecological common sense in the face of mounting evidence of the approaching global environmental crisis.

The Blueprint demanded a radical change in our approach to the environment, necessary if we are indeed to avoid 'undermining the very foundations of survival' for our species and the planet, citing the rise in global population, the increase in per capita consumption, disruption to ecosystems and depletion of resources at a rate that was not supportable. These trends, they estimated, would inevitably lead to a collapse in society if nothing was done about it. They, interestingly, foretold that politicians would tend to act to exacerbate the problems rather than act to solve them:

At times of great distress and social chaos, it is more than probable that governments will fall into the hands of reckless and unscrupulous elements, who will not hesitate to threaten neighbouring governments with attack, if they need to wrest from them a larger share of the world's vanishing resources.[16]

The book was, however, largely concerned with the impacts of overexploitation of the Earth's resources, the underlying problem that lies at the very root of our dilemma today. It provided excellent benchmarks against which we can measure the extent to which our species has effectively degraded the natural capital of our planet and polluted its ecosystems. But the authors also mention, in a couple of paragraphs, the potential for CO_2 emissions to lead to significant climate change:

The CO_2 content of the atmosphere is increasing at a rate of 0.2 per cent per year since 1958. One can project, on the basis of these trends, an 18 per cent increase by the year 2000, i.e. from 320 ppm to 379 ppm. SCEP considers that this might increase temperature of the earth by 0.5°C. A doubling of CO_2 might increase mean annual surface temperatures by 2°C.

They were subsequently proved to be very close to the actual recorded warming between 1947 and 1997 of between 0.25 and 0.5°C.

In the early 1970s, several other large-scale atmospheric issues came to the attention of the general public. Notable among these were acid rain, upper-atmospheric pollution problems raised by supersonic transport and stratospheric ozone depletion. What is so difficult to grapple with is the issue of who exactly is the invisible enemy in this war, where are they, who owns the problem and how does one fight against air?

FIRST ENCOUNTERS

While the scientists of the world have long been wrestling with the theoretical problem of climate change and resource depletion, for the general public the first of the 'environmental shocks' that brought home the reality that the twentieth century dreams of infinite cheap energy and limitless resources were unrealistic was the Energy Crisis of the mid-1970s. With it came the dawning realization that oil, the magic energy source from which the wealth and enjoyment of nations was built, of which every barrel can do the same 'work' as 540 man-hours of effort,[17] would one day run out. Futurologists then claimed we only had 30 years of oil left, a prediction that has proved to be, perhaps, less than half right, but globally, people started counting the barrels, and comparing them to the available reserves, and understandably, investing in renewable energy programmes.

The first public blow had been struck; mankind was perceived to be vulnerable and, by now, officially engaged in a battle, not against the air, but against their own fossil fuel dependency and time, two equally powerful adversaries. And the richest nations, ironically, became the most vulnerable.

THE WEAPONS ARE HONED

In 1971 SMIC had recommended that a major initiative in global data collection, new international measurement standards for environmental data, and the integration of existing programs to form a global monitoring network should be developed. The ozone challenge provided the perfect opportunity to see how effectively mankind, communally, could respond to what appeared to be a rapidly developing, global, catastrophe.

Ground-based measurements of ozone were first started in 1956, at Halley Bay, Antarctica. Satellite measurements of ozone started in the early 1970s, but the first comprehensive worldwide measurements started in 1978 with the Nimbus-7 satellite. In addition to the physical measurements, in 1974 M.J. Molina and F.S. Rowland published a laboratory study[18] demonstrating the ability of chlorofluorocarbons (CFCs) to catalytically break down ozone in the presence of high-frequency ultraviolet (UV) light. Further studies estimated that the ozone layer would be depleted by CFCs by about 7% within 60 years.

Based on the recommendations of such studies, the USA banned CFCs in aerosol sprays in 1978, showing a level of real leadership at this stage, which spoke of the courage of the then US administration. Slowly, various nations agreed to ban CFCs in aerosols but industry fought the banning of valuable CFCs in other applications. A large shock was needed to motivate the world to get serious about phasing out CFCs and that shock came in a 1985 field study by Farman, Gardiner and Shanklin[19] that summarized data that had been collected by the British Antarctic Survey showing that ozone levels had dropped to 10% below the normal January levels for Antarctica.

The severity, and rate, of the global ozone depletion spurred the UN to sponsor a resolution called the Montreal Protocol that was originally signed in 1987, based on negotiations started between European–Scandinavian countries and the USA over CFCs in aerosol sprays in 1983. The protocol went through a series of revisions, each one named after the city where the revision committee met, as new information from science and industry has become available. The meeting in Copenhagen in November 1992 laid down the most stringent phase-out schedule of CFCs for the world to date; and was signed by over 100 nations representing 95% of the world's current CFC consumption. Trade sanctions on CFCs, halocarbons and products containing them, were imposed as of April 1993 on nations not signing the protocol, and in May 1993 this ban was extended to the export of halocarbon solvents such as methyl chloride and carbon tetrachloride. This protocol laid out a schedule for the phase-out of CFCs and related halocarbons by the year 2030. An additional impact of the protocol was to mandate the sharing of technology between countries in order to speed the replacement and recycling of CFCs.

In 1988, Sweden was the first country to legislate the complete phase-out of CFCs, with a scheduled phase-out in all new goods by 1994. In March 1989 environmental ministers of the European Parliament announced a total phase-out of CFCs in Europe by the year 2000.[20] What the ozone problem demonstrated, to the world, is that when faced with a challenge as large as that of the stratospheric ozone problem, the global community has the science, the strategy, the will and the fiscal, legal and statutory mechanisms to contain that problem. It provided a precedent study for the larger challenge of containing climate change. It does offer some hope that we can act communally to maximize our chances of survival.

There has been significant variation in the size of the ozone hole over the past decade and while in August 2003, ozone values over Antarctica were already below 200 Dobson Units (DU), they rose sharply until 2006, when they descended to an almost record low. By 2007 they were back up at their 10-year average.[21] Scientists have predicted that with the reduction in ozone-depleting emissions the ozone hole could close up by 2070, but the actual scientific processes and climate impacts of the reduction in the size of the hole are only partially understood, for instance on surface wind speeds, although significant research is being carried out on the subject.[22]

THE COUNCIL OF WAR MEETS[23]

By the mid-1980s, the simulated predictions of the scientists on the warming climate began to demonstrate a close approximation to what was actually happening in the measured record, with clear evidence of increasing temperatures and the frequency and intensity of extreme weather events. The sheer scale of the problems humanity, and the planet, might face if, indeed, the climate was changing more than its natural variability would allow, began to manifest themselves, in the dollars spent in insurance payouts on climate events, the numbers killed in climate-related events, and the movement of species and deserts across the face of the globe.

In 1988, at the behest of national governments from around the world, the UN Environment Programme and the World Meteorological Organization, by now the 'War Council' leaders, established the Intergovernmental Panel on Climate Change (IPCC),[24] consisting of hundreds of leading scientists and experts on global warming. The Panel was asked to assess the state of scientific knowledge concerning climate change, evaluate its potential environmental and socio-economic impacts, and formulate realistic strategies to deal with the problem.

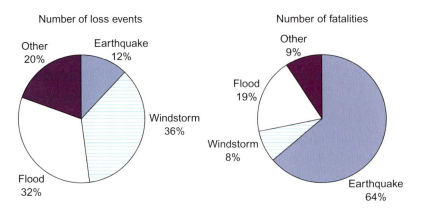

1.6.
Related number of insurance loss events and related fatalities by event types and number of fatalities in 2001.
Source: Munich Re, *Topics: Annual Review of Natural Catastrophes 2001*; for the 2002 review see http://www.munichre.com/pdf/topics_2002_e.pdf). Such figures underestimate climate-related deaths, as reported by other sources.

Two years later, in 1990, the IPCC published a report concluding that the growing accumulation of human-made greenhouse gases in the atmosphere would 'enhance the greenhouse effect, resulting, on average, in an additional warming of the Earth's surface' by the next century, with continued temperature increases thereafter unless measures were adopted to limit the emissions of these gases.

The findings of the First IPCC Assessment Report of 1990 played a decisive role in leading to the United Nations Framework Convention on Climate Change (UNFCCC),[25] which was adopted at the Earth Summit in Rio de Janeiro in 1992 and opened for signature. The Convention entered into force on 21 March 1994 and under it the industrialized countries agreed to aim to return their emissions to 1990 levels by 2010.

The relationship between the IPCC and the UNFCCC is worth clarifying. Under the UNFCCC a Subsidiary Body for Scientific and Technological Advice (SBSTA) was established. At the first of the annual Conference of the Parties to the UNFCCC (COP-1) in Berlin (February 1995), the functions of the SBSTA were clarified and SBSTA was requested to:

1. Summarize and interpret the latest international scientific research for the politicians (COP) and 'support' of the review of the adequacy of commitments (targets)
2. Assess the implications of research and advise on the development and improvement of comparable methodologies for:
   - National inventories of emissions and removals of greenhouse gases.
   - Projecting national emissions and removals of greenhouse gases and comparison of respective contributions of different gases to climate change.
   - Evaluating the individual and aggregated effects of measures undertaken pursuant to the provisions of the Convention.
   - Conducting impact/sensitivity analyses.
   - Assessing adaptation responses.

Since Rio, there have been annual follow-up COP meetings to try to establish agreements on exactly how emissions and impacts are going to be measured, and how to manage and programme the targets and tools used in the negotiations. On 11 December 1997, at the conclusion of COP-3 in Kyoto, Japan, more than 150 nations adopted the Kyoto Protocol. This unprecedented treaty committed industrialized nations to make legally binding reductions in emissions of six greenhouse gases:

- carbon dioxide.
- methane.
- nitrous oxide.
- hydrofluorocarbons (HFCs).
- perfluorocarbons (PFCs).
- sulphur hexafluoride (SF_6).

The called-for reductions varied from country to country, but would cut emissions by an average of about 5% below 1990 levels by the period 2008–2012. The USA agreed to reductions of 7%, Japan to reductions of 6% and the members of the European Union (EU) to joint reductions of 8%. Key to the US agreement to such a relatively ambitious target was a concurrent agreement that a system of emissions trading among industrialized countries be established, by which nations with binding limits could buy and sell, among themselves, the right to release greenhouse gases.

Much has happened since then, but by 12 August 2003, 84 parties had signed, including Canada, and 113 parties have ratified or acceded to the Kyoto Protocol.[26] In December 2003, COP-9 was held in Milan, to discuss the tricky issue of carbon sinks and emissions trading, and how to incorporate them in the global targets for the Protocol, an increasingly central issue as many countries attempt to avoid the need to make deep cuts in their own greenhouse gas emission inventories by investing in cheap 'carbon sinks' abroad. COP-10 in Buenos Aires in 2004 took stock of the achievements in terms of adaptation and mitigation strategies in the first 10 years of the Treaty. COP-11 in 2005 was held in Montreal in Canada, COP-12 in 2006 in Nairobi and COP-13 in 2007 in Bali.

On the 15 December 2007, in a last minute agreement at the COP-13 in Bali, all countries that are party to the Kyoto Agreement, and the USA (reluctantly), agreed upon a Bali Action Plan and Roadmap that outlined a broad range of actions relating to the mitigation and adaptation for climate change committing to:

- *Achieving* deep cuts in global emissions targets in accordance with the UNFCCC.
- *Reaffirming* as priorities economic and social development, and eradication of poverty.
- *Responding* to AR4 (Fourth Assessment Report) findings that global warming is unequivocal and needs urgent action.
- *Recognizing* that (really) deep cuts in global emissions will be required to achieve the ultimate objective of the Convention (avoiding climate chaos).

The sense of urgency at Bali was palpable and four main areas were dealt with in detail:

- A new framework for emissions inventories and reporting mechanisms for deforestation and land use.
- An adaptation fund and programme to enhance the ability of nations to adapt in time.
- Technology transfer mechanisms and financing reinforced and developed.
- Ad Hoc Working Group on Long Term Cooperative Action under the Convention set up to produce an action plan for presentation to COP-15 in Copenhagen in 2009, on which will be based the proposals for the post-Kyoto treaty.

A further function of the COP meetings is to report back on progress against targets and to this end in the Clean Development Mechanism arena, relating to projects whereby emissions reductions in one country can be claimed as carbon reductions by a funding country. For the year 2006/07 825 projects were reported, achieving 84 049 697 million certified emissions reductions and the development of 32 new agreed baseline and monitoring methodologies.

There have been four reports from the IPCC on the changing status of the science on climate change. In 2007 the IPCC was awarded a Nobel Peace prize for its work in climate change. The language used in the four successive reports of the IPCC tell of the alarming rate in the increase of this change. AR4, published in 2007, leaves little room for doubt about its mechanisms and causes.

The first volume of the Fourth IPCC Report, AR4, released in February 2007 in Paris, confirmed that global warming was happening, while the second, issued in April 2007 in Brussels, focused on the impact of the phenomenon on the world's populations and species.

The third volume of the AR4 report, dated May 2007, reported on the means of mitigating the worse impacts of global warming and focuses on the economic implications and technological options for tackling global warming. It states that emissions must start declining by 2015 to prevent the world's temperature from rising more than 2°C over pre-industrialized temperatures. The report also states that the low costs of buying insurance against these changes that would mean climate catastrophe in the coming decades, through the use of technologies currently available, is less than 0.1% of world gross domestic product (GDP) per annum.

AR4 of the IPCC had firmly established the link between anthropogenic emissions of greenhouse gases and climate change and reported step changes in the severity of their impacts. Many countries that were holding out for real targets for medium-term emissions reductions were thwarted, but it is felt that the COP-15 at Copenhagen will produce real targets for the post-Kyoto Treaty, driven on by the current US government.

AGENDA 21: THE ARMY IS FORMED

Once the decision to go to war was taken an army had to be assembled. This process started at Rio.

In 1992, the Earth Summit in Rio de Janeiro, properly titled the 'United Nations Conference of Development and the Environment', was profoundly influential. Twenty years after the first

Box 1.1 The language of the four IPCC reports has changed (see http://www.ipcc.ch/)

- 1st Report – 1990: 'We are now aware that *the general amplitude of the increase in the warming of the planet conforms to the predictions of the climate models*, but that this amplitude is comparable to that which occurs with the natural variability of the climate'.
- 2nd Report – 1995: 'In the corpus of the observations *lead us to believe* that there is a human influence on the climate of the planet'.
- 3rd Report – 2001: 'The recent observations provide *convincing indications* that the heating of the planet over that last five years is attributable to the activities of humans'.
- 4th Report – 2007: '*Warming of the climate system is unequivocal.* Most of (>50% of) the observed increase in globally averaged temperatures since the mid-twentieth century is very likely (confidence level >90%) due to the observed increase in anthropogenic (human) greenhouse gas concentrations'.

Box 1.2 The Bali Action Plan (See http://unfccc.int/meetings/cop_13/items/4049.php)

The Conference of the Parties,

Resolving to urgently enhance implementation of the Convention in order to achieve its ultimate objective in full accordance with its principles and commitments,

Reaffirming that economic and social development and poverty eradication are global priorities,

Responding to the findings of the Fourth Assessment Report of the Intergovernmental Panel on Climate Change that warming of the climate system is unequivocal, and that delay in reducing emissions significantly constrains opportunities to achieve lower stabilization levels and increases the risk of more severe climate change impacts,

Recognizing that deep cuts in global emissions will be required to achieve the ultimate objective of the Convention and emphasizing the urgency to address climate change as indicated in the Fourth Assessment Report of the Intergovernmental Panel on Climate Change,

1. Decides to launch a comprehensive process to enable the full, effective and sustained implementation of the Convention through long-term cooperative action, now, up to and beyond 2012, in order to reach an agreed outcome and adopt a decision at its fifteenth session, by addressing, inter alia:

   (a) A shared vision for long-term cooperative action, including a long-term global goal for emission reductions, to achieve the ultimate objective of the Convention, in accordance with the provisions and principles of the Convention, in particular the principle of common but differentiated responsibilities and respective capabilities, and taking into account social and economic conditions and other relevant factors …

   (b) Enhanced national/international action on mitigation of climate change …

   (c) Enhanced action on adaptation …

   (d) Enhanced action on technology development and transfer to support action on mitigation and adaptation …

   (e) Enhanced action on the provision of financial resources and investment to support action on mitigation and adaptation and technology cooperation including consideration of:

      (i) Improved access to adequate, predictable and sustainable financial resources and financial and technical support, and the provision of new and additional resources, including official and concessional funding for developing country Parties …

      (ii) Positive incentives for developing country Parties for the enhanced implementation of national mitigation strategies and adaptation action …

      (iii) Innovative means of funding to assist developing country Parties that are particularly vulnerable to the adverse impacts of climate change in meeting the cost of adaptation …

      (iv) Means to incentivize the implementation of adaptation actions on the basis of sustainable development policies …

      (v) Mobilization of public- and private-sector funding and investment, including facilitation of carbon-friendly investment choices …

      (vi) Financial and technical support for capacity-building in the assessment of the costs of adaptation in developing countries, in particular the most vulnerable ones, to aid in determining their financial needs …

2. Decides that the process shall be conducted under a subsidiary body under the Convention, hereby established and known as the Ad Hoc Working Group on Long-term Cooperative Action under the Convention, that shall complete its work in 2009 and present the outcome of its work to the Conference of the Parties for adoption at its fifteenth session

3–7. Setting out the terms of reference and financing arrangements for the COP14 in 2008.

Box 1.3 Carbon trading (by *Fiona Mullins*)

The United Nations Framework Convention on Climate Change (UNFCCC),[i] the Kyoto Protocol and emerging greenhouse gas emissions trading schemes are based on calculations of tonnages of each greenhouse gas (CO_2, CH_4, N_2O, HFCs, PFCs, SF_6). National greenhouse gas inventories of emissions are calculated and reported for UNFCCC compliance (and for future compliance with the Kyoto Protocol if it enters into force). The inventories are reported both in the tonnages of the actual gases (CO_2, CH_4, N_2O, HFCs, PFCs, SF_6) and also aggregated as a total CO_2 equivalent number. Each metric tonne of non-CO_2 gas is converted to CO_2 equivalents using a global warming potential number.

Greenhouse gas quantities are normally expressed in CO_2 equivalent units (CO_2e). Because each gas has a different impact on global warming, each non-CO_2 gas is multiplied by a Global Warming Potential (GWP) which reflects its impact relative to CO_2. The input data to this calculation are the tonnages emitted of each greenhouse gas, but the totals are reported in tonnes of CO_2 equivalent. For example each tonne of CH_4 is equivalent to 21 times a tonne of CO_2 because that is the standard metric used to approximate the effect of a tonne of CH_4 in the atmosphere compared to a tonne of CO_2 over a 100 year timeframe.

Emissions trading schemes for greenhouse gases use this same calculation methodology. For the UK emissions trading scheme, all greenhouse gases are potentially included, with some companies bringing N_2O and HFCs into the scheme as well as CO_2. The non-CO_2 units are translated into CO_2 equivalents for reporting and compliance purposes. For the EU emissions trading scheme, only CO_2 emissions are included in the first phase (2005–08) so the only relevant unit is metric tonnes of CO_2. Other gases may be added later as monitoring of them improves.

[i]See http://unfccc.int/index.html

global environmental conference in 1972 in Sweden, the UN sought to help governments rethink economic development and find ways to halt the destruction of irreplaceable natural resources and pollution of the planet.[27] One-hundred-and-eight heads of state were represented and the documents it produced included the *Rio Declaration on Environment and Development, Agenda 21*, the *Framework Convention on Climate Change*, and the *Convention on Biological Diversity*. Although these documents have not all achieved universal ratification, they have served as blueprints for the implementation of important sustainable development initiatives.

The Summit's message – that nothing less than a transformation of our attitudes and behaviour would bring about the necessary changes (harking back to Goldsmith's Blueprint of 1972) – was transmitted by almost 10000 on-site journalists and heard by millions around the world. The message reflected the complexity of the problems faced. Governments recognized the need to redirect international and national programmes and policies, in light of a 'grand survival plan' to ensure that all economic decisions fully took into account the environmental impacts of their actions, establishing for the first time in the context of international law, acceptance of the 'polluter pays' principle. The Rio Declaration set forth 27 universally applicable principles of sustainable development within which important themes were:

- Patterns of production: particularly the production of toxic components, such as lead in gasoline, or poisonous waste, many of which are major contributors to greenhouse gas emissions.
- Alternative sources of energy: to replace the use of fossil fuels which are linked to global climate change.

- A new reliance on public transportation systems: emphasized in order to reduce vehicle emissions, congestion in cities and the health problems caused by polluted air and smog. Transport emissions are a major contributor to greenhouse gas emissions.
- The growing scarcity of water: a major issue which is linked to a warmer climate as well as to increasing population and pollution.

The two-week Earth Summit in Rio was the climax of a sophisticated process, begun in December 1989, of planning, education and negotiations among all member states of the UN, leading to the adoption of Agenda 21, a wide-ranging blueprint for action to achieve sustainable development worldwide. Although Agenda 21 had been weakened by compromise and negotiation, it was still the most comprehensive and potentially effective programme of action ever sanctioned by the international community.

Much of the success of Agenda 21 has been derived from the training on environmental issues, instilled within its delivery, to the army of workers it has enlisted in the war on environmental degradation and climate change, from local council employees to heads of state. These forces have been armed, through the Agenda 21 process, with the units and measures, tools and methods, indicators and benchmarks that enable the most ordinary of people to be part of the most extraordinary monitoring project ever seen, the measuring of the rates and extent of the degradation of the planet on which we depend for our very survival. For, only by measuring the rates and extent of that degradation has it been possible to understand the risks we actually do face, and develop strategies to mitigate and avert them.

If one, simplistically, thinks of the climate change issue in terms of a war, then in overall command is the UN and its related organizations. Beneath it are the services represented by global treaties, gathered under banners such as Climate Change, Health, Poverty and Biodiversity, within which the laws, regulations and guidelines targeted at specific aspects of the global problem are developed. The IPCC and the World Health Organization (WHO) are definitely embedded in the intelligence unit at HQ, while Agenda 21 is responsible for the marshalling and training of the massed ranks of the forces. Nations act rather like battalion leaders commanding significant forces, under sectoral units such as transport, the environment and education. It is perhaps possible to compare other big players such as the World Trade Organization to parallel armies, acting, or not as the case may be, alongside the UN in its fight against climate change.

Within any army there are rogue commanders and infiltrators of the opposing forces who, for reasons of ignorance, convenience, malice or personal profit, attempt to impede the progress of the forces,[28] but no doubt, as the risks escalate, any restraint with which such counter-forces are dealt will decrease as the gloves come off. Internal fighting will break out and the obvious growing tensions between lobby groups will flare up. A case in point is the interests of the mining and agricultural sectors of Australia where the dominant coal industry has been able to protect their group interests, the selling of coal, against the weaker farmers' lobby who stand to lose everything as the great 'sunburnt country' gets browner.

Similarly, in the USA the oil lobby funds much government thinking on environmental issues while the farmers of the Mid-West who are slowly losing their lands to the droughts, floods and hurricanes, currently find it less easy to get a fair hearing at the top table in Washington. It is now happening that such minorities are turning to the law for recompense, just as those who were harmed by the knowing and malicious actions of the tobacco barons and the asbestos industry have recently won such major class actions in America.[29] It is certainly the case that in many

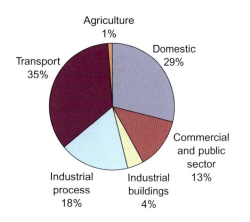
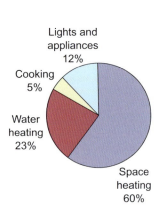

1.7.
Total UK delivered energy consumption by sector (*left*) and carbon emissions from buildings by source (*right*).
Source: Pout, C.H., MacKenzie, F. and Bettle, R. (2002) *Carbon Dioxide Emission from Non-domestic Buildings: 2000 and Beyond.* Watford: Building Research Establishment and Department for Environment, Food and Rural Affairs, p. 10.

places on the Earth the water wars between nations and interest groups have begun, and the parties are also resorting to the law to get justice in the face of environmental disputes.[30]

THE BATTLE RAGES

The battle, on many fronts, is growing more and more heated as the climate warms. The world is hotter now than it has been at any time in the past 2000 years. Eleven of the last 12 years (1995–2006) rank amongst the 12 hottest years on record, with temperatures in the Arctic increasing at over twice the average global rate over the past 100 years.[31]

The increase in the impact of climate change on the economy is well reflected in the magnitude and related costs for extreme climate events – up to 80% of all payouts by value – to the international insurance industry.[32]

The year 2003 proved to be a warning year. In July 2003 Sir John Houghton, former Chairman of the IPCC, informed the British public, in an article in the *Guardian* newspaper, that global warming was now a real weapon of mass destruction,[33] wielded by man himself:

The World Meteorological Organization warned in July 2003 that extreme weather events already seemed to be becoming more frequent as a result [of global warming]. The US mainland was struck by 562 tornados in May (which incidentally saw the highest land temperatures globally since records began in 1880), killing 41 people. The developing world is the hardest hit: extremes of climate tend to be more intense at low latitudes and poorer countries are less able to cope with disasters. Pre-monsoon temperatures in India reached a blistering 49°C (120°F)–50°C (9°F) above normal. Once this killer heat wave began to abate 1500 people were dead. While none can ascribe a single weather event to climate change with any degree of scientific certainty, higher maximum temperatures are one of the most predictable impacts of accelerated global warming.

In the following month of 2003, 35 000 Europeans died of heat stroke, with some 15 000 of those in France alone. The warning had already begun to come true.

THE COSTS OF THE WAR

In 2006 Sir Nicholas Stern's Review on the Economics of Climate Change was the first comprehensive UK review of the economic impacts of climate change. It clearly demonstrated that all countries will be affected by climate change, but the poorest countries will suffer earliest and

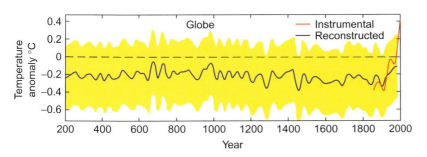

1.8.
Reconstructed global temperature anomaly (based on 1961–1990 instrumental reference period, adapted from Mann and Jones[31])

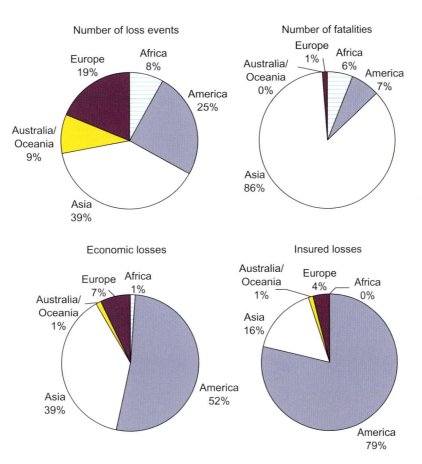

1.9.
Payouts by the insurance industry for natural disasters by geographical region.
Source: Munich Re, *Topics*: *Annual Review of Natural Catastrophes 2001*, see http://www.munichre. com/pdf/topics_2002_e.pdf.

most.[34] Its major conclusions were that average temperatures could rise by 5 °C from pre-industrial levels if climate change goes unchecked. His fairly dire conclusions are summarized below. He recommended *three elements of policy* for an effective response: carbon pricing, technology policy and energy efficiency. Carbon pricing, through taxation, emissions trading or regulation, will show people the full social costs of their actions. Technology policy should drive the large-scale development and use of a range of low-carbon and high-efficiency products. Climate change should be fully integrated into development policy, and rich countries should honour pledges to increase support through overseas development assistance. In December 2007 the UK Government pledged to put a carbon cost to every project it develops across government departments.

The Stern Review[34] concluded that 'business as usual' would cause a further 5.8°C rise in mean temperature, which would incur costs in excess of 20% of global GDP, while the cost of emission reduction measures to stabilize the temperature would be only 1% of GDP. The Stern Review, in conjunction with the IPCC AR4, marked a turning point in the global debate on climate change. It is impossible to state the extent to which Stern has caught the mood of the time, or created it, but either way there seems to have been a pronounced shift away from the debate over the science and towards the economics of mitigation versus adaptation.

The Australian climate change impacts report by economist Ross Gernaut for the Australian Government in 2007/08 further confirmed the potential extent of the social and economic impacts of a warming world,[35] but still politically corrective action was dilatory. Gernaut placed an emissions trading scheme (ETS) at the heart of the Australian response, but the value put on carbon is inevitably proportional to the amount of carbon that is needed to be saved and therefore traded. This is where it may be difficult to agree. One major problem in dealing with the issue is the widely varying and rapidly moving targets espoused by different groups.

Up until the Fourth IPCC Report there appeared to be some leeway in terms of the time available to achieve what were CO_2 emission reduction targets in the region of 450–550 ppm. However, in April 2007 the head of climate science at the NASA Goddard Institute for Space studies in New York, James Hansen, and his team shocked the scientific community by publishing a paper claiming that climate stability could only be guaranteed if we were to reduce CO_2 levels from the current level of 385 ppm in the atmosphere back to the 350 ppm mark.[36] The near-term impacts of not doing so are listed as including the inability of populations to adapt to rapidly changing temperatures, melting alpine glaciers, sea levels that rise several metres this century, and the loss of sea ice and coral reefs. The required levels of emissions reduction can be achieved, they propose, by phasing out coal generation except where the resulting CO_2 is sequestered, by adopting farming and forestry practices that sequester carbon from the atmosphere, and through the proposed costing of carbon.

One of the most effective books on the subject of what the impacts of the climate war will be was published in 2007 by Mark Lynas, on the impacts for humanity and the planet that may be caused by each degree that the global temperature rises.[37] It makes for grim reading and provided a basis, along with the Stern Report, for the form taken by our conclusions in the final chapter of this book.

THE WEAPONS ARE BEING HONED

As the rate of change in the climate accelerates to alarming levels the bid to meet more and more challenging targets is raised, and the weapons to meet deep cuts are being honed. Huge steps forward to tackle emissions regionally and by sector are being made around the world in an attempt to improve our mitigation defences, with the EU playing a real leadership role on the larger issues such as aviation.

Temp rise (°C)	Water	Food	Health	Land	Environment	Abrupt and Large-Scale Impacts
1°C	Small glaciers in the Andes disappear completely, threatening water supplies for 50 million people	Modest increase in cereal yields in temperate regions	At least 300 000 people each year die from climate-related diseases (predominantly diarrhoea, malaria, and malnutrition) Reduction in winter mortality in higher latitudes (Northern Europe, USA)	Permafrost thawing damages buildings and roads in parts of Canada and Russia	At least 10% of land species facing extinction (according to one estimate) 80% bleaching of coral reefs, including Great Barrier Reef	Atlantic Thermohaline Circulation starts to weaken
2°C	Potentially 20–30% decrease in water availability in some vulnerable regions, e.g. Southern Africa and Mediterranean	Sharp declines in crop yield in tropical regions (5–10% in Africa)	40–60 million more people exposed to malaria in Africa	Up to 10 million more people affected by coastal flooding each year	15–40% of species facing extinction (according to one estimate) High risk of extinction of Arctic species, including polar bear and caribou	Potential for Greenland ice sheet to begin melting irreversibly, accelerating sea level rise and committing world to an eventual 7 m sea level rise Rising risk of abrupt changes to atmospheric circulations, e.g. the monsoon
3°C	In Southern Europe, serious droughts occur once every 10 years 1–4 billion more people suffer water shortages, while 1–5 billion gain water, which may increase flood risk	150–550 additional millions at risk of hunger (if carbon fertilization weak) Agricultural yields in higher latitudes likely to peak	1–3 million more people die from malnutrition (if carbon fertilization weak)	1–170 million more people affected by coastal flooding each year	20–50% of species facing extinction (according to one estimate), including 25–60% mammals, 30–40% birds and 15–70% butterflies in South Africa Collapse of Amazon rainforest (according to some models)	Rising risk of collapse of West Antarctic Ice Sheet Rising risk of collapse of Atlantic Thermohaline Circulation
4°C	Potentially 30–50% decrease in water availability in Southern Africa and Mediterranean	Agricultural yields decline by 15–35% in Africa, and entire regions out of production (e.g. parts of Australia)	Up to 80 million more people exposed to malaria in Africa	7–300 million more people affected by coastal flooding each year	Loss of around half Arctic tundra Around half of all the world's nature reserves cannot fulfill objectives	
5°C	Possible disappearance of large glaciers in Himalayas, affecting one-quarter of China's population and hundreds of millions in India	Continued increase in ocean acidity seriously disrupting marine ecosystems and possibly fish stocks		Sea level rise threatens small islands, low-lying coastal areas (Florida) and major world cities such as New York, London, and Tokyo		
More than 5°C	The latest science suggests that the Earth's average temperature will rise by even more than 5 or 6°C if emissions continue to grow and positive feedbacks amplify the warming effect of greenhouse gases (e.g. release of carbon dioxide from soils or methane from permafrost). This level of global temperature rise would be equivalent to the amount of warming that occurred between the last age and today – and is likely to lead to major disruption and large-scale movement of population. Such "socially contingent" effects could be catastrophic, but are currently very bare to capture with current models as temperatures would be so far outside human experience.					

1.10.
Highlights from the Stern Report of 2005 showing the escalation in possible impacts or increasing global temperatures. *Source*: The Stern Report, 2005, HMSO.

Some areas have not been dealt with adequately, such as the emissions from shipping. The UN International Maritime Organization (IMO) reported in December 2007 on the emissions caused by its 47 000-strong global fleet. There has been a huge rise in shipping over the past decade and between 2008 and 2012, it is predicted that 6100 new container ships and bulk carriers, the world's largest ships, will be built, a 50% increase on total shipping capacity that is the same number in five years as the number of new jumbo jets expected to take to the skies in 10 years.

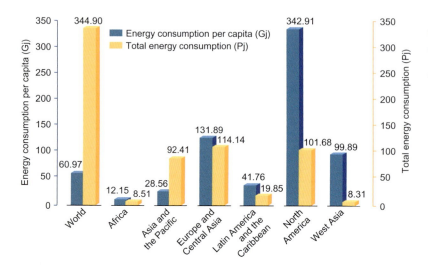

1.11.
Total and per capita energy consumption 1995 by region. *Source*: http://www.unep.org/geo2000/english/figures.htm.

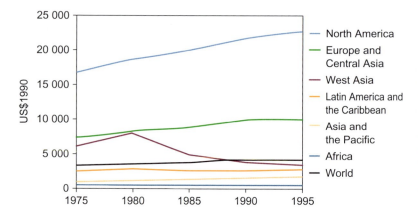

1.12.
Gross domestic product per capita 1995 by region. One of the problems faced is that the wealth of nations is directly related to their emissions in the tradition analyses of the trends in the twentieth century economy. This will change radically with the new predicted clean economies of the twenty-first century in which high emissions per capita will be a sign of poverty. *Source*: http://www.unep.org/geo2000/english/figures.htm.

Shipping appeared to have escaped scrutiny but it emits around 2% of global emissions, at least equal to airlines. And some say that it could account for twice the emissions of flying. Shipping, like aviation, falls outside the Kyoto Protocol but it accounts for almost 90% of all world trade, and this figure is rising.[38] But who owns these emissions and within whose borders do they lie?

On 27 May 2008, Members of the European Parliament (MEPs) on the environment committee voted overwhelmingly to include aviation in European ETS a year earlier than planned, in 2011 rather than 2012 as had been proposed by the Commission and the 27 national governments. They also lowered the cap from 100% of 2004/05 emissions to 90%. The plan would cost passengers £8 extra on EU flights and £32 on transatlantic routes, adding to the economic pressure on flying being experienced as a result of soaring fuel prices.[39]

Countries within Europe are taking enormous strides forward in building their own low-carbon economies. Germany has built the world's leading solar economy, being followed in this field by the massive investment in solar technologies by China.

Amongst European governments Spain has the highest dependency on fossil fuels, using them to meet 84% of its energy needs, and in 2007 it spent some 17 billion euro on oil imports. Rising fuel prices have been pushing up inflation. The Spanish Government is taking firm action to reduce energy consumption, and in 2005, taking a lead from the city of Barcelona and state of Catalan, introduced the first European solar law requiring all new homes to have solar hot water systems on their roofs. They calculate that they will save millions of euro spent on imported oil by cutting speed limits on dual carriageways outside major cities, bringing it in line with Barcelona, which already has a top speed limit of 50 mph. They are also handing out over 49 million free low-energy light bulbs, two per household, and by 2012 all light bulbs will be low energy. With these as part of a broad swath of measures between now and 2014, the Spanish Government hopes to reduce oil imports by 10% a year, cutting annual consumption by 44 million barrels. Air conditioning systems in public buildings will be set no lower than 26°C and in winter Spaniards, except in hospitals, will not be able to turn their heating higher than 21°C. Street lighting will be cut by 50% and the metro system will stay open later so that people can leave their cars at home. The government is planning to manufacture 1 million electric cars and all government vehicles are to meet at least 20% of their energy needs with biofuels. Commercial airlines will be allowed to use military routes to make routes 20% shorter.[40]

But the EU is not the only region taking firm action. Japan was the first country to introduce carbon labels on food, drinks, detergents and appliances from spring 2009, under a government-approved calculation and labelling system developed by the Trade Ministry. Again, this pioneering position has made them confront the questions of how to produce a robust calculation system that prevents 'in-house labelling schemes' being used that make some products appear to be more attractive than others. The carbon footprint for a bag of crisps, for instance, is:

1 bag of crisps $= 75\,g\ CO_2$
44% growing potatoes
30% chip production
15% packaging
9% delivery
2% disposal

The main driver for consumers to adopt low-carbon products appears to be the rush to be seen to be environmentally friendly, but there are obviously fairly firm limits to how much consumers would be willing to pay for eco-friendly goods. This is a problem that has been tackled in the UK, where high-carbon products are already being penalized under the tax regime (Table 1.1).

Table 1.1 Annual road tax for cars registered after 1 March 2001 (announced in the Spring Budget 2007)

Car band	CO_2 (g/km)	Diesel cars (£)	Petrol cars (£)	Alternative fuel cars (£)
A	Up to 100 g	0	0	0
B	101–120 g	35	35	15
C	121–150 g	115	115	95
D	151–165 g	140	140	120
E	166–185 g	165	165	145
F	186–225 g	205	205	190
G	226 g plus	300	300	285

Source: Vehicle Certification Agency's website: www.vcacarfueldata.org.uk

UK ministers were instructed to factor the shadow carbon costs into their financial calculations for any new plans, policies and investment decisions on transport, construction, housing, energy and planning. To do this they will use the shadow price for carbon, which represents the cost to society of the environmental damage done by carbon. The starting price for carbon in 2007 was put at £5.50 a tonne and it is predicted to rise annually to a price of around £59.60 a tonne in 2050. However, the theory that the carbon price will act against projects for new roads and power stations does not seem to have been effective, as the UK Government subsequently gave permission for a new generation of coal-fired power stations. One real problem this poses to the Government is how to do the calculations to ensure that they are universally consistent across departments.

TARGET LOCK-ON IS PROVING DIFFICULT

Another problem in trying to arrive at 'joined-up' thinking on how to reduce the impacts of climate change has been the lack of agreement on what reduction targets we should be meeting, before the question of how we meet them even arises.

The most credible method of achieving agreement on the required levels of emission reduction is that of 'Contraction and Convergence' (C&C), which has been described as looking increasingly like 'the only game in town'.

C&C, devised by Aubrey Meyer at the Global Commons Institute, is all about reducing the total global output of greenhouse gases, by gradually reducing national emissions to targets based on per capita quotas over time. To meet the more stringent atmospheric levels over the course of the century total global emissions would have to drop from an average of 1 tonne of CO_2 per person to below 0.3 tonnes per person over time depending on what is the final atmospheric level aimed at and how quickly it has to be achieved. C&C has the potential to smooth over the political and economic cracks that are threatening to tear down the Kyoto, and subsequent Protocols.

The convergence figures represent what it is estimated to be the carbon emissions reductions needed to stabilize climate change. The discrepancy between the reality of what we emit and what is required is being faced up to by some governments and the EU. On 23 January 2008 the EU put forward an integrated proposal for Climate Action in which a mandatory target of 20% of all energy use for the EU would come from renewables by 2020 and set a 10% minimum target for biofuels by 2020.[41] A plethora of action plans and associated targets has been proposed and adopted by many different groups and organizations, from local communities to towns and cites, states and countries, and over the next few years we may see these coalesce into a credible coordinated attempt by humanity to put in place the implementable strategies we need, quite simply, to survive. At the heart of such a targets framework, if it is to work, must lie the notion of C&C.

FIGHTING IN THE RANKS

Resistance to changing our own ways of life is enormous and is fought on many fronts. One of Former President George W. Bush's first actions when he came to power was to withdraw the USA from the Kyoto treaty. Despite the USA being one of the most vulnerable continents to extreme weather damage, the issues of global warming have been, by and large, presented to the

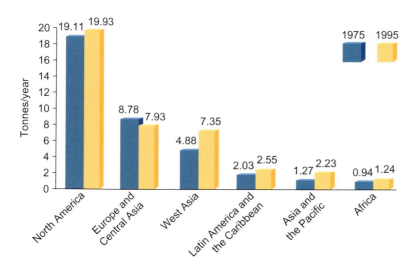

1.13.
CO_2 emissions per capita for the different regions of the world in 1975 and 1995 demonstrating how large the gap is between different countries and the scale of the challenges we face in trying to establish protocols for the equitable emissions of carbon dioxide.
Source: http://www.unep.org/geo2000/english/figures.htm.

Box 1.4 Contraction and Convergence (by *Aubrey Meyer*)[42]

ESSENTIAL PROPOSITION OF C&C

The C&C model[i] formalizes the objective and principles of the UNFCCC. It first proposes a reviewable global greenhouse gas (ghg) emissions 'contraction budget' targeted at a safe and stable future level for atmospheric ghg concentrations.

The internationally tradable shares in this budget are then agreed on the basis of 'convergence' from now, where shares are broadly proportional to income, to a target date in the budget timeline, after which they remain proportional to an agreed base year of global population. Recognizing that the bigger the budget, the greater the risks, and that decarbonization is further enhanced if revenue from emission

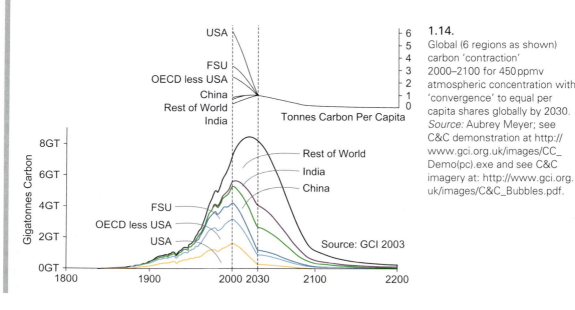

1.14.
Global (6 regions as shown) carbon 'contraction' 2000–2100 for 450 ppmv atmospheric concentration with 'convergence' to equal per capita shares globally by 2030.
Source: Aubrey Meyer; see C&C demonstration at http://www.gci.org.uk/images/CC_Demo(pc).exe and see C&C imagery at http://www.gci.org.uk/images/C&C_Bubbles.pdf.

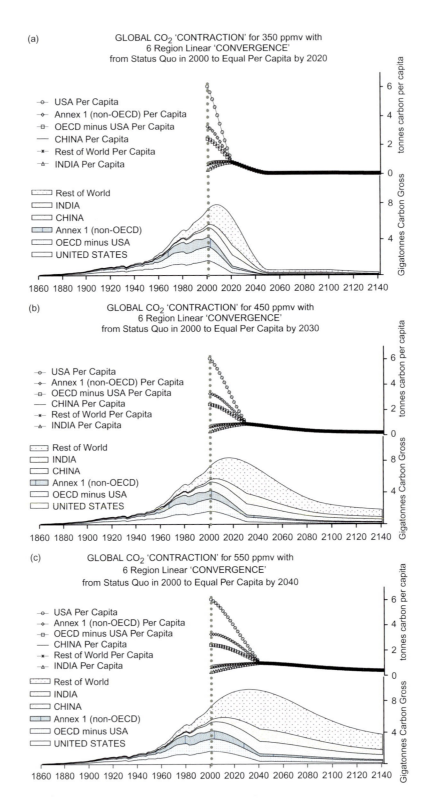

1.15.
C&C diagrams demonstrating the required emissions modification to stabilize the global carbon dioxide concentrations at (a) 350 ppm by 2020; (b) 450 ppm by 2030; and (c) 550 ppm by 2040.
Source: Aubrey Meyer.

trading is re-invested in zero emissions techniques. This reduces the randomness that has dogged negotiations since 1992 over future emissions commitments/entitlements, as it resolves the conflict between the GDP-led approaches and those emphasizing responsibility for the historic build-up of atmospheric concentrations.

CONTRACTION

On the basis of precaution, and guided by the scientific advice of the IPCC, all governments or regional groupings of governments jointly and severally agree to observe such an atmospheric target. With this it is possible to calculate the total diminishing amount of greenhouse gases that the world can emit for each year in the coming century. Whatever the rate chosen, C&C views this event as a whole as 'Contraction'.[ii]

CONVERGENCE

On the basis of equity, convergence means that each year's ration of this global emissions budget can be shared so that each country, or group of countries, progressively converges on the same allocation per inhabitant by an agreed date, for example by 2030. This recognizes the principle of globally equal rights per capita to the 'global commons' of the atmosphere, but achieved by smooth transition.[iii] Where countries or groups do have a diversity of natural endowments, C&C acknowledges this too by embracing, for example, the EU, which operates as a unit at the international level whilst creating its own convergence arrangements.

EMISSIONS PERMIT TRADING

Only emissions in excess of the total of permits created under C&C are not permitted ('hot-air'). Countries unable to manage within their agreed shares would, subject to the above and appropriate rules, be able to buy the unused parts of the allocations of other countries or regions. Sales of unused allocations would give low per capita emitting countries the income to fund sustainable development in zero-emission ways. High per capita emitting countries gain a mechanism to mitigate the premature retirement of their carbon capital stock whilst also benefiting from the export markets for renewable technologies this restructuring would create. All countries therefore benefit from more rapidly avoided global damages.

SUSTAINABLE GROWTH

Climate change increasingly augurs potentially catastrophic losses. C&C mitigates this by integrating the key features of global diplomacy and development necessary for long-term prosperity and security. C&C synthesizes the objective and principles of the UNFCCC in a constitutional rather than a stochastic manner, so that the necessary foundation for the transition to a new growth and prosperity is specifically guided by this agreement to the zero carbon energy technologies that make this prosperity with security possible.

[i] C&C options will calculate any rates of contraction and convergence for all countries' CO_2.

[ii] The example chosen shows global CO_2 emissions reduced to 40% of 1990 output value by 2100 giving a stable atmospheric concentration of 450 parts per million of CO_2 by 2100. Other contraction 'shapes' are possible for the same concentration outcome. Different rates of contraction are possible leading to different concentration outcomes but damages from climate change increase proportional to delay.

[iii] The example shows global pre-distribution of contraction through linear convergence so shares are proportional to international populations by 2050 with figures for population growth frozen from 2050 forwards. Different rates of convergence are possible and different dates of freezing population are possible. Both of these affect the pre-distribution of the tradable emissions entitlements.

American people as 'not an issue'. In October 2003 the US Senate rejected a plan, by 55 votes to 43, to curb CO_2 emissions from industry. The Bill, sponsored by John McCain (Republican) and Joe Liberman (Democrat), would have required industrial plants, not vehicles, to cut back emissions of CO_2 and other greenhouse gas emissions to 2000 levels by 2010. Larry Craig, the Idaho senator, said there was no need for a 'massive new regulatory process' for industrial CO_2. 'It is not a pollutant. It does not represent a direct threat to public health.' The White House opposed the Bill as it required 'deep cuts in fossil fuel use' to meet an 'arbitrary goal', and would drive up energy bills and pump prices. Since then there has been a change in US policy, led largely by pressure from below, from cities and their mayors[43] and industry,[44] and by the new Obama Administration.

Problems that were identified then for the USA are now rapidly changing:

- The voter is typically not concerned about environmental issues (and is very ill informed about them).
- Business lobbies, such as industry associations and ideological think-tanks, play a significant role in influencing policy.

The USA, which has known, in depth, about the problems and science of climate change for over 40 years and was the first nation in the world to sign the 1992 UN Climate Change Convention, has, with its blocking tactics over Kyoto, managed to prevent the world from 'locking-on' to clear and achievable targets that may provide the direct strike at the problem we need to survive, and meanwhile the problem grows in strength daily. However, many hope that the new administration may change all this in Copenhagen.

IS THE BATTLE LOST ALREADY?

What is clear now is that this war is the great war of all time for our own species. It is already too late for many others. We must act firmly and effectively in the face of the incontrovertible evidence

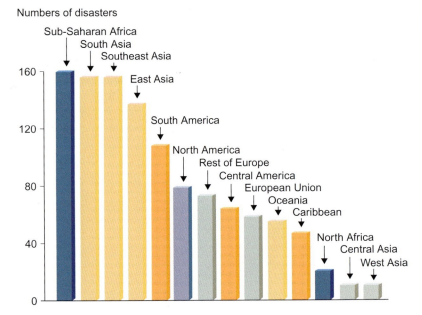

1.16.
The number of climate-related disasters experienced per continent, 1993–1997.
Source: http://www.unep.org/geo2000/english/figures.htm.

before us to fight it. We cannot trust to governments alone, or corporations, or councils to do what is necessary. There is no magic technical or surgical solution in this old-fashioned war. There is a crucial role in the frontline of this battle for every man, woman and child on the planet.[45,46]

There are some basic rules in this war. Rule number one is that: From those who have the most, the most must be expected. Equality and proportionality are the two key guiding principles that will help us survive through the twenty-first century. And because buildings use more energy than any other single sector in the developed world, it is from the building sector that the greatest cuts have been predicted as possible, and must be forthcoming. They use more energy than any other sector – they must make the biggest cuts.

This book shows that it may be possible to effect the 'radical change in our approach to the environment' called for by Goldsmith in 1972 and the authors of Agenda 21, 20 years later. These changes will cost real money, and cause real pain, but any war does. By March 2004 over $110 billion had already been spent by the USA alone on invading the single country of Iraq.[47] By the end of July 2008 the Iraq war had cost the USA over $542 000 000 000, or $1700 per person, $4600 per household and $341.4 million a day. By the end of 2009 governments globally had pledged trillions to save the banking system.

How much are we willing to spend on saving the world? It is money we have to spend, and pain we have to shoulder, because it is increasingly looking as if radical change of the contraction and convergence scale is necessary if we intend to survive on this planet in the long term.

So how long do we have to wait for answers to the key questions of the next two decades of the twenty-first century:

- Will that radical change happen?
- Can we adapt our buildings and cities to survive through the twenty-first century?
- Are we already too late?

Economist Ross Garnaut, in his 2008 report to the Australian Government,[48] pointed out that the 2007 IPCC report targets are based on unrealistically conservative emissions predictions, at a time when real CO_2 levels are increasing by 3% per annum globally. He does not believe that under that current treaties and emission reduction programmes we have any chance of meeting the ambitious European target of stabilizing atmospheric CO_2 levels at 450 ppm, when we are already at over 389 ppm and rising by at least 2 ppm per annum. It is considered that a target of 450 ppm will result in a temperature rise this century of 2°C, and the higher target of 550 ppm, which we are well on course to achieving and exceeding, will result in a mean global temperature increase of at least 3°C. Both figures, the report concludes, will result in runaway climate change. James Hansen of the NASA Space Institute now believes that if we are to enjoy a stable climate in the future we have to claw back the atmospheric CO_2 levels to 350 ppm.

To meet the 450 ppm target the USA and Australia would have to make annual reductions in emissions of 5% per annum in the next decade. The UK Climate Change Bill, the most ambitious in the world, calls for 3% per annum reductions to 2050.[49] Garnaut himself concludes that even to achieve the 450 ppm targets we will need far tighter constraints on emissions than are included in current agreements for both the developed and the developing world, but that achieving them 'does not appear to be realistic at this time'.

The following chapters outline how experts predict the climate will change. We include a wide range of evidence on what impacts those changes will have on our lifestyles and the buildings and settlements in which we live. Buildings are responsible for over 50% of all greenhouse gas emissions in the developed world, and much of the planning to date on the issue of climate change has centred around the challenge of mitigation, of reducing emissions of greenhouse gases from the built environment.

We now have to face the fact that it is more than likely that we will never achieve the required reductions to avoid climate chaos in the coming decades and centuries. It would be a wise plan now to prepare to adapt the infrastructure of our buildings and lifestyles to be able to withstand the extremes that will be thrown at us by a rapidly changing climate. This book is about developing an action plan for survival in the difficult decades ahead.

In Chapter 2 we look at idea of risk and how we can use an understanding of risk to inform the way we design the buildings and cities of the future.

NOTES AND REFERENCES

1   In January 2004 Sir David King, the Chief Scientific Adviser to the UK Prime Minister, made an address to the House of Lords in which he clearly stated that climate change was now a greater threat to humanity than terrorism. See <http://news.bbc.co.uk/1/hi/sci/tech/3381425.stm>.

2   On 22 February 2004 Mark Townsend and Paul Harris of the *Observer* published an article, on page 3, on a secret report produced by eminent scientists for the Pentagon which made chilling reading and warned of the very imminent threat of climate change that would ensure that 'disruption and conflict will be endemic features of life'. See <http://observer.guardian.co.uk/international/story/0,6903,1153514,00.html>.

3   A British study covering 40 years of comprehensive evidence reported that butterflies, birds and plants are in decline for around 70%, 54% and 28% of species, respectively. The study, published in the US journal *Science* on 19 March 2004, was said by Jeremy Thomas of the UK Natural Environment Research Council to add 'enormous strength to the hypothesis that the world is approaching its sixth major extinction event'. He pointed out that the other events were cosmic, coming from outer space, while this event appears to come from within, from our own species that 'through its overexploitation and its wastes, it eats, destroys, or poisons the others'. See Tim Radford's article on 'The Decline of Species', on page 1 of the Guardian, 19 March 2004.

4   Worldwatch Institute, State of the World Report 2008, see <http://www.worldwatch.org/stateoftheworld>.

5   M. Hulme, G. Jenkins, X. Lu, J. Turnpenny, T. Mitchell, R. Jones, J. Lowe, J. Murphy, D. Hassell, P. Boorman, R. McDonald and S. Hill, Climate Change Scenarios for the United Kingdom: The UKCIP02 Scientific Report, Appendix 2, published in conjunction with UKCIP, the Hadley Centre and the Climate Research Unit in the School of Environmental Science at the University of East Anglia, by the Tyndall Centre, Norwich, 2002.

6   For a full introduction to the process of climate change see <http://climatechange.unep.net/>.

7   For the global weather warning that extreme weather events are on the increase from the Secretary of the World Meteorological Organization on 3 July 2003, see <http://www.unic.org.in/News/2003/pr/pr111.html> and <http://www.guardian.co.uk/comment/story/0,3604,1007042,00.html>.

8   J.K. Galbraith, The affluent society, 1st ed, 1958., Penguin Books, Canada, 1999 p. 17.

9   For more information see the Mauna Loa Solar Observatory site on <http://mlso.hao.ucar.edu/>.

10 As early as 1965, three groups, all in the USA, had established ongoing efforts in general circulation modelling of the climate: Geophysical Fluid Dynamics Laboratory; UCLA Department of Meteorology; National Center for Atmospheric Research. Among the important Climate Circulation Modelling groups established in 1965–1975, two were in the USA, a country that has been aware, longer than any other, of the significance of climate change. These three were the RAND Corporation (Santa Monica, CA); Goddard Institute for Space Studies (New York, NY); and the Australian Numerical Meteorological Research Centre (Melbourne, Australia). For a fuller history of climate modelling see <http://www.aip.org/history/sloan/gcm/1965_75.html>.

11 The current climate models, building on the works of such earlier researchers, now use the commonly accepted 'general circulation models' (GCMs) or AGCMs ('atmospheric general circulation models'). These are complex models of the Earth's atmosphere and are time-consuming and expensive to run, usually funded by national governments. Early GCM scenarios were based on a doubling of the pre-industrial equivalent CO_2 concentration in the atmosphere. The models were run until a new equilibrium state was reached corresponding to this increased concentration of CO_2.

    In the 1990s GCMs began to incorporate submodels of the oceans, variously referred to as 'coupled ocean–atmosphere models' or CGCMs. Because the dynamics of climate change is dominated by the effect of the oceans, these models allow transient (time-dependent) simulations of the future climate to be made. Year on year these models are becoming more sophisticated and can now incorporate the impacts of aerosols in the atmosphere, and climate feedback, to a resolution of 50, down to even 5 km squares. For an explanation of the models used recently by the UK Climate Impacts Programme see <http://www.ukcip.org.uk/scenarios/pdfs/UKCIP02TechRep/Cover.pdf>.

12 <http://www.ipcc.ch/>.

13 D.H. Meadows, The Limits to Growth; A report for the club of Rome's project on the predicament of mankind, St Martins Press, London, 1972.

14 W.W. Washington, Study of Man's impact on the climate (SMIC), MIT Press, Cambridge, MA, 1971.

15 E. Goldsmith, R. Allen, M. Allenby, J. Davull, S. Lawrence, A Blueprint for Survival, Tom Stacy, London, 1972.

16 Goldsmith et al., A Blueprint for Survival, p. 27.

17 S. Roaf, Closing the Loop, RIBA Publications, London, 2004.

18 M.J. Molina, F.S. Rowland, Stratospheric sink for chlorofluoromethanes – chlorine atom catalysed destruction of ozone, Nature 249 (1974) 810.

19 J. Farman, B. Gardiner, J. Shanklin, Large losses of total ozone in Antarctica reveal seasonal ClOx/NOx interaction, Nature 315 (1985) 207–210.

20 <https://www.nas.nasa.gov/About/Education/Ozone/history.html>.

21 <http://www.theozonehole.com/> The Dobson Unit: one Dobson Unit (DU) is defined to be 0.01 mm thickness at STP (standard temperature and pressure). Ozone layer thickness

is expressed in terms of Dobson Units, which measure what its physical thickness would be if compressed in the earth's atmosphere. In those terms, it is very thin indeed. A normal range is 300–500 Dobson Units, which translates to an eighth of an inch – two stacked penny coins. In space, it is best not to envision the ozone layer as a distinct, measurable band. Instead, think of it in terms of parts per million concentrations in the stratosphere (the layer 6 to 30 miles above the Earth's surface). Such units, measurements, the targets they enable us to set are the basic weapons of our war on climate change. The unit is named after G.M.B. Dobson, one of the first scientists to investigate atmospheric ozone. This DU description was written by The Ozone Hole Organization and 'A Riddle inside a Conundrum within a Parable surrounded by an Enigma, and Up A Tree Again Productions'. For full details of their research, Dobson Units and current maps of the ozone hole see <http://www.theozonehole.com>.

22 One of the best sites on related science is that of the US National Oceanic and Atmospheric Administration. See <http://www.pmel.noaa.gov/>.

23 This section was written using some parts of the article by Leonie Haimson in *Grist* magazine on the Agenda 21 summit. See <http://www.gristmagazine.com/heatbeat/inshorta.asp>.

24 For a complete explanation of the processes of climate change and the related publications of the IPCC, modelling techniques and legislation see <http://www.ipcc.ch/> and for a potted and well-informed history see <http://www.doc.mmu.ac.uk/aric/eae/Global_Warming/global_warming.html>.

25 For a full state of play on the climate conventions see <http://unfccc.int/index.html>.

26 For a full list of parties signed up to the treaty see <http://unfccc.int/resource/convkp.html>.

27 <http://www.un.org/esa/sustdev/documents/agenda21/index.htm>. For a full list of the current Agenda 21 Action Programmes see <http://www.unep.org/>.

28 See the very interesting website for The European Business Council for a Sustainable Energy Future on <http://www.e5.org> for a run-down of the COPs.

29 A report compiled in 2002 by international law firm Baker and McKenzie warned that people are increasingly looking to lay blame for climate change costs and impacts and the main possible legal actions are either of a government suing a government, or an individual or an environmental organization suing a company for failing to do something, or alternatively, as we are now seeing in the USA, for governments or individuals suing the regulatory authorities for failing to deal with greenhouse emissions <http://www.abc.net.au/am/content/2003/s979176.htm>. The cases in the USA involve a group of environmental groups, joined by three American cities, suing the US export credit agencies for funding fossil fuel projects. Another group is suing the Environmental Protection Agency for a lack of action. Ironically it may be those companies who have publicly taken an anti-climate change line that are most vulnerable because their actions may be proved to have been in bad faith. For a good discussion on this trend see <http://www.legalaffairs.org/issues/September-October-2002/review_appelbaum_sepoct2002.html>. For a range of related issues raised see also <http://earthscience.surfwax.com/files/Global_Warming.html> and <http://www.iisd.ca/climate-l/Climate-L_News_17.html>.

30 People have long talked of the impending 'water wars', covered in Chapter 4 of this book, but they are already happening. Civil unrest within countries, and between countries and different interest groups on the subject of water, is an already chronic problem in many part of the

world, and long chronicled. See, for instance, P. Gleick (Ed.), Water in Crisis: A Guide to the World's Freshwater Resources. Oxford: Oxford University Press, 1993.

31 <http://www.ipcc.ch/ipccreports/ar4-syr.pdf>.

32 <http://www.zoca.com/swallowtail/articles/climate.html>.

33 Michael Meacher, Guardian, 28 July 2003, p. 14.

34 <http://www.occ.gov.uk/activities/stern.htm>.

35 <http://www.cgi.org.uk/briefings/Interim_Report_Feb_2008.pdf>.

36 For a link to the full paper see <http://.arxiv.org/abs/0804.1126>.

37 M. Lynas, Six degrees: Our future on a Hotter Planet, Fourth Estate, 2007.

38 Independent, 11 December 2007, Business, p. 38.

39 Guardian, 28 May 2008, p. 26.

40 Guardian, 31 July, 2008, p. 23.

41 <http://www.nature.com/nsu/031124/031124-14.html>. See also note 29 above and the concerns about trading in 'bad faith'.

42 <http://ec.europa.eu/energy/energy_policy/index_en.htm>.

43 For full details of C&C see the excellent website of the Global Commons Institute on <http://www.gci.org.uk/>.

44 See <http://www.kyotousa.org> and <http://www.citymayors.com/environment/usmayors_kyoto.html>.

45 See the World Business Council for Sustainable Development website: <http://www.wbcsd.org>.

46 <http://www.icount.org.uk> is a site run the very effective Stop Climate Chaos organization. See also <http://www.carboncounting.co.uk>.

47 See <http://www.costofwar.com> for an ongoing running total of the costs of the Iraq war to the USA.

48 For full details of the Ross Garnaut Review (2008) see <http://www.garnautreview.org.au/>.

49 See <http://www.defra.gov.uk/environment/climatechange/uk/legislation/> for details of the climate change bill.

2 RISK, SCENARIOS AND INSURANCE

INTRODUCTION

All of us are placed at risk by climate change. Some of us are more at risk than others, and for some that risk will prove catastrophic. It is fundamentally important to understand the nature of that risk in order to be able to future-proof the lives of individuals against it in the face of the rapidly changing circumstances of the twenty-first century.[1]

Risk, we believe, is composed of three elements:

1. The **vulnerability** of the person to a climate risk is influenced by the design and fabric of the buildings they occupy, and their habits, age, health and wealth. People in traditional buildings often have well-understood capabilities of adapting their buildings and seasonal and diurnal lifestyles to extend the range of climatic conditions they can occupy safely and comfortably. For those who live in settlements in already exposed locations such as hot deserts, in 'modern' houses with thin walls and roofs, large windows, dependent on air conditioning, they are either infinitely more vulnerable to changes in climate, or less so, than those in traditional, thick-walled houses with shading and deep basements. The ability of the modern house dweller to cope with extreme heat is dependent on their ability to pay for the energy to run coolers and the availability of electricity to run them. In the traditional house the ability to adapt the house lies with the homeowner, who is not at the mercy of the local grid and economy, utility prices, their own wealth and the global availability of oil. The young and the old, the weak and the sick are also more vulnerable to climate extremes.

2. The idea of the **exposure** of a person deals with the third element in the symbiotic triangle that ties people to their ecosystem and climate, and in turn to the bricks and mortar of their homes. The degree to which any population will be exposed to the worst extremes of climate change is related to their geographical location in relation to latitude, land masses and the patterns of the changes experienced. Some areas of the world will experience far faster and more extreme warming, in particular in the high latitudes of the northern hemisphere and towards the centres of land masses in areas with 'continental' climates. Geographically, the 'exposure' of Britain to swings of temperature has been damped by its island status, benefiting as it does from the thermal inertia of the vast oceans that surround it and are stirred towards

uniformity by the sea currents of the Atlantic Ocean. However, through its location on the edge of that ocean, the UK is one of the windiest countries in Europe and more exposed than most to storms. Those in Alaska, whose homes are on the melting tundra, and who face some of the most rapid predicted increases in temperature globally, are infinitely more 'exposed' to the risks of large-scale temperature increases than most, regardless of how much change their homes can accommodate.

3. The nature of the **hazard** is perhaps what will do for many of us in the long run. Hazard is a term that is typically described in terms of the size of the risk and the frequency with which it is experienced. How extreme the climate becomes, and how often will it be extreme are significant. If a river floods homes once in a century then those homes are under considerably less risk than homes that flood every year or two. It is on these two measures of hazard that the insurance industry largely bases its insurance premiums.[2] This can be illustrated with a case study. In 1993 Britain experienced one of the strongest storms in recent history. The 'Braer' depression ranged across Scotland for almost three weeks, reaching UK record-breaking lows of 915 millibars (the lowest pressure ever recorded in Europe is 912 millibars and hurricane Andrew, which cost the USA $30 billion in 1992, only reached 924 millibars). And yet its cost to the British insurance industry was (relatively) negligible, despite the strength of its *hazard*, for two reasons. First, it tracked across Scotland only, missing most of England, so the *exposure* of the British Isles to it was relatively low. Secondly, in Scotland building standards are higher than in England. Roofs still have to have sarking beneath the roof finishes and are more firmly constructed than required under English regulations, so reducing the *vulnerability* of individual buildings exposed to the storm.

It is, however, important to understand all aspects of the risks we face if we are to act effectively to reduce those risks over time.

RISK AND IMPACT

Risks ultimately either do, or do not, translate into damage to an individual, livelihoods, institutions, a landscape, a country or the planet. Risk is the potential for that damage to occur. The damage may take the form of a wide range of impacts, covered in chapters within this book on how hot, wet and windy it will get. The discussion on the insurance industry addresses the question of how much change we are faced with from the climate and also explores the idea of how vulnerable and exposed different peoples, settlements and buildings have been to such climate hazards in the past, to give an idea of how we may be affected by them in the future. Everything is connected in our world, so climate impacts on a landscape will affect, for instance, the insurance industry, which in turn impacts on regional development and the future of buildings and cities in such regions. Our understanding of future risk is still informed by past experience of related impacts.

2.1.
The risk triangle.
Source: Crichton, D. (1999) The risk triangle. In Ingleton, J. (ed.), *Natural Disaster Management.* London: Tudor Rose.

Risk can be calculated thus:

$$(possible)Hazard \times Vulnerability \times Exposure = (possible)Impact$$

The point to be emphasized here is that if any one of the three factors is zero then there is no risk. If risk is measured by the area of an acute angled triangle, a reduction in any one side will reduce risk. Risk management then becomes a case of examining each of the three sides in turn to look for the most cost-effective solutions.

For example, if one imagines the flood risk for a coastal town built on low-lying land at the mouth of a major river, how should the flood risk be managed? Does one tackle the vulnerability, hazard or exposure of the town?

Vulnerability

This is perhaps the obvious solution: build a flood barrier and flood walls; construct flood-proof buildings; put buildings and evacuation routes on stilts; consider floating buildings as in The Netherlands. Some years ago, a village in North Wales was repeatedly flooded and the children could not get to school. The children were issued with stilts, and this produced a cheap solution to the problem.

Hazard

While there may not be an immediate solution to increased rainfall events, rivers can be modified to cope with heavier rainfall. In Europe, meanders have been reinstated in the River Rhine in Germany, in order to reduce the flood risk for The Netherlands, for example. Unfortunately, the environmental lobby has succeeded in producing a European Directive (the Water Framework Directive) which is intended to prevent the modification of rivers.

Exposure

Simply move to higher ground, perhaps, and eliminate the exposure. This is not always easy as we have inherited a legacy of many cities built on low-lying land, but the threat of climate change and sea level rise will increasingly make relocation an unavoidable option. The capital of England may have to move to Birmingham, the only major English city which is not on low-lying land.

SCENARIO PLANNING

Traditionally people measured risk by applying to particular situations the lessons learnt through past experience. Historic events provided adequate experience against which to evaluate future risk. We now believe from the climate models, touched on in Chapter 1, that if current trends continue, the future climate will be very different from that today. But those future trends will be influenced by the actions taken by us today, because much of the increase in global temperatures is known to be strongly driven by anthropogenic, or human-made, emissions of climate change gases.

If we are to model future climates we must include the potential influences of our own actions on the trends. The way this is currently done is by using scenarios of what the future may be like, extrapolated from trends in the current climate and in social and economic activity. Against these we can measure the potential costs and benefits in the future of continuing with our 'business as usual' approach, or modifying our behaviour.[3]

Scenario planning involves looking at a range of alternative futures, using projections of current trends, and applying different boundary conditions and strategies to case studies. Brainstorming and think-tank techniques are often used to identify stepping stones and tripwires, ways in which strategies might fail, and what the key drivers for change are most likely to be.

Contrasting scenarios can then be scripted and tested out on decision makers to help them develop more effective policies with which to minimize the impacts of current decisions on future societies.

Scenarios are plausible descriptions of how things may change in the future, built to reflect what is possible, not what is preferred, desirable or undesirable. They are meant to be politically and morally neutral constructs.

The quality of life of future societies in, and around, buildings depends very much on the quality of the decisions we make about the choice of location and technologies for buildings, the form and fabric of the built environment and the lifestyles we adopt in them. The buildings we will live in, in 20 or 50 years' time, will be, by and large, those we occupy or are building today and so our choices, today, must be based on such descriptions of a probable future, because they are the best chance we have of designing buildings that go some way, at least, towards being the most appropriate long-term solutions in a rapidly changing world.

Three of the most influential scenario sets in Britain are those of the UK Foresight Programme, the Royal Commission on Environmental Pollution and the UK Climate Impacts Programme (UKCIP).[4] For a detailed outline of how these scenarios were derived see the companion website: http://books.elsevier.com/companions/0750659114

Foresight scenarios

The UK Foresight Programme began in 1993, drawing on the expertise of thousands of people from the UK's leading businesses, universities, government and other institutions.[5] It was designed to identify technical opportunities and social drivers in a changing world and has helped to shape research priorities in both the private and public sector. Thus, for example, it is now standard practice for research organizations seeking funding from the UK Government to be requested to identify how their research will fit in with the foresight scenarios. In addition, it is known that the UK Government Cabinet Office makes use of the foresight scenario methodology in formulating strategies and policies.

The scenarios are only two-dimensional, that is they consider only two dimensions of change, namely social values and governance systems. These scenarios were very important in building up a range of possible social and economic descriptions of the future that might arise if certain decisions were taken today and these scenarios have been widely used as the basis for other more complex scenarios.

A central aspect is the four social and economic scenarios described below.[5] The scenarios are not prescriptive; they simply describe how the world might look in the near future, exploring alternative directions in which social, economic and technological changes may evolve. These descriptions are for the UK and are based on various sources edited by the authors from an insurance perspective.

- *World markets: high economic growth and high greenhouse gas emissions.* This is a world where economic growth is paramount. Businesses merge to form ever-bigger groups and

UK gross domestic product (GDP) grows by 3% a year. There may be an accelerated nuclear energy programme but if not, global delay in any serious efforts to reduce greenhouse gas emissions means that climate change will accelerate dramatically with many more flood events. Nature is seen as a random factor and there is little desire to spend money on specific risk prevention strategies. Income and other inequalities increase substantially. Levels of social exclusion are high, but concern about issues of social equity or inclusion remains at low levels. Wealthy sections of the population can afford to protect themselves but increasingly the less well-off sections bear the losses of climate change impacts. The scope of planning in this scenario is narrowed towards supporting economic development. Insurance will be widely available for those who can afford it, but not in high-risk areas.

- *Global sustainability: low economic growth and low emissions.* This is where the big non-governmental organizations like WWF become more powerful and forge partnerships with governments to influence policy. UK GDP will grow at a slightly slower rate of around 2% a year with the fastest growing sectors being renewable energy and e-commerce. There will be improvements in air quality and water quality, biodiversity will stabilize and there will be strong climate management, but with reduced standards of living and more dependence on intermittent sources of energy like solar and wind. The government will provide assistance to those who are unable to access insurance.

- *National enterprise: low economic growth, but medium to high emissions.* This is the world of the fragmented business economy where the consumer is king. UK GDP will grow at 1.5% a year but there will be a decline in the financial services sector and in high-tech specialist services. Air and water quality will decline rapidly and biodiversity will deteriorate. Attempts to control climate change will collapse. While insurance is widely available, high premiums in vulnerable areas will mean that uptake becomes more scattered and uneven.

- *Local stewardship: low economic growth and medium to low emissions.* This is a world where stronger local and regional governments allow social and ecological values to be demonstrated to a greater degree at local level. Strict planning controls and sustainable flood management may reduce flood risks in some areas. Income and other disparities decline, as does social exclusion, and there is a very strong emphasis on equity, social inclusion and participatory democracy. Access to insurance and forms of risk sharing is fairly even. There are fairly high levels of welfare provision, and significantly higher levels of informal social security. Economic growth is not an absolute political priority.

In all scenarios, foresight research shows that some parts of England are particularly exposed to flood risks. These are the Lancashire/Humber corridor, parts of the coast (particularly in the southeast) and major estuaries.

While the scenarios are not prescriptive it is interesting to consider the pros and cons of each. One way to do this is to look at the results of a major research programme which tries to predict the future costs of flooding for different foresight scenarios. The results are shown in Table 2.1.

It is clear that the 'World Markets' scenario produces the highest levels of flood damage, but not the highest percentage of GDP. In other words, rapid economic growth can compensate for the property damage. The 'Local Stewardship' scenario has the lowest levels of flood damage but as a percentage of GDP it is no lower than 'Global Sustainability', owing to lower economic growth. 'National Enterprise' has the highest levels of loss as a percentage of GDP, because it suffers from high flood losses and low economic growth.

Table 2.1. Predictions for annual average costs of UK flooding by 2080 (£ billions)

Scenario	Drainage floods	River/coastal	Total	Percentage of GDP
World markets (high growth)	15	27	42	0.19
Global sustainability	3.9	7	10.9	0.08
National enterprise	10	20	30	0.41
Local stewardship (risk management)	1.5	4	5.5	0.08

Source: Thorne, C.R., Evans, E.P. and Penning-Rowsell, E. (eds) (2006) *Future Flooding and Coastal Erosion Risks.* London: Thomas Telford.

So what is best? It should be borne in mind that just looking at the totals does not reflect other issues such as social justice. The 'World Markets' scenarios will make some people very rich, but it will produce a larger number of people suffering from flood or storm damage. The issues go beyond social justice when it comes to flooding. There are issues of public health, social cohesion, and law and order to consider as well. It is these issues that concern the insurance industry. Insurance companies are nimble and sure footed. If they recognize an area has a particular flood problem and nothing is being done about it, they can simply refuse to renew or offer cover. It is less easy for them to control the dramatic growth they are seeing in looting, vandalism and insurance fraud after a flood or storm event, often driven by a breakdown in social cohesion.

Various statements from UK Government might lead one to believe that it is following the path of 'World Markets'. On the other hand, since Devolution in 1999, it seems clear that the Scottish Government is following the 'Local Stewardship' route.

RCEP 2000

The Royal Commission Report on Environmental Pollution (RCEP),[6] published in June 2000, has proved to be one of the most influential of all scenario sets for the built environment. The report suggested what appeared to be, then, deep cuts necessary in emissions from buildings of 60% by 2050 and 80% by 2100, to contain climate change. These dramatic cuts, only nine years down the road from publication, are now taken for granted and used as target values in government emissions reductions programmes. The RCEP scenarios introduce issues of what energy sources will be used and the impacts of related choices on future climates.

The UKCIP02 scenarios: background

These are the scenarios on which are based the following descriptions of future climates in the UK. The UKCIP02 scenarios build on the work of previous scenarios published by UKCIP in 1998, and have been updated to take into account:

- A series of climate modelling experiments completed by the Hadley Centre using their most recently developed models for the UK climate covering four alternative future climates, based on social and economic scenarios, labelled:
  - Low Emissions
  - Medium Low Emissions

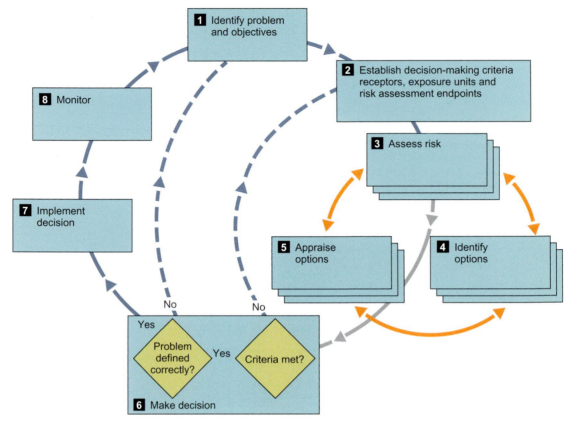

2.2.
Scenarios are essential for risk analysis, where they are used to define the problem and then for the assessment of its associated risks. For every major decision a detailed risk analysis that takes into account the impact on, and from, climate change will be increasingly a requirement. This proposed model for such an analysis is based on the UKCIP report on Climate Adaptation, Risk Uncertainty and Decision-Making.
Source: Willows, R.I. and Connell, R.K. (eds) (2003) *UKCIP Technical Report*. Oxford: UKCIP.

    — Medium High Emissions
    — High Emissions
- New global emissions scenarios published in 2000 by the Intergovernmental Panel on Climate Change (IPCC).

The UKCIP scenarios provide detailed information on future climates in Britain in relation to different geographical locations in the UK, extremes of weather and rises in sea level. What is presented below are just the headlines of the important UKCIP Summary Report, which fronts a vast amount of scientific research, and thousands of simulation runs, carried out in the UK and abroad in this complex field of trying to predict the future climate.

    There is a difference between a *climate scenario* and a *climate change scenario*. The former describes possible future climates rather than *changes* in climate. Climate scenarios usually combine observations about present-day climate with estimates of the change in climates, typically using the results from global or regional climate model experiments.

Many of the future changes that will happen over the next 30–40 years have already been determined by historic emissions and because of the inertia in the climate system. We therefore have to adapt to some degree of climate change however much future emissions are reduced.

The climate of the second half of the twenty-first century, and beyond, will be increasingly influenced by the volume of the greenhouse gases emitted by human society over the coming decades. By the 2080s, the UKCIP02 scenarios suggest that the atmospheric carbon dioxide (CO_2) concentrations may be between 525 parts per million (ppm) and 810 ppm, as shown in Table 2.2.

In the 1961–1990 record, the concentration of CO_2 of 334 ppm was significantly greater than the pre-industrial concentration of 280 ppm and by 2000 the atmospheric concentrations of CO_2 had reached around 370 ppm. Even if global emissions fall again below today's level, as assumed in the UKCIP02 Low Emissions scenario, the future rate of global warming over the present century may be about four times that experienced during the twentieth century. If the emissions rate increases to approximately four times today's level, the High Emissions scenario, the future warming rate may be about eight times that experienced during the twentieth century and such a change in climate will be extremely difficult to adapt to, and will have huge impacts on every person, building, settlement, society and country in the world.

In the following chapters we have used the outputs of the UKCIP02 scenarios because they are the ones that have been used as the basis for the current UK future projections that are included in the following chapters. However, the global models from the 2007 AR4 from the IPCC are out and they show a clear increase in the current and projected emissions and temperatures over the 2002 datasets. They have, however, not yet been applied to the UK level scenarios, so the UKCIP02 models stand.

How seriously should we take such predictions?

Temperate Britain has perhaps less to fear than many other countries with more continental climates, while the future scenarios for the USA and Australia,[7] two heavily energy-dependent continents, show a much bleaker picture. There is a vast amount of emerging knowledge on future climates freely available on the Internet[8] and many reputable institutions in countries around the world are working to help develop strategies with which to fight for the future.

We should take such climate change predictions very seriously indeed, and particularly because fears have been expressed that the hot summer of 2003, the hottest on record for Europe, is a

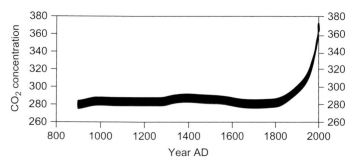

2.3.

Increasing historic concentrations (parts per million) of CO_2 in the global atmosphere. The line thickness indicates uncertainty in the concentrations.
Source: IPCC, from *UKCIP02 Briefing Report*, summary, p. 5.

Table 2.2. Changes in global temperature (°C) and atmospheric carbon dioxide concentration (parts per million or ppm) for the 2080s period (2071–2100 average) for the four UKCIP scenarios. The carbon dioxide concentration in 2001 was about 370 ppm and in mid-2008 stood at 385 ppm

SRES emissions scenario	UKCIP02 climate change scenario	Increase in global temperature (°C)	Atmospheric CO_2 concentration (ppm)
B1	Low Emissions	2.0	525
B2	Medium Low Emissions	2.3	562
A2	Medium High Emissions	3.3	715
A1FI	High Emissions	3.9	810

Source: UKCIP02 Briefing Report,[3] p. 6.

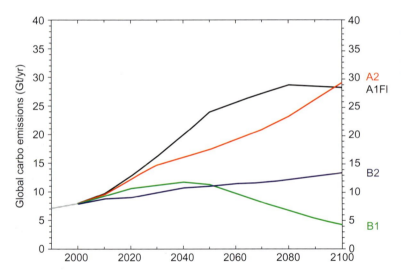

2.4.
Global carbon emissions from 2000 to 2100 for the four chosen SRES emissions scenarios with observed data to 2000.
Source: UKCIP02 Briefing Report, p. 6.

sign that not only is climate change speeding up but 'the parching heat experience [in the summer of 2003] could be consistent with a worst case scenario [of global warming] that no one wants to be true'. These are the words of Professor John Schnellnhuber, former scientific adviser to the German government and head of the Tyndall Centre. He added: 'What we are seeing is absolutely unusual. We know that global warming is proceeding apace, but most of us were thinking that in 20–30 years time we would see hot spells [like this]. But it is happening now'.[9]

THE INSURANCE INDUSTRY

One group that is taking climate change very seriously is the insurance industry, and their deliberations and decisions over the coming years could put millions, who can no longer get insurance for their homes, at the greatest economic risk of their lives.[10]

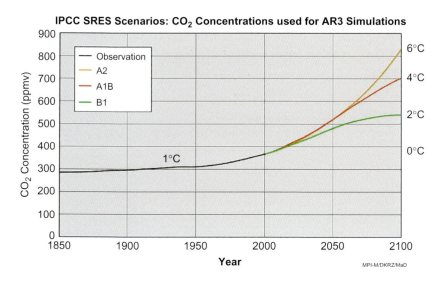

IPCC SRES Scenarios: CO₂ Concentrations used for AR3 Simulations

2.5.
Global carbon emissions
from 2000 to 2100 for the
three chosen AR4 emissions
scenarios with observed data
to 2005.
Source: www.ipcc.
ch/ipccreports/ar4.

If the huge (US$1.5 trillion per year) fossil fuel industry is the only industrial lobby that actively engages in the climate battle, it is likely to prevail and progress in addressing the global climate dilemma will continue to stall. Few industries are capable of doing battle with the likes of the fossil fuel lobby. But the insurance industry is. In financial terms the global insurance industry is three times bigger than the fossil fuel industry and has much greater potential political clout.

As new risks emerge, insurance cover is either provided for them at increased premiums or excluded from existing policies, and the number of uninsurable buildings increases. Insurers in the USA, for instance, now typically require building owners to take out special policies to cover the mould threat, described as the 'new asbestos' issue for the industry. Although the UK and Australia have not followed the USA in mould exclusion clauses yet, they may well do so over time.[11] Risks in the environment escalate because of changing conditions, building types and materials, chemicals, biological threats and even trends in agriculture.[12]

The insurance industry itself is now at risk in this rapidly changing risk environment. In 2003 the global insurance industry paid out more money over the year than ever before in history, and made record profits! This is because premiums have been rising rapidly and across the board to pre-empt catastrophic payouts that may actually bring the industry to its knees. The fear is that if allowance is made for a £15 billion event, from a terrorist or climate-related event, a £25 billion event will occur. The value of the buildings at the World Trade Center was $1.5 billion a tower but the total costs of the event, it is thought, will eventually reach $50 billion. The cost of London flooding has been put anywhere between £30 and £80 billion.

But every year the costs soar, and the numbers of lives blighted rise exponentially: on 25 June 2007, 20 000 people in Hull, England, were made homeless in floods in the American Mid-West. Figures from the 2007 Annual Report of the reputable Center for Research in the Epidemiology of Disasters (CRED) show that overall in 2007, nearly 10 000 people died in flooding world wide, with more than 5000 of these in Bangladesh. CRED's Annual Report for 2008 shows that in May 2008, nearly 140 000 people died in flooding in the wake of Cyclone Nargis in Myanmar.

The year 2003 was the worst on record for payouts from the industry. Munich Re's annual bulletin[13] was a sobering analysis of natural catastrophes in 2003 and concluded that economic and insured losses continue to increase at a high level. The year 2003 was marked by a series of severe natural hazard events, with the number of fatalities far exceeding the long-term average. It reinforced the fact that in view of the deteriorating risk situation, the insurance industry must continue to act rigorously; for example, by agreeing on limits of liability and risk-adequate premiums.

Highlights of the bulletin included:

- More than 50 000 people were killed in natural catastrophes worldwide, almost five times as many as in the previous year (11 000); such a high number of victims has only been recorded four times since 1980. The heatwave in Europe and the earthquake in Iran each claimed more than 20 000 lives.
- The number of natural catastrophes recorded in 2003 was around 700 and thus at the same level as in the previous year.
- Economic losses rose to over $60 billion (2002: $55 billion). These were mainly the result of tornadoes, heatwaves and forest fires, but also severe floods in Asia and Europe.
- Insured losses increased to about $15 billion (previous year: $11.5 billion). The series of tornadoes in the Mid-West of the USA in May alone cost insurers more than $3 billion.

The year 2003 was marked not only by natural catastrophes but also by other remarkable events: the power outages in the USA, the UK, Denmark and Italy, for example; total losses involving two satellites; numerous terrorist attacks; and a major leak of poison gas in China shortly before the end of the year. However, the extent of the losses caused by these events was much smaller than that caused by the natural catastrophes and they claimed fewer lives. Munich Re found that while windstorms and severe weather in 2003 accounted for only about a third of the approximately 700 events recorded, they were responsible for 75% of all the insured losses caused by natural catastrophes.

Insurance companies, virtually without exception, are convinced that the increasingly severe weather-related events are linked to changes in climate generating new types of weather risks and threatening greater losses. The insurance industry is preparing itself for increasing risks and losses, but the call is now for 'above all, transparency and a limitation of the risks'. This is not an easy prospect, as it does not just mean putting up premiums and making more profits but also, for instance, informing one home or office block owner in London that they will flood if the Thames Barrier overtops, while the one at the other end of the street will not. Today they are both charged the same rate to insure their office or house, as the risks are spread across the portfolio. Building owners are not informed that they are vulnerable to such events, or for instance dam breakage, or increasingly to litigation from building owners and occupiers on properties that become too uncomfortable in hot weather. The impact on property prices and insurability, when such information does become available in an increasingly 'transparent' marketplace, could be profound.

The insurance industry: viability

The insurance industry has the skills to provide the assessment, quantification and mapping of risks, prompt disaster recovery, fraud control, avoidance of duplicate administration and the access to international financial resources. It can thus contribute considerably to an efficient risk management system. The insurance industry also provides strong financial incentives for loss prevention and mitigation to their clients and the public, for example by means of deductibles (United Nations Environment Programme Insurance Industry Initiative paper on the Kyoto Protocol).[14]

Box 2.1 2003 Insurance industry payouts related to climate

Windstorms:

- Hailstorms hit the US Mid-West in April and May: cost insured losses of $5 billion.
- Tornadoes in May in the USA cost over $3 billion (one of the 10 most costly storms in insurance history).
- Hurricane Isabel, in the second half of September, swept over the US East Coast and devastated more than 360 000 homes with an economic loss of around $5 billion, of which $1.7 billion was insured.
- Europe suffered comparatively little damage from windstorms, with economic losses of around $1 billion and insured losses of $300 million.

Heatwaves:

- Germany alone recorded temperatures from June to August corresponding to a 450-year event in climatological terms. Predictions are that if the atmosphere continues to warm up unchecked, such a heatwave could become a mere 20-year event by 2020 in large areas of western and central Europe and large parts of the western Mediterranean region.
- Costs: approx. $13 billion, an extremely large amount, but the burden imposed on insurers by, for example, drought-related losses is relatively small because reduced yields in the agricultural sector as a result of dry weather are mostly not yet covered for insurance within the European Union.

Wildfires:

- In Australia, southwest Europe, Canada and the USA fires swept through whole region. In October and November alone, thousands of homes fell victim to the flames in California.
- Costs: $2 billion for the insurance industry, representing almost 60% of the economic losses.

Floods:

- In China, the swollen waters of the Huai and Yangtze flooded 650 000 homes and caused an economic loss of almost $8 billion.
- Southern France was under water in many parts at the beginning of December, when numerous rivers, including the Rhône, flooded their banks after extreme rainfall.
- Costs: insured losses $1 billion and economic losses of around $1.5 billion.

The concerns of many insurers are not just about the uncertainties around the increase in the frequency and severity of storms and floods which could cause problems, but also about the implications of changing responses and attitudes of governments and corporate clients. The activities of pressure groups and concerns of individual consumers are also very important and will increasingly affect insurers' strategies.

For many years insurers have accepted risks with surprisingly limited information about the natural hazards that impact so much on their claims costs. Increases in the frequency and severity of natural disasters and concerns about the effects of climate change are resulting in a new and healthy dialogue developing between the research community and the insurance industry.

In 1994, a study group set up by the Society of Fellows of the Chartered Insurance Institute published a very significant report entitled 'The Impact of Changing Weather Patterns on Property Insurance'. For the first time, there was a comprehensive analysis of the potential effects of climate change on the UK insurance industry. This study was followed by further, more detailed reports in 2001 and 2009[15] and by a range of widely available reports from different perspectives.[16] These reports raised questions about whether insurers would be able to continue to provide flood cover in the UK in the light of climate change.

Flood is not the only issue, of course; other perils could cause problems for insurers. In particular, buildings will be vulnerable to storm and subsidence damage and damage caused by driving rain, and research by the Building Research Establishment using insurance claims data has resulted in recommendations that building standards should be reviewed in the light of climate change impacts.[17] Both the English and Welsh governments need to urgently consider and implement changes to building standards along the lines already implemented in Scotland.

In June 2000 the Royal Commission Report on Environmental Pollution was published,[18] shortly followed by the World Disasters Report 2000 from the International Federation of Red Cross and Red Crescent Societies. Both these reports have re-emphasized the need for action to mitigate climate change and to adapt to its impacts, and will put renewed pressure on governments and insurers to take firm action.

How big is the problem? Average annual insured losses from global natural disasters have increased from $0.6 billion in the 1960s to $9.8 billion in the 1990s (all at 1998 values).[19] Such increases in the costs of natural disasters are not necessarily due to climate change. As Munich Re point out, they are due to a combination of factors such as population growth, rising standards of living, concentration of population in urban areas, settlement in hazardous areas, vulnerability of modern societies and technologies, as well as changes in climate and environment. The point is that in the future, climate change is likely to accelerate the rate of increase in the losses.

Of all the causes listed above, the future impacts of climate change are the hardest to predict. It seems clear now that global mean temperatures are rising and that sea levels will continue to rise, but how will this affect claims experience? In the UK the experts predict that there will be more droughts and subsidence, but also more coastal flooding in the southeast and more river and drainage flooding everywhere. While it is not yet clear whether there will be more frequent and more severe storms, there is increasing evidence to suggest that storm tracks will move south. This will mean more severe storms in the south of England where construction standards are lower than in the north, where storms have traditionally been more frequent. This will lead to higher damage levels and claims problems for insurers.[20]

In the past, historic claims experience was a good measure for predicting future risk. The increases in numbers and costs of natural disasters indicate the need for a new approach to underwriting. Insurers are therefore investing heavily in Geographical Information Systems (GIS), detailed databases and sophisticated modelling techniques to fine-tune their underwriting.

In addition to traditional risk management skills, insurers will increasingly find the need to work with academia and government, and this process has already started. Insurers are uniquely placed to contribute to society's efforts to reduce the impact of natural disasters, but they will have to learn new skills if their contribution is to be effective. Insurers will need to continue to work to improve their understanding of science and the built environment. They need to measure and manage their exposures, and reduce the vulnerability of the assets they insure if they are to be able to continue to write business at the premium levels people are prepared to pay. The issue of availability and affordability of insurance will become much more important, with possible threats of government intervention should an 'insurance underclass' develop.

If the climate is changing as rapidly as some of the latest scenarios suggest, it could present one of the biggest potential threats faced by insurers over the next 20 years and beyond. It could also present some of the biggest opportunities: not just new business opportunities, but opportunities for a new spirit of dialogue and cooperation between insurers, governments and the research community.

As public concern about greenhouse gas emissions and polluting industries increases, so insurers can expect pressure groups to demand that insurers use their power in the stockmarket to influence the policies of the companies they invest in. After all, the insurance industry, especially its pension funds business, controls some 30% of all the stocks and equities in the world's stock exchanges. The United Nations Environment Programme's Insurance Industry Initiative is an imaginative way for insurers around the world to work together and to demonstrate their commitment to corporate responsibility.

The UK is changing rapidly and over the next 20 years there will be major demographic, social and economic changes. Government and business are increasingly turning to scenario planning to develop their long-term strategies.

The insurer can reduce the risk of flood claims by reducing the number of flood plain properties it insures. It is estimated that in England and Wales, there are some 1.3 million homes in flood plains. This is not surprising, given the tendency to want to build near river crossings, or along transport corridors, such as river valleys. What should be of great concern to insurers is that this number is still increasing, despite improved knowledge of the hazard. The reason lies in the way the planning systems operate.

Greenhouse effect

2.6.
Imagine being in a metal car with the windows shut on a hot day, with no air conditioning and not being able to park in the shade. Edward Mazria's diagram shows how passive solar heating works as well as the greenhouse effect, because, as with glass, the re-radiated heat cannot pass back out through the upper atmosphere, which is why the world is warming. Being stuck in a glass and steel building with no opening windows would be rather like that when the electricity fails: impossible to occupy. And yet insurers demand the same premiums for such offices as they would for low, naturally ventilated, well-shaded buildings, if they are in the same postcode area. As the world warms anomalies like this in premiums will be questioned.
Source: Mazri, E. (1979) *The Passive Solar Energy Book*. Emmaus, PA: Rodale Press.

The UK Environment Transport and Regional Affairs Select Committee on Climate Change, in their report published in March 2000, stated that 'there is evidence that climate change concerns have not been fully incorporated into current planning practices' (Section 8.8) and further stated:

We urge the Government to continue researching the impacts of climate change and to use this to develop a strategy for adaptation. We note the start made on this in the Draft Programme. If future costs are to be minimized, it is critical that changes are made in some policy areas, for example land use planning in coastal areas and flood plains.

Managing risk

To reduce the risk, it is only necessary to reduce one of the sides of the risk triangle (Figure 2.1), but it is obviously better to try to reduce all three. Dr A. Dlugolecki has developed what he calls an 'Integrated Property Damage System'[21] in which he shows that as the risk increases, insurers move from a 'passive system' of simply paying for the damage. First, they progress to a 'reactive' system and then evolve into a 'planning' system. In other words, as the risk increases, insurers begin to act collectively to feed back information to the other components of the economic system, and if the risk becomes severe enough, insurers will insist on risk mitigation or will reduce their exposure.

There are clear signs that the UK market is beginning to move from a passive system to a reactive system, with UK insurers starting to work together to collect information and commission research. In the USA, however, largely as a result of Hurricane Andrew in 1992, the industry is already beginning to move into a 'planning' system. Perhaps the best example of this movement by the insurance industry can be found in Scotland, where the industry is represented on 'Flood Liaison and Advice Groups' around the country. There are 19 such groups, covering 94% of the Scottish population. They are set up by local authorities and meet regularly to discuss all aspects of flooding issues, including planning, flood management, sustainable drainage and insurance problems. All key stakeholders are invited and issues can be resolved in an informal and amicable way before decisions are reached.

Not all risks are insurable, of course, and risk aversion is one of the main driving forces for disaster mitigation, and one of the main hindrances for investment.[22] If insurers are not prepared to accept the risk of, say, a new factory to be built in a flood plain, then the developer is unlikely to proceed.

Will the insurance industry be able to weather the storms ahead? Will it have enough capacity for the claims costs that could arise? The answer is almost certainly 'yes', at least for the time being. If anything, the insurance industry has recently been suffering from too much capacity, and during the late 1990s this kept premiums low; not only insurers but reinsurers were cutting premiums for some years. This was happening around the world; premium rates were going down while exposure values were going up. This is nothing new for insurers who are used to 'the underwriting cycle': in times of profit, capital is attracted into the industry, capacity increases and, according to the laws of supply and demand, price falls until losses result in a reduction of capacity as weaker insurers drop out. The influx of capital was restricted to some extent by the barriers to entry in the insurance industry created by regulations such as the need for government authorization and a good solvency margin.

There are four major differences now:

- There has been a general move towards deregulation of rates, especially in Japan and continental Europe, which has led to strong price competition.

2.7.
The Pompidou Centre in Paris was designed by Renzo Piano, Richard Rogers and Gianfranco Franchini for a design competition in 1970. Construction started in 1972, cost 993 million francs, and the building was opened in 1977. Nineteen years later in 1996 the building closed for four years for a total refurbishment, for which the final bill was a further 576 million francs (one pound sterling was worth 9.44 francs at early 2004 exchange rates) (see: www.centrepompidou.fr). Offices pay the same insurance premiums regardless of their day-to-day maintenance or long-term refurbishment requirements.
Source: Sue Roaf.

- The growth of the securitization market in the 1990s makes it easier for capital to flow into the market if the returns are good enough. This means that as soon as premiums start to rise, capital immediately starts flowing into insurance bonds, thus driving premiums down again.
- Previous cycles have been against the background of continuous growth in demand for insurance as society becomes wealthier. In the 1990s, multinational corporations increasingly decided not to insure at all because for them it was just 'pound swapping' over time, and the exchange rate was not favourable.
- Last, but certainly not least, in the past, strong insurers could ride out bad times by realizing capital gains on investments, thanks to a healthy stockmarket. The stockmarket is anything but healthy at present, and there is no longer the cushion of investment profits.

Catastrophes are normally good for insurance business; they result in increased demand for insurance and make it easier for insurers to carry rate increases. Capacity has not been a problem right up to quite recently. The market was confident even in 1999 that the combination of another Northridge earthquake, another Hurricane Andrew and another 1987-style stockmarket crash would still not wipe out overcapacity in the industry.[23] Since then we have had the terrorism attack on the World Trade Center and confidence has taken a nosedive.

CONCLUSIONS

It is certainly clear that a new era of insurance is starting. In an important paper published by the Royal Geographical Society, Professor Clark has pointed out that insurance can have an important role to play in managing flood risks.[24] It offers much needed support to accelerate economic and social recovery following a disaster, but with pricing policies or restrictions on availability of cover, could discourage new development in flood plains. As insurers obtain access to better data, so the uncertainty of the identification of high-hazard areas reduces and these areas become less insurable. Clark supports a closer relationship between insurers and planners, and refers favourably to the Scottish planning system where an insurance expert is consulted by the planning authorities on land-use strategies.

In the long run, the price of insurance should reflect the degree of risk. If insurers are unsuccessful in managing risk through controlling exposure and vulnerability, rising hazard will mean increased risk, which means increased pricing or less cover. At a micro-level, insurers will become increasingly selective, using GIS technology and stiffer price discrimination based on differences in exposure and vulnerability. For example: lower 'premium' incentives for buildings built to higher standards and inspected at each stage of construction; higher premiums for buildings that are more vulnerable to terrorist attack being 'target' buildings by dint of their form, location or construction; and higher premiums for climate-vulnerable buildings that are more exposed to wind, flood and excessive heat gain from solar radiation, such as those that rise above the urban canopy of a city, are located on the flood plain or are overglazed.

The irregularity of extreme events makes it hard to assess the probability of loss for any one year, and if the frequency is changing then traditional actuarial methods may be of little help. In such a situation, there will be pressures for a conservative approach to underwriting; the 'when in doubt, throw it out' syndrome will become more common for high-hazard, high-exposure or high-vulnerability cases. However, if the industry takes this approach too far, there will be social and political pressures and the ultimate threat of nationalization. The behaviour of the insurance industry over the coming years will provide a litmus paper for us all, of the rate of growth of the climate change hazard.

We are all at risk from the impacts of the changing climate. Our *vulnerability* to it will depend on the infrastructure of our lives, the buildings we live in and the investments we make. Our *exposure* to that risk will depend on where that infrastructure is in relation to the hazards perpetrated on us by the changing climate. In order to plan judiciously to minimize risk to ourselves we need to know more about the scale of the climate *hazard* that may affect us, and it is those hazards that are explained in the following chapters.

NOTES AND REFERENCES

1   There are many different definitions of what risk is and for a fuller discussion of climate change and risk see <http://www.ukcip.org.uk/risk_uncert/main_risk_uncert.htm/>.

2   D.C. See Crichton, in: J. Salt (Ed.), The Implications of Climate Change for the Insurance Industry, Building Research Establishment, Watford, 2001. Also many of the descriptions, contributed to by David Crichton, are based on the following sources from an insurance perspective: C.R. Thorne, E.P. Evans, E. Penning-Rowsell (Eds.), Future Flooding and Coastal Erosion Risks. London: Thomas Telford, 2006.

3   For a full outline of the UK Climate Impacts Programme (UKCIP) work on current and future climates see <http://www.ukcip.org.uk/publications/pub.html> including: M.J. Hulme, J. Turnpenny, G. Jenkins, Climate Change Scenarios for the United Kingdom: The UKCIP02 Briefing Report, 2002. Published in conjunction with UKCIP, the Hadley Centre and the Climate Research Unit in the School of Environmental Science at the University of East

Anglia, by the Tyndall Centre, Norwich; M. Hulme, G. Jenkins, X. Lu, J. Turnpenny, T. Mitchell, R. Jones, J. Lowe, J. Murphy, D. Hassell, P. Boorman, R. McDonald, S. Hill, Climate Change Scenarios for the United Kingdom: The UKCIP02 Scientific Report, Appendix 2 published in conjunction with UKCIP, the Hadley Centre and the Climate Research Unit in the School of Environmental Science at the University of East Anglia, by the Tyndall Centre, Norwich, 2002. For information concerning local climate impacts contact the Hadley Centre on <http://www.meto.gov.uk/research/hadleycentre> or for detailed information on flood risks contact The Environment Agency on <http://www.environment-agency.gov.uk/contactus/?lang>. For datasets for future climates for use in building performance simulations, contact the Chartered Institute of Building Service Engineers and ask to be put in contact with their climate data group or via: <http://www.cibse.org>.

4   <http://www.ukcip.org.uk/scenarios/index.html>.

5   Details of Foresight can be obtained from <http://www.foresight.gov.uk/> The scenarios have been, and continue to be, further developed as part of the EPSRC/UKCIP Building Knowledge for a Changing Climate (BKCC) programmes. See for instance: C.L. Walsh, et al., Building knowledge for a changing climate: collaborative research to understand and adapt to the impacts of climate change on infrastructure, the built environment and utilities, Newcastle University, 2007.

6   RCEP, Energy – the Changing Climate: Summary of the Royal Commission on Environmental Pollution's Report, HMSO, London, 2000. A full copy of the report can be downloaded from: <http://www.rcep.org.uk/energy.html>.

7   See <http://www.cru.uea.ac.uk/~mikeh/research/usa.pdf> and <http://www.cru.uea.ac.uk/~mikeh/research/australia.pdf>, respectively.

8   Good starting points for researching future climates are the sites of the Intergovernmental Panel on Climate Change (IPCC) on <http://www.ipcc.ch/> and related sites: <ftp://ftp.ecn.nl/pub/bs/OpenProcess/gridded_emissions/> and <http://sres.ciesin.org/> and <http://www.grida.no/climate/ipcc/emission/index.htm>. For a full outline of the limits to future emissions set under International Treaties see the site of the United Nations Framework Convention on Climate Change since its inception: <http://unfccc.int/>. The UK government climate change research is coordinated by the Hadley Centre on: <http://www.meto.gov.uk/research/hadley-centre>. A full UK greenhouse gas inventory 1990–2000 is available at: <http://www.aeat.co.uk/netcen/airqual/reports/ghg/ghg3.html>. An excellent introductory site is that of the Climate Research Unit of the University of East Anglia on: <http://www.cru.uea.ac.uk/>.

9   <http://www.greenpeace.org.au/features/features_details.html?site_id545&news_id51147>.

10   <www.aag.org/HDGC/www/hazards/supporting/supmat2-4.doc>.

11   <http://www.aar.com.au/pubs/prod/recall2mar03.htm#Insur>.

12   Guardian, 8 October 2003, p. 6.

13   <http://www.munichre.com>.

14   I. Knoepfel, J. Salt, A. Bode, W. Jacobi, Potential Implications for the Insurance Industry. UNEP Insurance Industry Initiative for the Environment, The Kyoto Protocol and Beyond, 1999.

15   A. Dlugolecki, M. Agnew, M. Cooper, D. Crichton, N. Kelly, T. Loster, R. Radevsky, J. Salt, D. Viner, J. Walden, T. Walker, Climate Change and Insurance, Chartered Insurance Institute Research Report, London, 2001 (available on <http://www.cii.co.uk>) D. Crichton, 'General

Insurance for Personal Lines Business'. Chapter 7 of Dlugolecki (Ed.), 'Managing risk in the context of climate change'. The Chartered Insurance Institute, London, Available form <http://www.cii.co.uk/research>, 2009.

16   D. See Crichton, Flood Risk and Insurance in England and Wales: Are There Lessons to be Learnt from Scotland? Technical Paper No. 1, Benfield Hazard Research Centre, University College London. A range of other papers is available for free downloading from: <http://www.benfieldhrc.org/SiteRoot/activities/tech_papers/flood_report.pdf>. See also RICS Working Party (2001) Flooding: Issues of Concern to Chartered Surveyors. London: RICS, 2003.

17   See Building Research Establishment (BRE) (2003) Assessment of the Cost and Effect on Future Claims of Installing Flood Damage Resistant Measures. Commissioned and published by the Association of British Insurers, London, May 2003. Available from <http://www.abi.org.uk/Display/File/78/Flood_Resistance_report.pdf>. See also Scottish Executive, Improving Building Standards: Proposals. Edinburgh: Scottish Executive (available from www.scotland.gov.uk), 2002.

18   <http://www.rcep.org.uk/energy.html>.

19   <http://www.munichre.com>. See Munich Re, Topics 2000, Published January 2000.

20   D. See Crichton, Flood Appraisal Groups, NPPG 7, and Insurance, in: D. Faichney, M. Cranston (Eds.), Proceedings of the Flood Issues in Scotland Seminar held in Perth in December 1998. Scottish Environment Protection Agency, Stirling, Scotland, 1998, pp. 37–40; D. Crichton, UK Climate Change Programme. UK Insurance Industry. Minutes of Evidence to the Select Committee on Environment, Transport and Regional Affairs. 25 March 1999 <http://www.publications.parliament.uk/pa/cm199899/cmselect/cmenvtra/171/9832410.htm>, 1999; also I. Davis, personal communication; and D. Crichton, Floods, Who Should Pay? Lessons for Central Europe. Proceedings of a conference on 7 March 2003 on European Flood Risk, Benfield Greig Hazard Research Centre at University College London, 2003.

21   A. Dlugolecki, Overview of Insurance System re Extreme Events. Paper presented at the IPCC Workshop in Toronto, Canada, April/May 1998.

22   M. Kok, J. Vrijling, P. Van Gelder, M. Vogelsang, Risk of flooding and insurance in The Netherlands, in: W. Baosheng, et al. (Eds.), Flood Defence 2002. Proceedings of the 2nd International Symposium on Flood Defence. New York: Science Press, 2002.

23   The Economist, 16 January 1999.

24   M. Clark, Flood insurance as a management strategy for UK coastal resilience, Geographical Journal 164 (1998) 333–343.

3 HOW HOT WILL IT GET?

CLIMATE CHANGE

We now have unequivocal evidence that the climate is changing, in the words of the Fourth Assessment Report (AR4) published by the authoritative United Nations (UN) body, the Intergovernmental Panel on Climate Change (IPCC) in 2007. AR4 sets out clearly mechanisms and causes of climate change and tells of a rapidly warming world.[1]

IPCC 2007 projections for the rest of the century:

- *Probable* temperature rise between 1.8°C and 4°C.
- *Possible* temperature rise between 1.1°C and 6.4°C.
- Sea level *most likely* to rise by 28–43 cm.
- Arctic summer sea ice disappears in second half of century.
- Increase in heatwaves *very likely.*
- Increase in tropical storm intensity *likely.*

Twenty of the hottest years ever measured occurring in the atmospheric record have come since 1980 and the 13 hottest have all occurred since 1990. The year on record was 2005, whilst all five of the hottest years ever recorded were in the past decade. The five hottest years in ascending order were: 2005, 1998, 2002, 2003, 2004.

The last 10 years, globally, has been the warmest decade in the last 100 years, and it is likely that the last century was the warmest in the last millennium. Sea level has risen by 250 mm (10 inches) since 1860. What we have measured before can be taken as certain but the science of predicting what will come in the future is by no means perfect. However, the science of AR4 tells of trends that cannot be ignored by the responsible and concerned citizens of the planet. Some claim that there are systemic errors in the reporting on the subject and the IPCC, as an inevitable consequence of requiring political and scientific consensus, does come down on the side of cautious conservatism rather than the opposite. Other first class scientists are more forthright.

HOW HOT WILL IT GET IN TEMPERATE BRITAIN?

Before we embark on the impacts of a warming world it is worth mentioning that while climate change will produce generally warmer temperatures, the UK will still be at risk of cold temperatures too.

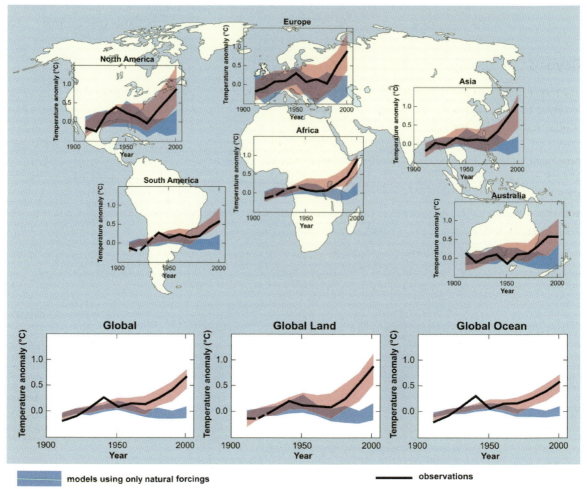

©IPCC 2007: WG1 AR4

3.1.
Temperature changes relative to the corresponding average for 1901–1950 (°C) from decade to decade from 1906 to 2005 over the Earth's continents, as well as the entire globe, global land area and the global ocean (lower graphs). The black line indicates observed temperature change, while the coloured bands show the combined range covered by 90% of recent model simulations. Red indicates simulations that include natural and human factors, while blue indicates simulations that include only natural factors. Dashed black lines indicate decades and continental regions for which there are substantially fewer observations. Detailed descriptions of this figure and the methodology used in its production are given in the Supplementary Material, Appendix 9.C.

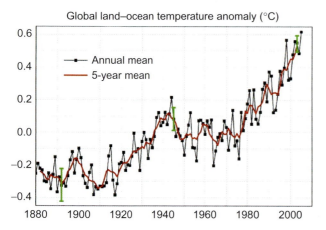

3.2.
Global temperature has increased by around 1.0°C in the past 100 years, with about 0.4°C of this warming occurring since the 1970s. The green bars show 95% confidence intervals.
Source: Hansen, J. et al. (2006) *PNAS*, 103, 14288–93.

Beyond the tipping point?

Two important studies have recently brought to public attention the possibility that we are already 'beyond the tipping point' and facing runaway climate change. Professor Bob Watson, chief scientific officer for the UK Department of the Environment, Food and Rural Affairs (DEFRA), spoke to the press on 7 August 2008 after the publication of a two and a half year analysis by the UK Foresight programme, and said that he thought we should now plan to adapt to temperature rises of up to 4°C. Sir David King, the former chief scientific officer to the UK Government, concurred with these findings, pointing out that there is now a 20% risk that we may reach these temperatures and that if we do it may well push up over dangerous climate tipping points resulting in knock-on effects such as the release of the methane hydrate deposits in the Arctic.

At 4°C we are basically into a different climate regime. I think that is a dangerous mindset to be in. Thinking through the implications of 4 degrees of warming shows that the impacts are so significant that the only real adaptation strategy is to avoid that at all cost because of the pain and suffering that it is going to cost. There is no science on how we are going to adapt to 4 degrees warming. It is actually pretty alarming.[2]

This comes after the seminal paper by James Hansen et al., entitled: 'Target atmospheric CO_2: where should humanity aim?' In it he and his co-researchers conclude that if humanity wishes to preserve a planet similar to that on which civilization developed and to which life on Earth is adapted, palaeoclimate evidence and ongoing climate change suggest that carbon dioxide (CO_2) will need to be reduced from its current 385 ppm to at most 350 ppm. The largest uncertainty in the target arises from possible changes in non-CO_2 forcing like the methane released from the melting tundra. An initial 350 ppm CO_2 target may be achievable by phasing out coal use except where CO_2 is captured and adopting agricultural and forestry practices that sequester carbon. If the present overshoot of this target CO_2 is not brief, there is a possibility of seeding irreversible catastrophic effects.

The IPCC, in their Second Report, and others had included several 'reasons for concern' to estimate that global warming of more than 2–3°C may be dangerous. The European Union (EU) adopted 2°C above pre-industrial global temperature as a goal to limit human-made warming and Hansen and his team had earlier argued for a limit of 1°C global warming (relative to 2000, 1.7°C relative to pre-industrial time), aiming to avoid practically irreversible ice sheet and species loss. This 1°C limit, with nominal climate sensitivity of ¾°C per W/m^2 and plausible control of other greenhouse gases, implies maximum CO_2 ~450 ppm. Hansen's 2008 paper gives clear evidence

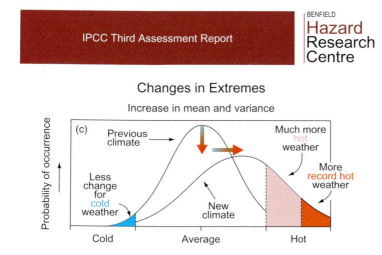

IPCC Third Assessment Report

BENFIELD
Hazard
Research
Centre

3.3.
The IPCC Third and Fourth Assessment reports showed that the issue will be changes in the mean and variance of temperatures, meaning that not only will it get hotter but it will be hot for more of the time, as shown in Figure 3.4.
Source: IPCC 3rd Assessment Report.

Changes in Extremes

Increase in mean and variance

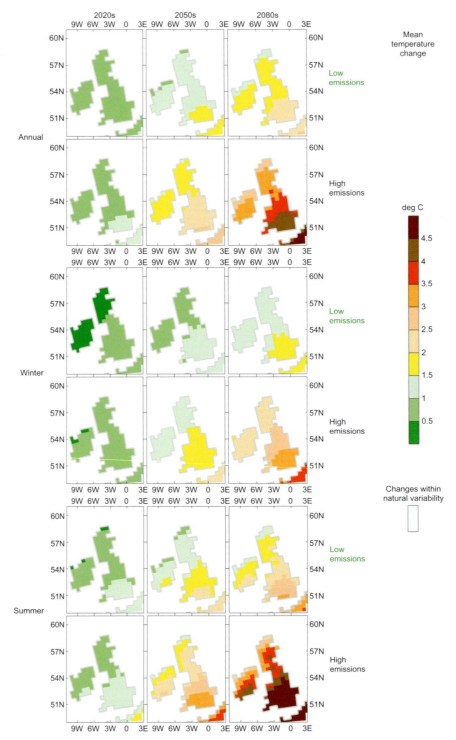

3.4.
Changes in average annual, winter and summer temperature for the 2020s, 2050s and 2080s for the *Low Emissions* and *High Emissions* scenarios showing that the southeast of England will get very hot indeed by 2080 under *Low* and *High* scenarios.
Source: UKCIP02 Climate Change Scenarios, funded by DEFRA, produced by Tyndall and Hadley Centres for UKCIP)
For a review of how such scenarios are developed see http://books.elsevier.com/companions/0750659114.

of the need for even lower levels of greenhouse gases because he believes that the key question is not what temperatures we can adapt to but at what point we cross the trigger point to inevitable climate chaos.[3]

Commonly published and cited sources show that predicted temperature changes vary significantly according to which scenario is adopted and also on a region by region basis. The best data we have in the UK to date are those of the UK Climate Impacts Programme scenarios (UKCIP02), which predict that average annual temperatures across the UK may rise between 2 and 3.5°C by the 2080s, depending on the scenario. In general, there will be greater warming in the southeast than the northwest and there may be more warming in summer and autumn than in winter and spring, a prediction that seems to have been leant credence by the hot summer and warm autumn of 2003.[4]

Under the High Emissions scenario, the southeast may be up to an astonishing 5°C warmer in the summer by the 2080s. During the last Ice Age, only 10 000 years ago, temperatures were only just over 3°C colder than today, so who knows what such predictions for future climates hold in store for our children and grandchildren in terms of actual climate extremes.

These are average figures and the mean maximum temperatures will be far higher. Figure 4.3 shows four different localities, representing four different climatic regions in the UK. The graphs show that on any given day, the daily maximum temperature will exceed a certain value. For example, the Berkshire graph shows that, under the Medium High Emissions scenario, there is around a 5% probability that, in the 2080s, the area will experience a summer maximum temperature of above 35°C and a 1% probability that it will go over 40°C. These maximum temperatures are simulated by the model for areas of 50×50 km in size. They are again lower than temperatures that would be actually measured at a specific site. The frequency of extreme hot spells will also increase, as shown in Table 3.1.

One clear pattern that has emerged is that the temperatures at night over many land areas are increasing at about twice the rate of daytime temperatures, and as one reads through this book many designers will be flagging design-related issues. So, for example, warmer nights mean that special care will have to be given to the environmental conditions in bedrooms. Another design problem relates to west-facing rooms with windows facing the low western sun when the ambient temperatures are at their highest in the afternoon so combining incoming sun with higher air temperatures.

Table 3.1 More and more years will be extremely hot over time. The table shows the percentage of years experiencing various extreme seasonal anomalies across central England and Wales for the Medium High Emissions scenario, with the anomalies shown relative to the average 1961–1990 climate

	Anomaly	2020s	2050s	2080s
Mean temperature				
A hot '1995-type' August	3.4°C warmer	1	20	63
A warm '1999-type' year	1.2°C warmer	28	73	100
Precipitation				
A dry '1995-type' summer	37% drier	10	29	50
A wet '1994/95-type' winter	66% wetter	1	3	7

Source: UKCIP02 Briefing Report,[5] p. 10.

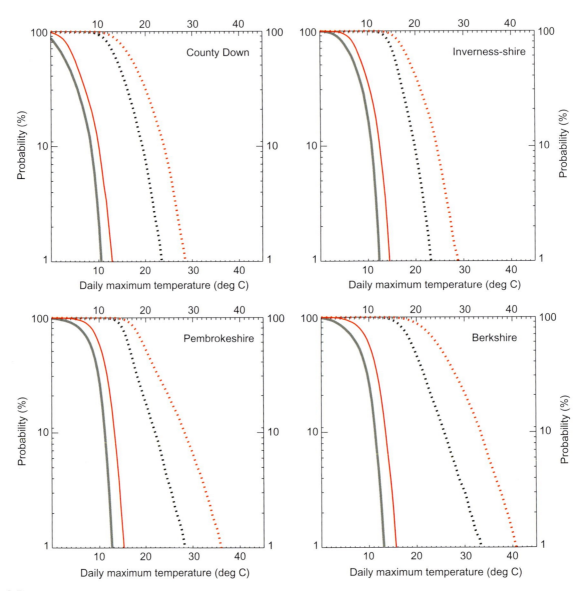

3.5.
The probability of a given daily maximum temperature in summer (*dashed*) and winter (*solid*) being exceeded on any given day. Dark grey = present climate; red = the *Medium High Emissions* scenario for the 2080s. This shows that in Berkshire even temperatures of 40°C may be exceeded by 2080 under the *Medium High* scenario.
Source: UKCIP02 Climate Change Scenarios, funded by DEFRA, produced by Tyndall and Hadley Centres for UKCIP.

A further consideration, that will considerably worsen future climates, particularly in London, is that of the urban heat island effect,[5] which makes the centres of heavily built-up areas warmer than their hinterlands. Heat islands are very much influenced by:

- The amount of building there is in a neighbourhood. This influences how much heat they can store in a day, week, month or season. It represents the thermal capacity of the area, rather like having more bricks in a storage radiator.

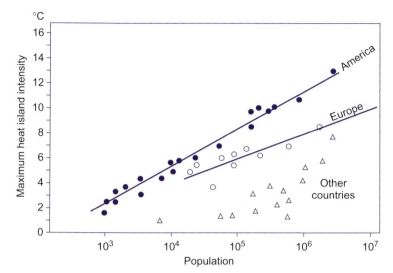

3.6.
Comparison of the strength of the heat island effect between American and European cities showing that the high-rise, highly serviced buildings of North America generate significantly higher heat island temperatures than lower, denser European cities.
Source: Littlefair, P. et al. (2000) Solar access, passive cooling and microclimate in the city: the Polis Project. *ACTES Proceedings*, Lyon, France, pp. 983–8.

- How good a heat exchanger individual buildings are. Buildings like the Barbican development in London make perfect exchangers, sticking up into the air with lots of fins and concrete balconies to absorb heat and lose it.
- The absorptivity or reflectivity of buildings, which influences how much heat they take in and how much they reflect back to the sky or the building opposite.
- The streetscape and how easy it is to dissipate the heat from the city by wind. If all the streets are linked to roads that channel the constant sea breezes, as in Naples, then heat can be regularly flushed out of the city. If the main streets impede the natural flows of air, then heat will be trapped in the city.
- How densely the area is populated. More people, each producing around 50–100W of heat, also means more machines and cars that give out heat.

The increases in temperature vary from region to region, but in cities such as Athens it can be between 8 and 13°C warmer inside than outside the city. For London, in the centre of the city it can be as much as 8°C warmer than the surrounding countryside. The heat island is highly changeable, most pronounced at night and weakening with increasing wind speed and distance from the city centre; the location of the thermal maximum of the heat island shifts with slight changes in wind direction. The number of nights with intense heat islands (greater than 4°C warmer than the surrounding countryside) has been climbing steadily since the 1950s.

The heat island effect may be influenced by the amount of cloud in the sky and simulations suggest large decreases in summer cloud cover over the whole of the UK, but especially in the south. Reductions in cloud cover under the Low Emissions scenarios are around 10% by 2080, but as large as 25% or more under the High Emissions scenarios, which will make solar energy technologies more viable but also may exacerbate the heat island effect.

Cloud cover increases slightly in winter, by no more that 2–3%, over the whole country. Autumn and spring become sunnier, particularly in the southeast. In summer, solar radiation increases by 10, 20 and even 30W/m over southern England, consistent with rainfall predictions and the increase in the predicted diurnal range of the temperature. This was apparent in the summer of 2003 where the mean Central England Temperature (CET) was 17.3°C over the summer,

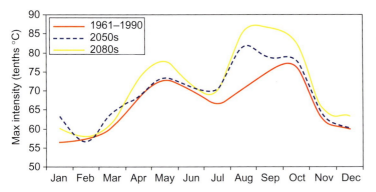

3.7.
The predicted maximum intensity of the London heat island over the year increases from the 1961–1990 record to 2050 and the 2080s when the temperature in central London will be over 8°C hotter than the surrounding countryside at times.
Source: Wilby, R.L., The Environment Agency.

making it the fourth warmest summer period on record. But the record for the highest maximum temperature ever recorded in the UK was broken on 10 August 2003 when 38.5°C (over 100°F) was recorded at Brogdale, near Faversham in Kent. The CET between March and August was also the warmest March to August ever on record, at 1.73°C above the long-term average.

Nights will warm more than days during the winter, and days warm more than nights during summer. It will stay warmer longer in summer, with up to 3–4°C night-time warming experienced, with a temperature that would now occur at 7.00 pm occurring at 11.00 pm under the High Emissions scenario.

The temperature of the heat island experienced in London will also be influenced by wind speeds, a factor that is influenced by pressure gradients across the country. The largest average wind speeds predicted, in the London's Warming Technical Report, occur along the coast, where between 4% and 10% increases in the average may be experienced in winter, but with smaller increases in summer. This is one of the more difficult factors to predict using current models.

WHAT WILL THE EFFECT OF THIS BE?

The wide range of impacts outlined below gives an indication of the variety and the extent of the influence of climate change on the lives of individuals in their own homes, around the world. Many of the issues raised link to points in other chapters and demonstrate the interconnectivity of the buildings we live in, the metabolism of the planet at large and the social, political and economic environments we inhabit.

Heat discomfort can interrupt work

Although Britain was not the most exposed country in Europe to the catastrophic August 2003 heatwave, time is money, and even in temperate London businesses will have to increasingly look to reduce their *vulnerability* to high temperatures in the workplace if such summers become commonplace. Offices that are vulnerable to high temperatures, such as highly glazed buildings, suffered very badly in the heatwaves of 2003 and 2005 and the Trades Union Congress (TUC), in response to wide-scale heat discomfort, called for legal maximum temperatures for workplaces.

Current legislation sets a minimum temperature below which no one should have to work, at 16°C or, where severe physical work is required, 13°C. The TUC suggested a maximum working temperature of 30°C, or 27°C for those doing strenuous work. In London in 2003, even in more traditional offices temperatures were exceeding these limits. It was also suggested that more breaks and a more relaxed dress code would help considerably.

One employment lawyer suggested that employers should think twice before sacking staff who walk out of their workplace because of the heat, as they may find themselves accused of unfair dismissal. Workers can protect their work conditions by local negotiation covering the provision of air-cooling systems, shading for windows and an adequate supply of drinkable water.[6]

Problems of poor internal climates are exacerbated by poor climatic design of buildings and their services. This was emphasized by all the staff of the refurbished HM Treasury building in London (July 2003), who were sent home after lunch because the building was simply too hot to occupy. It is unclear whether this was the fault of the designer of the refurbishment, the service engineers or the construction firm that did not properly commission the air conditioning system, but as temperatures increase designers will have to learn how to design and manage to avoid such overheating.[7] The need to put the building occupiers back into the equation of what makes an adequate building has made people more interested in the process of *post-occupancy evaluation* of building performance to ensure that lessons are properly learnt from such failures.[8]

Since then there has been considerable work done on how to reduce overheating in the workplace and at home, and an excellent document one can view online is 'Beating the Heat' by Jake Hacker and a team funded by UKCIP.[9] This report shows the clear advantage of ventilation overheating in UK summertime temperatures.

Heat and health

A study by scientists at the World Health Organization (WHO) in 2003 found that 160 000 people die every year from side-effects of global warming, such as increased rates of death resulting from a range of causes from malaria to malnutrition, and predicted that the number would double by 2020. Diseases spread by animals such as rats and insects are more common in warmer climates and issues such as the increasing scarcity of clean water with hotter, drier climates will also play a major part in increasing deaths from illness and malnutrition. In addition, the combination of increasing warmth and more standing water resulting from storms creates conditions conducive to epidemics, such as those of malaria, by providing breeding grounds for the insects and speeding up the life cycle as a result of the warmer conditions.[10]

Climate change will introduce three different types of health impact:

- **Direct impacts** through death and injury from heatwaves, storms, floods and drought.
- **Indirect impacts** through the occurrence of health conditions exacerbated by changing weather conditions, e.g. respiratory diseases exacerbated by atmospheric pollution, or ensuing outbreaks of disease, such as typhoid and cholera, related to climate events such as floods.
- **Migratory impacts** resulting from the movement of sources of infection resulting from the diaspora of diseases via various carriers with warming climates, e.g. malaria and trypanosoma.

The direct health impacts of climate change we see all around us on a regular basis, including deaths resulting from fires, floods and drought.

Heat and cold stress are the main direct causes of death from extremes of temperature and they are dealt with in Chapter 9 on the human thermal response and Chapter 14 on energy and fuel security issues.

Climate warming also causes a shift in regions where diseases can survive. Italy, a country that was declared malaria free in 1970, now sees numerous cases every year. Tick-borne encephalitis, visceral leishmaniasis carried by sandflies and potentially fatal, and other diseases are being reported as southern Italy in particular dries out. Concerns increase with climate change, increasing travel and the growth of densely populated cities about the rate of spread of a host of diseases, including tuberculosis, severe acute respiratory syndrome (SARS), Ebola, West Nile virus, malaria, plague, cholera, yellow fever, bird flu or influenza H5N1, Weil's disease, equine encephalitis, *Escherichia coli* 157, Lyme disease, *Cryptosporidium*, Lassa fever and Rift Valley fever.

The importance of shade for health

We can also see indirect impacts around us in the news as the changing climate begins to affect our lives and deaths. The increasing strength of solar radiation is also affecting even 'rainy' Britain. In September 2003 the UK government issued a warning to local authorities to remove sunbeds from every leisure centre in the country amid accusations that they are profiting from treatments that endanger the health of the public. Members of the Chartered Institute of Environmental Health, many of whom work for local councils, raised the alarm because they believe that sunbeds are contributing to the rise in the incidence of skin cancer. Research published by the *Journal of the National Cancer Institute* in 2002 shows a strong link between tanning lamps and skin cancer. They called, in their 2003 annual conference, for the inclusion of 'shade provision' to become a requirement for all big planning developments. School playgrounds would be required to provide children and teachers with shaded areas.[11]

Surprisingly, skin cancer is actually a major problem in the UK and exposure to ultraviolet rays and direct strong sunlight increases the risk of contracting skin cancer, by damaging the immune system and causing premature ageing of the skin. Skin cancer is now the second most common form of cancer in the UK. There are 40000 cases a year and the number of new cases annually rose by more than 90% in the 15 years between 1974 and 1989. Three-quarters of these result from malignant melanoma. Most skin cancers are not life-threatening but must be promptly removed surgically to avoid serious problems.

There are no published statistics available on how many melanomas are linked to travel abroad or tanning lamps or are contracted owing to exposure to the sun in the UK. Here again the combination of factors may place a crucial part, for instance holidays in Spain, tanning at the health club, gardening in summer and overexposure to direct sun in the workplace. In highly glazed buildings care should be taken to ensure that staff are not sitting in direct sun during their working day.

Insect infestations impact on our buildings

Insect populations can explode in certain conditions, including particular temperature bands. The smallest of animals can cause severe impacts. When such infestations strike they spread very rapidly; when sudden oak death spread from Oregon and California to Britain, it spread to more than 280 sites within months in England.[12] The same is true of moulds and fungi, which can have a devastating effect on people and buildings, as can termites, spreading north from Devon even now with the warming weather, and mosquitoes that are now found in parts of Kent. Such infestations may well affect our health, timber sources and the structures of our buildings.

The SARS effect: the effects of overcrowding

It is often the combination of conditions that really makes for serious epidemics, as many found out on the troop ships in the First and Second World Wars when thousands of weak and injured soldiers were crowded together in hot ships, providing ideal breeding grounds for a range of potent killers ranging from typhoid and cholera to the other lethal stomach bugs.

In late October 2003, 430 people were stuck down with a chronic stomach complaint caused by the norovirus, or Norwalk-like virus (NLV), on the cruise ship *Aurora*, carrying 18000 passengers and 800 crew. There was talk at that time of a £2.5 million claim against P&O, who operated the ocean liner, by some 250 of the infected passengers. Greece refused to let the liner dock in their waters to take on board provisions and medical assistance. NLV is the most common cause of stomach complaints in the UK, where 600000 to 1 million people suffer from it every year, particularly in schools and hospitals and where people are confined in close quarters. Similar viruses have disrupted other cruises.

Similarly, incidences of SARS, caught first from chickens, were concentrated in areas of high-density occupation, in hotels and high-rise housing estates in Hong Kong. SARS is caused by a coronavirus, a relative of the common cold, and was responsible for over 400 infections and 200 deaths in Southeast Asia and Canada in 2003. It spreads very rapidly and across large distances thanks to air travel, and is thought to spread primarily on droplets of water, through coughing and sneezing. Evidence from a large cluster of cases on a single housing estate in Hong Kong suggests that it can be spread in buildings, and in outdoor locations. Prevention measures for its transmission included the wearing of face masks and the thorough washing of hands.[13] With both the norovirus and the coronavirus the higher density of a population in one area will significantly increase the risks of infection of that population in that area.

The outbreak of SARS had a major impact on eastern markets in 2002. Economists cut the gross domestic product (GDP) forecast for Hong Kong alone by 2.5% in the wake of the outbreak,[14] while some estimate that the total costs may rise into billions rather than millions of dollars as travellers simply did not want to visit the infected regions. Travel insurers placed an exclusion zone on policies covering Canada, Hong Kong and China, and warned people they would not be covered if they caught the infection.[15]

Such outbreaks, on land or sea, demonstrate the potentially huge and growing risks to life and economic welfare arising from densely populated buildings and cities, in combination with rising temperatures.

Air pollution

Air pollution is already a growing health problem in many cities, including London, largely because of rising traffic levels, and will get worse in large urban areas under conditions of climate change. Recent studies show that relatively small rises in urban air pollution can trigger an increased number of potentially fatal heart attacks in people with vulnerable arteries.

During heatwaves air quality reduces, and on 7 August 2003 the UK government issued an official heath warning to asthmatics and the elderly, stating that air pollution in London had risen to the highest level for a decade as record temperatures were recorded in the capital. Air-quality monitors in Enfield recorded pollution levels of 131 parts per billion (ppb), almost three times the safe limit set by the WHO, as temperatures soared over 35°C.

Air quality in the UK in 2003 was the worst ever recorded, with the worst place in Britain for air pollution being a stretch of London's Marylebone Road, between Baker Street station and the

Madame Tussaud's exhibition, which exceeded pollution guideline levels 48 times in the first three months of 2003 and 11 times in 2002.[16]

Ozone levels also soared to 80–100 ppb in London at that time, while the highest levels ever recorded in Britain were 250 ppb in Harwell, Oxfordshire, in 1976 before strict EU laws restricting vehicle emissions were introduced.[17] However, there has been a gradual rise in the background levels of ozone in Europe since 1940. Government studies show that around 1600 people with breathlessness problems die prematurely every year due to high levels of air pollution and a further 1500, mostly asthma suffers, are admitted to hospital because their symptoms become worse during periods of poor air quality.[18]

An increasingly significant factor in the past few years, particularly in Southeast Asia, has been the contribution to urban air pollution of smoke from large fires experienced in countries around the globe, exacerbated by heatwave conditions.

Predicted future increases in the number and intensity of hot anticyclonic weather events in summer will favour the creation of more temperature inversions trapping pollutants in the near-surface layer of the atmosphere. It is estimated that a 1°C rise in summer air temperatures will result in a 14% increase in surface ozone concentrations in London.[19]

But the warming cocktail of atmospheric pollutants is being – incredibly – added to by the decisions of politicians who seem hell bent on worsening the already severe pollution problems we face. In August 2003, it was announced that, in the drive to meet the ever-increasing demand in America for energy, around 50% of which goes to power buildings, the Bush Administration opened a huge loophole in America's air pollution laws allowing an estimated 17 000 outdated power stations and factories to increase their carbon emissions with immunity. Critics of the draft regulations unveiled by the US Environmental Protection Agency claimed they amounted to the death knell for the Clean Air Act, the centrepiece of US Environmental Regulations. The proposed new Regulations were challenged by 13 states, including New York, but if adopted would provide a multi-million dollar victory for US energy corporations. Many of the objectors are particularly concerned about the health impacts of this loophole on the cities and populations in the vicinity of such plants.[20]

In Britain the Labour government has been very open about its desire to promote the interest of the aviation industry, with well-publicized plans for three major new airport developments over the next decade, at the expense of the well-being of ordinary citizens, particularly in southeast England.[21] Cheap air travel has a bread and circuses ring to it that appeals to politicians seeking re-election, but all political parties have possibly underestimated the intelligence of the local voters and their levels of knowledge on the issues involved. A major concern of people who live near runways, after noise, is the serious health consequences of poor air quality resulting from increased plane activity overhead.

Passenger flights emit more than 8 million tonnes of CO_2 every year in the UK, so playing a major part in climate change. This figure is predicted to rise to 19 million tonnes by 2030 if the airline industries are not checked, and ways to do this were the subject of a major review by the Department of Transport in 2003/04.[22]

Fuels burnt in aviation have a wide range of toxic emissions that directly affect human health. Aviation emissions include nitrogen oxide, hydrocarbons, sulphur dioxide, naphthalene, benzene (a known carcinogen), formaldehyde (a suspected carcinogen) and dust particles that harm human health and contribute to global warming. This 'poison circle' can extend for 6 miles around a single runway and run 20 miles downwind. Studies have linked airport pollution to cancer, asthma, liver damage, lung disease, lymphoma, depression, myeloid leukaemia and tumours.

The size of this problem is emphasized by the fact that today 70% of US residents live within 20 miles of a major airport. In the UK the figures for people living within 30 miles of the four London airports must be fairly similar. Aircraft pollution has been implicated in higher rates of child mortality, premature deaths and cancer deaths in a number of reputable studies.[23]

In the UK, air pollution, including that from aircraft and the surface traffic pollution associated with airports, is estimated to kill up to 24000 people every year and requires medical treatment for thousands more. The health costs of air pollution from the UK aviation sector are estimated at more than £1.3 billion a year.[24] As with vehicular air pollution, the impacts of this pollution will be accelerated with the higher temperatures that are associated with global warming. The traditional view that aviation is a 'sacred cow' and should not be restricted by legislation because it may slow down global economies, is now being questioned, as is the need for more and more airports and air travel, which seems dependent also on oil prices remaining at their current costs.

What is sure is that increasingly warm summers will affect the air quality and in turn the quality of life of millions of citizens in Britain as the weather becomes hotter. Some engineers argue that issues of air quality from transport, industrial and acid rain pollution are a good reason to use air conditioning in buildings, but the most damaging of the fine particulates in air pollution are too small to be removed by air conditioning filters, so invalidating this solution (more of which in Chapter 11).

Those who are interested in locating sources of air pollution in relation to a particular site in England or Wales can enter a postcode on the 'What's in your backyard' feature on the Your Environment page of the Environment Agency website; it will also show where pollution is being emitted from industrial sites and landfill sites.[25]

Water pollution

As water temperatures rise they often lead to an increase in toxicity. During periods of drought as water levels drop so do oxygen levels in water courses that can occasionally lead to large-scale death of fish stock in rivers and streams. This is exacerbated by increasing toxicity as there is less water to dilute any existing pollutants.

An increasing problem is also the impact of warming water on the growth of algal blooms in both fresh and sea water. There are growing fears that human-made pollution is producing 'dead zones' caused by critically low oxygen levels in the oceans of the world. By 2007 over 400 coastal dead zones were recorded, up from 300 in 1995 and 162 in the late 1980s. Dead zones are caused when massive algal blooms, feeding off pollutants such as fertilizers, die and decay. Marine bacteria feed on the algae in the blooms after they have sunk to the bottom, and use up much of the oxygen dissolved in the water. The resulting 'hypoxic' seabeds can asphyxiate sea-bed organisms like clams and worms, and in turn disrupt fish stock. The problem can be exacerbated by periods of heavy rain that flush out more of the chemical pollutants in the soils, into the streams and rivers and down into the sea.

Waste

Increasing temperatures all year round will affect many aspects of our lives. For instance, building, office, household and industrial waste may increasingly become an issue with climate because of:

- greater outdoor odour problems associated with waste disposal due to higher summer temperatures, and
- waste containment problems associated with heavy rains and floods.

There may be a need for more frequent waste collection in certain areas owing to high summer temperatures, and more protection of, and care in selection of, landfill sites.

The city with the greatest waste collection in the world is Naples which, as a result of systemic corruption in the council and waste collection industry, regularly suffers from garbage strikes. In May 2007 the rubbish had built up to a depth of 3 m on some streets, in some places people had set fire to it and the stink and resulting pollution was all pervasive. The dumps in the region are apparently full but the problem is one that will in time lead to major health problems for the citizens, not least because of the increase in rat populations as the waste piles grow.

In the UK 200 000 homes are close to landfill sites and were thought to be worth, on average, £5500 less because of the nuisance caused by dust, noise, small vermin, and water and air pollution caused by the neighbouring rubbish dumps. In the first comprehensive study of the effect of landfill sites on house prices it was found that Scottish homes lost a staggering 41% of their value if they were within a quarter of a mile of a site, while in the East Midlands only a 10% reduction within a quarter of a mile and 8.75% reduction within half a mile were recorded.

Noise

With climate change, a wide range of physical and social adaptations in the population may well affect noise issues in cities. For example, with warmer outdoor temperatures, the growth of the 'café society' may increase activity at all times of year in the streets of cities, and sensible planning of open-air eating facilities in relation to residential areas is necessary as the warmer evenings may well pre-date the adaptation of populations to higher street noise levels. Thought should also be given to the greater need to open windows in warmer weather and the need to ensure that the noise and pollution impacts of street life and traffic noise do not encourage a move towards the climatically unnecessary air conditioning of buildings. The increased need for traffic-free zones in open restaurant areas of a city may become a feature of future inner city planning strategies, to ensure that local office buildings can be naturally ventilated without excessive noise levels. So noise and pollution should be increasingly included as key concerns for urban designers and local councils alike. Even fashionable buildings on sites with high noise and traffic pollution levels are problems, like the £13 million Hammersmith Ark building. It is nearly three decades old, very elegant, with low rents per square foot, but because of its noisy location on a traffic island, it has proved over those years a challenge to rent out.

Fires

Fire hazards are significantly increased with hotter dry seasons, which add to the frequency, and the intensity, of bush and forest fires, creating a greater hazard to life, limb and property. Such fires occur generally in association with extreme dry periods and strong winds, as was the case with the Great Fire of London in 1666.[26]

Every month from November 1665 to September 1666 was dry. By August 1666, the River Thames at Oxford was reduced to a 'trickle'. The dryness extended to Scotland, at least from May to mid-July. The drought over these two months is noteworthy because it preceded the Great Fire of London, and apparently the east wind, which prevailed during that period, had dried the wooden houses of London until they were like tinder. When the fire started on 12 September, the east wind drove the flames before it, causing great problems with fire-fighting and helping the fire to spread rapidly, causing smoke from the fire to reach as far as Oxford.

The prevailing weather was noted as 'hot and dry', and on the first day of the fire John Evelyn noted in his diary, a 'Fierce' eastern wind in a very dry season. It is not clear though whether the wind was caused by the fire, or was there anyway. However, Evelyn did note that there had been a 'long set of fair and warm weather'. On 14 September Evelyn noted: 'The eastern wind still more impetuously driving the flames forward'. On the 15th, he noted that the wind was 'abating', but this may have been due to the fire burning itself out. In any case, this was effectively the end of the Great Fire, and when the rains came on the 19th the fire was quenched and a rainy autumn followed, although Evelyn claimed that smoke could still be seen rising out of the odd basement six months after it ended.

The climate in a particular year is crucial to the local and global fire hazard. Between 1997 and 2002 there were 209 000 fires in England. In the exceptionally dry summer of 2003 alone there were 110 460 with a number of catastrophic fires occurring that year around the world:

- April 2003: In Huddersfield, UK, hundreds of hectares of National Trust moorland were left charred by fires that swept through the tinder-dry hills near the city.
- July and August 2003: In Portugal, a national disaster was declared as more than 2300 fire-fighters tackled 72 blazes across the country.
- August 2003: In Canada, 30 000 people had to flee their communities in the Okanagan Mountain Forest Fire, 185 miles east of Vancouver, which had 100 m high flames moving at 30 m a minute across the countryside, leaving at least 200 homes as smouldering rubble in its wake. The fire began to 'crown', moving rapidly from tree top to tree top, and was seen to leap from building to building, some of which exploded in the intense heat. The fire started on 16 August with a lightning strike in the mountains.
- September 2003: On the French Riviera, huge forest fires destroyed over 1000 hectares of woods, following two devastating blazes in July that killed four people, including two Britons, and destroyed more than 18 000 hectares of pine and oak.
- October 2003: The final death toll in the southern Californian fires of October 2003 rose to over 22, including some of the 12 000 fire-fighters who battled with the blazes. Estimated damage from the fires, covering over 275 hectares and destroying nearly 3000 homes, could top £1.17 billion. Large fires also raged at the same time in the south of Denver and near Jamestown, Colorado.

Perhaps the most devastating of recent fires occurred in Greece in 2007, where 670 000 acres (270 000 ha) of land were burnt in one summer. The USA has the highest incidence of annual fire outbreaks and the highest insurance payouts for fire damage in the world, with the worst recorded fires in California's history occurring in autumn 2008. However, even in the UK it is anticipated that we could suffer from impacts as devastating as those in Turkey, where 100 000 acres (40 500 ha) of Antalya were destroyed in 2008, and Greece in recent years because rural Britain is becoming increasingly dry over time and fire chiefs are expecting catastrophic fires in the not too distant future.

The issue of what materials buildings are made of is an important one. In countries such as the USA and Australia, where buildings are typically constructed of timber, or timber-based components, not only is more of the building destroyed during a fire, and the strong winds associated with it, but such buildings add fuel to the fire and intensify the event. Europe is extremely fortunate to have traditional building industries in which buildings have been largely constructed of heavy masonry and are less vulnerable to the catastrophic devastation experienced in many bush and forest fires, where whole suburbs can ignite in fireballs as the timber houses literally explode with the heat. In Britain, the medieval cities were to a far larger extent made of timber-framed construction, which was replaced in London largely by brick buildings after the Great Fire in 1666.

Biodiversity impacts

Plant and animal species are being lost around the world with rising temperatures at a rate that has alarmed many scientists. Every year the numbers rise inexorably and with the dire warnings about the melting of the Arctic ice sheet there has been growing concern about the loss of whole species such as polar bear and other Arctic animals. For a full list of species loss take a look at the Red List of the International Union of Conservationists (IUCN).[27] There are estimated to be around 1.8 million species on Earth, but of those only around 41 000 have been assessed for their extinction potential.

Some of the most notable extinctions that are anticipated for the near future are those of the coral reefs, the Sumatran tiger, the Malaysian bear and the western gorilla. For some of these species there will no longer be anywhere suitable to live. Others will be unable to reach places where the climate is suitable to breed, feed or avoid thermal stress.[28]

THE RESTRUCTURING OF ECONOMIES IN THE WARMING WORLD

The impacts of biodiversity changes on regional economies

The loss of species has often catastrophic impacts on local economies. Fishing industries around the world will be highly impacted as river and ocean waters warm, changing centuries of tradition in their fishing practices. Every species has a temperature window within which it thrives and as temperatures change they will migrate to occupy their 'survival' temperatures. An extra 1°C in temperature pushed haddock, cod, plaice and lemon sole 200–400 miles north, according to the WWF (formerly the World Wildlife Fund). There have been more frequent sightings of species such as hammerhead sharks, triggerfish, sun fish and even red mullet, cuttlefish and black bream

3.8.
Bushfires on the eastern shores of Hobart, Tasmania, on 12 October 2006.
Source: Bill Bordass.

in the waters of the Isle of Man. Fishermen in Cornwall may have to start breeding lobsters in captivity to prevent them from being eaten by triggerfish when very young. Scuba divers regularly find octopi along the south coast and Japanese oysters have also started breeding in British waters. These trends may affect the economic welfare of the fishermen of Britain and the communities they support.

Even more catastrophic is what is predicted will happen to the world's coral reefs. More than 100 million people around the world depend on reefs for their livelihoods. Corals are very temperature sensitive and are dying over large areas as ocean waters warm. In the El Niño year of 1998 unusually high temperatures in the Indian Ocean killed more than 90% of the corals on shallow Indian Ocean reefs and future high temperatures could finish the reefs off completely. Sixteen per cent of all coral reefs globally were calculated to have been destroyed but the worst affected were those in the Indian Ocean. The corals that died were up to 100 years old and would take centuries to recover if sea temperatures stabilized at the current levels. It is predicted that the higher temperatures may be reached every five years now and for the latitudes 10–15 degrees south, by 2020 all corals species may be extinct.[29]

The economic costs of such extinctions are enormous. To combat such devastation legislation has just been introduced to make two-thirds of the Great Barrier Reef, off the east coast of Australia, into a protected area under conservation plans announced by the Australian Government in December 2002, forming the largest network of protected marine areas in the world. Strong opposition was brought by the Queensland fishing industry, where it was estimated that 250 jobs would be lost. Fishing on the reef generates only around £46 million, while tourism in the region is worth £1.7 billion.

In May 2003, Hamdallah Zedan, Secretary to the Convention on Biological Diversity, ratified by 187 nations, said that at the Earth Summit at Johannesburg it had been recognized that our health and our lives depend on biodiversity and that:

The millions of species on earth have evolved complex interactions that allow for their mutual survival. Man has disrupted this at such a rate that nature can no longer adapt. Scientists agree that the incidences of plagues and pandemics will increase as we battle to find ways of controlling these human health challenges.

Wolves at the gates of the city?

Animals are very ingenious, and even as one ecological niche closes, another may open up. The significance of a range of factors may influence how animals behave in a changing climate. Already we have the phenomenon of wild animals becoming adapted to live in cities, as was clearly outlined in David Baron's book *The Beast in the Garden*.[30] He cites cases of bears moving into New Jersey suburbs, raccoons in Los Angeles, and in the UK the urban fox is a common occurrence. The animals are drawn to feed off rubbish bins, a particular problem in the USA where, because of urban sprawl, the suburbs are moving into what was wilderness. Animal numbers have risen owing to restrictive laws in some states on the hunting and trapping of a range of larger animals, for instance lynx, bobcats, bears, beavers, foxes, wolves and cougars. There are black bears in the suburbs of Boston for the first time in 200 years and in New Jersey they have multiplied to over an estimated 3300. In December 2003 New Jersey authorized its first bear hunt in 33 years. Coyotes are multiplying too, and their cheek was demonstrated when one ran into the federal building in Seattle, through reception and into the lift! They routinely eat cats and dogs. In Florida the alligator population is growing at an unprecedented rate, helped by people

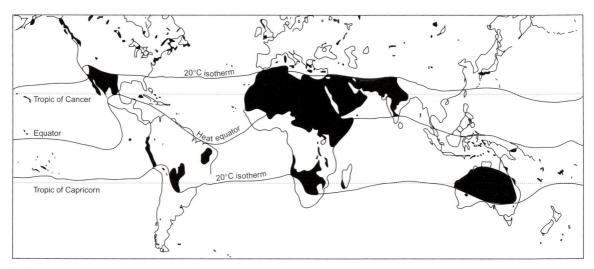

3.9.
Deserts of the world covered 22% of the world's landmass in 1970, and in 2000 this had risen to 33%.
Source: Isaac Meir.

buying up large plots and embracing the wilderness life and feeding the animals. David Baron maintains that the USA (and humans in general, the most pervasive species of all) is engaged in a grand and largely unintentional experiment. The 'range', on which Americans were once so happy to be 'at home', has moved from the plains to the car park at the mall and shows no sign of withdrawing back to the plains and the mountains.[31]

The death of mountain communities?

As jobs go, so too do the communities they supported. Global warming is already affecting many mountain communities as winter sports are pushed higher and higher up. Fifteen years ago it was possible to guarantee good skiing over Christmas in the Alps, even in the lower resorts. Today this can only be done for sites over 1750 m, and even then this is not certain. Many ski resorts at lower altitudes face bankruptcy, and increasing environmental impacts are recorded as there is more and more pressure put on providing services at higher altitudes.

A research group from the University of Zurich looked at the situation in relation to predicted future climates and concluded that while today 85% of the 230 resorts in Switzerland are 'snow reliable' (if seven out of ten winters had at least 30–50 cm of snow on at least 100 days between 1 December and 15 August), by 2030 to 2050 this would drop to 63%. If the snowline rises from 1200 to 1800 m one in four resorts in many areas would face ruin, with losses of £925 million a year.

In Austria the snowline is expected to rise 200–300 m by 2030–2050, making many resorts in the central and eastern parts lose their winter industry; and in Italy only resorts above 1500 m can expect reliable falls of snow, that is around half of the winter sports villages. Many such villages are facing major problems already. Many German resorts are also at low altitudes. In Australia an increase of 0.60°C would hit four of the nine ski resorts and a rise in global temperatures of 3.4°C, predicted under some scenarios, by 2070 would mean that no Australian resort could operate at a profit.

Even the summer climbing industry in the Alps is suffering. For the first time since records began in 1786, the summer 2003 heatwave made the Matterhorn too dangerous to climb. The mountain was closed in August 2003, with its naked slopes covered with heaps of rubble and scree. Two climbers died just trying to get to the restaurant at the start of the climbing routes. The permafrost that holds the mountain peaks together had melted to a depth of 7 feet (2.1 m), making ski lifts and cable cars unstable. The problems became apparent in July 2003, when an enormous rock avalanche hurtled down the mountain's east face, and within two hours another rocked the north face. More than 70 climbers had to be hauled from the mountain, one of the biggest mountaineering rescues in history. The mountain had actually begun to fall apart under their feet. Ice as it warms, but before it melts, may be more unstable than when it is turning to water. There is a growing realization that there is going to be a lot more of this type of devastation in mountainous regions as the foundations of the mountains, and their ski lifts and cable cars, become unstable.[32]

Agriculture

In 2008 a global food crisis broke upon an unsuspecting world. Hunger riots broke out from Haiti to Indonesia. Crop belts are moving north, and many English farmers are already growing maize and sunflower as the cost of staple crops soared, exacerbated by the shift in production to bio-fuel crops, widespread drought and a warming climate. Higher temperatures have led to failures not only in crop production but also in fish production, animal productivity and in some parts far higher than normal deaths of birds in poultry farms that were ill-prepared for heatwaves.

In the short term there may be some agricultural benefits for temperate or colder climates as the world warms. One is the ability to produce more than one crop a year and expand the range of species grown. One example is the potential for the increased production of British wine. In the Campsie Hills, near Glasgow, the Cumbernauld vineyard is thriving and, banking on a good dose of global warming in the area, locals eagerly await the advent of Scottish wine made from Caledonia grapes. It was claimed in 2004 that if the Champagne region of France were to overheat and has to return to making more traditional Bordeaux types of wine, southern England could become the home of sparkling wine. The geography of wine is set to change dramatically with climate change and those who will suffer most will be the growers of southern France and Italy who may have to move their grapes to higher elevations or change their grape stock plants. In Scotland grapes such as Muller-Thurgau and Bacchus may do well, while in the southern areas Pinot Noir and Chardonnay grapes may thrive best in the warming climate. Vine growers will have to be very adaptable to survive what climate change is throwing at them.[33]

The problems for agriculture are also numerous. Warmer winters have also allowed aphids to survive in much larger numbers, forcing growers to spray crops earlier, and a new range of insects, wasps and spiders has invaded Britain from across the English Channel.

In 2007 the real scale of the impacts of climate change on crop production began to become clearer when a whole range of factors came together to almost double food prices across the world in a dramatic few months. Worldwide cereal stocks fell to 111 million tonnes, the lowest in 30 years, and wheat prices rose from £65 a tonne in 2006 to £117 a tonne in 2008. The International Grains Council predicted that the industrial use of grains would rise in 2008 by 23% to 229 million tonnes, of which around 107 million tonnes would be absorbed by ethanol producers for biofuels. The price of rice rose by 50% in two weeks in May 2008, triggering food riots in many countries around the world as people began not to be able to buy basic foodstuffs. Food shortages are severely affected by extreme weather events and the extensive flooding in south China, Indonesia and the Philippines in summer 2008 heralded conditions of growing food poverty.[34] Widespread droughts and flooding in Australia, Africa and America also contributed to growing food shortages. Population growth around the world is also a factor in rising food prices, as are the rising standards of living in many emerging countries.

A loaf of bread in the UK rose from 53 pence in 2002 to 129 pence by summer 2008.
A tonne of rice on world markets rose from $145 in 2002 to over $700 by summer 2008.

Climate change has already created a global food crisis that is affecting everybody on the planet, and it is destined only to get worse. Prince Charles, in August 2008, made a controversial plea for humanity to turn away from the use of genetically modified crops because it put too much power in the hands of a few international corporations. What is increasingly apparent is that everyone from the lower and middle classes, in fact all but richest minority of the world's population, will have to turn their hands to growing or accessing as much of their own food locally as possible because of the growing cost of centrally provided food in the shops. Climate change is making food security as challenging an issue as that of energy security. For both these key challenges local storage solutions offer the individual more hope of survival in all but the most extreme of catastrophes. A local saying in the city of Mosul in northern Iraq is 'One day honey, one day onions', meaning one day plenty, one day basic rations. Every family should plan, perhaps, to locate their own stash of onions in a rapidly changing world.

Gardening

In 2008 the Royal Horticultural Society built their garden at the Chelsea Flower Show around the theme of climate change. Plants such as tender perennials did not feature and there were very few cacti to be seen. There were two future scenarios including a 'low emissions' and a 'high emissions' garden. The former had plants that can be grown in sheltered positions in today's gardens but the latter was populated with species that one would find in Mediterranean gardens today such as bougainvillea, succulents and a wide range of drought-resistant species.

Plants, like humans and other animals, are being influenced by the changing climate. In even the hottest and driest places on Earth the garden has always been an important climatic design feature, to enhance the enjoyment of life, through the richness of colour and texture, perfumes and appearance, but also a very effective way of providing cooling. The earliest dynasties of Mesopotamia were renowned for their gardens. The Garden of Eden was placed by historians at the confluence of the Tigris and the Euphrates and the poetry of the Sumerians, living over 5000 years ago in that region, lyrically details the beauty of the trees, plants and flowers enjoyed at the time. Most have also heard of the Hanging Gardens of Babylon and many will have read the rich poetry of the Persians, singing tributes to the beauty of the gardens and their contents with ponds and streams set, in an ordered fashion, in the great walled domains and parks.[35]

On such a great tradition of gardening were built the Roman gardens, as one can see today in Pompeii, where many have been reconstructed from the archaeological evidence garnered from the uncovered city. Vines and fruit trees, woods and flowers and herbs flourish, still reflecting the wall paintings around the houses.[36]

The secret of the success of gardening in some of the hottest places on Earth was to create a micro-climate fed by very selective watering systems and strategies and protected from the barren deserts beyond by high walls that kept out the hot winds and sun and contained the moister micro-climate within. Cold and moist air sinks, and many such gardens contain sunken sections, often covered by a canopy of trees to reduce evaporative transpiration rates and contain the coolth. Perhaps the greatest achievement of any urban gardeners is in the Chinese Desert Oasis city of Turfan, where the main crop of the town, grapes, is also used as an air conditioning system for the whole city: all the pavements and courtyards of houses in the old city are planted with vines that keep out the sun and provide a luxurious micro-climate beneath the vines. Other strategies for gardening in deserts include the planting of only drought-tolerant species and minimizing water loss rates by very careful diurnal and seasonal strategies for planting, watering and harvesting species.[37]

Just as we will rely increasingly on imported wisdom on appropriate building technologies as the climate warms, as traditional approaches to gardening cease to be viable in future climates, with drier and hotter summers and frost-free winters, many of the lower latitude approaches to garden design and upkeep will have to be incorporated into our strategies for maintaining gardens. Many of the species in British gardens today may have to be replaced in the future by more drought-tolerant plants, and for inspiration a good place to look for species appropriate to future climates in the UK is to the gardens of southern Europe today.[38]

THE PROBLEMS OF FREEZE

Increasingly, extreme weather events are associated not only with higher temperatures but also with the problems of freeze. Extreme cold events cause real challenges for many homes. The 'big freeze' of December 1995 and January 1996 caused widespread damage from burst pipes and water mains. The evidence submitted by the Scottish and Northern Ireland Plumbing Employer's Federation to the subsequent Scottish Affairs Committee Inquiry[39] highlighted the concern that many householders did not know how to or could not shut off the cold water supply. Many flats and tenements had no isolation valve for individual properties. The scale of burst

3.10.
In the summer of 2003 the American Mid-West suffered from an all-time record number of tornadoes, indicating a trend in the increasing frequency of storm events in the region. The frequency and intensity of storms increase as land masses heat up.
Source: Extreme Climate Calendar.

water pipe damage was reflected by the estimate from the Association of British Insurers (ABI) that the claims in Scotland would amount to some £350 million. Following this, the ABI produced a set of television commercials and a free schools pack on precautions to be taken to prevent burst pipes, in the hope that the school children would educate their parents. This was the most successful schools pack the ABI had produced, and almost every school in Scotland asked for supplies.

The ironic fact about all this is that other countries such as the USA have no great problems with burst pipes despite more severe winters, simply because of the design of their plumbing systems. Properties in the UK could be made similarly resilient by a simple modification[40] to the pipe work using materials costing less than £5, plus around 15 minutes' labour. If the North Atlantic circulation changes as a result of climate change, freeze could become a growing problem in the UK.

One chronic problem the USA does suffer from is the vulnerability of its power supply lines. Every winter there are communities around America where winters storms bring down power lines, leaving buildings without electricity for weeks, as in MacAlister, Oklahoma, in spring 2007 where the whole town was without electricity for three weeks. Planning to survive comfortably through a big freeze is essential too.

CONCLUSIONS

Every aspect of the way we live will be affected by climate change: the regions and settlements we live in, the air we breathe, the food we eat, our jobs, our holidays and the buildings we live in. We face a wide range of design challenges to accommodate such rapid changes. But one concern must cross our own minds as we see the rate and extent of the warming and note the extent of the changes that may well be wrought on the landscapes and on other species, and that is: Will we ourselves stay comfortable, safe and ultimately survive in the changing climate?

This question is addressed in Chapters 8 and 9.

NOTES AND REFERENCES

1   <http://www.wmo.ch/web/Press/Press.html>. IPCC, Climate Change 2007: The Physical Science Basis. Summary for Policymakers: Contribution of Working Group I to the Fourth Assessment Report of the Intergovernmental Panel on Climate Change. Geneva: IPCC. IPCC (2007b) Mitigation. Contribution of Working Group III to the Fourth Assessment Report of the Intergovernmental Panel on Climate Change. Geneva: IPCC, 2007a.

2   Guardian, 7 August 2008, p. 1.

3   J. Hansen, M. Sato, P. Kharecha, D. Beerling, R. Berner, V. Masson-Delmotte, M. Pagani, M.L. Raymo, D.L. Royer, J.C. Zacho, Target atmospheric CO_2: where should humanity aim? Science, 6 August 2008. Full paper available on: <http://arxiv.org/ftp/arxiv/papers/0804/0804.1126.pdf>. See also J. Lovelock, The Revenge of Gaia. London: Penguin, 2006.

4   For all related UKCIP reports see <http://www.ukcip.org.uk/publications/pub.html>, including: M. Hulme, et al., Climate Change Scenarios for the United Kingdom: The UKCIP02

Briefing Report, 2002, published in conjunction with UKCIP, the Hadley Centre and the Climate Research Unit in the School of Environmental Science at the University of East Anglia, by the Tyndall Centre, Norwich; M. Hulme, et al., Climate Change Scenarios for the United Kingdom: The UKCIP02 Scientific Report, Appendix 2, published in conjunction with UKCIP, the Hadley Centre and the Climate Research Unit in the School of Environmental Science at the University of East Anglia, by the Tyndall Centre, Norwich, 2002.

5   There is an increasing amount of work being done on the heat island effect. Some good references for those interested to start with are: H. Graves, R. Watkins, P. Westbury, P. Littlefair, Cooling Buildings in London, 2001. BR 431. London: CRC (see <http://www.brebookshop. com>); T.R. Oke, Urban climates and global environmental change, in: R.D. Thompson, A.H. Perry (Eds.), Applied Climatology: Principles and Practice. London: Routledge, 1997, pp. 273–287; see also London's Warming: The Impacts of Climate Change on London, Technical Report, published by the London Climate Change Partnership in November 2003 and available in pdf form, from the UKCIP website on <http://www.ukcip.org.uk/publications/pub. html>.

6   Guardian, Jobs and Money, 9 August 2003, p. 17.

7   Guardian, 9 August 2003. For more information on the building design see <http://www.betterpublicbuildings.gov.uk/hm_treasury.html>.

8   S. Roaf, Closing the Loop: Benchmarks for Sustainable Buildings, RIBA Publications, London, 2004.

9   J. Hacker, Beating the Heat, <http://www.arup.com/europe/newsitem.cfm?pageid=7234> 2005.

10   <http://www.who.int/globalchange/climate/summary/en/and>; see also <http://www.ukcip. org.uk/publications/pub.html> for a pdf version of: Department of Health, Health Effects of Climate Change in the UK: An Expert Review for Comment. Leicester: Institute for Environment and Health, 2001.

11   There are many concerns about the impact of radiation on the skin, and for a discussion on the subject see <http://www.biol.sc.edu/~elygen/Andrea%20Stanley.htm>. The WHO sees the establishment of a sun protection programme as a high priority as the young are most vulnerable to skin damage from the sun. See <http://www.who.int/uv/publications/en/sunprotschools. pdf>.

12   Guardian, 29 October 2003, p. 9

13   Guardian, 21 April 2003, p. 3

14   Independent on Sunday, 27 April 2003, p. 11.

15   Guardian, 25 April 2003, p. 19.

16   Independent on Sunday, 27 April 2003, p. 27

17   Guardian, 19 April 2003, p. 3.

18   Independent, 8 August 2003, p. 5.

19   London's Warming, The London Climate Change Impacts study, 2002, p. 63 <http://www.ukcip. org.uk/London/main_London.htm>; and particularly badly affected are cities in basin locations such as Sheffield and, surprisingly, Sydney, Australia.

20 Guardian, 23 August 2003, p. 1.

21 The UK Government in its 2003/04 White Paper on air transport made a range of recommendations to increase the capacity of UK airports including that two new runways should be built, the first at Stansted airport by 2012 with a second extra runway at Heathrow airport by 2020, providing 'stringent environmental limits' can be met. The paper rules out additional runways at Stansted, Gatwick and Luton and an airport at Cliffe. It does not rule out new runways and/or terminal capacity at Bristol, Birmingham, Edinburgh, Glasgow, Belfast, Cardiff, Manchester, Liverpool John Lennon, Leeds, Bradford and Newcastle airports.

22 The White Paper contains no evidence that the 'external' health impacts of such decisions have been taken into account during the decisions, as many had hoped for; see <http://www.dft.gov.uk/aviation/whitepaper/>.

23 It should be noted that a range of simple strategies could be employed to reduce the unsustainably high levels of air pollution resulting from aviation.

24 Taxiing by using two engines instead of four would reduce hydrocarbon emissions by 80% and carbon monoxide emissions by nearly 70%. Hydrocarbon and other emissions could be further cut by towing aircraft to and from terminals, using fuel vapour recovery procedures, and modifying jet fuel itself (which could reduce nitrogen oxide particulate emissions by 30%). Flying 6000 feet lower than their present cruising altitude, airlines could cut the damage caused by vapour trails by 47% – although they would burn 6% more fuel. Air traffic control stratagems could cut emissions by a further 10% if planes no longer had to fly 'zig-zag' patterns and were able to avoid queuing for take-off and landing slots <http://www.guardian.co.uk/uk_news/story/0,3604,1098385,0.html>.

25 <http://www.environment-agency.gov.uk/homeandleisure/37795.aspx>.

26 There are a number of excellent books on the Great Fire. See Clout, H. (ed.) (1999) The Times History of London. London: Times Books; Berresford Ellis, P. (1986) The Great Fire of London: An Illustrated Account. London: New English Library; Porter, S. (1996) The Great Fire of London. Gloucestershire: Sutton Publishing; and for full accounts of the contemporary diary entries of Samuel Pepys and John Evelyn see <http://www.pepys.info/fire.html>.

27 IUCN Red List: <http://www.nature.com/nature/links/040108/040108-1.html>.

28 See <http://www.biodiv.org>.

29 C. Sheppard, Coral grief. Nature, 18 September 2003. For a full text of this paper see <http://www.nature.com/nature/links/030918/030918-8.html>. See also R. Stone, A world without corals. Science 316 (2007) 678–681.

30 D. Baron, The Beast in the Garden: A Modern Parable of Man and Nature, W.W. Norton and Co, New York, 2003.

31 Guardian, 3 December 2003, p. 3. For more on this issue see www.unep.org

32 <http://www.int-res.com/abstracts/cr/v20/n3/p253-257.html> and for the melting Matterhorn story see <http://observer.guardian.co.uk/international/story/0,6903,1001674,00.html>.

33 R. Shelley, The winelands of Britain: past, present and prospective, 2008. Published by Petravin. See <http://www.winelandsofbritain.co.uk/book>.

34 For more information on this subject see <http://www.fao.org>, and an excellent site on the impacts of desertification see <http://www.grida.no/climate/ipcc/regional/166.htm>.

35 D.N. Wilber, Persian Gardens and Garden Pavilions, Second ed. (first published 1962), Dumbarton Oaks, Washington, 1979.

36 E.B. Macdougall, W.F. Jashmemski, Ancient Roman Gardens, Dumbarton Oaks, Washington, 1981.

37 T. Cochrane Ali, J. Brown, Landscape Design for the Middle East, RIBA Publications, London, 1978.

38 R. Bisgrove, P. Hadley, Gardening in the Global Greenhouse: The Impacts of Climate Change on Gardens in the UK, 2002. Technical Report. Oxford: UK Climate Impacts Programme (see <http://www.ukcip.org.uk>).

39 Scottish Affairs Committee Inquiry, Big Freeze: Lessons to be Learned, HMSO, Edinburgh, 1996.

40 J.R. Gordon, An investigation into freezing and bursting water pipes in residential construction. School of Architecture–Building Research Council at University of Illinois. Prepared for the Insurance Institute for Property Loss Reduction, USA, 1996.

4 HOW WET WILL IT GET?

INTRODUCTION

Water is the most fundamental building block of life itself and as we approach the years of the water wars an excess, or lack, of water may present the greatest hazard we face in building durable settlements in the future, even in 'rainy' Britain.

Flooding is the most evident impact from climate change. In Europe alone there have been major flooding disasters every year for more than 10 years (Table 4.1). Several of these have been in England and Wales.

PRECIPITATION TRENDS IN BRITAIN

The wettest places in the UK collect approximately eight times as much rain as the driest in an average year. In the Scottish Highlands, the average annual rainfall ranges from 5100 mm in the west to 585 mm in the east. London's average is 600 mm, or 1.6 million tons per square mile.

Table 4.1 Catastrophic European floods

Year	Location
1997	Oder (Germany/Poland)
1998	English Midlands and Wales, Sarno (Italy), Central Europe
1999	Danube, Northern Alps, Denmark (5 m coastal storm surge)
2000	England/Wales (twice), Switzerland, Italy
2001	England (twice), Wisla (Poland)
2002	England and Wales, Dublin, Danube and Elbe (100 deaths), Central Europe
2003	Rhône (France)
2004	Boscastle (Cornwall), Conwy Valley (North Wales), Derry City (Northern Ireland)
2005	Conwy Valley (again), Carlisle, Hawick, Alpine regions of Switzerland, Germany, Austria
2006	Danube (highest river level since 1895), Alps, Romania and Black Sea, Turkey (39 deaths)
2007	Malta, Yorkshire, Humberside, Midlands and South West of England
2008	Dublin and Belfast (widespread flooding in August costs the Irish insurance industry over (€96 m); record August rainfall in UK

Just because the west is wetter than the east does not mean that the west is a higher flood risk. People have adapted; they have learned to build bigger drains and to avoid using flat roofs or building on low land near rivers or coasts. What matters will be the extent to which society, especially in the east and the south, will be able to adapt to the increasingly severe rainfall events predicted with climate change. There will be particular problems in urban areas near the coast from flash floods in the summer, because as the sea surface temperature increases, this could lead to more frequent and severe thunderstorms. Such pluvial floods could happen anywhere, even on high ground, as in the Llandudno floods of June 1993, and cannot be mapped in advance.

British coastal waters are at their warmest in September when the land is already cooling. This is why autumn convection storms are common on the south coast in the autumn. These added to the flood problems in Sussex and Kent in October and November 2000. Summer 2006 was the warmest extended summer in England since instrument records began in 1659 and November 2006 recorded a record number of thunderstorms on the south coast of England. Damaging tornadoes were recorded in London in December 2006.

Britain is fortunate in its verdant landscapes and its future predicted climates. While the changes to predicted precipitation over the next decades appear to be severe for us, they are survivable, with prudent and judicious management.

Under the 2002 UK Climate Impacts Programme (UKCIP02),[1] winter precipitation in the UK is predicted to increase for all periods and for all climate change scenarios. By the 2080s, this increase ranges from between 10% and 20% for the Low Emissions scenario (depending on region) to between 15% and 35% for the High Emissions scenario. Conversely, the summer pattern is reversed and almost the whole of the UK may become drier, with a decrease in rainfall for the Low Emissions scenario of up to 35%, and for the High Emissions scenario of a staggering 50% or more. The highest changes in precipitation in both winter and summer are predicted for eastern and southern parts of England, while changes are smallest in the northwest of Scotland.[2] What we are looking at here is the increasing risk of summer droughts and winter flooding.

It should be noted that UKCIP02 is not the only source of climate change predictions. A major European research project involving 19 leading universities has produced a different set of scenarios under the 'Prediction of Regional scenarios and Uncertainties for Defining EuropeaN Climate change risks and Effects' (PRUDENCE). This predicts heavy winter precipitation in central and northern Europe and decreases in the south, and heavy summer precipitation increases in northeastern Europe and decreases in the south. Longer droughts will happen in Mediterranean countries. The floods in the summer of 2004 in Boscastle and 2007 in north and west England were very much in line with the PRUDENCE predictions, but not in line with UKCIP02.

Perhaps a more worrying prediction from the PRUDENCE project relates to winter storms. It is predicted that extreme wind speeds could increase between 45 and 55°N, that is as far north as Carlisle and Newcastle. These changes are associated with reductions in mean sea level pressure and more North Sea storms, leading to increases in storm surge along the North Sea coast, especially in England, Holland, Germany and Denmark. The worry is that while Scotland has adapted to severe storms over many centuries, England is not used to them. Thus when a major storm hit Carlisle in January 2005, the resultant rainfall had a devastating effect. The drainage system could not cope, electricity was cut off for 10000 homes for a week, and the police, fire and rescue services, which were located in the lowest part of the flood plain, were crippled. Even the emergency control centre and the depot for spare police uniforms were flooded. Carlisle became an effective 'no go' area for the police and many citizens stayed for several nights in their cold, wet homes or businesses with no light or heating simply to protect their property against looters.

Annual average precipitation changes across the UK may decrease slightly, by between 0% and 15%, by the 2080s, although there are likely to be large regional and seasonal differences in the changes.

It should be noted that these are averages. If one were to take extreme events into account, according to an analysis published in *Nature*[3] in 2002, there is a consensus in the results from all the 19 major climate change models around the world that the chances of a very wet winter in Britain could increase five-fold by the end of the century. This means that flood events are likely to show a dramatic increase in frequency, and this has been reflected in the work being undertaken under the Foresight scenarios initiative in Britain.

Rainfall is likely to also become more intense. Figure 4.1 shows that in both winter and summer the patterns of rainfall will change enormously, except perhaps for northwest Scotland. The figure shows there is over a 50% probability that more or less intense rainfall will be experienced in a given year and season for the different regions of the country. So for the southeast in particular, in winter, there will be much more rain, falling more intensely, leading inevitably to much higher flood risks for the region.

There is an important adaptation issue here: the west of the UK has traditionally had much higher precipitation levels than the east, and buildings, drainage systems and rivers have adapted or been adapted accordingly over centuries. If extreme precipitation suddenly increases in the east of the country, it will not be sufficiently prepared and will be unable to cope.

In August 2008 scientists issued a fresh warning after scientists from Reading and Miami Universities used satellite data from 1987 and 2004 to see how natural changes in surface and air temperatures caused by El Niño weather events influenced rainfall over the tropics. They found that warm periods were associated with the wettest periods, an effect that the models had underestimated by a factor or two or three. The heavier rainfalls experienced in the UK over 2007 and 2008 were certainly outside the range of normal precipitation events and may point the way to an age of heavier rains. Many of the downpours were classed in the 'most intense' category, defined (separately for each season and region) by an amount (mm) calculated from the 1961–1990 period, namely the daily precipitation exceeded on a minimally sufficient number of days necessary to account for precisely 10% of the seasonal precipitation.

Snowfall amounts will decrease significantly through the UK, perhaps by between 30% and 90% by the 2080s. There will be less snow over the whole UK and for all scenarios, with the largest percentage reductions, up to 90%, or perhaps more, by the 2080s for the High Emissions scenario, around the coast and in the English lowlands. In relative terms the Scottish Highlands will experience the smallest reductions, but even here total snowfall by the 2080s may decrease by 60% or more relative to present-day totals. Some areas of the UK are increasingly likely to experience quite long runs of snowless winters.

Humidity

As the climate warms, the specific humidity, the absolute amount of moisture in the atmosphere, will increase through the year, although the relative humidity may decrease, especially in the summer. Cloud cover in summer and autumn may decrease, especially in the south. Summer sunshine and solar radiation may correspondingly increase.

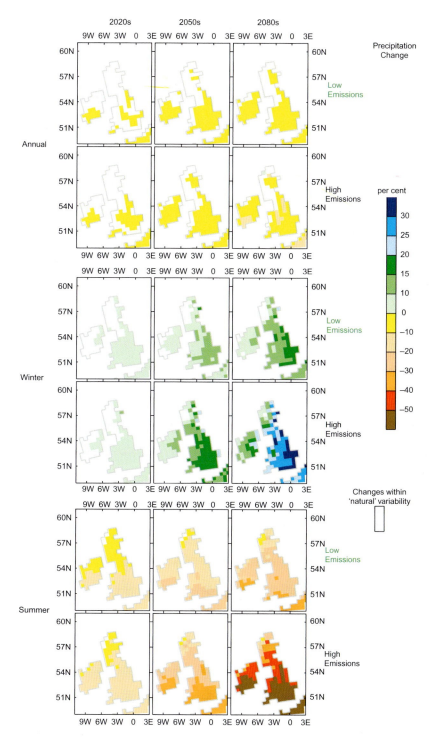

4.1.
Percentage change in average annual winter and summer precipitation for the 2020s, 2050s and 2080s for Low Emissions and High Emissions scenarios showing that the southeast of England will be very wet in winter and very dry in summer.
Source: UKCIP02 Climate Change Scenarios, funded by DEFRA, produced by Tyndall and Hadley Centres for UKCIP.

SEASONAL CHANGES

By the 2050s, typical spring temperatures may occur between one and three weeks earlier than at present (this statement relates to the means for the 1990s rather than 2003, which was already exceptional) and the onset of present winter temperatures may be delayed by between one and three weeks. This is likely to lead to a lengthening of the growing season for plants.

The heating and cooling requirements of buildings will also change, with less energy being needed to heat buildings in the UK through the winter and more energy needed to cool buildings, particularly ones that are poorly designed for the climate.

CHANGES IN WEATHER EXTREMES

High summer temperatures will become more frequent and very cold winters will become increasingly rare. A very hot August, such as experienced in 1995, and the record-breaking summer of 2003, with average temperatures many degrees above 'normal', may occur as often as once in five years by the 2050s and three years out of five by the 2080s for the Medium High Emissions scenario. Even for the Low Emissions scenario about two summers in three may be as hot as, or hotter than 1995 by the 2080s, or even perhaps than 2003. The southeast of England is predicted to become 50–60% drier in hot summers.

If UKCIP02 is correct and PRUDENCE is wrong, a drier summer climate will mean that summer soil moisture by the 2050s may be reduced by about 30% over parts of England for the High Emissions scenario and by 40% or more by the 2080s. This has obvious implications for soil shrinkage and related building damage. This will be further exacerbated by significant regional differences in rainfall, and the southeast of England, where the clay soils are particularly susceptible to shrinkage, will be badly affected.

Drought could even increase the flooding risk: in Amsterdam in summer 2003 the drought conditions weakened a raised river embankment so much that it gave way, causing localized flooding. In Shetland in summer 2003, prolonged drought conditions weakened the peat covering a hillside, and when there was a heavy shower of rain it resulted in a peat slide which engulfed several houses.

Extreme winter precipitation will become more frequent and by the 2080s daily precipitation intensities that are experienced once every two years on average may become up to 30% heavier, and that means the increasing likelihood of flooding and increased severity of flooding.

Already, the percentage of winter precipitation in England and Wales from three-day events has increased from 15% in 1930 to 30% today (Figure 4.4).

Very dry summers, like 1995, may occur in half the years by 2080, while very wet winters may occur on average almost one a decade for the Medium High Emissions scenarios. The combination of hot and dry conditions in summer will also become more common and by the 2080s virtually every summer over England and Wales, whether for the Low Emissions or High Emissions scenario, may be warmer and drier than the summer of 2001.

Some basic precautions need to be taken for individual buildings to protect them from very wet or dry spells. For periods of heavy rainfall wide storm gutters should be provided, walls, and especially their feet, should be protected from driving rain and splash back, and rain water retention features, such as green roofs, absorbent ground surfaces and water storage facilities for individual buildings or localities, should be designed in. A very simple precaution is simply to keep

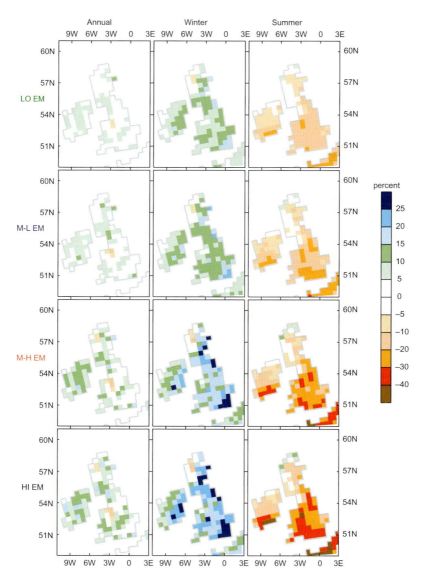

4.2.
Percentage change in the 2080s in the maximum daily precipitation amount which has a 50% chance of occurring in a given year, showing that dry summer weather in the south of England and Ireland will be a problem by the 2080s.
Source: UKCIP02 Climate Change Scenarios, funded by DEFRA, produced by Tyndall and Hadley Centres for UKCIP.

watercourses and drainage gullies clean, but there are no statutory duties on local authorities to do this (except in Scotland). So for example when there was heavy rain in the centre of Hull in England, the storm water gullies were soon overwhelmed, leading to houses in over 200 streets being flooded (Figure 4.5). Road resurfacing work had partially covered up many of the gullies, indicating that they had not been opened for cleaning for a considerable time. In addition, many were blocked by dead leaves from the previous year and grass cuttings. The gullies appear to have been contemporary with the surrounding housing that is over 80 years old, and had not been updated to modern standards.

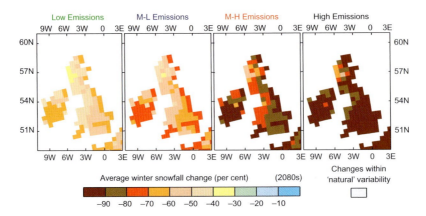

4.3.
Percentage change in average winter snowfall amount in the 2080s showing that White Christmases will be a thing of the past in most places by the 2080s.
Source: UKCIP02 Climate Change Scenarios, funded by DEFRA, produced by Tyndall and Hadley Centres for UKCIP.

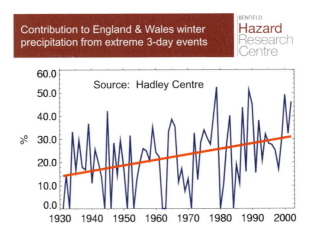

4.4.
Graph showing the increased contribution to winter precipitation from extreme three-day events in England and Wales.
Source: Hadley Centre.

It is difficult to imagine Britain as suffering from a 'drought' problem, but images of nearly empty reservoirs filled our papers in the UK in the winter of 2003 and are becoming commonplace. One manifestation of the increasing scarcity of water in the UK system is the rising prices, with charges for water and sewage set to rise by an average of over 40% by the end of the decade. Another is subsidence.

SUBSIDENCE

While the actions of planners in allowing development in flood plains are a concern, perhaps an even bigger concern is the outlook for future subsidence exposures. Subsidence claims currently cost insurers an average of £1 million per day, and this is likely to increase. At least planners

4.5.
On 25 June 2007 15 900 houses in 240 streets in Hull were flooded after a record downpour of 96 mm in two hours, a sixth of the city's annual rainfall. This was 235% of the average rainfall for that month, giving the event a return period of 150–200 years. Some areas flooded simply because drains like this were inadequate and partially blocked.
Source: David Crichton.

in England and Wales now have to consult with the Environment Agency about flood risks, but there is no obligation on them to consult with the British Geological Survey (BGS) about subsidence risks. Not only is there the issue of increasing droughts due to climate change causing subsidence on shrinkable clay soils, there are also issues of building on unsuitable ground. There are planning policy guidelines for unstable land (PPG14) and contaminated land (PPG23A), but often the ground conditions stem from very old workings where only BGS, with its huge archive of 640 000 borehole samples, is aware of problems. The 1991 Building Regulations under the 1984 Building Act focus on the structure, not the site, and the only regulations relating to the site are those dealing with radon gas (BR211). The position is rather different in Scotland, where planners are obliged to consult with BGS and Building Regulations are very different too.

The government has said that to save using too much agricultural land, 60% of the 3.8 million projected new houses will have to be built on 'brownfield' sites. Many of these sites will contain made-up ground, landfill, old mine workings and contamination. While the government has indicated that assistance may be available to remediate some sites for housing, many authorities are too small to have the expertise or the finance to obtain the information needed about the site. If the planners do not know of the problems and do not ask about them, then adequate remediation will not take place, and the planning policy guidelines will not be applied. The issue of increasing subsidence risk caused by climate change-induced droughts has already been outlined in this study; this risk would be greatly compounded if there are many more houses built on unsuitable ground. This could create major problems for insurers, and there is a very real danger that irresponsible local authorities may earn such a bad reputation for this that all new housing in their area might become an unacceptably high risk for subsidence cover.

The potential scale of this problem was outlined in October 2003, when the city of Shanghai announced that the land of the city was subsiding at a rate of 2.5 cm a year because so many new tower blocks were being built and so much water was being pumped from the underground

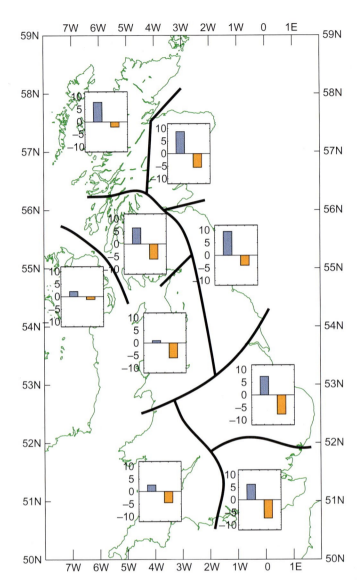

4.6.
UKCIP02 suggests the trend will be for winters to become much wetter, and summers drier, but this will vary significantly in the different regions of the UK. This figure presents the trend (1961–2000) in the fraction of the total seasonal precipitation contributed by the 'most intense' precipitation events in winter (*left hand bars*) and in summer (*right hand bars*) for a number of regions. Positive (*blue*) numbers indicate an increasing trend in the proportion of the total precipitation that comes from the 'most intense' events, i.e. the most intense events are increasing either in intensity or in frequency. (For more detail see note 3.)
Source: Figure produced by Tim Osborne. UKCIP02 Climate Change Scenarios, funded by DEFRA, produced by Tyndall and Hadley Centres for UKCIP.

reserves to provide drinking water for the exploding population of over 20 million people. These problems may be significantly increased with changing rainfall patterns.[4]

In the UK an indication of the growing problem was given in the long hot summer of 2003, when the Direct Line insurance company stated that, owing to the six dry months experienced in the south and east of the country, they saw increases in subsidence claims of 38% in June and 15% in July compared to the same periods in 2002.[5]

These are some of the problems faced by the UK. How much worse for those countries of the world where there is already a chronic water shortage, causing civil unrest and threatening war!

CIVIL UNREST

Civil unrest because of water is a growing problem in many countries, as the following examples confirm.

In Spain there have been a number of bitter demonstrations over the diversion of a staggering 30% of the waters of the river Ebro in the northeast of the country through a new canal to the parched southeastern provinces of Murcia, Valencia and Andalucia, where the great tourism centres of the Costa del Sol are based. Six dams have flooded the unique wildlife habitats in the north and the flatland habitats of the Ebro delta are disappearing at an alarming rate. Over 80% of the total Spanish budget for environmental projects has recently been channelled into the canal scheme, which is designed to take water from what is seen as the poorer provinces to fill the swimming pools of the rich in the south.[6] One of the main problems with the project, objectors claim, is that the calculations of river flows were done based on historic climates from the middle of the twentieth century, while conditions in the twenty-first century will be very different, leading to potentially catastrophic consequences for the future of the whole of eastern Spain.

In Spain the solution to increasingly chronic water shortages will also have further impacts on greenhouse gas emissions as more desalination plants are built to meet ever rising demand. In 2008 there were 950 plants around Spain, with plans to build more. They currently produce 2 million cubic metres of water a day, enough to supply 10 million people. Each plant produces a staggering million tonnes of carbon dioxide (CO_2) a year and is extremely energy expensive to operate. Desalination may not be affordable in the longer term as fossil fuels become scarcer.

The fact that water shortages can lead to local environmental crime waves was highlighted by the strange case of stealing water in Australia during a drought of 2003. Robbers used a range of equipment, including earth movers, to steal water in over 146 reported cases, often from neighbouring dams and billabongs. One of the advantages of stealing water from neighbours is that it gets around the draconian Australian water laws that put very strict conditions on the drilling of boreholes or taking water from rivers, so the law may, as here, encourage environmental crime. Statistics in Australia suggest that some 40000 jobs have already been lost because of the 2003 drought and it was expected to cost the country over £1.3 billion in that year alone.

But politicians in the UK have already provoked ire, and some civil unrest as people have taken to the streets in frustration at not being able to return to their homes over a year after they were flooded. In June and July 2007, 55000 properties were flooded. Around 7000 people were rescued from the flood waters by the emergency services and 13 people died. The floods caused the largest loss of essential services since the Second World War, with almost half a million people without mains water or electricity. Transport networks failed, a dam breach was narrowly averted and emergency facilities were put out of action. The insurance industry expects to pay out more than £3 billion, with other substantial costs for repairs to infrastructure largely being met by central government and the public utility companies responsible for water and power.

A year later civil servant Sir Michael Pitt was appointed to produce a review that was published on 25 June 2008. It is detailed but cleverly constructed to ensure that no one is any clearer as to who is actually accountable for these consequences. Even a year after the floods over 4000 people were still not back in their homes. The trauma and anguish suffered by hundreds of thousands has been enormous but Sir Michael still promoted the need to build on the flood plains. To quote from his review:

Many submissions to the Review call for a complete end to building on the flood plain.
  This is not realistic. The country cannot end all development along the Thames, or bear the costs of siting critical infrastructure, such as water treatment works or power stations, away from the water supplies they need to function.

Following this event, and concern over the condition of flood defences, the insurance industry threatened to deny cover completely to houses built on flood plains, which would have a drastic effect on property values and impede government plans for major house building programmes in such areas. In full knowledge of the risks of major new developments on flood plains John Prescott promoted the building of around 200 000 homes in the Thames Gateway area on land that will one day flood, and he knew it.

According to statistics around 10% of houses in England are at a risk of flooding at least once every 100 years. According to a House of Commons report between 2000 and 2006, the proportion of new houses being built in flood hazard areas in England averaged 11%. England still allows development in the flood plain, even under the government's 2006 Planning Policy Statement on flooding. Scotland stopped in 1995, Wales in 2004, and Northern Ireland in 2006. Building in the flood plain not only puts lives at risk, it makes the flooding hazard worse downstream.

Sir Michael's report says: 'Where there is development on the flood plain, buildings should be made flood resilient. The Government has recently produced guidance to developers on flood-resilient construction.' There is no way of making buildings flood resilient, unless you rename them boats. Such cavalier disregard for human suffering and the devastation wrought on lives and communities by ignorant policy making will eventually drive people onto the streets, but they won't knock on Sir Michael's door and he knows that, which gives us an inkling why so many people in power act with impunity in such matters to condemn the lives of others. The types of building being built in England on flood plains are social housing, schools, hospitals and care homes, the types of buildings occupied by the most vulnerable in our society and those least likely to riot, until they are desperate.

What will inevitably drive civil unrest is that lack of accountability. By contrast, on the issue of flooding, in Norway or France if a planner or mayor gives permission to develop in the flood plain then they are held liable, and may go to prison. In Norway insurance companies were recently able to successfully obtain damages from a provider of drainage whose poor management of the drains caused flooding to homes. Perhaps the insurance companies in the UK will sue on behalf of their customers where negligence can be shown to have caused flood damage.

The Environment Agency, which over the years has been systematically ignored by the government and planners in its recommendations not to build on the flood plains, famously in the Thames Gateway, appears to be developing legal teeth. In the case of the *Administrative Court in R (Environment Agency) v Tonbridge & Malling District Council*, the Council's decision to allow sheltered housing to be built on a flood plain was struck down as failing to take policy guidance sufficiently into account. The case *Bloor v Swindon Borough Council* also considered the relevance of flood plain policy to overall development planning policy, and in a more recent 2007 the Environment Agency won in the High Court against a local Council that wanted to put a new development for 63 sheltered housing apartments on the flood plain on a site that had been recently severely affected by flooding. The Council was shown not to have followed the Sequential test laid down under planning policy guidance.

If ordinary people wanted to sue for damage cause by developments in the flood plains they could use the legal precedent set by *Ryeford Homes v Sevenoaks District Council*, where a claim was made for damages against the planning authority in respect of flooding caused by allowing overdevelopment. The court in this case suggested that the developer of the adjoining site would be responsible for overloading the drainage system, not the planning authority for granting permission. So it implies that it should be possible to take a developer of the homes to court for that damage.[7]

Dealing with such a plethora of people involved in the phenomenon of developing in the flood plain, causing so many lives to be blighted and inevitably causing civil unrest and potentially violent responses is difficult, but who will people make the victims of their ire? The planners, councillors, developers, utilities and politicians all have a hand in the short-sighted actions that will increasingly blight people's lives as the climate changes. Rather than attack the town hall, efforts should be made to open up routes through litigation to ensure that the proper people are held to account for the damage they do through their own ignorance, lack of foresight or greed.

WATER WARS

Much can be learnt from incidents that occur between national boundaries where the unrest is dealt with by law. When the incidents involve two countries they may trigger a war. The global water wars have long been predicted and there are a number of flashpoints for such conflicts around the world, from the Mekong to the Rhône.

One high-profile region where chronic water shortages combine with political instability is around the River Jordan. Despite a far-sighted programme to bring Jordanian, Palestinian and Israeli hydrologists together to improve water quality in the river, and manage water demand and supply in the region, water availability will inevitably remain a flashpoint, particularly as populations in the regions continue to grow rapidly and rainfall can be virtually non-existent during periods of drought and under conditions of drier summers with climate change. One hope lies in the development of desalinating technology, such as already supplies much of the water for the city of Eilat, with its population of 56000 people, and the 80% of the water requirements of the Kibbutzim of the Negev desert adjacent to the Dead Sea, which has already dropped a massive 17m since 1975, according to the *Times Atlas of the World*.

On an even larger scale, the Aral Sea has been described as the worst environmental disaster in the world and it is predicted that within 10 years it will be the cause of armed conflict. The saline inland sea, divided between the former Soviet Republics of Kazakhstan and Uzbekistan, has been drying up for the past 25 years since the former USSR began a vast irrigation scheme drawing water from its two tributary rivers to grow cotton and rice in the desert. The irrigated area expanded from 6 million hectares in the 1960s to 8 million hectares and the sea began to shrink. It is now reduced to three separate parts and is still evaporating. The shoreline has receded on average by 250km and the salinity has increased dramatically, making the water a viscous salt paste in many parts, containing pesticides and minerals. High levels of liver and kidney cancer around the sea have become commonplace. Although an action plan has been introduced there seems to be little agreement between the five countries that border the lake on how to move

4.7.
Droughts are increasingly threatening not only agriculture but also the availability of water from ground and surface sources. It is settlements on the land between the desert and the sown that will dry first, and those where groundwater pumping has caused a sudden dropping of the water table, as in the villages around the central Persian desert.
Source: Sue Roaf.

forward, and a proposed dam to the north of the sea, to be built by Kazakhstan, may prove the final straw that leads to an inevitable water war in the region.[8]

Again and again such examples can be shown, as in the constant struggle among Turkey, Syria and Iraq over the waters of the Tigris and Euphrates rivers. India plans to divert large quantities of water from major rivers, including the Ganges and Brahmaputra, threatening the livelihoods of more than 100 million people downstream in Bangladesh. The ambitious plans to link major rivers flowing from the Himalayas and divert them south through drought-prone areas are still on the drawing board but so concerned is Bangladesh that it is considering appealing to the United Nations to redraft international law on water sharing. The project is vast: it is projected to cost between £44 and £125 billion and will take at least 14 years to complete. If the project goes ahead Bangladesh may have to build a huge network of canals to irrigate the farmlands now watered by the Brahmaputra, but it claims that the whole scheme would have catastrophic effects on the country. Another water war brewing perhaps?[9]

But the struggles can occur on a much smaller scale too. What happens when water supplies on one side of an island dry up but not on the other? What will that do to local tensions? For instance one really unexpected impact of warmer temperatures was that Scotland began to run out of water. In July 2008 half of the 10 whisky distilleries on the Isle of Islay in northwest Scotland had to be closed because the layer of peat from which their water supplies are derived became dehydrated, causing several burns or streams to stop flowing and causing the loch levels to fall. Distilleries on the north end of the island suspended production for two weeks while those on the southern end, such as the world-famous brand Laphroaig, remained in production. There are huge sums riding on the whisky markets, as on many others. Here we see the phenomenon whereby micro-climate and micro-location may become increasingly key to the viability of crops and production in a region and also to local wars over water.

In 2007 catastrophic droughts become entrenched in the USA and Australia, and in 2008 in China the waters of the Yangtze fell to their lowest levels since 1866. This river alone provides drinking water to hundreds of millions of people and thousands of factories in a delta that accounts for 40% of the economic output of China. The drastic falls in river levels are feared not only for their economic impacts but also for the increasing toxicity of the water that remains and the potential of the drought to destroy the habitats of species such as the finless dolphin, the Chinese sturgeon and many bird species. One dreadful impact of the drying of lakes and rivers is the way it drives the march of rats inland from the dried-out reed beds towards human populations in their search for food.

BOREHOLE WATER

One of the problems with borehole drilling is that it leads to a reduction in the resource. Groundwater is the main supply for more than 2 billion people in the world and is diminishing almost everywhere. Beneath Mexico City the water table has fallen on average by 2 m and in the American Mid-West water tables have fallen by 3 m in a decade, and 30 m in some places. So much has been pumped from beneath Florida that in some places the aquifers are at risk from being flooded by sea water. Twelve cities of more than 10 million people rely on underground water reserves, including Shanghai, Bangkok, London and Calcutta. Water is used for the rapidly growing global population, in industry and agriculture. It takes 1000 tonnes of water to grow a tonne of wheat, 2000 tonnes to grow a tonne of rice, and small farmers in many regions will be the first to suffer as aquifers dry up. The estimated percentages of populations dependent on groundwater for different regions include 75% in Europe, 32% in Asia Pacific, 29% in Central and South America, and 32% for the world on average.[10]

WHO OWNS THE WATER?

Here we have the problem of who owns the water in the ground, a question rather like who owns the air? One thing is for sure – that it is not Coca-Cola. In Kochi, India, in December the local 'Davids', in the form of a group of villagers, took the 'Goliath' of the major soft drinks corporation, Hindustan Coca-Cola Beverages, to the Kerala High Court to direct it to stop drawing groundwater for use in its bottling plant at Plachimedu in the Palakaad district. David won, and the court directed the local council and the state government to ensure that the plant does not extract groundwater after a specified time. The court decreed that the groundwater beneath land is not owned by the landowner. Normally, every landowner can draw a 'reasonable' amount of groundwater which is necessary for their domestic and agricultural requirements. But here, 510 kilolitres of water was extracted per day, converted to products and transported out of the state, thus breaking the 'natural water cycle', and causing the drying up of village fields for miles around the plant. Extraction of the groundwater, even up to the admitted limit by the company, was illegal, the court held. The company had no legal right to extract this much natural wealth and the Panchayat and the government were bound to prevent it. The court held that the groundwater belongs to the general public and the company had no right to claim a huge share of it. The government also has no power to allow a private party to extract such a huge quantity of groundwater, the result of which could be drying up of water tables. So let the buyer beware for high water use industries in the future.[11]

The Coca-Cola case is an issue of the overexploitation of the capacity of the environment to provide enough water to sustain soft drink production at the required level, while supporting the expectations of the traditional local community. This basic calculation of capacity should have been done and reviewed at the planning stage of the factory development.

WHO OWNS THE WATER PROBLEM?

There are two issues here:

- The first is unsustainable development – the project exceeding the environmental capacity of the area to support it. This should, from what we have seen in the Coca-Cola case above, be done using calculations of current water resources, under future climate scenarios, to evaluate the reducing capacity of the environment to support too great a demand on it. The capacity calculations should be produced at the planning stage as part of the sustainability statement of a project and the decisions to reject plants like that at Kochi taken before too great a loss is incurred.
- The second issue is that clear laws should exist on the apportioning of the available water to ensure that the basic human right to clean water is maintained for as long as is humanly possible.[12]

But these issues are pertinent even here in Britain, where the government should be asked questions like:

- Was the chronic water shortage in the southeast, now and in the future, taken into account when permission was given to build the Thames Gateway development, east of London, with 200000 new homes?
- What are the extra infrastructural costs of placing those new homes in the southeast, where new dams and water plants have to be built to cope with the increase, as opposed to the northwest, where there will be more water in summer, and the long-term costs will be lower for the ordinary householder, and who pays for them?
- Does the ordinary householder agree to pay the increased water bill costs so that an extra 200000 homes can be built in the Thames Gateway?
- How has the serious problem of more homes exacerbating summer droughts in the southeast been dealt with in the planning process?
- Will farmers who have less and less water available to them, and who are already suffering from drought stress in arable crops, with irrigation water having to be saved for higher value vegetable and salad crops,[13] be able to claim compensation from the politicians who unwisely approved developments that exceeded that capacity of the regional environment to support them?

FLOODING IN BRITAIN

Flooding is an increasingly chronic problem globally. In the UK it is predicted to increase significantly owing to:

- Increased winter rainfall, and possibly increased summer rainfall as well, according to the PRUDENCE research.

Table 4.2 Predictions by 86 leading UK flood experts for annual average costs for UK flooding by 2080 in billions of pounds

Scenario	Drainage floods	River and coastal	Total (% of GDP)
World markets (high growth)	15	27	42 (0.19)
Global sustainability	3.9	7	10.9 (0.08)
National enterprise	10	20	30 (0.41)
Local stewardship risk management	1.5	4	5.5 (0.08)

Source: Foresight Project, UK Cabinet Office.

- Higher sea levels, in conjunction with higher wave heights and bigger storm surges.
- More intense and frequent winter storms. It is difficult to predict storm incidence and while the Hadley Centre model predicts an increase, several other models do not. It is safe to say that storms will be wetter, however. It should be noted that PRUDENCE predicts more frequent and severe storms in England as far north as Carlisle and Newcastle.

The UK Cabinet Office has commissioned a major piece of research to examine the likely future costs of flooding in the UK under different UKCIP02 scenarios and the four Foresight socio-economic scenarios (Table 4.2).

The high costs of drainage floods should be a concern. Such floods can happen anywhere, but especially in places where the drainage system is old, overloaded, or poorly cleaned or maintained. The floods of June and July 2007 demonstrated this clearly. UK drainage systems often date back to Victorian times. The problem is not so bad in Scotland, where developers are not allowed to build unless there is spare capacity in the existing drainage systems, but in England and Wales, development is allowed even if drainage systems are already overloaded.

This can cause problems for insurers in that the inadequacies of drainage systems are difficult to map. Many major insurers have geographical information systems with maps of areas at risk of flooding from rivers or the sea, but these do not include areas at risk of drainage floods. For example in June 2007, the whole of the village of Toll Bar in South Yorkshire was flooded, but this was outside the flood zones of one of the leading insurance companies (see Figure 4.8).

PUBLIC HEALTH RISKS FROM FLOODING

Nearly half of the world's population is infected by vector-borne diseases. Many are associated with standing water. Diseases like malaria, chikungunya fever, West Nile virus and dengue fever are all dependent on warm temperatures and humidity. Climate change bringing warmer weather and flooding could increase the risk in the UK. In the meantime there are serious health risks from flooding due to zoonoses and water-borne pathogens. Zoonoses are diseases that can be spread from vertebrate animals. These include anthrax and Weil's disease, spread by flood waters. Water-borne pathogens like *Cryptosporidium* can come from sewage or from the bodies or excreta of animals and can be spread by flood waters often reaching drinking water supplies through reservoirs. *Cryptosporidium* is not destroyed by normal water treatment plants and there

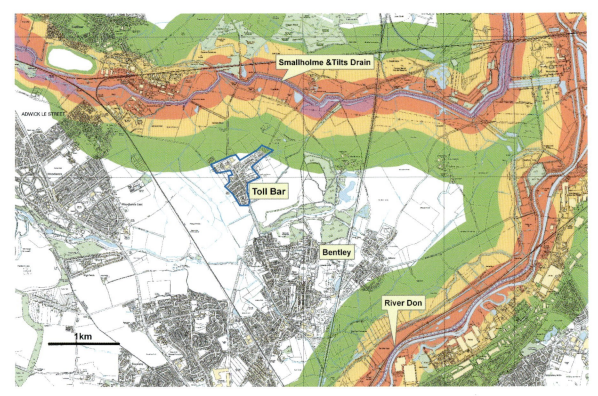

4.8.
Map of the Toll Bar area showing different levels of hazard by different colour shading. This is the type of map that is currently owned by insurance companies for all UK flood areas and it has been supplied on condition that the insurance company is not identified.
Source: David Crichton.

is a particular risk from swimming in or touching contaminated water, or even touching the sand from used sandbags.

According to research by the Middlesex Flood Hazard Research Centre, 20% of flood survivors suffer from gastrointestinal upsets and these can be fatal for the elderly or young children or those without sufficient immune response.[14] One the saddest stories to emerge from the 2007 summer floods in the UK was that of Edward Hopkins, 66, who died of multiple organ failure as a result of septicaemia, 18 days after he was trapped in filthy flood water for four hours after a torrent flowed through his house on 20 July.

The safest approach is to avoid building in flood hazard areas at all, and this is the approach taken in most developed countries, including Scotland, Wales and Northern Ireland.

There are around 28 significant differences in the way flood risk is managed in Scotland compared with England. Differences in legal and planning practice and policy, differences in working with all key stakeholders, and above all a sincere desire on the part of local and national government (except for Moray) to reduce flood risks.

In England the position is very different, and the priority is to build millions of new homes, regardless of whether they are at risk of flood or not. An estimated 2 million homes are situated in flood hazard areas in England (Table 4.3).

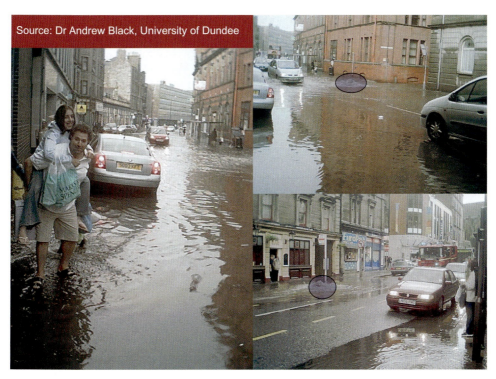
Source: Dr Andrew Black, University of Dundee

4.9.
Drainage systems can sometimes actually provide a pathway for flood waters to back up directly into built-up areas, as shown in these images in which raw sewage is flowing out from the drains marked with the purple ovals.
Source: Andrew Black, University of Dundee.

Table 4.3 Flood exposure in Britain

Country	Proportion of existing properties at risk	Proportion of new build in flood hazard areas
England	10%	11%
Wales	12%	Negligible (since 2004)
Scotland	3.9%	Negligible except for Moray (since 1995)

The biggest problem of exposure to floods is in England, where a shocking 11% of new-build projects are located on the flood plain. Planners typically prefer to put homes on the flood plain rather than in the green belt, but the human cost of this trend is inestimable.

Since 1 January 2003, the issue of insurance for properties at risk of flooding in England has been addressed by an Association of 'British' Insurers' (ABI) 'Statement of Principles'. According to the ABI, around 350 000 properties 'in the flood plain' are at a risk of flooding greater than the 1.3% probability. (It is not clear whether this figure includes low-lying coastal properties, non-domestic properties or properties outside England.) These properties will not be acceptable for new insurance but for properties already insured, provided improvements to reduce the risk to

1.3% are 'scheduled for completion within the next five years' (a rolling time limit), cover will normally be maintained by the existing insurer. This means that such property owners will be less able to shop around for cheaper cover, but for houses the current insurer will maintain cover if the property is sold (subject to normal underwriting criteria) and the current insurer may maintain cover on small businesses where they are sold. At the time or writing, the ABI has never officially stated whether the Statement of Principles applies to Scotland, Wales or Northern Ireland, as well as England, but it can be assumed that that is the intention.

The insurance industry agreement does not limit premium increases, and after the 2007 floods home owners in many low-lying parts of England saw their premiums rise, with excesses going up to £1000–5000, or more, and even been denied cover. It will become more difficult to sell such homes, particularly if lenders require insurance cover. In summer 2007 nearly 15000 homes were flooded and the risk under climate change scenarios is set to rise considerably.[15]

SOCIAL RESILIENCE

The design of buildings and social systems can affect social resilience and eventual overall flood losses. There are several areas of concern in England, for example:

- 89 hospitals and 2374 schools are on flood plains in England. Over 70% have no flood defences. Hospitals are difficult to evacuate, especially intensive care units, where evacuation could put lives at risk. Hospitals are also important resources during flood events, when water-borne pathogens can cause widespread illness.
- There is a legal duty to protect flora and fauna, but not people. Thus watercourses are often not cleaned in case this disturbs nesting birds, even if this increases the flooding risk.
- In many areas the fire and rescue services have no training or equipment for flood rescue. This is a statutory duty in Scotland, but in England these services are often dependent on volunteers from the Lifeboat service.
- The Disability Discrimination Act requires level access on new properties for wheelchairs. When builders are faced with the need to put in ramps for doorways, there seems to be a tendency for them to lower the floor level of the property to save money on ramps. This of course makes the property more vulnerable to flood damage. The morality of building homes for disabled people in flood risk areas does not seem to be considered.
- Post Offices, small shops, hairdressers and other small businesses are important for social cohesion and local employment. As these close, communities will become increasingly prone to social problems.
- England will face high costs of integrating the 191000 immigrants currently entering the country each year as it becomes an increasingly multicultural society. Already the population of England has increased by a million in the past three years.

Another major problem that may also result from flooding is the contamination of land. A key feature of many pollutants is that they are more likely to move in wet than in dry soil. Many sites on flood plains with a history of soil toxicity may become more toxic if the soil is flooded. In this case, even if a portion of the topsoil has been removed and replaced, if regularly flooded, pollutants may leach through the new topsoil towards the surface. So the worst conditions are provided by a combination of contaminated land and regularly inundated sites, highlighting the problems of containing contamination from industrial sites on flood plains.

4.10.

The River Dee at Maryculter, November 2002: one of a series of photographs taken by Aberdeenshire council officers from a helicopter at the height of the flooding. The council boundary runs down the middle of the river with Aberdeenshire on the right and Aberdeen City on the left. Note the flooded caravan site in the centre of the picture. The normal path of the river can be seen near the top of the picture, where the farmer had constructed riverside flood banks. The Aberdeenshire strategy is generally to encourage farmers to remove flood embankments beside rivers. It is more sustainable to allow fields to flood, thus storing flood waters and attenuating the downstream flow to reduce flooding elsewhere.
Source: reproduced with the kind permission of Aberdeenshire Council.

A major concern in England, prone as it is to flooding, continues to be that of new developments in flood plains being permitted regardless of the risk (Table 4.4).

It is not clear why local planning officers in England continue to allow development in flood hazard areas: it could be a combination of factors:

- Planning policy in England allows flood plain development in certain circumstances, namely if there is nowhere more suitable.
- Many parts of the southeast of England are short of land for development and what land there is is often in an area of prime agricultural land, or a Site of Special Scientific Interest, a Conservation Area, Green Belt or similar. As such it is protected against development by powerful interest groups with legal backing.
- Planning officers do not have to worry about the hassle of designing or financing flood defence schemes, as they do in Scotland. Instead, they can pass this on to the Environment Agency.
- Planning officers are under pressure from property developers, who have made huge profits in recent years, and who often have undue influence over local or national political parties. Perhaps it is coincidental that developers are often found to be major contributors to the funds of some political parties.
- Planning officers are also under pressure from local elected members who want to see more development in their councils because that brings in more income and wealth.
- Planning officers almost never consult with key stakeholders like the insurance industry, landowners, residents' associations, flood survivor groups or others over flood risks as they do in Scotland, so they get an entirely one-sided view of the problem.

Table 4.4 Percentage of all new dwellings built in flood-risk areas in England, by region, 1996–2005

Region	1996	1997	1998	1999	2000	2001	2002	2003	2004	2005[*]
North East	6	5	2	3	1	2	2	3	2	2
North West	5	5	7	5	6	9	6	8	5	4
Yorkshire and Humber	11	12	7	10	13	12	11	15	10	13
East Midlands	10	12	6	7	9	11	13	13	11	9
West Midlands	7	4	6	6	2	4	5	4	5	3
East of England	6	7	8	7	7	6	7	8	7	13
London	27	25	26	24	23	20	21	28	26	18
South East	6	8	9	10	9	10	8	10	7	7
South West	5	6	6	8	7	8	10	7	8	7
England	9	9	9	9	9	9	10	11	10	9

Source: Land Use Change Statistics, Department of Communities and Local Government
[*]Provisional figures.

4.11.
Not only settlements are vulnerable to river and coastal flooding but also transport routes, agriculture and health, from the spread of pollution and sewage. The scale of the problem is hinted at by this view of the River Severn in flood.
Source: R.L. Wilby, Environment Agency.

- Many planning officers and members of committees on local councils simply do not understand the issues involved because they are not presented with adequately explained information and do not bother to talk to key stakeholders such as insurance companies which could help them to understand the implications for local communities. By contrast, local authorities in Scotland regularly take advice from the insurance industry and in return the industry helps to resolve possible local difficulties of availability and affordability of insurance.

Even the 'experts' do not agree on how correctly to calculate flood-related impacts, as is evidenced by a bitter battle being fought over a series of new developments by Kohn Pederson

Fox, RMJM and Nicholas Grimshaw & Partners on the banks of the River Clyde in Scotland. The project requires the filling in of some dock basins, which it is claimed will increase the risks of major flooding in Glasgow, according to a report by Clyde Heritage Trust. The report concludes that Glasgow may be at risk of floods similar to those that caused extensive damage in Prague and Dresden in 2002. All of the riverside developments cumulatively add to the narrowing of the river, which reduces its flood water storage capacity, pushing water elsewhere in the city. The Clyde Heritage Trust also demanded a comprehensive and robust flood plan to be integrated into the overall redevelopment of the city, similar to the construction of the Thames Barrier in 1984.[16]

The developers and experts disagree with the findings of this report and the battle rages. But there is an ethical issue here: on what side does one come down, on the precautionary side that would tend to hold off from committing to a project that may have catastrophic impacts for the surrounding communities, or on the side of increasing the value of the whole area through fashionable development? Two groups of people will have to suffer any disastrous consequences from such developments: the local council-tax payers and those whose buildings would lose their value if flooded. It would appear that there is a moral onus on ensuring that both groups properly understand the calculations on each side of the argument so they can best decide on their own future. Developers have no vested interest in the long-term well-being of the community in the area, but the insurers of those properties will be involved in the future of such developments, and that is why their take on such developments is crucial.

Urban flooding is on the increase around the world, as cities expand and water-absorbent fields and forests give way to impervious roads, buildings and car parks. Torrential rains can lead to flash flooding with devastating consequences, and the phenomenon of urban flooding is becoming a problem in cities that for centuries have been untouched by it previously.[19] This is largely due not only to more hard surfaces, but also to the continuing practice of building on the flood plain and the increasing intensity of rainfall with climate change. Failing storm water and sewage infrastructure is also a problem in the UK and some councils in England and Wales now employ SUDS, 'SUstainable Drainage Systems', to reduce the risk of urban flooding, although it should be noted that these do not work on flood plains where there is nowhere for the water to go, as any water 'sinks' are often already below the water table during flood events. SUDS are standard practice for all new developments in Scotland, which arguably leads the world in this respect, especially in retrofitting of SUDS for existing properties. However, in Scotland there is no perception of SUDS as a flood alleviation tool; instead SUDS are rightly seen purely in the context of reducing diffuse pollution.[17] Also in Scotland there are statutory duties for the maintenance of SUDS installations, whereas maintenance responsibilities in England and Wales are still unresolved and many SUDS ponds for example have been filled in for parking or used for fly tipping. A key problem with urban flooding is also the speed of run-off and the 'flash flood' effect that catches people unaware and is responsible for many of the drowning deaths associated with floods as people try to escape in their cars down flooded roads.

Rising sea levels

The problem of flooding in the southeast of England is made worse by the fact that the land mass is sinking in the region and by the fact that relatively large areas in the southeast are already prone to coastal and riverine flooding. Many regions of the world share this problem.

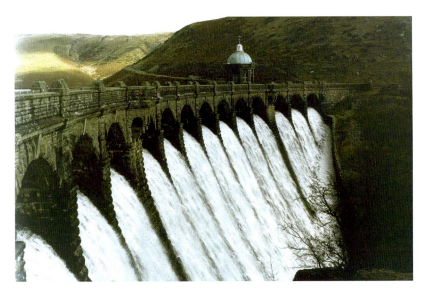

4.12.
Many of the great British reservoirs were built during the drought years of the late-nineteenth century, like the dam at Craig Goch Reservoir, one of a series in the Elan Valley, Mid-Wales, built to provide a safe water supply for Birmingham, 72 miles away. The scheme was the brainchild of the late Victorian Mayor of Birmingham and has a reservoir capacity of 2000 million gallons of water. The Elan Valley dams are now owned by Welsh Water.
Source: Charles Knevitt.

Worldwide, approximately 400 million people live within 20 m of sea level, and around 23% within 20 km of a coast. However, this figure is difficult to calculate properly from existing data. Eleven of the world's largest cities are on the coast and in the USA a staggering 53% of the population live near the coast and may therefore be vulnerable to surges in sea levels.[18]

Venice is one of the many cities that face the same problem as London, that as sea levels rise the city itself is sinking on its alluvial soils. In 1900 the central area of Venice around St Mark's Square flooded around 10 times a year. Today it is closer to 100 times a year and over the century Venice has actually sunk by around 20 cm. If scientists are right and sea levels rise between 40–60 cm over the next century and the city continues to sink at the same rate, then the eventual inundation of the city is inevitable and it will, it is predicted, be uninhabitable by 2100.[19] Many are sceptical that the proposed barrier around the lagoons of the city will ever materialize, not least because of its cost, which is put in the billions rather than millions.

WATER QUALITY

Water quality will be very much affected by climate change:

- Decreased summer rainfall will affect water availability and quality, increasing also the concentrations of CO_2 and pollutants in river, dams and lakes.
- Higher sea levels will interfere with natural drainage patterns, coastlines and water and sewage supply networks.
- More intense and frequent storms may pollute water supplies.
- Changing groundwater levels affect water supply.

- Increased water temperatures will accelerate the growth of water-borne bacteria, plants and fungi.
- Decreased oxygen levels in water, with higher temperatures and less water in rivers, may kill river species, including fish, which are also physiologically temperature sensitive in their habitats.
- High levels of rainwater run-off from increased levels of rainfall and storm incidence will exacerbate pollution incidences in built-up areas.

An example where a combination of factors is killing large stretches of water is occurring in Lake Tanganyika in Central Africa, where the nutrient balance of the lake's water has been so altered that due to a lack of vital nutrients fish stocks have fallen drastically, with a dramatic impact on the local fishing economy. In an area where between 25% and 40% of the protein needs of local people in the four bordering countries traditionally come from the lake, the slumping of the fish numbers, in a large part due to higher water temperatures and changing wind patterns, will have a catastrophic effect on local populations.[20]

DAMS AND RESERVOIRS

Levels of precipitation, and periods of droughts and rain, have direct impacts on the infrastructure of water catchment, storage and supply systems. Climate change may well prove a real threat to the integrity of such systems.

There is, for instance, a very real and hidden problem in many countries of the overtopping of dams, reservoirs and canals. On 2 November 1925 there was a blow-out of the lower section of a portion of the Eigiau dam in the Conwy Valley in North Wales. The water scoured a channel 70 feet wide and 10 feet deep, as 50 million cubic feet of water surged down to the Coedty reservoir below. The reservoir was nearly full at the time and the spillway had to cope with a surplus discharge well in excess of its designed capacity. The dam was overtopped, washing away the embankment, and the core collapsed. There was an almost instant release of 70 million gallons of water. A wall of water, mud, rock and concrete hit the village of Dolgarrog at 9.15 pm that Monday evening.

Fortunately, many of the villagers were attending a film show at the village Assembly Hall, out of the path of the flood, and 200 workers were working late in the nearby aluminium factory, otherwise more lives would have been lost. As it was, 10 adults and six children were killed and many houses were destroyed.[21]

Huge boulders, the size of houses, can still be seen in the village. It later transpired that the general manager and board of directors of the company which owned the dams knew that there were defects in them from the beginning, but chose to keep the facts secret. No one was ever held to account, and two of the streets in the rebuilt village were named after directors of the company.[22]

It should be emphasized that no lives have been lost in the UK from dam failure since the Dolgarrog disaster in 1925; however, failures do occur around the world. In 1959 the Malpasset dam in France failed, resulting in the deaths of 421 people, and in 1963 the overtopping of the Vaiont dam in Italy due to a landslide caused 1189 deaths, even though the dam itself remained intact. In 1972 a dam in West Virginia, USA, failed causing 125 deaths. Modern dams and reservoirs are designed and built to very high standards in Britain, and are designed to last for 50–75 years, but the average age of large British dams is 110 years, and in the future the safety margins will increasingly be eroded by climate change. So far as current safety standards are concerned the main concern is the secrecy surrounding the condition of dams and raised embankments.

There are also concerns about the secrecy surrounding dam break inundation maps, and the lack of preparedness of the emergency services in dealing with a catastrophic failure.

The information in the public domain is enough to illustrate the scale of the issue.[23] The Reservoirs Act 1975 applies to all reservoirs holding or capable of holding more than 25 000 cubic metres of water. There are over 2500 such reservoirs in the UK, of which 530 are large enough to be included in the World Register of Large Dams. Owners of dams covered by the Act are obliged by law to have them inspected every 10 years by a civil engineer from a special panel, but the law does not specify the details of the inspection or that the results should be published. In practice, the thoroughness of the inspection depends almost entirely on how much the dam owner is prepared to pay, and the author is not aware of any case where the results have been published, or even given to local authority emergency planning officers or the emergency services. At the time of writing, dam owners in England and Wales also refuse to issue dam break flood inundation maps. This could mean, and indeed this has happened, that planning officers for the local authority might grant planning permission for new housing developments within the area that would be flooded if the dam failed, simply because they did not know that the area was within the danger zone. Dam owners in Scotland are obliged to make such maps available to emergency planners, fire and rescue services and the police, so that evacuation plans can be made.

By contrast, in France, everyone living in areas at risk from dam break is fully aware of the fact, and these areas are subject to frequent evacuation exercises. Informal comments from engineers would seem to indicate that they believe the British are more likely than the French to panic if they were given such information.

Climate change could well lead to an increased risk of failure of British dams, some of which are as much as 300 years old. Failure can be caused by many factors, for example climate change, could lead to subsidence of the dam foundations, landslip into the reservoir or overtopping due to heavy rainfall.

Around half of the 2500 large UK dams have earth embankments, most of them constructed before heavy soil compaction equipment was available. Little is known about the content of such embankments, especially the core, or the extent of internal settlement or disturbance, for example from rabbit burrows.

Droughts could lead to cracking of the embankment wall, and climate change will lead to more droughts in the summer, followed by more rain in the autumn. This could impose additional loads, which were not considered when the reservoir was planned. There could also be additional loadings from increased snowfall in upland areas, followed by rapid snowmelt due to rainfall. Higher windspeeds over the reservoir surface could cause more frequent overtopping, leading to erosion of earth embankments unless suitably protected.

Other possible causes of failure include vandalism of valves, pipe work or controls, terrorism or aircraft crashes. Many dams are in or near urban areas, for example there is a large reservoir in Brent in London which is very close to housing and aircraft flight paths. Most UK dams are over 100 years old. A detailed record is kept of defects in dams but this is not published. The reasons for the secrecy surrounding the condition of the nation's dams is not clear, but prudent insurance underwriters are always inclined to assume the worst when information is withheld. The record of dam safety in the UK has been excellent since 1925, but climate change fears might cause some underwriters to reassess the situation. It would seem quite likely that there are people living and working within the danger zone of large dams in the UK. In the USA, where information is more readily available, more than 2000 communities have been identified as being at risk from dams that are believed to be unsafe.

Growing population and wealth, especially in the southeast of England, will lead to greater demand for water, while supply will be reduced by summer droughts. Demand management controls such as water meters can only have a limited effect and groundwater abstraction is near its limit. It is therefore likely that more dams will need to be built, and in southeast England these are likely to be near urban areas. Meanwhile, in 2000, government introduced a research programme for dams, with some of the survey work subcontracted to the Transport Research Laboratory because of their expertise in checking earth embankments.

More dams are likely to be built because of climate change, either retention dams as part of flood alleviation measures, or reservoirs for hydro power (in response to the moves away from fossil fuel power generation) or water supply (in response to increasing summer droughts).

Meantime, so long as dam condition reports and inundation maps remain secret, insurance companies may be increasingly likely to assume that properties near to reservoirs may be at risk of flooding from a breach, particularly in the case of older earth embankments, or concrete dams constructed more than 50 years ago.

CANALS AND WATERWAYS

British Waterways owns and manages over 540 km of navigable rivers and 2600 km of canals, which interact with the major river basins and land drainage systems of the UK.[24] Most of the canals were constructed more than 200 years ago, and are very vulnerable to flood events. Often the waterways cross different catchments and can thus transfer flows from one catchment to another. British Waterways also owns and manages 89 reservoirs in the UK, some of which are managed entirely for flood storage. Canals are usually 'still' waters, and do not clean themselves as with flowing rivers, so pollution is a particular problem, for example from sewage back-up from drains, and one that is exacerbated in hot summers.

Canals generally operate with only 300 mm of freeboard, and there are over 650 km of embankments to be maintained. Overtopping of embankments, especially those over 200 years old, can lead to failure, which could have a catastrophic impact, particularly in urban areas.

British Waterways is very aware of the risk and has a system of sluices, weirs, pumps and floodgates to control the flow into canals. It has a thorough system of emergency procedures that have worked well so far, but climate change, with the predicted increasingly intense periods of rainfall, is going to impose a major challenge to our 200-year-old network of canals, and this challenge does not yet seem to be fully recognized by government. Despite the extent of the risk, canals are exempt from the safety requirements of the Reservoirs Act.

CONCLUSION

The levels of rain and snow falls in regions have complex and wide-ranging impacts on our built environment and lives. The drive to reduce exposure to the hazards they can bring may increasingly influence the location of populations in the future, just as major steps are taken to reduce the vulnerability of individuals and buildings to those hazards. The time has now come to put into place national plans for managed retreat from coastal and riverine flood plains and extreme precipitation-related events. The social and economic costs of not doing so are unaffordable in the short, medium and longer terms. Accountability must be brought into the system and those with the power ultimately to put into place the necessary laws must be made to do so in the interests of the voters who put them into power, rather than the loudest lobby groups who may well hold them in their sway.

It may be possible to plan intelligently to keep populations largely out of harm's way from flooding; however, it may be impossible to move people away from the unpredictable track of a storm.

NOTES AND REFERENCES

1   M. Hulme, J. Turnpenny, G. Jenkins, Climate Change Scenarios for the United Kingdom: The UKCIP02 Briefing Report, Tyndall Centre for Climate Change Research, School of Environmental Sciences, University of East Anglia, Norwich, UK. 2002 Available in pdf format on: <http://www.ukcip.org.uk/publications/pub.html>. For the updated version of the UKCIP02 predictions see the UKCIP2008 predictions, due to be published in November 2009: <http://www.ukcip.org.uk>.

2   See <http://prudence.dmi.dk/>, accessed 25 May 2008. See also M. Beniston, D.P. Stephenson, O.B. Christensen, C.A.T. Ferro, C. Frei, S. Goyette, K. Halsnaes, T. Holt, K. Jylha, B. Koffi, J. Palutikof, R. Scholl, T. Semmler, K. Woth, Future Extreme Events in European Climate: An Exploration of Regional Climate Model Projections climate change Journal, 81 supplement 1. (2007).

3   T.N. Palmer, J. Rälsänen, Quantifying the risk of extreme seasonal precipitation events in a changing climate, Nature 415 (2002) 512–514.

4   Observer, Cash, 31 August 2003, p. 5.

5   Guardian, Society, 27 November 2002, pp. 8 and 9. For desalination see Guardian, 6 April 2008, World, p. 37.

6   For Legal references see Tate v Duffy, EWHC 361TCC; Ryeford v Sevenoaks, 46 Building Law Reports 34 or 16 Construction Law Reports 75 or 1990 J. Plan. Environ. Law 36 or 1990 6 Constr. Law J. 170: R v Tonbridge, 2001 49 EG 118.

7   Guardian, 14 November 2002, p. 25; Guardian, 29 October 2003, p. 13.

8   Guardian, 24 July 2003, p. 15.

9   <http://www.unep.org/Documents/Default.asp?DocumentID = 321&ArticleID = 4026>.

10 <http://timesofindia.indiatimes.com/articleshow/362916.cms>.

11 'The human right to water entitles everyone to sufficient, affordable, physically accessible, safe and acceptable water for personal and domestic uses', states the Committee document. 'While uses vary between cultures, an adequate amount of safe water is necessary to prevent death from dehydration, to reduce the risk of water-related disease and to provide for consumption, cooking, personal and domestic hygienic requirements', <http://www.globalpolicy.org/socecon/ffd/gpg/2002/1127water.htm>, see also the Indigenous Peoples' Kyoto Water Declaration, from the Third World Water Forum, Kyoto, Japan, March 2003, <http://www.treatycouncil.org/new_page_52112111.htm>.

12 Guardian, 27 August 2003, p. 10.

13 Observer, Cash, 12 October 2003, p. 11.

14 D. Crichton, C. Ditchburn (submitted) Flooding: social resilience, health, and evacuation issues. J. Inst. Civil Eng. Urban Design and Planning edition.

15 The Environment Agency's 'What's in your backyard' feature on the Your Environment page of its website shows the flood risk in Britain at any particular post code at <http://216.31.193.171/asp/1_introduction.asp>. The Environment Agency service only applies to England and Wales, but there is a commercial website that provides a free post-code search facility for the whole of Britain. It can be found at: <http://www.home-enviro-search.com>.

16 Building Design, 13 September 2002, p. 2.

17 S. Roaf, Closing the Loop: Benchmarks for Sustainable Buildings. London: RIBA Publications, Chap. 19, 'Flooding'. On SUDS in particular see North East Scotland Flood Appraisal Group (2002) Drainage Impact Assessment: Guidance for Developers and Regulators. Stonehaven: Aberdeenshire Council. Available from Aberdeenshire Council. Keep an eye out for Floods and SUDS: A Guidance Note for Local Authorities on SUDS Issues by David Crichton, not yet published, but available free by e-mail from david@crichton.sol.co.uk. See also two important websites. First, the Foresight Flood and Coastal Defence Report, launched on 22 April 2004, looks 30–100 years ahead and uses the UKCIP02 Climate Change Scenarios and Foresight Future socio-economic scenarios. It outlines the possible risks for the UK from flooding and coastal erosion, and highlights the decisions that need to be made to protect people, homes, businesses and the environment in the future. In each scenario, if flood management policies remain unchanged, the risk of flooding increases significantly, and the damage could be very costly. Under the most extreme scenario, the annual cost of damages could increase 20-fold from the current level. Copies of the report can be downloaded from <http://www.foresight.gov.uk/fcd.html>. Secondly, Flooding and Insurance – Information and Advice from ABI. The Association of British Insurers has developed a dedicated web page as a gateway to information on flooding and insurance issues, including details of ABI's views and reports, and a flood resilience fact sheet with information for householders on how they can reduce flood damage. Visit <http://www.abi.org.uk/flooding>.

18 <http://www.giss.nasa.gov/research/intro/gornitz_04/>.

19 Observer, 5 January 2003, p. 2.

20 Independent, 14 August 2003, p. 11.

21 D. Thomas, Hydro Electricity in North West Wales, National Power plc, Llanrwst, 1997.

22 C. Draper, Walks in the Conwy Valley, Gwasg Carreg Gwalch, Llanrwst, 2002.

23 See The Babtie Group and the Centre for Ecology and Hydrology 2002 Climate Change Impacts on the Safety of British Reservoirs, Report commissioned by the Department of the Environment, Transport and the Regions (DETR), now DEFRA, through their reservoir safety research programme (unpublished) and A. Hughes, H. Hewlett, P. Samuels, M. Morris, P. Sayers, I. Moffat, A. Harding, P. Tedd, Risk Management for UK Reservoirs. Construction Industry Research and Information Association (CIRIA) Research project report C542. London 2000.

24 Much of this section is based on the following paper: S. Sim, L. Morgan, D. Leftley, (British Waterways) British Waterways' role in flood mitigation and emergency response. Municipal Engineer, 151 (2002) 305–311.

5 WINDSTORMS

THE DESTRUCTIVE POWER OF WIND

Of all the hazards that the climate can throw at us, none equals the power of an angry storm. Despite the fact that there is much greater uncertainty about future changes in wind speed and direction, recent studies have demonstrated that the UK is becoming windier and storm incidents are increasing. This reflects a pattern throughout the world, in which not only are hurricanes and storms increasing in number and intensity but storm seasons are extending into months where storms were previously unrecorded. Worldwide more than a third of all natural disasters are caused by windstorms in an average year, causing around a third of all fatalities and economic losses from natural disasters. Munich Re claimed that 'The evidence points to critical extreme wind speeds and precipitation being exceeded with increasing frequency, so that for this reason alone there will inevitably be a stark increase in the loss burdens as well.'[1]

The year 2008 alone saw the highest number of deaths from winter storms in the USA as scores of people were killed and thousands left homeless in January and February from the deadly night storms that caught many people sleeping. Around the world death tolls and damage rise annually, and more so, as seen in the Burmese Delta region during the 2008 cyclone, where people lived in flimsy huts.

A windstorm provided the most obvious example of the importance of using resilient construction techniques. The great British storm of October 1987 caused £1400 million of damage claims for insurers. The storms in January and February 1990 cost insurers £2500 million. Yet these storms were not particularly severe, compared with the Braer storm in 1993.

The Braer storm was probably the most severe storm to hit Britain in the past 300 years.[2] It lasted continuously for 22 days (17 of which were at severe storm force 12 or higher) with an atmospheric pressure at a record-breaking low of 915 mb, the equivalent of a category 5 hurricane (Hurricane Andrew in the USA in 1992 was only a category 4, with an atmospheric pressure of 924 mb, but caused US$30 billion of damage). By comparison, the October 1987 UK storm was trivial: it lasted only 24 hours, with atmospheric pressure only down to 960 mb. Yet the damage from the Braer storm, apart from the damage to the ship after which the storm was named, was negligible to the insurance industry.

5.1.
Wind damage is responsible for the largest payouts from the insurance industry in Britain and globally. A cause for further concern is that for the first time in recorded history a tropical hurricane arose in December in the Caribbean in 2003, indicating an unprecedented lengthening of the storm season for the Americas.
Source: Sue Roaf.

One of the reasons for this is resilient construction. It has been calculated that the damage caused by Hurricane Andrew would have been reduced by 40% if buildings had been constructed to current building codes.[3] The Braer storm mainly affected the Shetland Islands, where traditional Scottish or Scandinavian designs are used, and all the building companies are local. As a result, almost all the buildings are constructed of thick stone walls and Welsh slated roofs, with sarking boards.

The use of sarking boards has two major advantages. First, if the roofing tiles or slates are blown away, there is a secondary covering underneath to prevent the wind from entering the loft. Secondly, the smooth surface of sarking boards means that each tile or slate has to be individually nailed in place or it will fall off during construction. Without sarking boards, tiles can simply be hooked onto battens and will stay in place without nailing, so the absence of fixings is not noticed until the wind blows. Unfortunately, sarking boards are rarely used now, at least in England and Wales, yet the cost of using them during construction is relatively low.

During 1997 and 1998, the Department of Environment, Transport and the Regions, and the Scottish Office, funded a project with the Building Research Establishment in Scotland to review the impacts of climate change on the construction industry and on building standards.[4] The report highlighted the need for the design and planning of new buildings to change to 'future proof' new construction, and that failure to adapt existing buildings to cope with future climate would result in increased maintenance and repair costs, and inevitable increases in insurance premiums. Further research and impact assessments were required. Unfortunately little has been done since then.

Perhaps this is because of the widely held perception that older buildings are more vulnerable to storm damage than new ones, especially if they have not been well maintained. The Building Research Establishment was stating this as recently as 2003, but how much of this is fact and how much is assumption? David Crichton was only able to find one UK research project based on the large insurance industry database of storm damage cases, and this shows that the perceptions may be wrong. Research for the Loss Prevention Council (now part of the Building Research Establishment) in 1998 shows that:

- Poor maintenance is not a major factor.
- It is not old buildings that are vulnerable, but new ones, especially those built after 1971.

There is a desperate need to carry out further research into this, using insurance claims data. Before the days of building standards, local builders tended to 'overengineer' buildings, in the light of local knowledge. They also used local stone and timber, plus heavy Welsh slate. Now with building codes, the construction industry builds to the code, which only has a 10% cushion for extreme events. This could explain why older buildings that have already survived many storms are likely to be more resilient than brand new buildings built to the standards set out by codes but no higher.

Work at the University of Aberdeen, part supervised by David Crichton and funded by the Loss Prevention Council, involved a detailed impact assessment of the vulnerability of different types of buildings to windstorm. Using insurance claims data, the research[5] indicates that modern housing may even be more vulnerable, particularly housing built after 1971. One reason for this could be the introduction of prefabricated rafters around this time. Originally rafters were installed without cross-bracing, and if subjected to sideways pressure, could collapse like a set of dominoes, bringing down the gable wall. It is interesting to note that after the October 1987 storm, a study[6] found that between 60% and 80% (depending on area) of houses damaged had roofing damage, and 'an unusually high proportion of gables had both leaves of masonry sucked out'. In recent years the insurance industry around the world has suffered from mounting losses from wind damage. In the USA, it has been found that the majority of damage has occurred in conditions where the mean recurrence interval was less than 50 years.[7] There has subsequently been a whole programme of measures from the US insurance industry to reduce the vulnerability of buildings to windstorm.

In a supplement to the Aberdeen study mentioned above, in the UK, damage was found from wind speeds that had a recurrence interval as low as three or four years in the case of modern buildings. So far the insurance industry has left it to local government to ensure proper construction through the adoption and enforcement of appropriate building codes. If the findings of the Aberdeen study are representative – and more work is clearly needed to establish whether this is the case – this would indicate that building codes and enforcement may already be inadequate in the UK. Unless major changes are made to the Building Regulations to make buildings more resilient to windstorm (and this is very unlikely in the short term), insurers will have to be more selective in their pricing. They can do this using their detailed data on designs and types of building stock, combined with very sophisticated windstorm models.

Windstorm modelling by insurers has improved significantly in the past decade. The latest techniques now model the geostrophic wind first, that is the wind at an altitude where it is not affected by surface roughness factors, and then vary the model for local conditions where gusts are affected by the topography and the nature of the buildings. This work is being undertaken by a number of reinsurers, insurers and reinsurance brokers independently. However, the job is so large that there is a need for some central expert body, with access to large-scale computing power, to provide definitive answers on behalf of the whole insurance and construction industry.

INSURANCE AS A TOOL TO IMPROVE RESILIENCE

The built environment will have to become more resilient to natural hazards. As shown above, research has indicated that UK building stock in some areas is particularly vulnerable to windstorm, for example. Insurers could potentially have an important role, using premium incentives and other means, to help to raise standards of construction and inspection of new buildings, and retrofitting older ones. To target these efforts, more data are needed about what happens in a flood or windstorm.

At present, when an insurance customer reports storm damage, insurers capture just enough information to enable them to deal with the claim. It would be much more far-sighted to start to capture additional information about the local wind conditions and the reason for the failure of the structure. A database of even just a few thousands of such claims could be of value to the engineers reviewing building standards. In the UK in 1987, the industry had 1 million storm claims, in 1990 it had 3 million. If details of each of these claims had been captured along with local wind speeds, the construction industry would be in a much better position now to understand what needs to be done to improve building resilience to storm damage. When the next major storm happens insurers would be no better placed to capture such information than they were in 1990. While insurers have been capturing details of UK flood claims since 1995 and now have the biggest flood damages database in the world, there is no financial incentive for them to capture windstorm claims in such detail and the costs of capturing and analysing storm data are prohibitive at around £30 000 per year.

WHEN THE EXTREME STORM HITS

Getting out

Many have lost their lives because, when a storm hits, they simply could not get out of buildings in time. One of the most vulnerable of all building types to storm dangers is, surprisingly, the most 'modern' type: the thin, tight-skinned, air-conditioned building with no opening windows and no escape route onto the roof. If such buildings are located on a flood plain where there is any risk of water rising to block the only doors on the ground floor, then people have no way out. If the air conditioning then fails, if there is, for instance, a blackout or the plant room is in a flooded basement, and there is little breathable air in the building (this happened in New York during the August 2003 blackout), then things become critical. If you add to this situation exposure to pollutants, perhaps a broken sewage mains or gas pipes damaged in the basement as furniture is banged against them by flood water, or similarly broken toxin containers, then that building may be a death trap, in which, unless occupants are willing and able to smash a glass cladding panel (virtually impossible with some modern 'bomb proof' glasses) they could well die. Risk assessments encompassing such likelihoods should be done for all buildings of this type.

Another problem that has caused deaths during the flooding associated with windstorms is the location of the means of escape underground, in a car park or an exit route or a subway, as these flood first and trap occupants within a building – or kill them on their way out. During floods in Houston, Texas, in 2001 a secretary was travelling down in a lift when a power blackout occurred, and as is standard in many lift programmes, the lift lowered her gently to the basement, which was full of water and she drowned.[8] The advice is, during floods and storms, as in fire, do not use the lifts.

Also, buildings on flood plains must be increasingly closely regulated. Experience has shown that it should be compulsory for bungalows to have escape routes, with accessible windows fitted in their roofs to enable occupants to clamber onto the roof in the case of a rapid inundation of their homes.

People in ordinary buildings can also be very vulnerable to storms. This was shown in December 2003 when five people died in a torrential rainstorm with 90 mph winds in the south of France in a region that had suffered catastrophic floods the winter before. One elderly man was found drowned in his basement flat while others were killed as their cars were washed off roads. Some 8000 people were evacuated from their homes, and roads and railway lines were closed. Flood waters caused two buildings to collapse in Marseille, where 47 people were evacuated to a local sports centre. In Lyon 200 people spent the night in a gymnasium after their train was cancelled. ASN, the National Nuclear Authority, closed four Rhône valley nuclear reactors because of the storm, as a precaution, showing again, as during the drought of August 2003, the vulnerability of this technology to extreme weather events. Floods also disabled a water purification plant in the Haute-Loire region, leaving 4000 without drinking water.[9] These events give a taste of the range of impacts that can accrue from a bad storm. A detailed report on the causes of the event, requested by President Chirac, cited global warming as a cause. Chirac ordered that solutions to the problem of flooding be found that would reduce the scale of the impacts in future years.

Floods, logging and landslides

Every year 90 000 square kilometres of forest are being lost due to logging, the equivalent area of the British Isles, according to the *Times Atlas of the World*, for use in industry and commerce and for cooking and heating. During wind and rain storms, the slopes exposed by logging are washed away, and then major landslips occur that, in recent years, have been claiming increasing numbers of lives around the world.

For instance, when Hurricane Mitch hit land in 1998, the highest numbers of casualties were caused by landslides, a direct result of logging. Officials estimated about 7000 had died in the region. The greatest losses were reported in Honduras, where an estimated 5000 people died and 600 000 – 10% of the population – were forced to flee their homes after the storm as floods and landslides erased from the map many villages and households as well as whole neighbourhoods of cities. In neighbouring Nicaragua, the death toll was also high. Official preliminary figures showed 1330 dead and 1903 missing nationwide. As many as 1500 people may have died in mudslides when the crater lake of the Casitas Volcano collapsed, sending a wall of mud and debris onto villages below.[10]

In November 2003 a staggering 72 people were killed by a flash flood that washed through a tourist resort on the island of Sumatra, Indonesia, sparked off by several days of heavy rain in the Leuser National Park. The river Bohorok overflowed its banks, washing away many of the flimsy buildings of the area and leaving only around 10% standing. Officials claimed that the flood was caused by 'massive logging' in the Leuser National Park, a widespread problem in many regions of the world,[11] including, in recent years, Spain, Italy, France and Switzerland. Hence maintenance and replanting of forests may be one way of saving lives during storms.

EVACUATION

In his excellent book *Florida's Hurricane History*, Jay Barnes, former Director of the American National Hurricane Center in Florida, described his concerns about the increasing population of the state and the decreasing ability of people to be evacuated from it in the case of a major hurricane.[12] Even though Florida has been battered by hurricanes many times over the years, most Florida residents today have not experienced a major hurricane. Barnes sums up his concern:[13]

Certainly Andrew in 1992 was a tremendous wake-up call for South Florida. The Panhandle had Eloise in 1975 and most recently Opal in 1995, but the peninsula itself has been spared during the last 25 years. As we look back at Florida's hurricane history, we find a flurry of activity in the late 1920s, 1930s, and 1940s. There was the powerful 1926 hurricane in Miami, the 1928 storm that killed many people at Lake Okeechobee, and the fierce Labor Day storm of 1935 that swept across the Florida Keys. Then a series of major hurricanes rolled through the Florida Peninsula in the 1940s. From 1941 to 1950, eleven hurricanes struck, seven of which were category 3 or greater. Of course, most of them didn't have names. Few people talk about them anymore, largely because most Florida residents weren't around back then. Some have been forgotten and are no longer part of Florida's 'hurricane culture.'

Florida has always been vulnerable to hurricanes, but the explosive growth that has occurred in the past few decades has made the coastal areas even more precarious. The population has more than doubled in the past 40 years, and in many communities, it has been that long since the last significant hurricane. Many coastal areas are especially vulnerable because of their unique evacuation problems. In the Keys, for example, only one highway offers escape for many thousands of residents. The 1935 hurricane, which moved through the central Keys on Labor Day, illustrates the evacuation dilemma. As it approached Andros Island in the Bahamas it was a category 1 storm. It took just over 40 hours to become a category 5 storm and was the strongest ever to hit the United States. Today, the time required for evacuation of the Keys is more than 24 hours, and evacuation times for the southeastern and southwestern counties may exceed 40 hours. For many of these areas, the lead time required is too great and the population too large for the highway system to handle all of the traffic.

What I fear most is a scenario similar to what happened in 1935 – a storm that approaches Florida as a minimal hurricane, then explodes in intensity as it accelerates toward the coast. Andrew and Opal were somewhat like that, although fortunately Opal weakened before it came ashore. If a rapidly intensifying hurricane strikes an area that has a long evacuation time, thousands of residents could be caught in the storm's path, where they might be trapped in their cars or forced to remain in inadequate shelters. This is the nightmare that hurricane forecasters live with.

Unfortunately, hurricanes are increasing in intensity and severity right along the Eastern seaboard of North America and this fear has yet to be tested.[14]

Is there time to make it?

When Jay Barnes joined the National Hurricane Center staff, the average forecast error in a 24-hour period was 120 nautical miles, and when he left 25 years later it was down to only about 110 miles. During this time, the population of Florida's coastal areas was exploding. The increase in population has far exceeded any small improvement we have made in our ability to forecast hurricanes. Jay considers it unlikely that there will be any major breakthrough in the forecasting of hurricanes in the future. The atmosphere is too complex to allow the kind of precision forecasts that people who live on the coast today need.

A similar lack of precision in forecasting was a hallmark of the Great 1987 storm when forecaster Michael Fish famously said on the 6 pm news that there was no hurricane coming, before the rapidly developing storm struck early next morning. Here the unpredictability, as in Florida, becomes a factor in how many do, or could, die.

The basic reason for this is that it is still too difficult to forecast the weather accurately:[15]

5.2.
The Royal Palm Park in downtown Miami was littered with boats and debris after the September hurricane of 1926.
Source: Photograph courtesy of Special Collections Department, University of South Florida Library, Tampa Campus.

We must remember, too, that the mathematical models used in numerical weather forecasting, though remarkably successful, can never fully represent the complexity of the real atmosphere. And complete observational coverage of the atmosphere over the oceans west and south of the British Isles will probably never be achieved.

The question here is: will people be given enough warning time to evacuate an area? In some cases, the answer is no. If they have to remain in a city in an extreme windstorm they should be very careful to choose a robust building and never remain in a brittle one. Lightweight buildings with thin glazed or clad skins may be the most dangerous buildings to remain in, as evidenced in Figure 5.3. People should take time to choose wisely and shelter in a low heavy building with smaller windows and solid walls to protect them.

Evacuation plans

Whom to contact in emergencies
Many buildings and communities at times of flood do get cut off from their escape routes by the rapidly rising water and need to know an emergency number to call, such as the British service 'Floodline' – the Environment Agency Emergency hotline.[16] An added risk factor, however, is that if an electricity blackout occurs mobile phone systems can also go down and this should be factored in to escape plans.

Where to go
Another factor to consider is that people have to know where they can go to be safe. They should be told in advance that at times of flood, fire, heat and storms a safe centre has been established

at a particular location that has links with the emergency and health services, perhaps heating or cooling, dry clothes, bedding and food. Every community should have an emergency centre identified, where access is possible without electric swipe cards or locking systems, and everyone should know who is in charge.

Causes of evacuation failure

There may be a number of causes of people refusing to evacuate. For example:

Risk perception: Human perception of risk is often very different from actual risk. Professor Paul Slovic has spent a lifetime studying and trying to explain this phenomenon.[17] Flood defences can give a false sense of security, as was found in the Grafton incident[18] in Australia in 2001, where residents refused to leave because they were convinced the defences would protect them (in the event they did, but only just.)

Companion animals: Professor Heath at Purdue University, Indiana, USA, has carried out extensive research on the evacuation behaviour of pet owners in the USA.[19] He found that the main threats to public health from pet ownership in disasters are:

- Pet owners who fail to evacuate.
- Pet owners who evacuate without their pets and later try to rescue them.
- Mental stress arising in owners separated from their pets.

Purdue University researchers studied human behaviour after mandatory evacuation from flooding in Marysville, California, in January 1997. They compiled details of 400 disaster survivors.

(a)

5.3.
(a) Image of the Marriott Hotel in New Orleans just after Hurricane Katrina, with virtually every window blown out by the wind. The robust low concrete City Hall below had not lost a single window.
Source: AP images/PA photos.

The overall evacuation rate was 80%. Of the persons who failed to evacuate, nearly 80% owned pets.

- 30.5% of human evacuation failures could be attributed to dog ownership.
- 26.4% to cat ownership.

In Weyauwega, Wisconsin there was a train derailment in 1996 and burning propane tank wagons were at risk of exploding. There was a compulsory evacuation of the entire town for 18 days.

(b)

5.3. Continued (b) The Marriott Hotel 18 months later with the windows not even repaired. The City Hall had been in continual use during the same period. One is a robust building and one is a brittle building that breaks easily in extreme winds. Investors should be very wary of investing in brittle buildings in a future of more intense windstorms if they wish their investments to retain their value.
Source: AP images/PA photos.

Approximately one-third of pet owners took their pets with them, one-third evacuated without their pets then attempted to rescue them, and one-third left their pets in their homes for the entire 18 days. Many who rescued pets did so in defiance of evacuation orders and at great risk to themselves.

The main lesson from Heath's research is that emergency planners should allow pet owners to evacuate with their pets and should provide appropriate transport, accommodation, cat carriers, bird cages and small animal boxes.

Evacuation strategies for urban neighbourhoods

The problem in cities is that there are so many people to evacuate, at times of crisis, that sheer numbers become the problem, particularly when urban neighbourhoods are already overcrowded. In London it may be possible to cope with 300 extra commuters every morning at rush hour on the existing tube system, but if the local population increases by perhaps 2000, or even 10 000 people from a couple of new tower blocks on a street (100–200 people a floor on 50 floors), then transport services may not cope with them even without an emergency. This problem was seen in the World Trade Center, where the capacity population of the Twin Towers was around 20 000 people, and although less than half full, there was a significant problem with getting the people away from the towers, one of which collapsed within three-quarters of an hour.

In the crowded city of Shanghai a new generation of super scrapers was planned to house up to 100 000 people. This is a city prone to floods and typhoons, sitting as it does at the tip of the Yangtze river, and as its mayor has admitted, it is badly prepared for any such emergencies[20] and could be struck by widespread flooding at any time, although it is hoped that the Three Gorges Dam upstream will significantly reduce the risk to this burgeoning city from fluvial flooding in the future. One problem is that the dam will reduce the amount of silt flowing through the delta into the sea. This silt has always been a defence against cyclones hitting the city and if it is not replenished, the city may be in greater danger of coastal flooding.

Overpopulation problems result in 'funnelling' effects, for instance of multiple commuters from district lines converging on single stretches of line at particular hours of the day/week causing gridlock. It is the 'surge' of moving people that debilitates systems of movement around a city, and before any new buildings are constructed in a city a very detailed study of the carrying capacity of a city, and calculations of the optimal evacuation strategies for every locality, should be undertaken.

The problem is that not only are there too many people in one place but the routes into and out of the city are dysfunctional. The mathematician Nickos Salingaros outlined how such movement systems work in his paper on 'urban webs'.[21] Salingaros outlined structural principles for

5.4.
Great Yarmouth after the peak of the flood in 1953. On 8 November 2007 a tidal surge of similar height threatened the coastline of East Anglia. *Source:* Sue White.

urban form. The processes that generate the urban web involve nodes, connections and the principles of hierarchy. Among the theoretical results derived from his work was a pattern of 'multiple connectivity', in which a city needs to have a variety of 'connections' so that people have a range of alternative routes through the city to avoid the problem of bottlenecks.

He investigated the city in terms of the types of uses the buildings are put to in the different areas of the city and a key risk factor he identified is that areas of the city become dominated by 'monofunctionality', a prime example being that of the single-use 'megatower' or skyscraper. Not only do these create a 'mathematical singularity' where one or more quantities become extremely large or infinite, so detracting from the quality of the streetscape and city, but because such towers do, en masse, one thing only, as a result their occupants will behave en masse, needing to be evacuated all at the same time, if at all.

We have also learnt much from 9/11. The idea that any building could be evacuated three floors at a time (the principle on which building evacuation strategies for large buildings are now designed), after 9/11 is ludicrous. As soon as an emergency happens (like the blackouts of August 2003) everybody thinks it may be another 9/11 and gets out of the building straight away, regardless of what is said on the loudspeaker system because no one now has faith in what they say on loudspeakers. Also many building evacuation strategies are based on having 'pressurized' staircases, that in reality do not work once three or four doors onto that staircase are opened, and would not work once the energy in the buildings fails. This is an apparently clever idea that has to be rethought.

On a street, large monofunctional buildings drown out any of the human outflows from adjacent buildings in a district, when evacuation of an area is necessary, because of the sheer force of their outflow, rather as a gas or liquid would behave under the laws of fluid dynamics. Other people emerging from smaller adjacent buildings would need to find a quiet space in the slipstream of the dominant flow to hang onto, in order to have the chance of being carried away from the event. Put several such towers together and basically no one will get out safely because of the confusion, or turbulence, created at the meeting of major flows. Certainly the occupants of any smaller building between them would have to fight hard (so retarding the outflow of the major building) to have a chance of escape at all. So it is the nature of the interactions of people outflows from adjacent buildings (determined by mathematics), during periods of evacuation, as well as the simple numbers versus routeways calculations (determined by mathematics) that will determine who escapes from an area, as well as the fighting abilities of the evacuees. More men than women would probably escape, because they are stronger and the urge to survive is deep, so to some extent this could be modelled; but then British men may, perhaps, be more chivalrous, so this also would have to be factored into the equation.

In answer to a question from a major employer in a city on whether people will get out of the organization's building safely, many issues will have to be factored into the response, including:

- What is the carrying capacity of the existing routes and transport systems in the city?
- What are they escaping from, e.g. floods, fire, bombs, excessively hot indoor temperatures?
- Are their escape routes likely to be blocked?
- How long is the warning time they will get?
- What are the adjacent buildings like?
- Who are the people who want to escape?
- What is the use pattern of the building?

- Where will they go?
- Do they know where to go and how to get there?

Such planning is essential, not only for employees who want to survive, but for councils and businesses who need to demonstrate they have behaved responsibly in the face of risk, for insurance companies who need to know they are containing the risk they cover, and for the government which needs to contain the growing risks of climate change, and terrorism.

The stakes are high. For instance, in the case of London, a 2004 estimate suggested that if a tidal surge comes over the top of the Thames Barrier, the cost would be in the region of £30 billion, or 2% of UK GDP.[22] Could one not now put another 0 at the end of that figure? What would be the cost of paying for loss of life resulting from what could have been predicted by proper planning? Where does the legal buck stop in such an event?

Owing to the increasing unpredictability of global storm tracks, no new, or existing, development or neighbourhood should now be without a strategy for dealing with the eventuality of encountering an extreme windstorm, no matter where in the world they are built.

NOTES AND REFERENCES

1   See <http://www.munichre.com/pdf/TOPICSgeo_2003_e.pdf>.

2   R. Stirling, The Weather of Britain, Giles de la Mare, London, 1997.

3   <http://www.ibhs.org/publications/view.asp?id=455>.

4   S.L. Garvin, M.C. Phillipson, C.H. Sanders, C.S. Hayles, G.T. Dow, Impact of Climate Change on Building, Building Research Establishment, East Kilbride, 1998.

5   V.K.S. Mootoosamy, M.J. Baker, Wind Damage to Buildings in the United Kingdom. University of Aberdeen, Department of Engineering. Loss Prevention Council, Watford, Paper LPR 8:1998.

6   P.S.J. Buller, The October Gale of 1987: Damage to Buildings and Structures in the South-East of England, Building Research Establishment, Watford, 1988.

7   Sparks, Peter, Defending Against the Wind. Paper presented at the National Committee on Property Insurance Annual Forum, Boston, MA, December 1990.

8   Guardian, 4 November 2003, p. 16.

9   Guardian, 24 September 2001.

10 <http://www.turkishdailynews.com/old_editions/11_04_98/for2.htm>.

11 Guardian, 4 December 2003, p. 19.

12 J. Barnes, Florida's Hurricane History, University of North Carolina Press, Chapel Hill, NC, 2003 (1st edn. 1998).

13 <http://www.ibiblio.org/uncpress/hurricanes/fl_foreword.html>.

14 S.B. Goldenberg, C.W. Landsea, A.M. Mestas-Nunez, W.M. Gray, The recent increase in Atlantic hurricane activity: causes and implications, Science 293 (2001) 20 July.

15 <http://www.met-office.gov.uk/education/historic/1987.html>.

16 See <http://www.environment-agency.gov.uk/floodwarning>; the British Floodline is on 0845 988 1188.

17 P. Slovic, Perception of Risk, in: R. Lofstedt (Ed.), Risk, Society and Policy Series, Earthscan, London, 2000.

18 N. Pfister, Community response to flood warnings: the case of an evacuation from Grafton, Aust. J. Emerg. Manage. 17 (2) (2001) 19–29.

19 S. Heath, Animal Management in Disasters, Mosby, St Louis, MO, 1999.

20 <http://www.china.org.cn/english/12537.htm>.

21 N. Salingaros, Theory of the urban web, J. Urban. Des. 3 (1998) 53–71. For the full paper see <http://www.math.utsa.edu/sphere/salingar/urbanweb.html> © Taylor & Francis Limited. See also Kunstler, J.H. and Salingaros, N. (2001) The end of tall buildings, on <http://www.peoplesgeography.org/tall.html>.

22 Guardian, 9 January 2004, p. 11.

6 SEA LEVEL RISES

INTRODUCTION

Since the end of the last Ice Age, some 18 000 years ago, the sea level has risen by over 120 m as the land ice melted and flowed back into the sea. Britain, then, was joined to the continent by its entire eastern coastline. On average, sea levels have risen at a rate of around 0.1–0.2 mm per year over the past 3000 years globally, but in the twentieth century this has increased to 1–2 mm per year in an upward trend.

Around 2.5 billion people live within 100 km of a coastline, nearly 39% of the world's population, and many of these people will be directly affected by rising sea levels in three ways:

- As seas rise many areas of the coast will be inundated.
- With increasingly severe and frequent storms and wave damage, shoreline retreat will be accelerated.
- Catastrophic coastal inundation events may be caused by a combination of climate events such as heavy flooding, high tides, and windstorms in combination with higher seas and storm surges.

This issue of how much of a low-lying shoreline retreats as sea levels rise is a complex one and depends very much on the behaviour of incoming currents, wave patterns, the structure, materials and form of the shoreline, and wave heights in that area and the care with which the coastline is managed.[1]

While sea level is predicted to rise almost everywhere, there is considerable spatial variation resulting in part from whether the land itself is rising or sinking; in some regions the rise is close to zero, while others may experience as much as twice the global average value. The predicted patterns show large increases in sea level in parts of the north Pacific and to the west of Greenland, but is should be noted that sea level rises are more difficult to predict than temperature rises.[2]

As the world warms, it was predicted in the Third Intergovernmental Panel on Climate Change (IPCC) report that global average sea levels may rise by between 7 and 36 cm by the 2050s, by between 9 and 69 cm by the 2080s and 30–80 cm by 2100. The majority of this change was predicted to result from the expansion of the warmer ocean water. However, in the past few years the phenomenal and increasing rate of land ice melt has made people rapidly revise upwards their estimates

Table 6.1 Historic rates of vertical land movement and estimated net change in sea level by the 2080s using the low end of the Low Emissions scenario (9 cm global sea level rise) and the high end of the High Emissions scenario (69 cm rise)

	Vertical land change (mm/year)	Sea level change 2080s (cm) relative to 1961–1990	
		Low emissions	High emissions
NE Scotland	+0.7	1	61
SE Scotland	+0.8	0	60
NE England	+0.3	6	66
Yorkshire	−0.5	15	75
East Midlands	−1.0	20	80
Eastern England	−1.2	22	82
London	−1.5	26	86
SE England	−0.9	19	79
SW England	−0.6	16	76
Wales	−0.2	11	71
Northern Ireland	n/a	9[*]	69[*]
NW England	+0.2	7	67
SW Scotland	+1.0	−2	58
NW Scotland	+0.9	−1	59
Orkney & Shetland	n/a	9[*]	69[*]
Global average	n/a	9[*]	69[*]

Source: UKCIP02 Climate Change Scenarios, funded by DEFRA, produced by Tyndall and Hadley Centres for UKCIP.
[*]These estimates of the sea level change exclude the vertical land changes.

of sea level rises. If the land ice on Greenland melts it is estimated that global sea levels will rise by 7 m, and if the West Antarctic ice sheet melts it will contribute as much as 70 m to global sea levels. The Antarctic acts as a storage area for snowfall, and by doing so currently acts help to mitigate rising sea levels.

ACCELERATING RATE OF ICE MELTS

In August 2008 scientists reported that the ice at the North Pole had melted at an unprecedented rate over the summer, leading to a dire warning that if this rate of melt continues the Arctic could be ice free by 2013.[2] Satellite images showed that a large storm over the Beaufort Sea at the end of July 2008 had caused the sea ice to break up dramatically, resulting in the loss of more than a million square kilometres of ice, more than the record-breaking losses of summer 2007. In 2003, when the first edition manuscript of this book was submitted, computer models of ice melts showed that the Arctic ice was predicted to last until 2070. Current models and imaging now show that the sea ice may only have a few more years before it disappears completely other than a few outcrops of islands near Greenland and Canada. Some put this as soon as 2013. This will have huge consequences for weather and climate and, of course, sea levels. The Arctic ice melts are the first and most obvious large-scale indicator that global warming is happening far more rapidly and more dramatically than previously predicted.

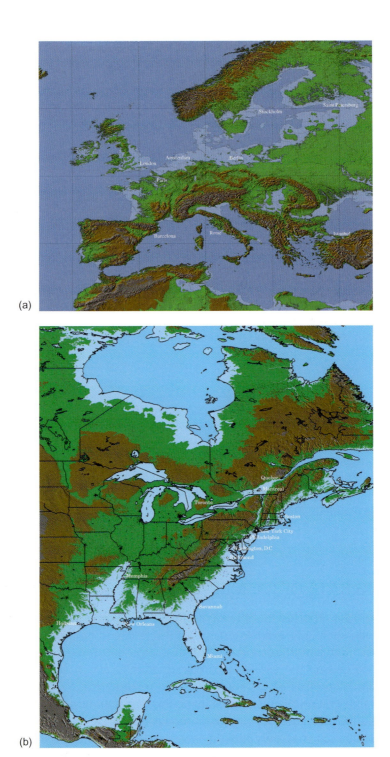

6.1.
Computer models of what (a) Europe and (b) North America may look like if the global ice reserves melted raising the sea levels by 100 m.
Source: Williams, L.O. (2002) *An End to Global Warming*. Pergamon, reproduced with permission.

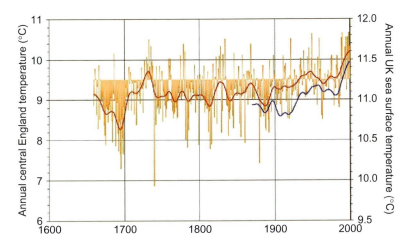

6.2.
As the global climate warms so the seas of the world warm too. This is reflected in this graph showing the warming of the climate in central England (red) and the surrounding UK coastal waters (blue). The deviations here are relative to the 1961–1990 average, and not the different scale for each.
Source: UKCIP02 Climate Change Scenarios, funded by DEFRA, produced by Tyndall and Hadley Centres for UKCIP.

James Hansen, director of climate science at NASA/Goddard Institute for Space Studies in New York, published a paper in 2008 that sets out the evidence for making cuts on today's carbon dioxide (CO_2) levels back to 350ppm. He points out that 'Equilibrium sea level rise for today's 385ppm CO_2 levels in the atmosphere is at least several meters, judging from paleoclimate history and accelerating ice mass losses from Greenland and West Antarctica heighten concerns about ice sheet stability' and in turn the potential to trigger climate tipping points that may lead to catastrophic sea level rises.[3]

The temperatures of UK coastal waters are increasing, although not as rapidly as temperatures over the land, with again the greatest warming in the south of England. Offshore waters in the English Channel may warm in summer by between 2°C and 4°C by the 2080s.[4]

The relative sea level will continue to rise around most of the UK shoreline, with the rate depending on the scenario and the region. This is because some parts of the UK land mass are actually rising, in the northwest of Scotland for instance, while other areas like southeast England are sinking relative to sea levels. This is due to isostatic rebound in Scotland as the land recovers from the weight of the glaciers of the last Ice Age, leading to a lowering of land in the south due to 'tilting' of the tectonic plate. By the 2080s, and depending on the scenario, the UKCIP02 models show that sea levels may rise be between 2 and 58cm above the current level in western Scotland and between 26 and 86cm above the current level in southeast England.

Extreme sea levels, occurring though combinations of high tides, sea level rise and changes in winds, will be experienced more frequently in many coastal locations. For some English east coast locations, for example, a water level that at present has a 2% probability of occurring in any given year may have an annual occurrence probability of 33% by the 2080s for the Medium High Emissions scenario. Sea level rises may also lead to deeper water in the near-shore zone allowing waves greater energy to reach the shoreline, so significantly increasing storm damage to shorelines.

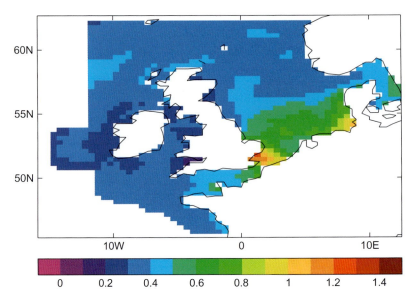

6.3.

One of the most dangerous areas of sea around the British Isles is that between southeast England and France, where the extreme water height is higher than in any other stretch of British waters. The figure shows the change, by the 2080s, in the height (metres) of the extreme sea level that has a 2% chance of occurring in any given year for the Medium High Emissions scenario, with the mid-range estimate of 30 cm global sea level rise.

Source: UKCIP02 Climate Change Scenarios, funded by DEFRA, produced by Tyndall and Hadley Centres for UKCIP.

Even if greenhouse gases in the atmosphere are stabilized, further substantial increases in sea level over many centuries remain inescapable owing to the extremely slow response of the oceans to air temperature.

The question has been raised in the media of the effect of climate change on the 'Gulf Stream', one of the three main ocean conveyors, the great currents that drive the seas – the Atlantic, the Pacific and the Indian Oceans, also known as the 'thermohaline' loops.

The ability of the oceans to convey heat is dependent on the salinity of the water. If the oceans become more saline, they become more efficient in transporting warm water from the equatorial regions to the temperate zones. The North Atlantic Conveyor, also called the North Atlantic Drift but commonly referred to as the Gulf Stream, brings warm weather to the UK from the tropics and via the north American and Canadian coasts. It also melts Arctic ice, reducing the amount of sunshine reflected back into space (the albedo), and this has a global warming effect. As the Conveyor becomes more active, more heat is taken from the Southern and Indian Oceans. (The South Pole is insulated from the Conveyor by the Antarctic Circumpolar Current and is not affected by this.)

There comes a point where the amount of freshwater from Greenland and Arctic ice melt plus the increase in freshwater flows from rivers in Siberia reduces the salinity to the stage where the flow of heat is reduced or interrupted for a spell. This happened around 1900 in the North Atlantic, for example, and again around 1960 ('The Great Salt Anomaly'). Each time this was followed by several years of unusually cold weather in the UK (1900–1905, and 1963–1971), a phenomenon also described as 'oceanic flip flop'. There is not yet a scientific consensus on the question of whether climate change will interrupt the flow of the Gulf Stream,[5] but if it did the consequences would be very serious, especially for the British Isles.

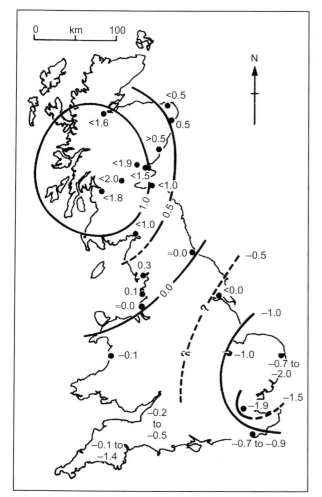

6.4.
Estimate of the present (late Holocene) rates of relative land changes (mm/year). Positive values indicate relative land uplift, negative values are relative land subsidence. Contours have been drawn by eye. The effects of sediment consolidation are not included.
Source: UKCIP02 Climate Change Scenarios, funded by DEFRA, produced by Tyndall and Hadley Centres for UKCIP, and Ian Shennan, 1989.

The UKCIP studies point to the fact that the Gulf Stream will continue to exert a very important influence on the UK climate. Although its strength may weaken in the future, perhaps by as much as 25% by 2100, it is unlikely that this would lead to a shutdown of the Gulf Stream and a resulting permanent cooling of the UK climate within the next 100 years since the warming from the greenhouse gases will more than offset any cooling from a weakening of the Gulf Stream. All of the changes included in the UKCIP02 report reflect this predicted weakening of the Gulf Stream. However, not enough is known about the factors that control ocean circulations to be completely confident about this prediction, especially in the longer term.

WHAT MAKES SEA LEVELS RISE?

Sea level changes are caused by:

- The thermal expansion of the oceans.
- The melting of glaciers.
- Changes to the major Greenland and Antarctic ice sheets.

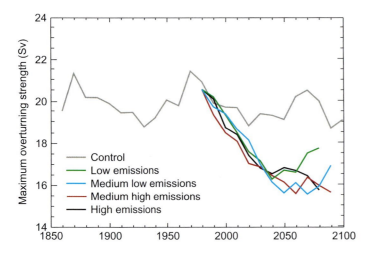

6.5.
Simulations by the Hadley Centre show a weakening of the Gulf Stream during the twenty-first century although 'flip flop', the shutting down of the flow, is not considered likely this century.
Source: UKCIP02 Climate Change Scenarios, funded by DEFRA, produced by Tyndall and Hadley Centres for UKCIP; *Briefing Report*,[15] p. 14.

The thermal expansion of the oceans

As the temperature of the waters in the oceans rises and the seas become less dense, they expand and will spread, occupying more surface area on the planet and causing inundation of low-lying areas. Increased temperature will accelerate the rate of sea level rise. Since the end of the last Ice Age, 18 000 years ago, the sea level has risen by over 120 m.

The melting of the glaciers

This is occurring at an alarming rate, with glaciers on five major continents disappearing rapidly. The ice cap on Mount Kilimanjaro may be gone in 20 years and the summer of 2003 saw melting of the permafrost levels in many parts of the Alps, destabilizing mountain slopes and closing off the Matterhorn to visitors for the first time in its history. Temperature changes are already causing 90% of the world's glaciers to retreat and some to disappear completely, with potentially catastrophic consequences for communities that rely on meltwater for irrigation, hydroelectric power and drinking water, and also communities affected by sea level rises.

In the Alps, where summer temperatures have risen by 2.1°C since the 1970s, summer flows in glacier-fed rivers have doubled, enabling hydroelectric dams to remain full and power stations to generate at maximum capacity, helping to take up the load slack from the nuclear power stations that, owing to low river flow elsewhere, could not generate at full capacity during the heatwave of 2003 in Europe. So there are many other knock-on effects from such melts.

In the longer term many glaciers will only survive at the highest altitudes. Only Scandinavian and Alaskan glaciers are not receding, and in some cases are increasing owing to increased snowfall locally, another side effect of climate change.

Another problem is that because of the higher atmospheric pressure experienced in the Alps there is now less snowfall there, resulting in glaciers not being replenished as before. Scandinavia, by contrast, is in the path of the changed track of the Atlantic depressions, as is Britain, resulting in extra rainfall in these countries. In other regions of the world the picture is much worse; the glaciers of Central Asia are disappearing at a rapid rate, threatening severe future drinking water

(a)   (b)

6.6.
(a) When Mark Lynas's father photographed this fan-shaped glacier in the Jacabamba valley in the eastern Cordillera Blanca in Peru in 1980 he little thought that his son would revisit it 20 years later to find that it had completely disappeared (b). Note the severe thinning of the ice field on the skyline above the lake.
Source: (a) Bryan Lynas; (b) Tim Helweg-Larsen in Lynas, M. (2004) *High Tide: News from a Warming World.* Flamingo.

deficits in countries such as Kazakhstan as the river run-off is reduced. A further problem is the mounds of rubble left behind them, in which meltwater accumulates in dams that could burst and cause catastrophic flooding to settlements downstream.

Changes to the major Greenland, Arctic and Antarctic ice

At very high northern latitudes, in and around the Arctic Sea, ice loss will be dramatic, although in the southern oceans around Antarctica that rate of ice loss will be slower. The maximum melt of the Greenland ice sheet has increased on average by 16% from 1979 to 2002. The melting in the winter of 2002/03 was unprecedented, in a year when the sea ice in the Arctic was at its lowest level ever recorded. The warming of Greenland and the Arctic is already increasing the rate of sea level rises, mainly owing to the dynamic response of the large ice sheet rather than just the melting of the ice. For every degree increase in mean annual temperature near Greenland, the rate of sea level rises increases by about 10%.[6]

Monitoring has shown that currently the oceans are rising by around 5 cm every 10 years. Both sea and glacier ice cool the earth, reflecting back into space about 80% of the springtime and 40–50% of summertime sunshine. The winter sea ice cover is extremely important to the global climate as it slows heat loss from the relatively warm ocean to the cold atmosphere and without the large sea ice masses at the poles to moderate the energy balance, global warming will escalate.

In 2003 Professor Johannessen of Nansen Environmental and Remote Sensing Centre in Bergen, Norway, wrote that 'At the current rate of thawing the Arctic sea ice could disappear completely by the end of the century having a serious effect on the wildlife of the region, such as the 22000 polar bears that depend on the pack ice during their seal hunting seasons.' The estimated fall in sea ice of up to 60% on Canada's east coast is also having a devastating effect on the seal populations that rely on the ice during the pup rearing season.[7] Norwegian scientists now believe that the evidence indicates this may happen in less than 10 years because of the accelerated thaw.

The Antarctic Peninsula is one of the fastest warming places on Earth and it is the speed of such local warming that could trigger unexpected events. Not only are the breeding grounds for many rare species, such as the penguin colonies and seals, shifting with the warming climate, but the pattern of snowfall is changing and threatening the nesting habits of the birds. Many Antarctic species are susceptible to very small changes in climate.[8]

The Antarctic is the world's largest remaining wilderness region; it is larger than the USA and drier than the Sahara. Parts of it are covered by 3000 m of compacted ice and snow and the continent is the repository of nine-tenths of the world's freshwater.[9]

IMPACTS OF SEA LEVEL RISES

Inundation of coastal communities

Sea levels will rise almost everywhere but at very different rates, with some areas having very little rise and others over the twice the global average rises. The predicted patterns show large increases in sea level in parts of the north Pacific.[2]

Many islands around the world will disappear as sea levels rise. Tuvalu may be the first large inhabited island to be lost forever. It comprises nine coral atolls located between Australia and Hawaii. Their highest point is 5 m (15 feet) above seal level. As sea level has risen, Tuvalu has experienced lowland flooding. Salt water intrusion is adversely affecting drinking water and food production. Tuvalu's leaders predict that the nation will be submerged in 50 years, but this may be very optimistic as much of the island is already covered by water at regular intervals during the year. In March 2002 the country's prime minister appealed to Australia and New Zealand to provide homes for his people if his country is washed away, but the plight of this nation is being ignored.[10]

Other threatened island nations include the Cook Islands and the Marshall Islands. During the past decade, the island of Majuro (Marshall Islands) has lost up to 20% of its beachfront.

In addition to island nations, low-lying coastal countries are threatened by rising sea level. A 1 m rise in sea level, inevitable under current CO_2 emissions scenarios, would inundate half of Bangladesh's rice land and flood large areas of rice-growing nations such as Vietnam, China, India and Thailand. There are areas of large-scale population particularly vulnerable to sea level rise in the Philippines, Indonesia and Egypt.

In 2008, we saw the utter devastation brought to Myanmar, where 140000 people died, already undernourished as a result of the a destroyed economy, living often in huts made from bamboo and palm fronds and abandoned by their government. It took the intervention of private individuals and charities to bring relief to the decimated communities and it is they who are still attempting

(a)

(b)

6.7.
Arctic perennial sea ice has been decreasing at a rate of 9% per decade. The first image (a) shows the minimum sea ice concentration for the year 1979, and the second image (b) shows the minimum sea ice concentration in 2003. The data used to create these images were collected by the Defense Meteorological Satellite Program (DMSP) Special Sensor Microwave Imager (SSMI).
Source: NASA and http://www.gsfc.nasa.gov/gsfc/earth/pictures/2003/1023esuice/STILLsea79.jpg.

to build some resilience to these poorest of the world's poor who live so close to the surface of the world's rising oceans, as do getting on for 43% of the world's population.

No one is immune to inundation, not least the USA as we saw with Hurricane Katrina. The eastern coastline of the USA is extremely vulnerable to coastal erosion, with shorelines constantly and rapidly retreating in a number of regions, resulting in the narrowing of beaches and washing out of vacation houses, exacerbated by the more frequent and intense hurricanes along the eastern seaboard. The problem is reflected in the soaring insurance costs for coastal homes, and

6.8.
Woman carrying a bowl of food through the flood waters in the centre of Funafuti atoll of the South Pacific to a gathering in the nearby community centre. The tidal floods, brought on by rising sea levels, were up to a foot deep in places.
Source: Lynas, M. (2004) *High Tide: News from a Warming World*. Flamingo.

in Florida for instance basic insurance for the average home costs between $1000 and $4000 depending on its location, not least in relation to the sea.

Coastal flooding in the UK

In Britain the impacts of the combination of sea level rises and stormier weather are set to take a high toll. Much of the British coastline will experience rising seas and stormier weather, and amongst others, the National Trust, which owns 600 miles of coastline, is engaged in a 'managed retreat' from threatened coastlines. A number of its key sites will be threatened; seaside properties in the picturesque villages like Porthleven, Mullion, Birling Gap and Brownsea, as well as major sites like Lindisfarne Castle and St Michael's Mount, are at risk.[11]

Settlements have evolved with defences designed to cope with historic sea levels and extreme heights of flood or storm surges. It is the surge height of a river or ocean wave that causes the most damage and overtops defences, and this height will be raised above previous historic levels, exacerbated by sea level rises and more intense storms. The risk of London flooding is increasing year on year. The Thames Barrier, built at a cost of £50 million in 1984 to protect the capital from tidal surges until 2030, is clearly not going to be able to protect London from a flood like that of 1953 by then.[12]

This area of southeast England has suffered throughout recorded history from catastrophic inundations, and London is particularly vulnerable, being sited on the conjunction of the mouth of the flood-prone Thames river valley and the end of a storm surge-prone estuary (Box 6.1).

In light of such a historic record of flooding and given that this area of Britain will see great rises in sea levels it is easy to understand why so many people are concerned over the plans for the Thames Gateway project for 200 000 homes to the east of London. The development, it is hoped, will provide 300 000 jobs in an area that already has no job shortages and one that is prone to serious flooding and contains some of Britain's most valuable wildlife sites, 42 of them Sites of Special Scientific Interest. It reaches some 40 miles on each side of the Thames east of London and as planned will be one of the biggest construction projects Britain has seen since the post-war boom, with a proposed new airport at Cliffe, a deep-water port at Shellhaven and a second bridge across the lower Thames landing on the south side of the river at Higham Marshes in the EU Special Protection Area.[13]

Box 6.1 Some examples of fatal floods in London's history[i]

1236 – Floods caused by a high storm surge tide in November drowned many people and a great number of cattle in the Woolwich area.

1242 – Heavy rain and thunderstorms on 19 November and on many days thereafter; the Thames flooded at Westminster and Lambeth.

1663 – A flood, driven by gales and produced by a high tide that was said not to have been exceeded for more than 200 years submerged Whitehall.

1703 – November: The Great Storm. The tidal flood affecting the Thames on 30 November was associated with this storm, though the tidal storm surge for this event was more significant on the Severn and along the Dutch coast. Twelve warships with 1300 men on board were lost in sight of land, Eddystone lighthouse was destroyed and practically all shipping in the Thames was destroyed or damaged. In London alone 22 people were drowned, 21 people were killed and 200 injured by falling and flying debris. It was estimated that 8000 people lost their lives in the floods caused by the storm in the rivers Thames and Severn and in Holland. The damage due to the storm and flood in London alone was estimated then to be £2 million.

1809 – January: A flood occurred, which may have been tidal in the lower reaches of the Thames, and carried away bridges at Eton, Deptford and Lewisham. Flooding was noted at Windsor.

1953 – 31 January to 1 February: The North Sea Storm Surge. A northerly severe gale/violent storm (mean speeds up to 70 knots/80 mph, with gusts in exposed areas in excess of 100 knots/115 mph) developed

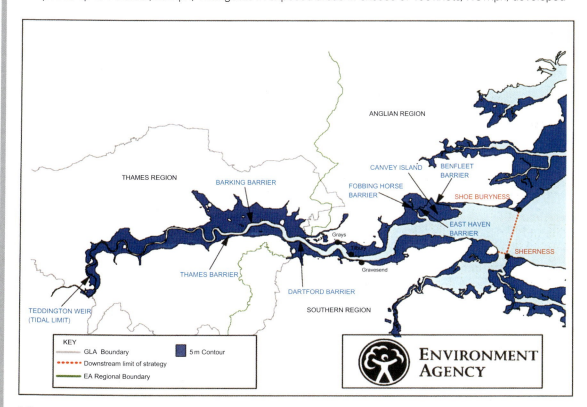

6.9.
The historic flood plain of the lower Thames Estuary showing the areas that have historically flooded during periods of tidal surges.
Source: Environment Agency.

as a depression deepened as it moved east–northeast just to the north of Scotland. Then on the 31 January, still deepening, it turned and accelerated southeastwards across the North Sea, making landfall in the Elbe–Weser estuary in northwest Germany late in the evening. As a result of the storm, the ferry *Princess Victoria* foundered during a crossing of the Irish Sea, with the loss of 132 lives. Much damage (loss of timber) was done to afforested areas in Scotland too. The major well-known effect of this storm was due to a combination of events, which brought tragedy to many living in low-lying areas on either side of the southern North Sea. The rapidly reducing pressure allowed a rise in water level; a sharp recovery (or rise) in pressure to the west of Ireland tightened the gradient on the western flank of the low pressure area; the state of the tide (spring/full-moon) and of course the driving of huge quantities of water towards the narrower southern portion of the North Sea gave rise to severe inundation of coastal areas in England (from the Humber estuary in the north to the Thames Estuary and east Kent coast in the south), Belgium and the Netherlands, with much loss of life. The situation was not helped due to the fact that the rivers were full, attempting to discharge greater-than-average quantities of winter rain-water against the wind-driven surge. The UK Storm Tide Warning Service was inaugurated after these floods,[ii] though the Dutch had had a similar service since the early part of the twentieth century.

[i]From the excellent site: http://www.booty.demon.co.uk/climate/wxevents.htm
[ii]The UK Storm Tide Warning Service can be contacted via the Environment Agency General Enquiry line: 0845 9333111; Floodline on 0845 9881188 gives information on all types of coastal and riverine flooding. For specific enquiries e-mail the EA on enquiries@environment-agency.gov.uk

The Association of British Insurers (ABI), which had not been consulted during the planning stages, was so concerned about the proposed location and the use of lightweight innovative construction methods such as timber and steel frame housing, which has proved to be high risk for insurers in the past, that they had not guaranteed to provide mortgages or house insurance for a single dwelling before plans were passed for the development. In a spectacular example of the lack of joined-up thinking the ABI was requiring that a substantial flood defence be placed around the whole development, possibly a double band structure. This would inevitably push up flood water levels in the Thames Estuary, so flooding other settlements on its coast and possibly, in conjunction with a storm surge and raised sea levels, push water over the Thames Barrier so flooding London. The Thames is the best defended river in the UK, with protection to a design standard of the 1000-year return period event. In The Netherlands they design for a 10000–20000-year event. Perhaps London should do the same.

At the very least, architects need training in more flood-resilient designs such as building on stilts (as seen on the waterfront in Dundee in Scotland) or building floating homes as in The Netherlands. However, even if this is done there is still the issue of flood rescue and evacuation. Many rescue services in England do not have training or equipment for flood rescue. (They have a statutory duty to do this in Scotland.) Emergency planners should be concerned that there is only one road in and out of the heart of the Thames Gateway development and not only will this lead to congestion but it also means that in the event of an emergency, evacuation of the region would be slow at best, and at worst be halted by a single road accident.

While confidence in the regional sea level rise predictions is not as great as for temperature,[14] there is sufficient evidence for people to make informed and sensible decisions about where, and where not, to develop 'sustainable' communities. Perhaps the French word here is better. They use 'durable', meaning that they will last.

For instance, in choosing inappropriate construction types the ABI is worried that houses in areas such as the Thames Gateway development are too *vulnerable* to damage in the event of

6.10.
The poor minorities, the sick and the elderly were left to die, whilst the dead were left to rot in New Orleans during the coastal inundation caused by Hurricane Katrina in 2005, by an administration that did not consider it worth their while to act decisively and in time to save many of them. The passive unwillingness of many authorities now to take decisive action to move populations out of the sea's reach is perhaps tantamount to acting in the same way.
Source: AP.

a flood, and that they are, being located in this flood zone, too *exposed* to the *hazard* of flooding. Increasingly, planning for 'sustainability' will require that the exposure of new developments to such hazards be minimized and this may well mean far tighter planning controls on who lives or works on flood plains, or ultimately moving people to those areas of the country that will not flood and are capable of being evacuated rapidly and safely if they do.

We have seen in the aftermath of Hurricane Katrina in New Orleans in 2005 the breakdown of civil society in the face of the scale of events associated with major coastal inundations. This was in the so-called richest nation on earth. We saw too how the matchstick houses of the regions were effortlessly swept away by the incoming tides, often leaving little evidence of their ever having stood at all. Poor housing, poor evacuation and emergency response planning and aftercare were eclipsed by the vision of the abandonment of the sick, the poor minorities, the disenfranchised, the elderly, the dying and the dead in the streets to die and rot. Those enduring images should inform decision makers at all levels and in every country in the world of the ill-advisedness of not intelligently pre-empting the growing destructiveness of climate change events. Coastal inundations by the sea pose perhaps the greatest threat of all to populations.

Responsible governments should now be putting in place and into action detailed plans for the managed retreat of people away from areas that are now, and increasingly will be in the future, prone to coastal inundation. Not to do so is irresponsible, but as with all natural hazards it appears that people never believe it will happen until it does. The scale of the threats now posed by rising

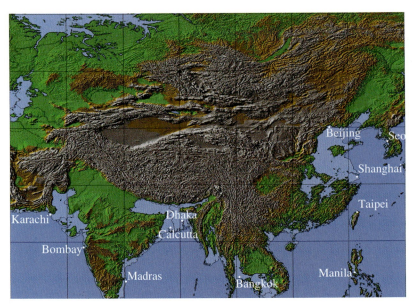

6.11.
China is one of the many countries that will be worst affected by rising sea levels. This image shows the new coastline of China if the Arctic, Antarctic and all mountain glaciers melt resulting in sea level rises of around 100 m.
Source: Williams, L. (2000) *An End to Global Warming.* Pergamon, reproduced with permission.

sea levels is too great to ignore. It is up to local affected communities to act to make politicians take their heads out of the sand and act. What they will do about the problem when the light is seen to dawn on them is as yet unclear.

NOTES AND REFERENCES

1   For a map of where these people live see <http://earthtrends.wri.org/text/POP/maps/196. htm> and for a detailed discussion of the impacts of shoreline management see <http://www.survas.mdx.ac.uk/pdfs/3mizutan.pdf>.

2   Observer, 10 August, 2008, p. 17.

3   J. Hansen, M. Sato, P. Kharecha, D. Beerling, R. Berner, V. Masson-Delmotte, M. Pagani, M. Raymo, D.L. Royer, J.C. Zacho, Target atmospheric CO_2: where should humanity aim? Open Atmospheric Science Journal, 2, 217–231. For full text see <http://arxiv.org/ftp/arxiv/papers/0804/0804.112b.pdf> Science, 2008.

4   M. Hulme, G. Jenkins, X. Lu, J. Turnpenny, T. Mitchell, R. Jones, J. Lowe, J. Murphy, D. Hassell, P. Boorman, R. McDonald, S. Hill, Climate Change Scenarios for the United Kingdom: The UKCIP02 Scientific Report, Appendix 2, published in conjunction with UKCIP, the Hadley Centre and the Climate Research Unit in the School of Environmental Science at the University of East Anglia, by the Tyndall Centre, Norwich, 2002. <http://www.ukcip.org.uk/publications/pub.html>.

5   For a fuller discussion of this phenomenon and related arguments see D. Crichton, The Implications of Climate Change for the Insurance Industry: An Update and the Outlook to 2020, Building Research Establishment, Garston, Watford, 2001. See <http://www.brebookshop.com>. For a concise website on the subject see <http://www.doc.mmu.ac.uk/aric/eae/Climate/Older/Gulf_Stream.html>.

6 Guardian, 11 January 2003, p. 9, quoting the work of Professor Konrad Steffan, a geographer at Colorado State University.

7 Independent, 10 March 2003, p. 5.

8 Guardian, 9 September 2003, p. 9.

9 <http://www.antarctica.ac.uk/About_Antarctica/Ice/index.html>.

10 For an excellent description of the current state of flooding in Tuvalu and a fascinating first-hand description of a wide range of climate change impacts around the world see M. Lynas, High Tide: News from a Warming World, Flamingo, 2004.

11 <http://www.nationaltrust.org.uk/coastline/save/coastal_erosion.html>.

12 Observer, 22 December 2003, p. 5.

13 Guardian, Society, 12 March 2003, p. 8.

14 See <http://www.metoffice.gov.uk/research/hadleycentre/pubs/brochures/B2000/predictions.html>.

15 M.J. Hulme, J. Turnpenny, G. Jenkins, Climate Change Scenarios for the United Kingdom: The UKCIP02 Briefing Report, Published in conjunction with UKCIP, the Hadley Centre and the Climate Research Unit in the School of Environmental Science at the University of East Anglia, by the Tyndall Centre, Norwich, 2002.

7 VULNERABILITY, EXPOSURE AND MIGRATION

MIGRATION

Definition (http://www.hyperdictionary.com/dictionary/migration):

1. the movement of persons from one country or locality to another, the periodic passage of groups of animals (especially birds or fishes) from one region to another for feeding or breeding.
2. (chemistry) the nonrandom movement of an atom or radical from one place to another within a molecule.
3. a group of people migrating together (especially in some given time period).

Over 175 million people now live outside the country of their birth – double the figure in 1975. Many are economic migrants, who may be fleeing poverty and severe deprivation. They are an important development resource for their home countries, remitting about US$80 billion per year to developing nations, compared to the $50 billion such countries receive in world aid.[1]

Environmental refugees currently outnumber those fleeing from war, political or religious persecution which, at the time of writing the first edition of this book in 2003, numbered below 20 million people a year, and by 2007 had risen a further 1.6 million to 26 million people. In 2006 some 9.9 million of these were under the care of the United Nations High Commissioner for Refugees (UNHCR) and by 2007 this figure had risen to 11.4 million. In October 2007 Sheffield University started a new Centre for the Study of Genocide and Mass Violence that was predicated in part on the idea that climate change has the potential to trigger genocide. Climate change is a key driver for mass violence as people begin to fight over increasingly scarce resources, be it habitable land or drinking water or the already troubling shortage of fossil fuels.

By 2050, the new Economics Foundation claim that around 150 million people will be displaced by the impacts of climate change and such refugees will be a major cause of global instability and a fertile breeding ground for bitterness and resentments, and terrorism.[2]

The Third Report from the International Development Committee of the House of Commons, on 'Global climate change and sustainable development' (2002), stated:[3]

Where vulnerability is extreme, often populations are left with no alternative but to migrate. It is often used as a means of last resort.

Migration is an important traditional coping mechanism to deal with climatic situations that are not surviv-able, and as such is an adaptation strategy. But the right to migrate is increasingly being contested and is a source of conflict in many societies. Many of those displaced in Bangladesh by rising sea levels will migrate to India, exacerbating already high levels of illegal migration. The immigration of populations of the Sahel into the Ivory Coast was on such a scale that the Ivory Coast had introduced legislation preventing foreign nation-als from owning land. There is no international recognition of environmental refugees; they are not entitled to the same rights as refugees from conflict and persecution. The UK Government has no specific policy to deal with them. The British Bangladeshi Professional Association called for a new convention to protect the rights of environmental refugees in the same way that refugees fleeing conflict or persecution are protected under international law. The need for national and international policies to deal with 'environmental' refugees will become greater as more people are temporarily or permanently displaced from their homes by more frequent and more intense climate disasters or by progressive climate change, such as rising sea levels or desertification. The UK Government was recommended by the Commons committee to push for a policy on 'environmental' refugees. Any policy response must recognize that this issue cuts across several [govern-ment] departments.

Migration has traditionally been seen as a 'reaction' to environmental disasters, but in an age where we have the tools and methodologies to predict, and imagine, future impacts the move-ment of peoples must be developed as a 'proactive' tool. For instance, the inhabitants of Tuvalu, mentioned in Chapter 6, know very well their plight, but even today as their islands flood they have nowhere to go.

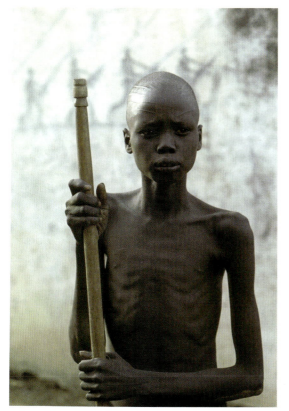

7.1.
Children across the world are becoming climate refugees, such as this young man in Sudan. Would you close the door on his future, which is now threatened by a combination of climate change and war?
Source: Adrian Arbib.

Every region and country should have well-developed models now of what climate change will do to their industries, populations and ecosystems over time, in order that humane political decisions on the movement of peoples in the future can be carefully planned to avoid the later devastation in extreme climate events.

Perhaps one of the most effective adaptation skills our society could develop would be to train enough climate modellers to be able to inform a generation of decision makers, and the communities they serve, on how to minimize the impacts of climate change on populations. But it would depend on who was being affected, because we all know that humane political decisions often do not win votes, regardless of who is doing the polluting. Such information may also be against the entrenched interests of some politicians and industries.

We know enough already, in many instances, for it to be arguably irresponsible not to act to engineer our future history to minimize the impacts of our actions today on the well-being of the children of tomorrow. The careful, pre-emptive planning, and movement, of future populations is one of the most effective methods we have of minimizing such impacts, across the world or just across a town.

The polluters should pay

The cost of supporting climate refugees is now a matter for open negotiations. Many are now questioning why, when it is the rich countries that are creating the pollution that is driving climate change, it falls on the shoulders of many of the world's poorest countries, and continents, to foot the bill for those peoples displaced by that climate change.

The New Economics Foundation warned in September 2003 that the rich countries of the world must be prepared to take their fair share of the refugees created by climate change, in an extension of the 'polluters pay' principle. This states that:[2]

People whose environments are damaged and destroyed and who are losing their livelihoods, should be recompensed and protected by those responsible.

The Foundation suggested that the Geneva Convention should be expanded to include those displaced by environmental degradation. They argue that, despite widespread denials of liability, where countries continue to pollute when they are fully aware of the damaging consequences, they should be made to reflect their liability by taking in climate refugees. To disregard knowledge should be classed as intentional behaviour, and could be considered as environmental persecution. Environmental refugees currently outnumber those fleeing from war, political or religious persecution and could reach 20 million people a year. The number of refugees taken in, they suggest, should be proportional to the amount of pollution a country generates.

The UK, for instance, produces around 3% of greenhouse gas emissions and of the 20 million refugees created a year they should be liable to take in 300000. The figure for the USA, which generates 25% of all greenhouse gases, would be 5 million refugees a year. They cite the fact that rich countries spend around £50 billion a year subsidizing fossil fuel industries but around £300000 helping poor countries manage their emissions and adapt to climate change.

The idea that the impacts and severity of climate change could, over the coming decades, become the subject of international litigation is interesting; that the polluters will have to pay could add billions to the budgets of countries as they face the challenges of footing the bill for climate change in the future. But it is also within countries that the issue of responsibility for paying for climate change impacts becomes critical.

In a desperate attempt to get the Bush administration to accept its responsibilities in relation to climate change, a dozen US states filed a suit against the US Government to force them to act on global climate change.[4] In the suit the states claimed that the agency was ignoring federal studies that demonstrate that climate change is causing 'disease, extreme weather, destruction of shoreline and loss of critical wetlands and estuaries'. What was not cited are the economic and human impacts of the desertification of tracts of the Mid-West and the huge costs of the inevitable, and happening, mass migration of people from stricken areas as agriculture is devastated by the climate.

In the UK could similar charges be levelled? The already stretched water reserves of the south-eastern area of England are to be required to supply a massive increase in homes and population in the region, imposed upon them by the current government, so threatening future availability of summer water supplies in the region.[5] Will such decisions be the source of law suits, either from water utility companies that will find it increasingly expensive to make less water go further, or from populations whose water bills rise to insupportable levels because of injudicious decisions by transient governments? Similarly, as whole neighbourhoods of a city have their transport, sewerage, water and electricity services compromised to support a monster building, for instance, whose developers have sold, profited and moved on without paying for any of the environmental impacts of that building, will the polluters, in these cases, be made to pay?

One of the core issues here is the extent of the vulnerability of communities to impacts.

VULNERABILITY

Many sources expand on the perception that the impacts of climate change will not be evenly spread across the globe and are likely to fall disproportionately on the poor.[3] Such studies typically outline the potential impacts on the developing world. The Tyndall Centre, of the University of East Anglia, conducted an excellent study in Vietnam,[6] demonstrating that those already marginalized in the economy were likely to suffer the greatest impacts as they had the fewest resources for coping with adverse change, a finding reflected in a number of other studies.[7]

In the Commons Select Committee report on global climate change referred to earlier, it was repeatedly stressed that climate change has the potential to increase further the inequality between developed and developing countries. As with corruption and HIV/AIDS, they claim, climate change could undermine development investment.[3] However, unlike corruption or HIV/AIDS, climate change is not widely recognized as an immediate problem because many of its impacts have been, to date, gradual and long term.

The relative economic severity of climate events in different regions may be influenced by a wide range of factors from the large difference in the value put on a life in different parts of the world, to multiple impacts resulting from the interaction of different factors and events in a particular region. The relative *vulnerability* of a settlement, as may be demonstrated by cost of property repair or death tolls during droughts or heavy rains, may accrue largely from the compounding of contributory factors to those deaths or damage by, for instance, the incidence of local land and water pollution, as much as to the relative *exposure* of a settlement to a flood/drought *hazard* in the region.[8]

Insurance statistics do not illustrate well the compounding of such physical factors or the inter-relationship of more complex human, historic or economic trends that might influence the level of impacts resulting from the slow desertification and abandonment of regions, the sinking of water tables, or many other aspects of climate change that will fuel human migrations. They also do not address the external costs that those regions will have to pay when accepting incoming refugees.

7.2.
Regional depopulation may be accelerated by a compounding of issues such as low rainfall, pollution of water, waste, overpopulation and high temperatures.
Source: Adrian Arbib.

There is also little evidence of work having been done on quantifying the vulnerability of populations to long-term internal costs. If, for instance, the Thames flooded, inundating riverside homes in the capital or fashionable riverside sites, many very rich people, including MPs, could lose their life's savings that are wrapped up in, say, a Westminster flat. How does one calculate the knock-on impacts on an economy of the loss of the lifetime investment of thousands of people?

In the UK, the Association of British Insurers (ABI) guaranteed availability of flood insurance for areas where the flood risk is less than one in 75 years in 2007. Whether the ABI now decides to insure the homes in an area will depend on whether the government has, or has not, constructed adequate flood defence works in that area by that time and tightened planning controls locally. In many areas such assurances will not be forthcoming and insurance will be withheld. Where are the economic impacts of that withholding then recorded? Who is responsible for the welfare of those flooded?

People who have, perhaps, £200 000 mortgages on such properties may spend the rest of their working lives paying off a mortgage on a property that is virtually unsellable. Such people may no longer be able to afford to live in expensive cities and may have to move to where they can afford housing in the future. Lives are already being ruined by such flooding.

Similarly, insurance companies and banks that have invested in inner city properties that are shown to be increasingly expensive to heat, cool and maintain as the climate warms and the costs of energy rise may find it impossible to sell such 'White Elephant' or 'Dog' buildings, and sections of the markets, where large amounts of equity are placed in real estate, could collapse, taking swathes of white collar workers and their families into poverty. Similar results could accrue from the direct impacts of catastrophic storms that destroy vulnerable buildings, or fires or urban flooding. Buildings, or whole areas of a city, are already subject to resulting negative equity.

What we learnt in the summer of 2003, as the lights went out in cities around the world (for millions of people in Italy because a single tree blew across a power line in a storm), was that in fact the people in the buildings of New York were the most vulnerable of all during power failures. High-rise buildings had to empty within minutes because the air was no longer breathable, according to some evacuees. Those in simple traditional buildings in cities in the developing world where the power failed often hardly noticed it, getting on with life as usual until the power went back on. What would have happened if the electricity had failed in New York in a blizzard? Perhaps it is time for the developed nations to look at the issue of vulnerability very closely in relation to their own cities and lifestyles.

As the pressures of climate change bite, the vulnerability of populations to it will spread, from the dried-out Mid-West of America, hurricane-struck Florida, the flooded coastal flats of the Thames Estuary, to the deserts of Africa and the Middle East. Populations will not stay where they no longer have homes they can afford to live in, food or water enough to survive, and they will bring their anger to town, as has happened throughout history. When the Nile or the Rhine flooded, people came to the nearest towns and cities in hope of surviving there, and were willing to take what they needed to survive.

We have seen from Katrina that the population of New Orleans dispersed to cities around the USA and many have not returned to the city. We are already looking at an age of major climate-driven diaspora. If national and international governments can intelligently anticipate such movements they may be able to substitute catastrophic human influxes with managed retreat to safer havens. We have the tools to do this. It is the political will that is lacking in the face of understandable reluctance of people to leave their homes before such climate catastrophes have actually affected them.

In an interesting study, written in the late 1930s, S.F. Markham, an extremely influential climatic determinist, mapped those areas of the world that could comfortably house European populations without too much heating and cooling.[9] He argued that all those areas without shading in Figure 7.3, above and below the tropics, would require large amounts of energy to keep 'civilised whitemen' comfortable, but, he opined, the domination of the white European in the world would be established with the uptake of air conditioning in those areas where it was too hot to survive in a 'civilised' fashion without it. He also went on to point out that air conditioning, even in the hottest climate, gave people the 'zest' to dance, eat, work, earn and spend money. It is an interesting line of thought to associate global politics, religion and capitalism with the joys of air conditioning. Recent studies, however, have begun to indicate that in some climates people will spend more time out of doors, shopping, eating and spending more money, in warmer weather. This is a field where much more work is needed on understanding exactly how such complex interrelationships among climate, economy and human behaviour can be manipulated to result in decisions with low environmental impacts that can also benefit local and regional economies.

Much is written about 'vulnerability' to climate change. The Commons Report describes it as being: 'determined by social, institutional and economic factors and the sensitivity of populations to climate impacts, as well as by institutional capacity, the ability to adapt, and location'. The Commons Report also states that:[3]

As the conditions within a country change, so does its vulnerability. National vulnerability will increase if the main centres providing economic growth are located in vulnerable areas.

Do they mean exposed areas, or both exposed and vulnerable areas? For example, those countries whose populations and economically productive enterprises are in coastal zones will face a higher risk.

The Intergovernmental Panel on Climate Change (IPCC) Working Group II[10] noted that the communities that are the most vulnerable to climate change were also subject to pressures from population growth, resource depletion and poverty.

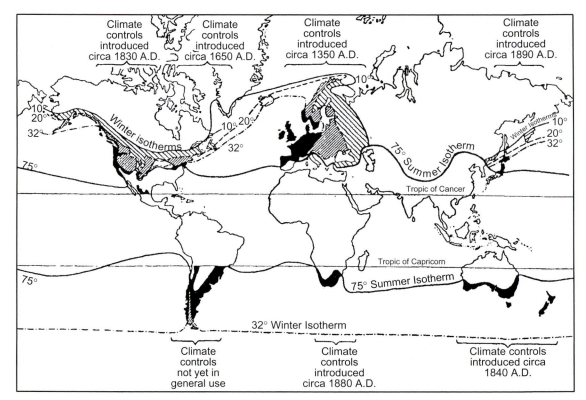

7.3.
Areas of the world where the warmest months do not exceed a mean of 75°F (23.9°C) and the mean for the coldest month does not fall below 32°F (0°C), 20°F (−6.7°C) or 10°F (−12.2°C). (Tropical areas within these limits have been excluded because of the greater intensity of solar radiation.) These were areas Markham considered of optimal climate, requiring minimal heating and cooling to maintain indoor comfort.
Source: Markham,[9] p. 98.

Rapid urbanization, land degradation, water pollution, water scarcity and the destruction of ecosystems are added pressures. All these factors affect vulnerability to variations in the current climate, as well as to future climate change.

These conditions would appear to be applicable to many coastal cities such as London, New York and Tokyo. What is not mentioned is that the short-sighted actions of politicians can add substantially to this catalogue of risk factors, and the vulnerability of populations, by not taking seriously the challenges of future-proofing buildings, cities and regions against such pressures. MPs who represent local populations should be given key positions on committees making decisions on such developments in their constituencies.

The Commons Report[3] goes on to claim that 'Developing countries have limited financial, human, technological, institutional and natural resources, making them less able to respond to the effects of climate change.' That may be true, but how prepared is the southeast for the knock-on impacts of three million new homes – the need to find more local waste dumping sites, to make scarce summer water supplies serve hundreds of thousands more people in the region, to increase sewerage capacity and build new power plants in an already well-populated region?

QUIS CUSTODIET IPOS CUSTODES?

Who guards the guardians? A major problem with the development of solutions to the problem of international climate refugees is that no single international agency, not even the UNHCR, exists to promote the rights and interests of environmental refugees.[3]

In the UK no single agency has the remit to promote environmental sustainability at the broad scale. One department deals with flooding, another with energy, waste and water supply. As early as 2003 the Institution of Civil Engineers (ICE) called for an Independent Chief Engineer (it could be a person in any profession with the right knowledge) 'to ensure that a co-ordinated, long term, sustainable approach is followed and that actions are not wholly driven by political agendas'.[5] The catastrophic floods of 2007 in the UK demonstrated that a lack of joined management and response exacerbated the damage caused by the floods and the suffering of many who were affected. What has not yet been ostensibly recognized by the British government, despite increasingly sophisticated scenario-based studies of future impacts,[11] is that the vulnerability of many people in the UK to adverse impacts of the changing climate is increasing more rapidly than anyone thought. What will happen to the ski resort communities of Scotland as the snow disappears? How will the agricultural and fishing industries be affected? Will enough water be available to the populations of the southeast, at an affordable cost, as the summers get warmer and drier? Can the Thames Barrier hold back the tidal surges until the new barrier is built? Will the Thames Gateway development increase vulnerability to flooding of the coastline communities of the whole of southeast England? Will climate refugees from the lower latitudes bring north with them smouldering resentments, fuelled by hardship and global inequality, and will migrations carry with them the potential for spreading political conflict?

To quote from Mark Mawhinney, in the conclusions of his book on sustainable development:[12]

the major issue remains the lack of clear evidence for decisions on development ... and the risk that arises as a result of this. The lack of clear evidence often leaves humanity with a choice – act before the event using preventative principles or leave it until the evidence is available.

Migration is often seen as a safety net to be used to ease population pressures after a catastrophic event; in fact, it may also be one of the most powerful tools we have for the pre-emptive planning for the mitigation of climate change impacts.

NOTES AND REFERENCES

1   Guardian, 30 September 2003.

2   <http://www.neweconomics.org/gen/uploads/nld2s2juqs2t34> mdhr31235506122003192037. pdf, see also <http://www.wmo.ch/web/Press/Press.html>.

3   Published on 24 July 2002. <http://www.parliament.the-stationery-office.co.uk/pa/cm200102/ cmselect/cmintdev/519/51902.htm>.

4   The Ecologist, December 2003, p. 6.

5   ICE, The State of the Nation: An Assessment of the State of the UK's Infrastructure by the Institution of Civil Engineers, See text on: <www.ice.org.uk>, 2003.

6   W.N. Adger, P.M. Kelly, N.H. Ninh (Eds.), Living with Environmental Change: Social Resilience, Adaptation and Vulnerability in Vietnam, Routledge, London, 2001, p. 314.

7   IPCC, Third Assessment Report: Impacts, Adaptation and Vulnerability, 2001.

8   A range of publications is available on planning for disaster mitigation and response. See P.K. Freeman, L.A. Martin, R. Mechler, K. Warner, P. Hausman, Catastrophes and Development: Integrating Natural Catastrophes into Development Planning, World Bank, Washington, 2001. See also <www.worldbank.org/dmf/files/catastrophes_complete.pdf>, and the International Federation of Red Cross and Red Crescent Societies, World Disasters Report: Focus on Reducing Risk, 2002, <www.ifrc.org/publicat/wdr2002/chapter8.asp>.

9   S.F. Markham, Climate and the Energy of Nations, Oxford University Press, Oxford, 1944.

10 Report of IPCC Working Group II: Summary for Policy Makers, 2001. Available from: <www.ipcc.ch/pub/spm22-01.pdf>.

11 Various agencies are undertaking excellent studies and scenarios of a range of impacts in a more or less coordinated fashion, but how the results of this work are fed to the general public or feed into the political decision-making process is less clear. See for instance <http://www.foresight.gov.uk/>, <http://www.ukcip.org.uk/publications/pub.html> and <http://www.rcep.org.uk/energy.html>.

12 M. Mawhinney, Sustainable Development: Understanding the Green Debates, Blackwell Science, Oxford, 2002, p. 171.

8 HEALTH IMPLICATIONS OF CLIMATE CHANGE

Janet Rudge and Sari Kovats

HEALTH EFFECTS OF HEAT AND COLD

As the climate changes, populations will increasingly fall victim to the trends in both weather and climate. They will be exposed to gradually warmer or cooler local conditions and occasionally to extreme weather events such as heatwaves or cold waves, fire, strong storms and flooding. During the most extreme events many people will die as a result of physical injury resulting from impact, immersion, poisoning or burning. These impacts vary regionally. In some parts of the world a high percentage of deaths during flooding result from snake bites. However, the greatest cause of death in a changing climate results simply from either gradual or rapid changes in temperature. This chapter deals with the tricky question of when those changes in temperature begin to affect the health and life expectancy of populations in general.

The impact of *hot weather* on human health in Europe, for instance, has gained importance in recent years owing to the major heatwave event that occurred in western Europe in 2003 when some 35000 people died as a result of the heat during 10 days in August.[1] Extreme weather events are predicted to become fairly normal by the middle of this century, signalling unpredictable temperature variations with further potential effects on health. The impact of cold weather, however, remains considerable, particularly in the UK. Therefore, this chapter will review the evidence for the direct effects of weather, and in particular both the heat and cold effects on health and their future implications in a changing climate.

COLD WEATHER EFFECTS ON HEALTH

There is a strong relationship between changes in outdoor temperature and numbers of deaths from chest and heart illness.[2] Cold-related deaths are consistently greater than numbers associated with high summer temperatures.[3] In European and other countries, most excess winter deaths are due to cardiovascular and respiratory disease, although the proportions vary.[4] In the UK, despite a persisting, widespread assumption that hypothermia (cooling of the body core) is largely responsible,[5] one-third of these deaths are attributable to respiratory disease and more than a half to cardiovascular events (mainly heart attacks and strokes).[6] Although circulatory (cardiovascular) disease accounts for higher absolute numbers, winter temperatures have a greater *proportional* effect on respiratory disease.[7,8] However, the relationships between respiratory and cardiovascular disease can confound the numbers attributed to each.[9,10] Temperature variability is also influential. According to a US study of 12 cities, this had more effect on respiratory mortality than extreme hot or cold days.[11]

Indirect effects of influenza, air pollution and season appear to explain part of cold-related mortality, but the fact that the remaining proportion occurs very soon after temperatures fall suggests that there is a direct effect of cold.[8] The relationship between low temperatures and mortality is therefore established, but the separation of indirect and direct effects is complex, as is the apportionment of effects of indoor, as opposed to outdoor, temperature. The effect of outdoor temperatures is investigated most widely, since those data are more easily obtained than indoor temperatures. Research on building-related cold temperature effects stems largely from the UK, with some focus also on Europe, while more recent work is being published from New Zealand.

Most studies relating to the association between cold ambient temperatures and respiratory illnesses have focused on damp and mouldy living conditions rather than cold house temperatures.[7] However, dampness and mould are often related to cold indoor conditions which, consequently, are related to allergic response respiratory conditions. The effects of ambient temperature on physiological function include asthma attacks, which can be triggered by breathing in cold air, reduced resistance to respiratory infection, and 'wheeze' in children associated with dampness and condensation on cold surfaces, which produce allergenic mould growth.[7] Both indoor and outdoor low temperatures can exacerbate respiratory illnesses in the presence of respiratory pathogens.[7]

Several factors that have seasonal variations have been identified as risk indicators for cardiovascular disease,[4] including winter increases in plasma cholesterol, plasma fibrinogen, blood pressure, and red and white blood cell counts. These changes in blood composition also occur during acute cold exposure, leading to the suggestion that short-term exposure to cold initiates a mild inflammatory reaction and an increased tendency for excessive blood clotting.[4] One study concluded that seasonal variation in blood pressure is related independently to both indoor and outdoor temperature, but that indoor temperature has the stronger impact.[12] If blood pressure is raised, as in response to cold, there is increased stress on the circulatory system and associated conditions.

Benchmark indoor temperatures have been identified for maintaining health:[13] between 18°C and 24°C, there is no risk to healthy, sedentary people; below 16°C resistance to respiratory infections may be affected; below 12°C there is an increased risk of cardiovascular events, due to raised blood pressure. Hypothermia is caused by prolonged cold and the risk increases appreciably below 5°C.[14]

PHYSIOLOGICAL EFFECTS OF HEAT

Healthy people have efficient heat regulatory mechanisms that cope with increases in temperature up to a particular threshold. The body can increase radiant, convective and evaporative heat loss by vasodilatation (enlargement of blood vessels in the skin) and perspiration. Heat can increase blood viscosity. Healthy volunteers exposed to 41°C for six hours experienced elevated platelet counts and increased blood viscosity.[15] Severe perspiration can also lead to a reduction in plasma volume. However, the pathophysiology of heat is not well understood, particularly in elderly people and those with chronic diseases.

The increased sweat production in the heat can lead to two types of problems: dehydration and hyponatraemia (caused by drinking large quantities of water with low salt concentrations). A significant proportion of heat stroke cases is due to exercise in hot weather in young healthy people, so-called 'exertional heat stress'.[16,17] For less fit subjects, heat illnesses can occur at low levels of activity, or even in the absence of exercise.[18]

CLIMATE AND ISSUES OF PUBLIC HEALTH

Excess winter mortality and indoor temperatures

Excess winter mortality is a particular problem in Britain, where it is thought to be associated with poorly insulated houses, in which internal temperatures track the external temperature, providing little protection against the cold, and where occupants cannot afford to adequately heat such homes to safe temperatures. Such a combination of circumstances, i.e. energy-inefficient homes and low household incomes, is known as *fuel poverty*. The current government definition of fuel poverty is where households need to spend more than 10% of their annual income on energy to achieve a standard heating regime.

Excess winter mortality is conventionally measured as the number of deaths occurring during the winter months (December to March) in excess of the average for the rest of the year. Alternatively, it is measured as a ratio of these figures. As an indication of the scale of the problem, in the decade up to 2007, annual numbers of excess winter deaths ranged from 23000 to 48500 in England and Wales.[19] This phenomenon is evident in most climates and is apparently associated with the relative seasonal fall in temperature from summer to winter and not necessarily with absolute low temperature levels.[20,21] It is a linear relationship and not simply a step increase in the winter period showing an effect of just the very coldest days,[22] although stories of escalating numbers may reach the headlines during cold snaps. Within any one country (in the northern hemisphere) excess winter mortality generally increases in areas farthest north, but there are differences between countries that do not follow this pattern according to latitude. Some with temperate climates and milder winters exhibit a greater relative excess than those with extremely cold winters.[23] British householders appear to be less well protected from the cold in their homes than many of their continental neighbours. Typically, the UK suffers up to three times the ratio of excess winter deaths compared with countries such as Sweden or Germany, where winters are colder but homes are warmer and better insulated.[24] Nor does it compare well with some countries that experience similar winter temperatures, such as France and Denmark.[25]

The closer relationship between outdoor and indoor temperatures in Britain, because of deficiencies in the building fabric, is argued as key to its relatively high numbers of winter deaths.[25] The Eurowinter Group showed that in some European countries with milder winters, indoor temperatures were lower and bedrooms were less often heated, at a given outdoor temperature, than where cold winters were normally experienced.[26] At the same time, other protective measures against the cold were less prevalent in these countries, such as clothing and outdoor activity, which the Eurowinter study also associated with higher winter mortality. Other research compared housing characteristics in several European countries in terms of energy efficiency measures and affordability of heating bills. It found that those with the poorest housing had the highest excess winter mortality and that this also coincided with countries that have milder climates.[27]

8.1.
The elderly are some of the most vulnerable in society to extremes of heat and cold.
Source: the Help the Aged British Gas partnership.

The use of central heating seems to reduce the incidence of winter deaths. The increased use of domestic central heating has been cited as the main reason for the decreasing excess winter mortality apparent in many developed countries,[28] although the direct evidence is possibly inconclusive.[29] In Britain, where central heating ownership spread later than in countries with very cold winters such as Canada, Norway and Sweden, excess winter mortality has begun to decrease later than in those countries and, as described, remains higher. The ability to pay to run the central heating, once it is in the building, would obviously be key to the resultant indoor temperature and its effect on health, and partly depends on the degree of insulation provided by the building fabric.

Insulating homes helps to improve conditions for health and well-being. Evidence from a housing intervention study in New Zealand has shown health benefits for housing occupants with respiratory conditions. Installing insulation led to significantly warmer and drier homes, significantly improved self-reported health and fewer general practitioners' visits and hospital admissions for respiratory conditions.[30]

Heatwave events and mortality

Hot weather has a greater impact on mortality than the number of deaths reported as due to classical heat illness. Heatwaves are associated with short-term peaks in mortality. Some heatwave events are very severe and can be considered a disaster if public services are overwhelmed. The heatwave in July 1987 in Greece was associated with 2000 excess deaths.[31] In France in 2003, where some 15 000 people died from the heat, the mortuary service and hospitals were unable to cope with the increase in mortality.

The mortality impacts of heatwave events have been estimated using episode analyses. Attributable mortality is estimated by subtracting the 'expected' mortality from the observed mortality during a pre-defined period. The expected mortality is calculated using a variety of measures, including moving averages, and averages from similar periods in previous years. Estimates are therefore sensitive to the method used to estimate the expected mortality.[32] Lower than expected mortality can sometimes be seen following heatwave events, indicating that some of the mortality during the heatwave is attributable to deaths brought forward by a matter of days or weeks (short-term mortality displacement).[33,34]

Heatwaves vary greatly in their impacts on health. The same temperatures can have different impacts depending on the duration of the event, or the time in the season. Heatwaves early in the summer (June/July) are associated with greater impacts on mortality than heatwaves of comparable or hotter temperatures in the same population in subsequent months.[35,36]

VULNERABLE GROUPS

Vulnerability to cold

Fuel poverty particularly affects older people who are especially vulnerable to the adverse health effects of cold living conditions. Yet, in the UK in particular, they are often least able to afford sufficient heating and are most likely to live in poorly insulated housing with inefficient heating systems. High numbers of excess winter deaths among those aged over 65 are associated with these factors. There is also evidence that increased risk of fuel poverty among older people is a predictor for increased excess winter emergency hospital admissions for respiratory disease.[37]

Pensioners are likely to spend more time at home than others and are therefore more susceptible to poor thermal conditions where they occur. The British Geriatrics Society recommends 21 °C as a suitable indoor temperature for older people.[14] Older people are most at risk because they are generally less mobile than others and because the body's thermoregulatory system can deteriorate with age. In the latter case, awareness of temperature extremes is affected, which influences a person's ability to take appropriate avoiding action when the temperature drops. 'Cold stress' exacerbates circulatory disease and results from fluctuations in temperature,[38] such as moving between warm and cold rooms. However, moving from a cold dwelling to the cold outside produces greater cardiovascular strain than going out from a warm house.[39]

Other groups vulnerable to cold-related illness are the very young and the chronically sick. Children are particularly subject to 'wheeze' in damp conditions, which often occur together with cold. Low temperatures will also slow reflexes and affect coordination, especially among older people, and can therefore be the cause of accidents in the home. Apart from the recognized physical effects of cold housing on health, mental health problems can arise from the compounded stress of living in debilitating cold and damp conditions. A UK study found that interventions to alleviate fuel poverty, resulting in improved home temperatures and thermal comfort, were significantly associated with improved mental well-being.[40]

Increasing central heating ownership has been linked with the declining numbers of excess winter deaths over recent decades, but the spread of central heating may not have benefited the most vulnerable groups.[41] After all, central heating ownership does not guarantee that its use can be afforded by householders. Research in the UK suggests that increased vulnerability to winter death from cardiovascular disease is linked to indoor temperature and thermal efficiency of housing.[42] Other work has shown that lack of central heating is associated with a higher risk of dying in winter but identifies the need to explore further the influence of socio-economic factors and other measures of housing quality.[43] Fuel-poor groups in Britain appear to be far more vulnerable to dying from cold in winter than those who can afford to heat their houses properly.

Vulnerability to heat

There are many physiological factors that impair temperature regulation and so can be predisposing factors for clinical heat illness:[44]

- Dehydration due to reduced food and liquid uptake or intestinal problems.
- Use of diuretics or alcohol abuse.
- Use of other drugs that affect thermoregulation (e.g. neuroleptics).
- Previous heat illness, low fitness, obesity, sleep deprivation, long-term high-level exercise and protective clothing.

Both individual- and population-level epidemiological studies provide strong and consistent evidence that age is an important factor for heat- and cold-related mortality. There appears to be a general increase in risk above middle age.[45,46] Elderly people in institutions, such as residential care homes, are also vulnerable to heat-related illness and death.[46,47] There is some evidence that mortality in hospital inpatients is also affected by heatwaves.[48] Many hospitals and care homes are still without space cooling in the UK and many have unshaded south- and west-facing windows.

There is currently little evidence for heat effects on mortality in young age groups (under 15 years) in European populations, as the underlying mortality in this age group is very low. There is anecdotal evidence of heat deaths caused by children being left in cars on hot days. Children are more prone to dehydration owing to the relatively high volume of fluid in their bodies compared to an adult. Hospital admissions in children increase in hot weather, primarily as a result of injuries associated with playing outside.[49]

Epidemiological studies from the USA have identified several socio-economic factors that affect heat-related mortality:[50]

- Living alone, or not leaving the house at least once per day.
- Housing characteristics (e.g. building type, floor level, use of air conditioning).
- Deprivation.

Case–control studies following the 1995[51] and 1999[52] heatwaves in Chicago both found that the strongest risk factor for dying in a heatwave was social isolation.

During a heatwave, mortality impacts are greater in cities than in the surrounding areas or in the country as a whole. This has been shown in the UK in 1995,[53] in Greece in 1987[54] and in Missouri, USA, in 1980.[55] Mapping of heatwave deaths in St Louis in 1966 found the highest rates in inner city areas where population density was higher, open spaces were fewer and socio-economic status was lower than in surrounding areas.[56,57] In Chicago, during the 1995 heatwave, over 700 hundred people died, particularly in blocks of flats. Many older people were found dead in their homes because security fears had prevented them from opening their doors to improve the cross-ventilation.[58] Individuals are more vulnerable to heat stress if they are in poorly designed housing, but there has been relatively little epidemiological research on housing characteristics as a determinant of heatwave mortality risk.

So far, heat-related mortality in the UK is not apparently related to income, i.e. the impacts of hot weather on health are distributed across income classes.[46] As with winter mortality, vulnerability may be more closely linked to social activity and housing types, which are not directly correlated with socio-economic status as measured by conventional deprivation indices.

BUILDINGS AS MODIFIERS OF TEMPERATURE

The capacity of humans to adapt to varied climates and environments is considerable. Physiological and behavioural differences between cultures have developed over many millennia as a consequence of exposure to vastly different climatic regimes. The design of vernacular, or traditional, buildings is also sensitive to climate, using a number of techniques to suit the building to the climate, and providing appropriate passive cooling or insulating techniques. In many areas the appropriate use of buildings is determined by the local culture. An instance in hot climates is the internal migration from one time of day to another, or from one season to another, between parts of the house that provide more comfortable (less stressful) indoor climates.

Humans undergo physiological adaptation to warmer climates. Many studies have illustrated this for people moving to hotter countries, and particularly for soldiers or sports people. The physiological adaptation can take place over a matter of days or weeks. The body responds by increasing the output of sweat and improving cardiovascular stability upon heat exposure. Both responses lead to reduced thermal and cardiovascular strain. The rate at which infrastructural changes will take place in response to climate change is likely to be much slower, however.[59]

British homes are often poorly built to withstand the cold. The Energy Report for the 1996 English House Condition Survey found that 38% of homes failed to reach the minimum standard needed to safeguard health,[60] according to Collins' benchmark temperature thresholds.[13] In typical winter conditions, over 10% of all homes in England have a living room temperature below 16°C. When the outside temperature is below freezing, the percentage increases to nearly 18% of all homes, including almost 4% with rooms below 12°C.[61] The UK government now acknowledges the link between cold homes and poor health, while the Department of Health recognizes that fuel poverty contributes to inequalities in health status.

Domestic building standards required in the UK are relatively poor compared with elsewhere, despite regular increases in demands of regulations concerning insulation and energy efficiency since 1974.[25] The lack of effective insulation is commonplace and many homes in Britain built before the First World War are separated from the elements by a wall only one brick thick. The housing stock is notoriously 'leaky', harking back to an era when homes were heated with open fires that required a good draught to burn well. Air infiltration is rife even in modern homes because of a number of influences, including poor design, methods of construction and quality of workmanship.[62] Boardman describes the problems of heat loss from British housing due to high ventilation rates and the consequent difficulties that arise in attempting to effectively draught-proof older dwellings.[25]

In the rest of Europe the picture is very varied. The Eurowinter Study was a large-scale epidemiological study designed to consider the effect of winter climate and protective behaviour on excess winter mortality.[26] Indoor temperatures were measured across regions and cities in a number of European countries, including Finland, The Netherlands, Germany, England, Italy and Greece. These were taken as one-off readings simultaneously with the administration of questionnaires on heating use, clothing and outdoor excursion behaviour. Among the authors' conclusions was the following, that:

striking differences indoors were higher living room temperatures and more frequent bedroom heating in the colder countries, all at a given level of outdoor cold.[26]

England was found to be nearer the 'warmer' end of the scale in terms of the average outdoor winter temperature (calculated from October to March) and with respect to this conclusion. This was not the case, however, when it was judged by the number of days in the year when the mean daily temperature falls below 18°C, which indicates the misleading nature of an 'average' temperature when comparing climates.

Consideration of average indoor temperature levels alone, with no reference to daily or other variations, allows no acknowledgement of the possible effect on comfort or health of a changeable climate, such as prevails in the UK, or of between-room differences.[63] Various research studies have presented evidence for the health effects of temperature changeability.[11,20] The fact that temperatures are changeable means that 'mild' averages disguise the extremes experienced, which, if buildings are energy inefficient, will be translated into similar indoor conditions. Even so, there is accumulating evidence that indoor temperatures vary across Europe and that in countries with 'mild' winters, buildings tend to offer less protection against the cold than where the winter climate is more extreme.[17,26,64] Similarly, certain existing housing types in regions with temperate climates may not easily protect against extreme heat.[65]

It is evident that the effect of climate on people and their health is modified – to varying degrees – by the buildings they occupy. In countries with more predictably extreme climates, buildings are generally better equipped to cope with extreme temperatures than in those where long periods of cold or heat are not the norm. Thus, insulation and energy efficiency are given higher priority in building regulations for countries like Germany and in Scandinavia. At the same time, it may be that buildings in such countries are traditionally designed to cope with the most uncomfortable seasonal conditions usually experienced, but at the expense of different comfort features required over shorter periods at other times of the year. This would explain the lack of adequate heating in southern European countries, where summer conditions are viewed as the priority but indoor temperatures are found to be low during the relatively brief winter season.

In the temperate climate of the UK, where extreme weather conditions are not normally experienced, space and prevention of damp have generally taken priority over insulation in the past, in terms of building regulations. Much of the housing stock is poorly insulated and 'leaky', with inefficient heating systems, so that indoor temperatures closely follow outdoor temperatures, particularly if the occupants are unable to afford sufficient heating for these homes that are hard to heat. Cold and damp conditions frequently occur together, especially where dampness is due to condensation. This occurs on cold surfaces, caused by poorly insulated fabric and lack of sufficient heating or appropriate ventilation.

Buildings that have poor insulation characteristics, or are lightweight, with low thermal capacity, will be as likely to produce uncomfortable indoor temperatures during hot summers as in cold winters. If ventilation possibilities through windows are limited, the potential for night cooling during hot weather would also be restricted. It is not likely, therefore, that buildings which, at present, are not well designed to cope with cool winters will be more able to produce comfortable conditions during the potentially more frequent hot summers. In fact, important factors for heat-related deaths in Paris in summer 2003 were shown to be lack of insulation and living on the top floor.[65] The risk was less where dwellings had more rooms (and opportunities to create draughts) and greater where there were more windows (and opportunities for solar heat gain). Orientation, window-opening behaviour, outdoor surface temperatures and vegetation indices were also implicated. These findings have significance for existing buildings and urban design in the light of likely higher summer temperatures in the future.

Local authorities and building professionals require education to appreciate the role that better building design can play in enabling buildings to remain cool in hot weather. This includes the use of tried and tested techniques as well as the incorporation of modern technological approaches. Schools of architecture and engineering have a responsibility to ensure that such considerations are an essential element in their curricula.

HEALTH EDUCATION AND WARNING SYSTEMS

Education to advise people of appropriate behaviour during hot weather is an essential component of heat-death prevention. Many governments in Europe have issued advice on how to avoid heat-related illness. An understanding of human behaviour during heat events is needed so that appropriate messages can be developed and targeted. There is a lack of qualitative research on behavioural responses to heatwaves and heatwave warnings.

There have been several campaigns aimed at getting people to be warmer in winter. The following components are required for an effective heat-health warning system:[66]

- Sufficiently reliable heatwave forecasts for the population of interest.
- Robust understanding in the cause–effect relationships between thermal environment and health.
- Effective response measures to implement within the window of lead-time provided by the warning.
- The community in question must be able to provide the needed infrastructure.

A range of methods is used to identify situations that adversely affect human health.[67] Heat warning systems, when accompanied by specific health interventions, are generally considered to be effective in reducing deaths during a heatwave.

IMPLICATIONS OF CLIMATE CHANGE ON BUILDINGS AND HEALTH

Future seasonal averages may be warmer and there are likely to be more extreme temperatures and greater variability within seasons, which could affect health. Although numbers of winter deaths could diminish as a result of warmer winters, it is likely that excess summer deaths will increase as summers become hotter, and the population most likely to be affected is older age groups.[68]

Wet buildings are harder to heat. Buildings will have to withstand increasingly frequent extreme events such as storms, strong winds and flooding. Strong winds affect building heat loss and draughts, with consequences for indoor temperatures and comfort. The predicted warmer, wetter winters would present less of a threat in terms of low temperatures and research to date has not found a relationship between rainfall and excess winter mortality. However, damp reduces the insulating effect of building fabric so, where buildings already have poor insulating qualities, these will be reduced further still by increased rainfall and become more frequently difficult to heat comfortably and affordably. The likelihood of condensation occurrence may also be increased, with possible implications for mould growth and consequent health problems.

Extreme summer temperatures can be exacerbated by certain building and urban environment characteristics, as found in Paris in 2003,[65] with disastrous results. There are lessons to be learned from this research, in particular for top floor urban apartments.

From the point of view of healthy indoor temperatures, buildings need to be insulated from both heat and cold. In summer, they should be capable of being well ventilated, with windows shaded from the hot summer sun. In winter, occupants should be able to heat them effectively, free from draughts but with controlled ventilation, with windows, fabric and configuration to take advantage of warming by the winter sun. The possibilities for ventilation need to be designed with recognition of occupants' concern for security.

CONCLUSIONS

The implications of climate change for health have been presented here in terms of temperatures in buildings. The temperature at which there is an increased risk of illness due to heat depends on the normal outdoor conditions. Countries with a cold climate, such as those in Scandinavia, have learned to insulate their buildings against the cold. Likewise, behaviour in hot climates is more appropriate to the heat. Some of this is related to learning appropriate behaviour, such as drinking more water or taking a siesta in the heat of the day. Some of it is in the provision of appropriate buildings, such as those that take advantage of thermal mass to reduce indoor temperature variability in temperate or desert climates.

For architects there are important lessons to be learned from the scientific analysis of buildings, and in the light of this the study of local vernacular buildings. For national and local authorities the study of buildings and the understanding of the effects of weather patterns in existing climates can give important clues for the provision of warnings and help to communities struggling with unexpected conditions.

The wrong conclusions can also follow, for instance an overreliance on the provision of mechanical systems to alleviate the more extreme conditions. These can add to the problem of climate change through the excessive use of fossil fuel energy. It is also becoming increasingly clear that the assumption that energy is always available can be misleading when extreme weather puts a strain on energy utilities.

For buildings to provide a safe and comfortable environment in the future they should:

- Provide the means for occupants to simply regulate the indoor climate.
- Avoid the use of mechanical cooling (or heating) where possible.

In addition, there is a need for:

- Education of building professionals on how to design buildings that meet these needs.
- Education of the public on the ways to avoid heat stress and cold stress in ways that require little energy use.
- The instigation of mechanisms for warning the public and the authorities when dangerous weather episodes are expected.
- Further medical advice to be issued together with weather forecasts (e.g. advice is currently given on pollen counts, ultraviolet exposure and wind chill; a Met Office scheme is already underway with general practitioners so that patients with chronic obstructive pulmonary disease can be targeted to take appropriate actions when a cold snap is predicted).
- Retrofitting of the existing housing stock to provide sufficient insulation (while maintaining appropriate ventilation) and to combat overheating through shading.

- Consideration of urban design to ameliorate extreme temperatures through the use of building layout, planting and appropriate surface materials, including water.
- Provision of 'climate havens' or refuges, i.e. cooled or heated communal spaces; for example, in the USA people often go to the malls to keep cool or warm during the day.

A fundamental challenge for those who are designing buildings and cities in a changing climate is that they must understand how the relationship among people, climate and buildings impacts not only on the health of humans but also on their comfort, the subject of the next chapter.

NOTES AND REFERENCES

1   S. Kovats, T. Wolf, B. Menne, Heatwave of August 2003 in Europe: provisional estimates of the impact on mortality, Euro Surveill. Wkly. 8 (11) (2004).

2   G.M. Bull, J. Morton, Environment, temperature and death rates, Age Ageing 7 (1978) 210–221.

3   W.R. Keatinge, G.C. Donaldson, E. Cordioli, M. Martinelli, A.E. Kunst, J.P. Mackenbach, S. Nayha, I. Vuori, Heat-related mortality in warm and cold regions of Europe: an observational study, Br. Med. J. 321 (2000) 670–673.

4   J.B. Mercer, Cold – an underrated risk factor for health, Environ. Res. 92 (2003) 8–13.

5   W.R. Keatinge, G.C. Donaldson, Cold weather, cold homes and winter mortality, in: J. Rudge, F. Nicol (Eds.), Cutting the Cost of Cold. Affordable Warmth for Healthier Homes, E&FN Spon, London, 2000.

6   M. Curwen, Excess winter mortality: a British phenomenon?, Health Trends 22 (1991) 169–175.

7   K.J. Collins, Cold, cold housing and respiratory illnesses, in: J. Rudge, F. Nicol (Eds.), Cutting the Cost of Cold. Affordable Warmth for Healthier Homes, E&FN Spon, London, 2000.

8   A.E. Kunst, C.W.N. Looman, J.P. Mackenbach, Outdoor air temperature and mortality in the Netherlands: a time-series analysis, Am. J. Epidemiol. 137 (1993) 331–341.

9   S. Stewart, K. McIntyre, S. Capewell, J.J.V. McMurray, Heart failure in a cold climate: seasonal variation in heart failure-related morbidity and mortality, J. Am. Coll. Cardiol. 39 (5) (2002).

10 D.L. Crombie, D.M. Fleming, K.W. Cross, R.J. Lancashire, Concurrence of monthly variations of mortality related to underlying cause in Europe, J. Epidemiol. Community Health 49 (1995) 373–378.

11 A.L.F. Braga, A. Zanobetti, J. Schwartz, The effect of weather on respiratory and cardiovascular deaths in 12 US cities, Environ. Health Perspect. 110 (2002) 859–863.

12 K.T. Khaw, Temperature and cardiovascular mortality, Lancet 345 (1995) 337–338.

13 K.J. Collins, Low indoor temperatures and morbidity in the elderly, Br. J. Hosp. Med. 38 (1986) 506–514.

14 S. Lowry, Housing and Health, BMJ Books, London, 1991.

15 W.R. Keatinge, S.R. Coleshaw, J.C. Easton, F. Cotter, M.B. Mattock, R. Chelliah, Increased platelet and red cell counts, blood viscosity, and plasma cholesterol levels during heat stress, and mortality from coronary and cerebral thrombosis, Am. J. Med. 81 (1986) 795–800.

16 Y. Epstein, Y. Shani, D.S. Moran, Y. Shapiro, Exertional heat stroke – the prevention of a medical emergency, J. Basic. Clin. Physiol. Pharmacol. 11 (2000) 395–401.

17 M.M. Fonseka, Heat stroke in young adults, Ceylon. Med. J. 44 (1999) 184.

18 G. Havenith, Y. Inoue, V. Luttikholt, W.L. Kenney, Age predicts cardiovascular, but not thermoregulatory, responses to humid heat stress, Eur. J. Appl. Physiol. 70 (1995) 88–96.

19 Office for National Statistics. Excess winter deaths by age group, Government Office Region and country of usual residence, England and Wales, 1991/1992–2004/2005 and 2005/2006. <http://www.statistics.gov.uk/statbase/Expodata/Spreadsheets/D7089.csv/> (accessed 1.05.07, 2007.

20 J. Rudge, British weather: conversation topic or serious health risk?, Int. J. Biometeorol. 39 (1996) 151–155.

21 A.S. Douglas, H. al-Sayer, J.M. Rawles, T.M. Allan, Seasonality of disease in Kuwait, Lancet 337 (1991) 1393–1397.

22 P. Wilkinson, M. Landon, S. Stevenson, Housing and winter death: epidemiological evidence, in: J. Rudge, F. Nicol (Eds.), Cutting the Cost of Cold. Affordable Warmth for Healthier Homes, E&FN Spon, London, 2000, p. 27.

23 K. Laake, J.M. Sverre, Winter excess mortality: a comparison between Norway and England plus Wales, Age Ageing 25 (1996) 343–348.

24 Help the Aged, Addressing Excess Winter Deaths: The Causes and Solutions, Help the Aged, London, 2001.

25 B. Boardman, Fuel Poverty: From Cold Homes to Affordable Warmth, Belhaven Press, London, 1991.

26 Eurowinter Group, W. Keatinge, G. Donaldson, K. Bucher, E. Cordioli, L. Dardanoni, K. Jendritzky, K. Katsouyanni, A. Kunst, J. Mackenbach, M. Martinelli, C. McDonald, S. Nayha, I. Vuori, Cold exposure and winter mortality from ischaemic heart disease, cerebrovascular disease, respiratory disease, and all causes in warm and cold regions of Europe, Lancet 349 (1997) 1341–1346.

27 J.D. Healy, Excess winter mortality in Europe: a cross country analysis identifying key risk factors, J. Epidemiol. Community Health 57 (2003) 784–789.

28 M. Sakamoto-Momiyama, Seasonality in Human Mortality, University of Tokyo Press, Tokyo, 1977.

29 M. Henwood, Fuel Poverty, Energy Efficiency and Health: A Report to Eaga CT, Eaga Charitable Trust, Keswick, 1997. p. 29.

30 P. Howden-Chapman, A. Matheson, J. Crane, et al., Effect of insulating existing houses on health inequality: cluster randomised study in the community, Br. Med. J. 334 (2007) 460–464.

31 K. Katsouyanni, D. Trichopoulos, X. Zavitsanos, G. Touloumi, The 1987 Athens heatwave (Letter), Lancet ii (1988) 573.

32 S. Whitman, G. Good, E.R. Donoghue, N. Benbow, W. Shou, S. Mou, Mortality in Chicago attributed to the July 1995 heat wave, Am. J. Public Health 87 (1997) 1515–1518.

33   F. Sartor, R. Snacken, C. Demuth, D. Walckiers, Temperature, ambient ozone levels, and mortality during summer 1994, in Belgium, Environ. Res. 70 (1995) 105–113.

34   M. Huynen, P. Martens, D. Schram, M. Weijenberg, A.E. Kunst, The impact of heat waves and cold spells on mortality rates in the Dutch population, Environ. Health Perspect. 109 (2001) 463–470.

35   S. Hajat, R.S. Kovats, R.W. Atkinson, A. Haines, Impact of hot temperatures on death in London: a time series approach, J. Epidemiol. Community Health 56 (2002) 367–372.

36   C.J. Skinner, Y.A. Kuleshov, Association between thermal stress and elderly mortality in Sydney – a comparison of thermal sensation indices, in: Proceedings of the 2001 Windsor Conference on Thermal Comfort, Cumberland Lodge, published by the Thermal Comfort Unit, Oxford Brookes University, Oxford, 2001, pp. 262–272.

37   J. Rudge, R. Gilchrist, Measuring the health impact of temperatures in dwellings: investigating excess winter morbidity and cold homes in the London Borough of Newham, Energ. Buildings 39 (2007) 847–858.

38   F. Enquselassie, A.J. Dobson, T.M. Alexander, P.L. Steele, Seasons, temperature and coronary disease, Int. J. Epidemiol. 22 (1993) 632–636.

39   J. Goodwin, Cold stress, circulatory illness and the elderly, in: J. Rudge, F. Nicol (Eds.), Cutting the Cost of Cold. Affordable Warmth for Healthier Homes, E&FN Spon, London, 2000.

40   G. Green, J. Gilbertson, Warm Front Better Health. Health Impact Evaluation of the Warm Front Scheme, Centre for Regional, Economic and Social Research, Sheffield Hallam University, Sheffield, 2008.

41   G. Raw, R. Hamilton, Building Regulation and Health, Building Research Establishment, Garston, Watford, 1995.

42   P. Wilkinson, M. Landon, S. Stevenson, Housing and winter death: epidemiological evidence, in: J. Rudge, F. Nicol (Eds.), Cutting the Cost of Cold. Affordable Warmth for Healthier Homes, E&FN Spon, London, 2000.

43   P. Aylin, S. Morris, J. Wakefield, A. Grossinho, L. Jarup, P. Elliott, Temperature, housing, deprivation and their relationship to excess winter mortality in Great Britain 1986–1996, Int. J. Epidemiol. 30 (2001) 1100–1108.

44   E.M. Kilbourne, Illness due to thermal extremes, in: J.M. Last, R.B. Wallace (Eds.), Public Health and Preventative Medicine, Appleton Lang, Norwalk, CT, 1992, pp. 491–501.

45   M. Sierra Pajares Ortiz, J. Diaz Jemenez, J. Montero Robin, J. Alberdi, I. Miron Perez, Daily mortality in the Madrid community during 1986–91 for the group between 45 and 64 years of age: its relationship to air temperature, Span. Rev. Public. Health. Review Espania Salud Publica 71 (1997) 149–160.

46   S. Hajat, R.S. Kovats, K. Lachowycz, Heat-related and cold-related deaths in England and Wales: who is at risk?, Occup. Environ. Med. 64 (2007) 93–100.

47   J.D. Faunt, T.J. Wilkinson, P. Aplin, P. Henschke, M. Webb, R.K. Penhall, The effete in the heat: heat-related hospital presentations during a ten day heat wave, Aust. N. Z. J. Med. 25 (1995) 117–120.

48 M. Lye, A. Kamal, Effects of a heatwave on mortality-rates in elderly inpatients, Lancet i (1977) 529–531.

49 K.K. Christoffel, Effect of season and weather on pediatric emergency department use, Am. J. Emerg. Med. 3 (1985) 327–330.

50 E.M. Kilbourne, Heat waves, in: M.B. Gregg (Ed.), The Public Health Consequences of Disasters, US Department of Health and Human Services, Centers for Disease Control, Atlanta, GA, 1989, pp. 51–61.

51 J.C. Semenza, C.H. Rubin, K.H. Falter, J.D. Selanikio, W.D. Flanders, H.L. Howe, J. Wilhelm, Heat-related deaths during the July 1995 heat wave in Chicago, N. Engl. J. Med. 335 (1996) 84–90.

52 M.P. Naughton, A. Henderson, M. Mirabelli, R. Kaiser, J. Wilhelm, S. Kieszak, C. Rubin, M. McGeehin, Heat related mortality during a 1999 heatwave in Chicago, Am. J Prev. Med. 22 (2002) 221–227.

53 C. Rooney, A.J. McMichael, R.S. Kovats, M. Coleman, Excess mortality in England and Wales, and in Greater London, during the 1995 heatwave, J. Epidemiol. Community Health 52 (1998) 482–486.

54 K. Katsouyanni, D. Trichopoulos, X. Zavitsanos, G. Touloumi, The 1987 Athens heatwave (Letter), Lancet ii (1988) 573.

55 T.S. Jones, A. Liang, E. Kilbourne, M. Griffin, P. Patriarca, S. Wassilak, R. Mullan, R. Herrick, H. Donnell Jr., K. Choi, S. Thacker, Morbidity and mortality associated with the July 1980 heat wave in St Louis and Kansas City, J. Am. Med. Assoc. 247 (1982) 3327–3331.

56 A. Henschel, L. Burton, L. Margolies, J. Smith, An analysis of the heat deaths in St Louis during July 1966, Am. J. Public Health 59 (1969) 2232–2242.

57 S.H. Schuman, Patterns of urban heatwave deaths and implications for prevention: data from New York and St Louis during July 1966, Environ. Res. 5 (1972) 59–75.

58 E. Kleinenberg, Heatwave: Social Autopsy of Disaster in Chicago, University of Chicago Press, Chicago, IL, 2002. pp. 54–65.

59 R.S. Kovats, G. Jendritzky, Heat waves and human health, in: B. Menne, K.L. Ebi (Eds.), Climate Change and Adaptation Strategies for Human Health, Steinkopff Verlag, Heidelburg, Darmstadt, 2005, pp. 63–98.

60 DETR, English House Condition Survey 1996, Energy Report. Stationery Office, London, 2000.

61 R. Moore, Personal communication, 2001.

62 D. Nevrala, The effect of insulation, mode of operation and air leakage on the energy demand of dwellings in the UK, in: Ventilation of Domestic Buildings, British Gas, London, 1979.

63 J. Rudge, R. Winder, Central heating installation for older, low income households: what difference does it make?, in: H. Levin (Ed.), Indoor Air 2002: Proceedings of the 9th International Conference on Indoor Air Quality and Climate, vol. 4, Indoor Air 2002, Santa Cruz, California, 2002, pp. 1078–1083.

64 J.P. Clinch, J.D. Healy, Housing standards and excess winter mortality, J. Epidemiol. Community Health 54 (2000) 719–720.

65 J. Ribéron, S. Vandentorren, P. Bretin, et al., Building and urban factors in heat related deaths during the 2003 heat wave in France, in: Proceedings of Healthy Buildings 2006, vol. V, Lisbon, Portugal, 2006, pp. 323–326.

66 N. Auger, T. Kosatsky, Chaleur accablante: Mise à Jour de la Littérature Concernant Les Impacts de Santé Publique et Proposition de Mesures D'adaptation, Régie régionale de la santé et des services sociaux de Québec, Direction de la santé publique, Montréal, 2002.

67 C. Koppe, G. Jendritzky, R. Kovats, B. Menne, Heatwaves: Impacts and Responses, World Health Organization, Copenhagen, 2003.

68 G.C. Donaldson, W.R. Keatinge, Direct effect of rising temperatures on mortality in the UK, in: R.S. Kovats (Ed.), Health Effects of Climate Change in the UK: An Update of the Department of Health Report 2001/2002, Department of Health, London, 2008, pp. 81–90.

9 CLIMATE CHANGE AND THERMAL COMFORT

We share with other mammals the mechanisms of temperature regulation – shivering, sweating and changing the distribution of blood between the body's peripheral circulation and the deeper organs. But we also use clothing and shelter and burn fuel to warm and cool us. The use of these cultural mechanisms to control our temperature has made it possible for our species to survive in almost all climates, but it has also created new kinds of vulnerability. Our body temperature now depends on the price of clothing or fuel, whether we control our own furnaces or have them set by landlords, whether we work indoors or outdoors, our freedom to avoid or leave places with stressful temperature regimes ... Thus our temperature regime is not a simple consequence of thermal needs but rather a product of social and economic conditions. (R. Levins and R. Lewontin, *The Dialectical Biologist*[1])

INTRODUCTION

The conditions that cause ill-health and mortality in populations as a result of the warming climate and related extreme weather events are at one end of the spectrum of impacts of the design of buildings and cities on people dealt with in Chapter 8. Whilst it is especially important to avoid dangerous indoor conditions, it is also important to avoid discomfort. Whether a person is comfortable, uncomfortable or even in danger will depend either on the quality of the building they occupy or alternatively on their ability to afford to mechanically heat or cool that building. In the latter case a local energy supply will also be needed. In a former age when there were few machines, and perhaps in a future age when few people on Earth can afford to run machines, it is imperative that designers relearn the fundamental lessons of the relationship between humans, buildings and the climate. This chapter deals with the effects of climate on the comfort of building occupants and how this might be altered by climate change.

The occupants of any building will respond to the thermal environment at three levels:

- Through unconscious physiological changes – sweating, shivering, muscle tension and changes in the blood flow.
- Through behavioural responses – consciously through the addition or removal of clothing, or semi-consciously such as changes in posture or moving to a more comfortable spot.
- Using the controls afforded by the building they occupy, some of them without the use of energy – opening windows, drawing curtains or blinds; others where mechanical building controls are used – fans, heaters or air conditioning.

This chapter starts by looking at the comfort issues: what constitutes a comfortable environment and how we can future-proof buildings against climate change. The chapter then considers the problems related to thermal health in relation to climate change. Climate change is generally characterized as 'warming' and an increase in heatwaves and their associated impacts might be expected, such as those experienced during the 2003 and 2006 in Europe. Some climate models also suggest that an increasingly cold climate in western Europe may occur, but in a much longer time frame. In Chapter 8 we looked at the effect these changes may have in increasing the illness and even deaths caused by the climate, which are already a feature of health in many parts of the world.

THERMAL COMFORT

The role of comfort

There are three reasons why thermal comfort is important to the design of buildings:

- Comfort (and particularly thermal comfort) is an important aspect of user satisfaction.
- The temperature which people try to achieve in their house is an important factor in deciding the amount of energy it will use.
- If a building fails to be comfortable, then the occupants will take actions to make themselves comfortable. These actions will usually involve the use of energy – possibly destroying a carefully constructed low-energy strategy.

The heat balance

In order to stay healthy, we have to keep our internal body temperature at an almost constant 37°C. To ensure a constant body temperature the heat produced by the body must, over time, be balanced by the sum total of the heat lost from it. The heat produced [the metabolic rate, generally measured in watts per square metre (Wm^{-2}) of body surface area] is related to a person's activity: the more active the more heat. There are essentially four avenues of heat loss:

- **Convection** – heat loss to (or gain from) the air. This depends on the temperature of the air and on the air velocity next to the body surface (skin or clothes) (see also Box 9.1).
- **Radiation** – heat loss direct to (or gain from) surrounding surfaces. This depends on the temperature of the surrounding surfaces (the radiant temperature) (see also Box 9.2).
- **Conduction** – heat loss (or gain) direct to surfaces in contact with the body which depends on temperature of the surface. In most cases this is a small contribution to heat loss.
- **Evaporation** – heat loss due to the evaporation of skin moisture. This depends on the amount of water in the air (humidity) and the air velocity next to the body (see also Box 9.3).

Heat is also exchanged from the lungs during breathing, this loss is partly convective and partly evaporative. The mathematical expression for the balance between heat production and heat loss is one way of calculating the thermal conditions to provide in a building. This is the heat balance approach to setting thermal conditions. The basic equation for heat balance is:

$$M - W = Ev + Ra + K + Co + Re + S \ (Wm^{-2}) \tag{9.1}$$

where M = rate of metabolic heat production, W = energy used in doing mechanical work, Ev = heat loss by evaporation from the skin, Ra = heat loss through radiation, K = heat loss by

Box 9.1 Heat loss by convection

We are surrounded by air. When the temperature of the air is lower than skin temperature we will lose heat from the body by convection. When air temperature is above skin temperature we will gain heat. In cool, still conditions air heated by the body will become buoyant when the body heats it. It will then rise up and form a 'plume' above the head and then disperse. Any movement of the air will add to the cooling by helping to strip the warmed air from the body at a greater rate, effectively cooling the air in contact with the body. Air movement is counted relative to the body surface so, for instance, walking will add to the effective air movement. Turbulence in the air stream can also have an effect, helping to increase the cooling effect of air movement.

These effects occur whether or not the body is clothed. Where clothing is worn the cooling effect of convection occurs at the clothing surface so instead of the skin temperature it is the temperature of the surface of the clothes that affects the rate of loss of heat. By insulating the skin the rate of heat loss is reduced. Air movement can also have some impact on the effectiveness of clothing as an insulator: a permeable material allowing the cool air to penetrate further and reduce the garment's effectiveness.

Where the air in contact with the body is hotter than skin temperature all these effects act in the opposite direction to heat the body.

In summary: the cooling (or heating) effect of the air depends on the difference between air temperature and skin (or clothing surface) temperature and on the air movement. The effect of air movement is generally considered to be roughly proportional to the square root of the air velocity.

Box 9.2 Heat loss by radiation

All bodies emit heat at their surface at a rate that is proportional to the fourth power of their absolute temperature (absolute temperature is equal to the centigrade temperature plus 273). At the same time surrounding surfaces are radiating to the body in a similar fashion. So the body loses heat if the surroundings are colder and gains heat if they are hotter. If the surroundings were all at one temperature the situation would be relatively simple. But of course they are not, in any real situation there will be cold windows or hot ceilings, radiators and even the sun. There is not space here to go too far into the details of radiant energy exchange.

The full picture integrates the effect of every part of the surrounding surfaces with every part of the body. The usual simplification is to talk in terms of the 'mean radiant temperature'. This is the temperature of a sphere which would exchange no net radiation with the surroundings. The notion of the mean radiant temperature is very useful. It can be used to assess the cooling or heating effect of the environment.

In a real situation the radiant temperature will vary from point to point in a room and the size of the human body means that it will even vary from point to point on the body. In general, a rough estimate of radiant temperature such as the average temperature of the room surfaces is all that can be achieved. The effect of any large surface with a different temperature needs to be taken into account, especially as people notice radiant asymmetry (often interpreting it as a 'draught' in the case of a cold surface).

There is only a relatively small temperature range in most buildings. The fourth power law for radiant heat exchange can therefore be approximated so that the radiant heat loss is roughly proportional to the temperature difference between the clothing surface and the radiant temperature.

conduction (generally negligible), Co = heat loss by convection, Re = heat loss by respiration (convective and evaporative), and S = heat stored in the body (= 0 over time).

More detail of the physical processes underlying thermal comfort is given in the appropriate boxes, which touch briefly on the main points. Don McIntyre's excellent book *Indoor Climate*[2]

Box 9.3 Heat loss by evaporation

When water evaporates it extracts a quantity of heat (the latent heat of evaporation) from its surroundings. The evaporation of water from the surface of the skin means much of the latent heat is extracted from the skin and cools it. This cooling effect is very powerful (the evaporation of 1 g/minute is equivalent to 41 W) and is used by the body for cooling when we sweat. It is not the sweating that cools us but the evaporation of sweat from the skin.

After the sweat has been evaporated it must move away from the skin if it is to be successful, in order that more evaporation can occur. The driving force for evaporation is the gradient of the water vapour pressure near the skin surface. The water vapour pressure is that part of the total pressure of the air that is caused by the molecules of water in it. The hotter the air, the more water it is capable of carrying. The maximum driving force is the difference between the vapour pressure at skin temperature and the vapour pressure in the air as a whole.

The heat lost by evaporation from the skin is usually caused by the amount of sweat produced and not the maximum that can be evaporated (this would require the body to be totally wet with sweat). So the sweat glands and not the physical conditions usually govern the heat loss by evaporation. Air movement tends to increase evaporation in much the same way as it increases convection. So the water vapour pressure in the atmosphere and the square root of the air velocity decide the possible heat loss by evaporation.

and Ken Parsons' *Human Thermal Environments*[3] are good starting points for those who want to know more.

Because of the importance of keeping the internal body temperature constant the body has a number of ways of controlling the rate at which heat leaves the body. These actions are referred to as thermoregulation. Such responses as changes of blood supply to the skin to increase or reduce heat loss, or in more extreme cases, sweating in hot conditions or shivering in the cold. See Box 9.4 for more detail on thermoregulation.

Thermal comfort is a psychological phenomenon defined by the American Society of Heating, Refrigeration and Air Conditioning Engineers (ASHRAE) as 'That state of *mind* which expresses satisfaction with the thermal environment [emphasis added]'. This psychological phenomenon is often taken to be a response to the physical environment and the physiological state of the body, but is almost certainly affected by the attitude of the person to their surroundings and their experience of thermal environment as well as its current state. See Box 9.5 for more detail on psychophysics.

Conscious ('behavioural') thermoregulation is generally triggered by thermal discomfort. Discomfort is usually the result of a change in the core temperature coupled with information from the thermal sense at the skin that the body risks continued thermal imbalance (e.g. a draught in a cold room). In contrast, a situation that is moving in a direction to restore thermal balance is considered comfortable or even pleasurable (e.g. a cool breeze on a hot day). Thermal sensation is therefore part of a feedback system to maintain thermal equilibrium, so that a comfortable environment is one where occupants can maintain thermal balance as a dynamic equilibrium. An uncomfortable environment is one in which we cannot prevent discomfort.

The complexity of the thermoregulatory processes and their dynamic nature has made them difficult to characterize mathematically. Steady-state formulations for thermal comfort such as that of Fanger[4] have been found to underestimate the extent to which people will naturally adapt to changes in the environment, particularly in variable conditions.[5,6]

Box 9.4 Thermal physiology: metabolic heat and the control of deep body temperature

We produce energy by 'burning' food to provide the energy we need to live. Most of this energy takes the form of heat. The body produces this 'metabolic heat' all the time: more is produced when we are active and the more active we are the more heat is produced (Table 9.1). Heat is transported around the body by the blood. The organs of the body, and particularly the brain, must stay at about 37°C. The body has mechanisms for controlling the deep body (or core) temperature. If our brain temperature exceeds acceptable limits, the body reacts to restore heat balance.

A drop in core temperature causes vasoconstriction: blood circulation to the surface of the body is reduced, and the temperature of the skin drops, cutting the heat loss. A further drop in core temperature leads to increased tension in the muscles and then shivering to increase metabolic heat. A rise in core temperature causes vasodilatation: the blood supply to the periphery is increased, increasing skin temperature and heat loss to the surroundings. A further increase causes sweating to increase heat loss by evaporation.

Table 9.1 Metabolic rate for selected activities

Activity	Wm^{-2}	Met
Reclining	46	0.8
Seated, relaxed	58	1.0
Sedentary activity (office, dwelling, school, laboratory)	70	1.2
Standing, light activity (shopping, laboratory, light industry)	93	1.6
Standing, medium activity (shop assistant, domestic work, machine work)	116	2.0
Walking on level:	110	1.9
2 km/h	140	2.4
3 km/h	165	2.8
4 km/h	200	3.4

Source: International Standard 7730. Moderate Thermal Environments: Determination of PMV and PPD Indices and Specification of the Conditions for Thermal Comfort (1994). Geneva: International Organization for Standardization.

Adaptive behaviour as a way of looking at comfort

Field studies and rational indices

One method that has been widely used to investigate the conditions we find comfortable is the field study. Take a group of subjects who are going about their normal everyday lives and ask them how hot they feel on a scale, such as those shown in Table 9.2 (i.e. their 'comfort vote'). At the same time, the physical environment (temperature, humidity, air movement) is measured. Over a period of time the way in which the subjective responses change can be related to these measured physical conditions.

Figure 9.1 shows the mean comfort vote of subjects from a field surveys plotted against the mean temperature recorded over the period of the survey. The rate of change of comfort vote with temperature is much lower from one survey to another than it is within any particular survey.

The reasons for this observation from field surveys have been the subject of considerable speculation and research, most of which has concentrated on the context in which field surveys

Box 9.5 Psychophysics: how we feel about the environment

The physiological actions described in Box 9.4 are augmented by the thermal sense in the skin. This adds information about the skin temperature, warning of conditions that might pose a danger. There are two types of skin temperature sensors, one concerned mostly with heat and the other with cold. Our impression of the warmth or cold of our environment arises in part from the skin sensors. It is integrated with the core temperature so that the sensation may be pleasing if the overall effect is likely to restore thermal equilibrium and unpleasant if it works against it. Thus a cold skin sensation will be pleasant when the body is overheated, unpleasant if the core is already cold. The sensation from any particular part of the body will depend on time, location and clothing, as well as the temperature of the surroundings.

Psychophysics is the study of the relation between the sensations we experience and the stimuli we receive from the physical world. The relationship between thermal sensation and the thermal environment is hard to model. Psychophysical experiments have concentrated on more defined relationships such as the warmth and cold of surfaces when they are touched. Nevertheless the thinking behind field studies of thermal comfort has been to relate thermal sensation to the stimuli of the thermal environment.

The comfort vote is a method of trying to assign numbers to our thermal sensation. However, an ability to say how we feel does not imply a one-to-one relationship between thermal comfort and the physical conditions that cause it. The pleasure given by a thermal stimulus depends not only on the physiological conditions at the time the stimulus is received but also on the social and other conditions prevailing and on the recent thermal experiences of the person concerned. So a particular stimulus can give rise to a range of sensations. We cannot say that a set of conditions will give rise to a particular sensation, only that there is a probability that it will.

are conducted. Nicol and Humphreys suggested, in 1973,[7] that this effect could be the result of a feedback between the thermal sensation of subjects and their behaviour and that they consequently 'adapted' to the climatic conditions in which the field study was conducted.

Unlike laboratory experiments, field studies include the effects of all the behaviours of subjects during their normal everyday lives. Some of the behavioural actions are concerned with the thermal environment, and will therefore affect the relationship between thermal comfort and the environment. The adaptive approach seeks to explain the differences between the field measurements and those obtained in the laboratory by looking at the cumulative effect of behaviour in this relationship.

People and indoor climate

The corollary of the effect shown in Figure 9.1 is that in field surveys the temperature that people find comfortable (the 'comfort temperature') is closely related to the mean temperature measured. This was found to be the case in surveys conducted over a wide range of indoor climates, shown in Figure 9.2.[8] The strong relationship between the comfort temperature and the mean temperature measured during the survey is clear.

As an example of how effectively adaptive actions can be used to achieve comfort, Figure 9.3 shows the actual proportion of subjects comfortable among office workers in Pakistan at different indoor temperatures. The data were collected over a period of a year so the comfort temperature was continually changing, as was the indoor temperature.[9] The major methods these workers had

Table 9.2 Seven-point ASHRAE and Bedford scales of thermal sensation. The −3 to +3 scale is generally used for mathematical evaluation of comfort in indices such as Fanger's Predicted Mean Vote (PMV); the 1 to 7 scale is used in survey work, to avoid confusion

ASHRAE descriptive scale	Numerical equivalent		Bedford descriptive scale
Hot	+3	7	Much too hot
Warm	+2	6	Too hot
Slightly warm	+1	5	Comfortably warm
Neutral	0	4	Comfortable, neither warm nor cool
Slightly cool	−1	3	Comfortable and cool
Cool	−2	2	Too cold
Cold	−3	1	Much too cold

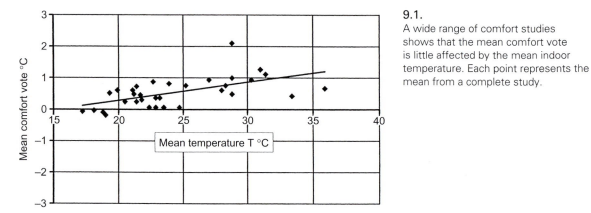

9.1.
A wide range of comfort studies shows that the mean comfort vote is little affected by the mean indoor temperature. Each point represents the mean from a complete study.

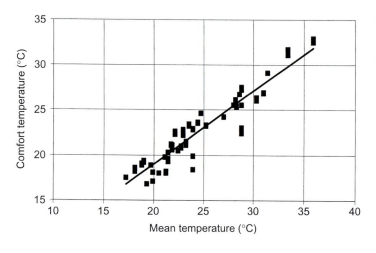

9.2.
The variation of comfort temperature with mean indoor temperature from surveys throughout the world.
(*Source:* data presented in Humphreys, 1976[8])

to control their comfort were changing their clothing and using air movement, fans being universally available in Pakistani offices. The curve shows the mean probability of comfort. Each point represents the proportion comfortable in a particular city in a particular month. Note that little discomfort is recorded at indoor temperatures between 20 and 30°C.

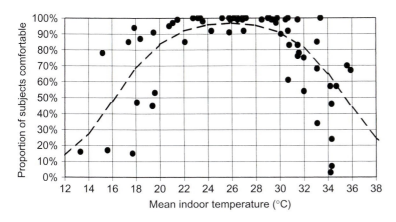

9.3.
Pakistan: the proportion of office workers who were comfortable at different indoor temperatures. Each point on the graph represents the results of one survey of about 20–25 people in a single office. It will be noticed that on many occasions the subjects recorded no discomfort. With a continually changing indoor temperature and comfort temperature Pakistani buildings were found to be comfortable at temperatures ranging between 20 and 30°C with no cooling apart from fans. (*Source*: Nicol et al., 1999[9])

Adaptive actions

Interest in the phenomenon outlined above has led to the development of the so-called *adaptive* approach to thermal comfort which attributes the effect to an accumulation of behaviours or other factors which, taken together, are used to ensure comfort. In a defining paper on the approach, Humphreys and Nicol[10] explained the meaning of adaptive actions (see Box 9.6).

Box 9.6 shows some of the actions which may be initiated in response to cold or to heat. The lists are intended to be illustrative of an indefinitely large number of conceivable types of action, and are by no means comprehensive. It will be noticed that the lists contain physiological, psychological, social and behavioural items. The lists have in mind the climate and culture of the UK and some items would need modification for other lands.

Box 9.6 Examples of adaptive actions

Some conceivable actions in response to cold:
- Vasoconstriction (reduces blood flow to the surface tissues)
- Increasing muscle tension and shivering (generates more heat in the muscles)
- Curling up or cuddling up (reducing the surface area available for heat loss)
- Increasing the level of activity (generates body heat)
- Adding clothing (reduces the rate of heat loss per unit area)
- Turning up the thermostat or lighting a fire (usually raises the room temperature)
- Finding a warmer spot in the house or going to bed (select a warmer environment)
- Visiting a friend or going to the library (hoping for a warmer environment)
- Complaining to the management (hoping someone else will raise the temperature)
- Insulating the loft or the wall cavities (hoping to raise the indoor temperatures)
- Improving the windows and doors (to raise temperatures/reduce draughts)
- Building a new house (planning to have a warmer room temperature)
- Emigrating (seeking a warmer place long-term)
- Acclimatizing (letting body and mind become more resistant to cold stress)

Some conceivable actions in response to heat:

- Vasodilatation (increases blood flow to surface tissues)
- Sweating (evaporative cooling)
- Adopting an open posture (increases the area available for heat loss)

- Taking off some clothing (increases heat loss)
- Reducing the level of activity (reduces bodily heat production)
- Having a beer (induces sweating, and increases heat loss)
- Drinking a cup of tea (induces sweating, more than compensating for its heat)
- Eating less (reduces body heat production)
- Adopting the siesta routine (matches the activity to the thermal environment)
- Turning on the air conditioner (lowers the air temperature)
- Switching on a fan (increases air movement, increasing heat loss)
- Opening a window (reduces indoor temperature and increases breeze)
- Finding a cool spot or visiting a friend (hoping for a cooler temperature)
- Going for a swim (selects a cooler environment)
- Building a better building (long-term way of finding a cooler spot)
- Emigrating (long-term way of finding a cooler place)
- Acclimatizing (letting body and mind adjust so that heat is less stressful)

The set of conceivable adaptive actions in response to warmth or coolth may be classified into five categories:

- Regulating the rate of internal heat generation.
- Regulating the rate of body heat loss (see Box 9.7 for more detail of the use of clothing).
- Regulating the thermal environment.
- Selecting a different thermal environment.
- Modifying the body's physiological comfort conditions.

Because there are very many conceivable adaptive actions, comfort is likely to be restored by means of a coordinated set of minor actions, rather than by means of a single mode of action. For example, a response to coldness might entail a slight increase in muscle tension, a barely perceptible vasoconstriction, a slightly 'tighter' posture, putting on a sweater and the desire for a cup of coffee. The effect of each might independently be small, but the joint effect can be large, not least because changes in heat flow and changes in thermal insulation are multiplicative in their effect on temperature differential. The more subtle adaptations are unlikely to be captured by questionnaire responses about clothing and activity, and would therefore be 'invisible' to the usually recommended procedures for the evaluation of predicted mean vote (PMV) and standard effective temperature (SET).

Adaptation can be regarded as a set of learning processes, and therefore people may be expected to be well adapted to their usual environments. They will feel hot when the environment is hotter than 'usual' and cold when it is colder than 'usual'. The adaptive approach is therefore interested in the study of usual environments. In particular, what environments are 'usual', how does an environment become 'usual', and how does a person move from one 'usual' environment to another? (The heat exchange equation is able to indicate what might be meant by a 'hotter' or a 'colder' environment, but has nothing to say about what might be a 'usual' environment.)

Not all researchers agree on the wide range of adaptive actions outlined by Humphreys and Nicol, and there is generally a feeling that adaptation is concerned with behavioural, more or less conscious actions.

The adaptive principle
The fundamental assumption of the adaptive approach is expressed by the adaptive principle: *If a change occurs such as to produce discomfort, people react in ways which tend to restore their*

Box 9.7 Clothing

Clothing plays a major role in enabling humans to survive outside the tropics. Clothing is of particular importance to the adaptive model of thermal comfort. In the physical model of the heat transfer the clothing is assumed to be a uniform layer of insulation between the body and the environment with a single surface temperature. Quite clearly this is an approximate treatment, since the clothing is anything but uniform. The face in particular is generally unprotected and the actual clothing insulation varies from place to place on the body according to the nature of the clothing ensemble. In practice, however, the assumption appears to work quite well, and the overall insulation of the clothing can be expressed as the sum of the contributions from the individual items of clothing being worn, as if they were each spread over the whole of the body surface. In this context the layers of air trapped between multiple layers of clothing and between the clothing and the skin are counted as part of the ensemble.

The insulation of the clothing is generally expressed in 'clo units' where 1 clo = 0.155 m^2 kW^{-1}. Tables of clo values for typical ensembles, and for individual clothing items, are given in Table 9.3. There is

Table 9.3 Clothing insulation for selected garments

Garment	I_{cl} (clo)	Garment	I_{cl} (clo)
Underwear		*Shirts – blouses*	
Panties	0.03	Short sleeves	0.15
Underpants with long legs	0.10	Lightweight, long sleeves	0.20
Singlet	0.04	Normal, long sleeves	0.25
T-shirt	0.09	Flannel shirt, long sleeves	0.30
Shirt with long		Lightweight blouse, long sleeves	0.15
Sleeves	0.12	*Dresses – skirts*	
Panties and bra	0.03	Light skirts (summer)	0.15
Trousers		Heavy skirt (winter)	0.25
Shorts	0.06	Light dress, short sleeves	0.20
Lightweight	0.20	Winter dress, long sleeves	0.40
Normal	0.25	Boiler suit	0.55
Flannel	0.28	*Jackets*	
Sweaters		Light summer jacket	0.25
Sleeveless vest	0.12	Jacket	0.35
Thin sweater	0.20	Smock	0.30
Sweater	0.28	*Outdoor clothing*	
Thick sweater	0.35	Coat	0.60
High-insulative, fibre pelt		Down coat	0.55
Boiler suit	0.90	Parka	0.70
Trousers	0.35	Fibre-pelt overalls	0.55
Jacket	0.40	*Shoes and gloves*	
Vest	0.20	Shoes (thin soled)	0.02
Socks		Shoes (thick soled)	0.04
Socks	0.02	Boots	0.10
Thick, ankle socks	0.05	Gloves	0.05
Thick, long socks	0.10		
Nylon stockings	0.03		

Source: International Standard 7730. Moderate Thermal Environments: Determination of PMV and PPD Indices and Specification of the Conditions for Thermal Comfort (1994). Geneva: International Organization for Standardization.

always a big problem with such descriptive tables: they are culturally defined and a thick suit in one climate might be counted as rather thin in another. In addition to acting as insulation against the transfer of dry heat, the clothing has an effect on the heat loss by evaporation. It affects evaporative cooling by introducing extra resistance to water vapour depending on its permeability to moisture and it can absorb excess moisture next to the skin. The absorbed moisture is then evaporated from the clothing and not from the skin, so it is not so effective in cooling the skin.

The way clothing works is often more complex than suggested. In some hot, dry climates, for instance, the inhabitants wear loose, multiple layered clothing to keep the high environmental temperatures away from the skin, whilst allowing heat loss by evaporation when dry air is pumped through the clothing as the body moves. Another complication in dealing with clothing is that its function is not purely thermal. Our social as well as our thermal needs determine the way we clothe ourselves. Wearing a jacket open or closed can make a significant difference to its cultural as well as its thermal characteristics. Chair upholstery may add as much as 0.2–0.4 clo to the standard methods for estimating clothing insulation. The need to specify the value of the clothing insulation and permeability is a source of considerable uncertainty in the heat balance model of human heat exchange.

comfort. This principle applies to field surveys conducted in a wide range of environments and thus legitimizes meta-analyses of comfort surveys such as those of Humphreys,[11] Auliciems and deDear[12] and deDear and Brager.[6] These meta-analyses have been used to generalize from the results of a number of individual thermal comfort surveys.

By linking people's actions to comfort the adaptive principle links the comfort temperature to the context in which subjects find themselves. The comfort temperature is a result of the interaction between the subjects and the building or other environment they are occupying. The options for people to react will reflect their situation: those with more opportunities to adapt themselves to the environment or the environment to their own requirements will be less likely to suffer discomfort.

The prime contextual variable is the climate. Climate is an overarching influence on the culture and thermal attitudes of any group of people and on the design of the buildings they inhabit. Whilst the basic mechanisms of the human relationship with the thermal environment may not change with climate, there are a number of detailed ways in which people are influenced by the climate they live in and these play a cumulative part in their response to the indoor climate. The second major context of nearly all comfort surveys has been a building, and the nature of the building and its services plays a part in defining the results from the survey. The third context is time. In a variable environment such as will occur in most buildings occupants will respond to changes in the environment. They will do this by taking actions to suit the environment to their liking or by changing themselves (for instance by posture or clothing) to suit the environment. This implies that the comfort temperature is continually changing. The extent of these changes and the rate at which they occur is an important consideration if the conditions for comfort are to be properly specified.

The relationship with outdoor climate

Humphreys (1978)[11] took the indoor comfort temperatures determined in a number of surveys conducted worldwide and plotted them against the outdoor monthly mean temperature at the time of the survey. The results are shown in Figure 9.4. He found a clear division between people in buildings that were free-running (neither heated nor cooled) at the time of the survey and

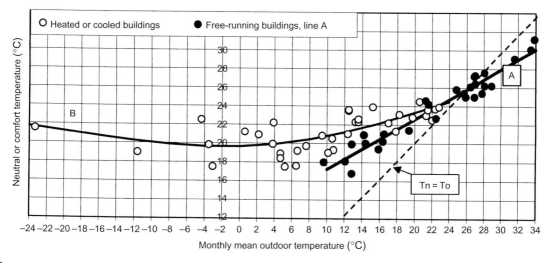

9.4.
The change in comfort temperature with monthly mean outdoor temperature. Each point represents the mean value for one survey (this graph is from Humphreys, 1978[11]). The buildings are divided between those that are climatized at the time of the survey and those that are free-running. Subsequent analysis of the ASHRAE database of comfort surveys[13] showed similar results.

those in buildings that were climatized (heated or cooled) at the time of the survey. The relationship for the free-running buildings was closely linear. For climatized buildings the relationship is more complex.

The feedback mechanisms create order in the relationship between indoor climate and comfort temperature. In a free-running building the indoor climate is linked by the building to outdoor conditions. When the building is being climatized the relationship changes, because the indoor climate is decoupled from that outdoors.

People in buildings: adaptive opportunities

Buildings differ in a number of ways: in addition to their individual physical form, they differ in their services, in what sort of heating or cooling system is provided and whether it is used, in the possibilities they offer for occupants to control their environment, and in the policies of management about whether there is a dress code and so on.

There are other aspects of building services that affect the comfort of occupants. Leaman and Bordass[14] have demonstrated that there is more 'forgiveness' of buildings in which occupants have more access to building controls. By forgiveness they mean that the attitude of the occupants to the building is affected so that they will overlook shortcomings in the thermal environment more readily.

A more robust characterization is that of Baker and Standeven.[15] They identify an 'adaptive opportunity' afforded by a building that will affect the comfort of its occupants. The premise is that the more opportunity occupants have to adapt the environment to their liking the less likely are they to experience thermal stress and the wider will be the range of acceptable conditions (Figure 9.5). Adaptive opportunity is generally interpreted as the *ability* to open a window, draw a blind, use a fan and so on. It must also include dress code working practices and other factors that influence the interaction between occupant and building. Changes in clothing, activity and

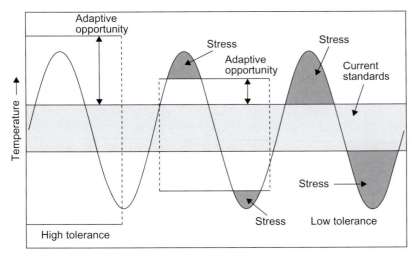

9.5.
Effect of adaptive opportunity: the greater the opportunity to control the environment – or the occupants' requirements – the less likelihood of thermal stress. (*Source*: adapted from Baker and Standeven, 1995[15])

posture and the promotion of air movement will change the comfort temperature. Other adaptive opportunities will have no direct effect on the comfort temperature, but will allow the occupants to change the indoor climate to suit themselves. Actual adaptive behaviour is an amalgam of these two types of action: changing the conditions to accord with comfort and changing the comfort temperature to accord with prevailing conditions. The range of conditions considered comfortable is affected by the characteristics of the building and the opportunities for individual adaptation by occupants.

In reality it has been found difficult to quantify the adaptive opportunity in terms of the availability of building controls. Nicol and McCartney[16] showed that the mere existence of a control did not mean that it was used, and that merely adding up the number of controls does not therefore give a good measure of the success of a building or its adaptive opportunity. It would seem that as well as the existence of a control a judgement is needed as to whether it is useful in the particular circumstances. For example, solar shading may be useless on one face of a building, but essential on another. In addition, the perceived usefulness of a particular control will change from time to time depending on conditions.[17]

Time as a factor in the specification of comfort temperatures

When people take actions in response to a thermal environment that is causing discomfort these actions take time to accomplish. A number of actions can be taken: some, like opening a window, take little time, while others, such as the change of fashion from winter to summer clothes, take longer. The change is fast enough to keep up with the fluctuations in the weather from season to season but not always quick enough to account for all the changes in the weather.[18] In his comparison between outdoor temperature and the comfort temperature indoors (see Figure 9.4), Humphreys (1978)[11] used records of the monthly mean of the outdoor air temperature as the defining variable as do deDear and Brager[6]. The weather can change dramatically within a month and both people and the buildings they inhabit change at a rate that will not be reflected by a monthly estimate. Box 9.8 suggests a way in which the effects of time can be included in the model of comfort and adaptation.

Box 9.8 Characterizing the effect of time on adaptive behaviour

Recent surveys have tried to determine the rate of change of comfort temperature using longitudinal comfort surveys conducted over a period of time.[i-iii] The exponentially weighted running mean of the temperature reflects quite well the time dependence of the comfort temperature or clothing insulation.
The equation for the exponentially weighted running mean at time t is:

$$T_{rm(t)} = (1 - \alpha)\{T_{t-1} + \alpha T_{t-2} + \alpha^2 T_{t-3} \ldots\} \tag{9.2}$$

where α is a constant such that $1 \geq \alpha \geq 0$, $T_{rm(t)}$ is the running mean temperature at time t, T_t is the mean temperature for a time t of a series at equal intervals (hours, days, etc.), and T_{t-n} is the instantaneous temperature at n time intervals previously. The time interval often used to calculate T_{rm} is a day. The rate at which the effect of any particular temperature dies away depends on a. Equation (9.2) simplifies to:

$$T_{rm(t)} = (1 - \alpha)T_{od(t-1)} + \alpha \cdot T_{rm(t-1)} \tag{9.3}$$

where $T_{od(t-1)}$ and $T_{rm(t-1)}$ are the mean temperature and the running mean temperature for the previous day. Today's running mean can thus be simply calculated from yesterday's mean temperature and yesterday's running mean. The time series gives a running mean temperature that is decreasingly affected by any particular temperature event as time passes. The larger the value of a the more important are the effects of past temperatures.
    The aim is then to find the value of α that gives the best correlation of outdoor running mean with the comfort temperature. The correlation of outdoor running mean temperature with comfort temperature rises gradually until α reaches about 0.8 and then starts to decrease. This suggests that although the peak in the correlation with comfort temperature is small, there is a real effect. The correlation with daily mean outdoor temperature T_{od} ($\alpha = 0$) and with the monthly mean of outdoor temperature ($\alpha \cong 0.95$) are both less than the correlation with T_{rm} where $\alpha = 0.8$. A similar effect has been found to apply to clothing insulation.[ii,iii]

[i]McCartney, K.J. and Nicol, J.F. (2002) Developing an adaptive control algorithm for Europe: results of the SCATs project. *Energy and Buildings*, 34, 623–35.
[ii]Morgan, C.A., deDear, R. and Brager, G. (2002) Climate clothing and adaptation in the built environment. In Levin, H. (ed.), *Indoor Air 2002: Proceedings of the 9th International Conference on Indoor Air Quality and Climate Indoor Air 2002*, Santa Cruz, USA, Vol. 5, pp. 98–103.
[iii]Nicol, F. and Raja, I. (1996) Thermal Comfort, Time and Posture: Exploratory Studies in the Nature of Adaptive Thermal Comfort. Oxford: School of Architecture, Oxford Brookes University.

An adaptive case study: avoiding discomfort in Pakistan and Europe

In the past, countries have been assumed to take a path of increasing technological sophistication. In the response to climate change it may be necessary to relearn skills that have fallen into disuse. As fuel prices increase, the ability to adapt to our surroundings is likely to be one of those skills.
    Several studies have been made of thermal comfort in Pakistan,[9] and of the use people make of the thermal controls that are available. Pakistan is a country where the incidence of air conditioning is low, and where a wide range of temperature is found, not only outside but also inside buildings. This is partly because the 'level of technology' is less developed in Pakistan, but

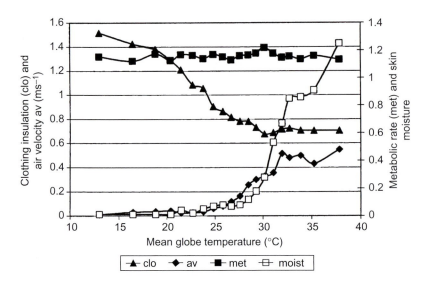

9.6
Use of adaptive actions to suit the subject comfort temperature to the environment in Pakistan.
(*Source*: Fergus Nicol)

crucially it is because the price of fuel is relatively much greater because of the exchange rate for the rupee against the dollar. Even for relatively well-off Pakistanis the cost of running the air conditioning can be prohibitive.

Five cities were identified in different climatic areas of the country and a study was conducted of office workers who were going about their normal work routine. Surveys of about 100 workers were made in each of the cities on a monthly basis for a period of one year. In addition to subjective responses from the subjects on the Bedford scale (Table 9.1) they were asked for their preference for a warmer or cooler environment and an estimate of the moisture of their skin. Details were collected of the clothing they were wearing, of their activity and of their use of building controls (windows, fans, lights and heaters). Measurements were made of the globe temperature, the air temperature, the humidity and the air velocity. Outdoor temperatures were collected from local meteorological stations.

From these measurements it is possible, among other things, to relate the extent to which different adaptive actions are taken by the subjects at different temperatures. Two types of adaptive actions are investigated: those that change the comfort temperature of the subject and those that seek to change the environment to suit the subject. Examples of the former are the use of clothing and metabolic rate, and the changes in these are illustrated in Figure 9.6. Also shown are the changes in air velocity and skin moisture. Changes in air velocity will be caused by the use of fans (which are found in all Pakistani offices) and to a lesser extent the opening of windows, but it will have the effect of increasing the temperature that occupants find comfortable. Skin moisture only serves to illustrate the physiological state of the subjects. A graph of discomfort at different values of the indoor temperature at the time of the survey is given in Figure 9.3. There is clearly little discomfort between 20 and 30°C. Most of the changes in clothing and air movement occur in the same range of temperatures.

A similar pattern occurs in the use of building controls (Figure 9.7). The use of heating ceases when the indoor temperature exceeds 20°C and fans are all running when the temperature reaches 30°C. Windows are more likely to be opened as the temperature rises, though at temperatures above 35°C they are likely to be heating rather than cooling the office and there is some

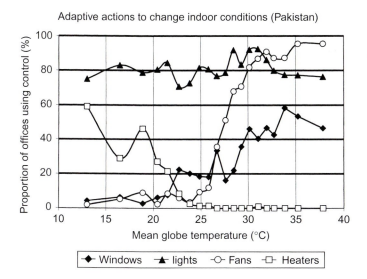

9.7.
Use of various controls to suit the environment to the subject in Pakistan.
(*Source*: Fergus Nicol)

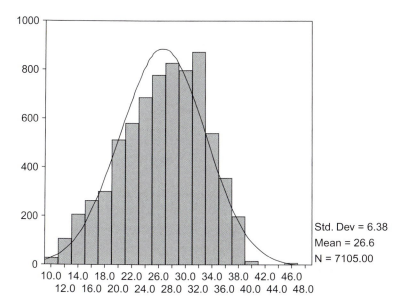

9.8.
Distribution of indoor temperatures in Pakistani buildings. Temperatures are largely constrained to the range of 20–32°C. The curve shows a normal distribution with the same mean and standard deviation.
(*Source*: Fergus Nicol)

evidence that fewer subjects are opening them at these high temperatures. Lighting is hardly affected by temperature – the use of blinds (which was not recorded) is often to exclude the solar heat and glare at high temperatures. Indoor temperatures are constrained to an 'acceptable zone' of 20–32°C for about 70% of the time (Figure 9.8).

A similar analysis of the results from the European SCATS survey[19] is shown in Figures 9.9–9.11. The results given apply only to buildings which were free-running at the time of the survey: many of the buildings were air conditioned and so the temperature of the building was not in the control of the occupants. Figure 9.11 suggests that there is more discomfort in European buildings but a range of indoor temperature from 19 to 27°C probably gives rise to little increase in discomfort. Figure 9.12 shows that the indoor temperature remains within these limits for over 80% of

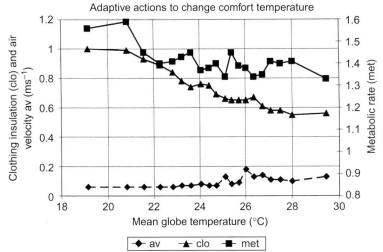

Adaptive actions to change comfort temperature

9.9.
Use of adaptive actions to suit the subject comfort temperature to the environment in Europe.
(*Source:* Fergus Nicol)

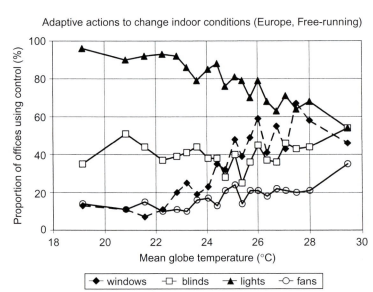

Adaptive actions to change indoor conditions (Europe, Free-running)

9.10.
Use of various controls to suit the indoor environment to the subject in free-running buildings in Europe.
(*Source:* Fergus Nicol)

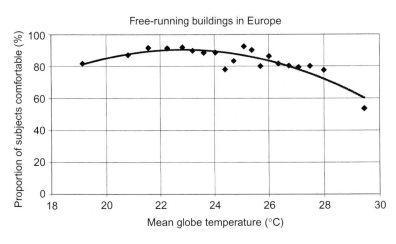

Free-running buildings in Europe

9.11.
Proportion of European subjects comfortable at different temperatures in free-running buildings. Separating the countries gives a higher level of comfort, but over a narrower band of temperatures.
(*Source*: Fergus Nicol)

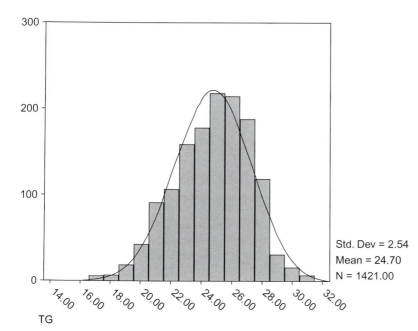

9.12.
Distribution of indoor temperatures in European buildings: the temperatures fit the range of comfort temperatures, falling mostly between 19 and 27°C. (*Source*: Fergus Nicol)

the time. Again much of the adaptive action takes place between these limits. The reason for the greater dissatisfaction in Europe is not clear, but there is a number of possible reasons, one being the international nature of the European survey population, another the more constrained work-force in Pakistan, where unemployment is high.

THE ADAPTABILITY OF BUILDINGS

How much of a challenge will climate change be to us? Surely we can adapt to the changes ahead with better buildings and technologies?

That humans are adaptable we know. They have settled in flimsy tents from the ice lands of the Arctic to the sand lands of the equator. They can live without machines in climates from 50°C below to 50°C above freezing point.

That buildings are adaptable we also know, and that people can live in the same tent, perhaps not comfortably, at the extremes is sure. But there is a fixed range of temperatures within which a building type will give adequate protection in extreme weather, flanked by thermal thresholds beyond which survival in such a building may not be assured. We also know that with clever design, building types can be modified and improved in one area to be safe in a significantly wider range of temperatures. Chapter 10 shows how this is the case in the Roman and the Baroque buildings of Naples. But there are climate thresholds beyond which buildings cease to be safe to occupy, with the vulnerability of the occupant depending on the form and fabric of the buildings, and the degree of its exposure to extreme climates.

The risk of not surviving in a particular building type and region will be largely dependent on the nature of that building and on how much the climate changes. Both are crucial in the challenge of designing buildings today in which people can be comfortable in 50 years' time.

The role of the building is three-fold:

- It should provide an indoor climate which is typical of local climate and culture.
- It should provide adaptive opportunities which mean that in extreme or unusual weather occupants can make themselves comfortable by such means as opening the window or switching on a fan, using technology that is familiar and effective.
- Occupants should also feel that they can change themselves (e.g. by clothing adjustments that are within the local social norms). This may be as much up to the building owner as to the building.

CONCLUSIONS

The implications of climate change for comfort and health have been presented. In the case of comfort, building occupants will be increasingly dependent on the opportunities that the social and physical characteristics of the building offer them to adapt to the changes. The effectiveness of these will depend on the ability of occupants to change their behaviour and attitude to the building as the changes occur.

The adaptive principle tells us that people will change themselves and their environment to achieve comfort, but this also assumes that their behaviour is appropriate in the changed circumstances. The tendency to open windows in hot weather, for instance, is only helpful if this has the effect of cooling the building; if the weather outside is very hot this may make things worse.

The temperature at which there is an increased risk of illness due to heat depends on the normal outdoor conditions. This suggests that similar cultural considerations apply to health as to comfort. Countries with a cold climate, such as Scandinavia, have learned to insulate their buildings against the cold. Likewise behaviour in hot climates is more appropriate to the heat. Some of this is related to learning appropriate behaviour (for instance by drinking more water) and some of it is in the provision of appropriate buildings, such as those that take advantage of thermal mass to reduce indoor temperature variability in temperate or desert climates.

For architects there are important lessons to be learned from the scientific analysis of buildings, and in the light of this the study of local vernacular buildings. For national and local authorities the study of buildings and the understanding of the effects of weather patterns in existing climates can give important clues for the provision of warnings and help to communities struggling with unexpected conditions.

The wrong conclusions can also follow; for instance an overreliance on the provision of mechanical systems to alleviate the more extreme conditions. These can add to the problem of climate change through the excessive use of fossil fuel energy. It is also becoming increasingly clear that the assumption that energy is always available can be misleading when extreme weather puts a strain on energy utilities.

For buildings to provide a safe and comfortable environment in the future they should:

- Provide the means for occupants to regulate the indoor climate.
- Avoid the use of mechanical cooling where possible.
- Avoid the need for large amounts of energy to provide comfortable interiors.

In addition, there is a need for:

- Education of building professionals on how to design buildings that meet these needs.

NOTES AND REFERENCES

1   R. Levins, R. Lewontin, The Dialectical Biologist, Harvard University Press, Cambridge, MA, 1985.

2   D.A. McIntyre, Indoor Climate, Applied Science Publishers, 1980.

3   K.C. Parsons, Human Thermal Environments, second ed., Blackwell Scientific, Oxford, 2003.

4   P.O. Fanger, Thermal Comfort, Danish Technical Press, Copenhagen, 1970.

5   M.A. Humphreys, Thermal comfort in the context of energy conservation, in: S. Roaf, M. Hancock (Eds.), Energy Efficient Buildings, Blackwell Scientific, Oxford, 1992.

6   R.J. deDear, G.S. Brager, Developing an adaptive model of thermal comfort and preference, ASHRAE Trans. 104 (1998) 145–167. See also ASHRAE Standard 55, in: Thermal Environment Conditions for Human Occupancy, American Society of Heating Refrigeration and Air Conditioning Engineers, Atlanta, GA, 2004; and R. Nevins, P. Gagge, The new ASHRAE comfort chart. ASHRAE J. 14 (1972) 41–43.

7   J.F. Nicol, M.A. Humphreys, Thermal comfort as part of a self-regulating system, Build. Res. Pract. (J CIB) 6 (3) (1973) 191–197.

8   M.A. Humphreys, Field studies of thermal comfort compared and applied, J. Inst. Heat. Ventilat. Eng. 44 (1976) 5–27.

9   J.F. Nicol, I. Raja, A. Allaudin, G.N. Jamy, Climatic variations in comfort temperatures: the Pakistan projects, Energy Build. 30 (1999) 261–279.

10 M.A. Humphreys, J.F. Nicol, Understanding the adaptive approach to thermal comfort, ASHRAE Tech. Data Bull.: Field Stud. Therm. Comf. Adapt. 14 (1998) 1–14.

11 See both M.A. Humphreys, Field studies of thermal comfort compared and applied. J. Heat. Ventilat. Eng. 44 (1976) 5–27; and M.A. Humphreys, Outdoor temperatures and comfort indoors. Build. Res. Pract. (J CIB) 6 (2) (1978) 92–105.

12 A. Auliciems, R. deDear, Air conditioning in Australia I: human thermal factors, Archit. Sci. Rev. 29 (1986) 67–75.

13 M.A. Humphreys, J.F. Nicol, Outdoor temperature and indoor thermal comfort: raising the precision of the relationship for the 1998 ASHRAE database of field studies, ASHRAE Trans. 206 (2000) 485–492.

14 A.J. Leaman, W.T. Bordass, Productivity in buildings: the 'killer' variables, in: Workplace Comfort Forum, London, 1997.

15 N.V. Baker, M.A. Standeven, A behavioural approach to thermal comfort assessment in naturally ventilated buildings, in: Proceedings CIBSE National Conference, Chartered Institute of Building Service Engineers, Eastbourne. London, 1995, pp. 76–84.

16 J.F. Nicol, K.J. McCartney, Assessing adaptive opportunities in buildings, in: Proceedings of the CIBSE National Conference, Chartered Institute of Building Service Engineers, London, 1999, pp. 219–229.

17 J.F. Nicol, M.R.B. Kessler, Perception of comfort in relation to weather and adaptive opportunities, ASHRAE Trans. 104 (1) (1998) 1005–1017.

18 J.F. Nicol, Time and thermal comfort, evidence from the field renewables: the energy for the 21st century, in: A. Sayigh (Ed.), Proceedings of the Fourth World Renewable Energy Congress, Brighton, Part 1, Pergamon Press, Oxford, 2000, pp. 477–482.

19 K.J. McCartney, J.F. Nicol, Developing an adaptive algorithm for Europe: results of the SCAT's project, Energy Build. 34 (2002) 623–635.

10 THE ADAPTIVE POTENTIAL OF TRADITIONAL BUILDINGS AND CITIES

INTRODUCTION

Traditional societies have for at least 10 000 years lived in adequate comfort in buildings and settlements in a wide range of climates, from the Tropics to the Arctic, without the use of mechanical cooling or the need for large amounts of energy. Until 120 years ago the only energy available to many societies to heat or cool their buildings was what they could find, mine, collect and carry home, be it dung, coal, wood, peat, water or ice. For 90% of the world's population this is still the case.

There were many ways in which buildings could be used and adapted to enable people to colonize the planet.[1] They could:

- Choose a different climate for a different season, by migrating between summer and winter lands in transhumant or nomadic migrations.
- Change the form and/or materials of the building to provide a range of indoor climates that keep out or in the heat or cold as is needed over the year.
- Choose a different part of a building or space for use at a particular time of day or season on planned intramural migrations around one building.
- Import heat or cold into the building in the form of firewood, coal (where available), ice, sun or warm or cool air.
- Evolve the buildings and lifestyles to accommodate climate change.

In the evolution of buildings people have always played a vital part in adapting themselves and the buildings around them to provide the comfort they seek. The question we must ask now is whether, in a rapidly changing climate, the majority of the world's population, who cannot afford mechanical cooling, can adapt their buildings fast and far enough to be able to remain in their traditional lands.

The last Ice Age occurred only just over 12 000 years ago, when the global temperature was around 3°C colder than today. Three degrees seems like a very small change to have such dramatic consequences on the global climate. After all, northern Europe was largely covered by ice

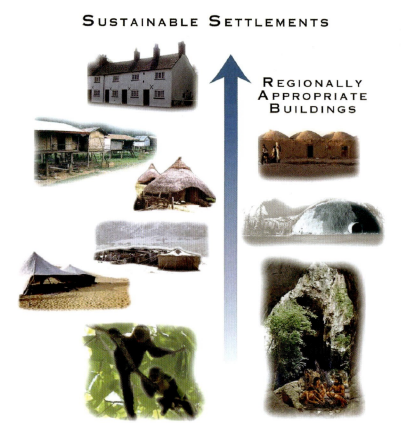

SUSTAINABLE SETTLEMENTS

REGIONALLY
APPROPRIATE
BUILDINGS

10.1.
Vernacular buildings have evolved over time to make the best use of local materials and conditions to provide adequate, and often luxurious, shelter for populations inhabiting even the most extreme climates of the world. *Source:* Sue Roaf, digitally produced by Claire Palmer.

caps then, and humans mostly lived in the lower temperate and equatorial regions of the world, in caves or in transient shelters that have left no archaeological record.

The earliest excavated settlements with buildings date from after this last Ice Age, and were found in the Zagros mountains in Luristan, western Iran, where at Gange Dareh, a settlement of small, oval mud-brick houses was carbon dated to around 7200 BC. Since then, great cities and civilizations have risen and fallen on many continents, leaving little trace of their original glory, invisible beneath the feet of passing generations.[2] All of these great civilizations were affected by the changing climates, and some, like the Mayans, may have disappeared because of years of droughts, or floods, in their heartlands. People, when their own lands become climate stressed, move, as we saw in Chapter 7. However, since the beginning of recorded history peoples have seasonally migrated to take advantage of beneficial climates and a diversity of feeding grounds.

SEASONAL MIGRATION: NOMADS

The basic reason for having buildings is to provide shelter against the climate. It is extraordinary how little of a building can suffice to provide adequate shelter in even the most arduous of climates. The tent, for instance, is used to house people from the deserts of Saudi Arabia to the tundra regions of the Arctic Circle. In fact, most areas in these regions are uninhabitable – cold

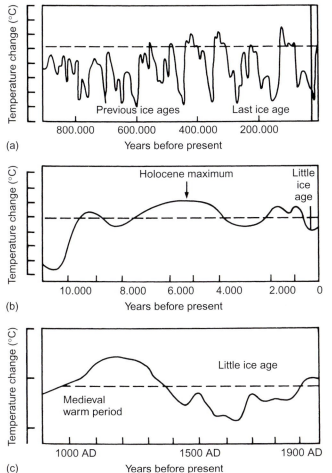

(a)

(b)

(c)

10.2.
Schematic diagrams of global temperature variations over the last (a) 1 000 000, (b) 10 000 and (c) 1000 years.
Source: Houghton, J.T., Jenkins, G.J. and Ephraums, J.J (eds) (1990) *Climate Change: The IPCC Scientific Assessment.* Cambridge: Cambridge University Press, p. 202.

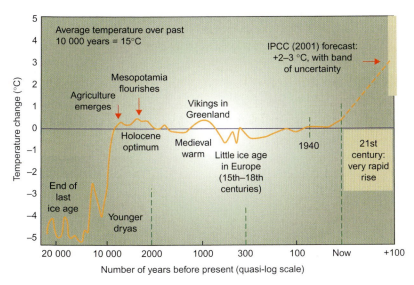

10.3.
Human societies have had long experience of naturally occurring climatic vicissitudes. The ancient Egyptians, Mesopotamians, Mayans and European populations (during the four centuries of the Little Ice Age) were all affected by nature's great climatic cycles. More acutely, disasters and disease outbreaks have occurred, often in response to the extremes of regional climatic cycles, such as the El Niño southern oscillation cycle.
Source: http://www.who.int/globalchange/climate/summary/en/.

or hot – at particular times of the year, when the tribes are elsewhere. Nomadic peoples often occupy peripheral lands that would not traditionally support communities all year around. Their secret is to travel in search of the heat, coolth and food they require to survive, a strategy also employed by the British upper classes who spent the summer in the country and the winter in towns in the 18th and 19th centuries, and in the early-twentieth century, winters in Nice or Capri.

The Beiranvand tribe of the Zagros Mountains, where permanent settlements perhaps began, is a case in point. The tribe migrates in spring from the hot plains of Mesopotamia near Dizful some 100 miles up into the cooler mountain plateau north of Khorramabad, where the wheat they have sown earlier will be ripening and the summer can be spent in cool comfort, weaving and celebrating weddings. This same mountain bowl could be metres deep in snow in winter, by which time the tribe will be safely back in their warm winter quarters on the low plains.[3]

The tent, or 'third skin', that divides the tribe from the elements is woven from black goat's wool. With the additional help of the clothes worn, quilted blankets and a small fire, the tent will be occupied in temperatures that range from below zero and up to the high forties centigrade. One tribal leader boasted that his tribe had a wonderful life because they were warm in winter and cool in summer when they drank iced water from their springs, while the town dwellers were cold in winter and hot in summer when they drank only warm water, which offered little or no relief from the heat.

In colder regions such as Mongolia or Central Asia, the yurt or the gher are tents made of much thicker materials, of beaten sheep's or goat's wool felt that is better able to withstand the biting wind and driving snow of those regions. The Sani live in animal skin tents. The form of their tents is also more compact, minimizing the surface area of the tent and so reducing heat loss from it. In colder regions tribal people also rely more on their second skin, clothes, for the extra warmth they need in winter. The Sani people of the Arctic not only occupy relatively small dwellings, rather of the proportion of the ice-built igloo, in which there is simply less air to heat, but like the Inuit, they wear full skin body suits lined with fur, even in the tent at night, in mid-winter.[4]

A tent is also eminently adaptable so that it can be closed down in winter to provide a snug, smaller, more windproof environment while in summer it can be expanded to provide little more than a well-ventilated shade awning. The actual form of the tent, the material and performance of its construction and the way in which it is used and adapted over a year are all indicators of the extent to which the people in a season and a region need to increase or decrease the difference between the indoor and outdoor climate. The more extreme the climate, the better the tent must be at keeping it out.

Adapting to new ecological niches in times of threat

The Beiranvand tribe has, over the past 70 years or so, been diversifying into a range of new 'ecological niches', as part of the settled populations of villages, towns and cities. This is part of a tribal strategy for survival in the face of a range of major changes in their habitat and society,[5] including those wrought by climate change and war.

ADAPTING THE FORM AND LIFESTYLES OF A PLACE

Buildings inherently occupy two main climates. They have access to the land and the sky. The earth has a steady, slow-moving temperature that gradually fluctuates over the year following

10.4.
The Beiranvand tribe on migration through the Zagros Mountains in spring, carrying their worldly goods on the backs of the pack animals, moving from the hot Mesopotamian plains to their cool high summer camp in the Zagros Mountains.
Source: Sue Roaf.

10.5.
The simple black tents that serve to keep the tribe warm in the winter snow and cool in the blistering summer heat.
Source: Sue Roaf.

the running mean of monthly temperature changes. The sky climate fluctuates from moment to moment at the whim of the weather and its passing clouds or showers or breezes, following generally the daytime and night-time temperatures dictated by latitude, altitude, continental location and the sun. Buildings have evolved to exploit both climates to a greater or lesser degree depending on location and the comfort requirements of populations.

Some of the greatest of all the passive buildings evolved from the great ancient empires of the Middle East. The mud-brick houses of the high desert city of Yazd, in central Iran, are some of the most sophisticated passive buildings in the world. Some, built of simple mud brick, are over 600 years old and still standing. They have on their roofs a very obvious sign of the great skills at climatic design in the form of the windcatchers that crown many of their settlements. In the densely inhabited towns and villages of this desert region these towers reach up above the roofs of buildings to catch the faster flowing upper air stream and channel it down to ventilate and cool the rooms below and their occupants. This they do, not only convectively by passing

SPRING	AUTUMN	TEMPERATURE		CAMP
		2080m.asl	PISH-E KUH	
AUG		36/20	37/19	SUMMER GARVESELLA CAMP
JULY		37/21	38/20	
JUNE		35/15	36/15	
		KHORAMABAD	30/14	30/14	TADJEREH
MAY		29/15	30/14	
		24/13	25/12	ANGUZ
APRIL		25/13	26/8	
MARCH				DADABAD
	SEPT	35/16	34/15	TRIBAL ROAD
		BADLANDS OF BALAGARIVEH		I L R A H
OCT		34/18	35/17	
NOV		25/13	26/12	PUSHT-E KUH
DEC		22/9	20/7	500m.asl	DELFIN WINTER CAMP
JAN		22/12	20/10	DIZFUL
FEB		24/13	22/11	
		PLAINS OF KHUZISTAN		

10.6.
Diagram showing estimated temperatures inside and outside the Beiranvand tents at different months, in the different locations, on the 200 mile annual migration along the '*il rah*', the tribal road. *Source:* Sue Roaf, digitized by Claire Palmer.

cooler air over the skins of building occupants, but also using radiant coolth. By taking the cold night air, and passing it over the heavy mud-brick walls of the rooms below, the warmth collected in those walls during the day is drawn out and dumped back to the sky, making the rooms below the windcatcher cooler during the day than the outdoor air temperature. In winter the free energy of the sun enters through the glass in the French doors of the south-facing winter room and is trapped inside, unable to escape the closed space, and this heat is stored in the massive mud-brick walls of the room, which re-radiate this free heat back into the room all through the night providing a remarkably steady indoor temperature. This collecting, storing and dumping of energy, heat, by the structure of the building itself is done 'passively', requiring no 'active' input of energy by building users at all.

By using the form of the building and understanding the available resources they can harvest the environmental yields available at a site of coolth and heat from the sun, the wind, the earth, water and plants. By doing so elegantly and efficiently the Yazdi could live an often luxurious life

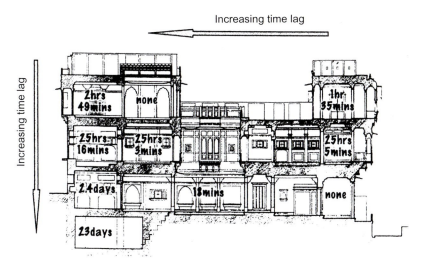

10.7.
The time required for indoor room temperatures to respond to outdoor temperature changes varies enormously according to the extent to which the room is coupled to the earth or the sky temperature.
Source: Jane Matthews.

in arid dry desert lands, but this was only possible through a symbiosis among building, people and climate.

In permanent settlements people do not have the choice to move to more comfortable climates, but they can practise a different form of migration, as they move around their own homes in search of optimal microclimates. Annually, the family migrates horizontally around a courtyard. In winter the family will spend most of the day and night in a south-facing glazed winter room overlooking a warm, sheltered courtyard. In summer, the living room shifts to the north-facing end of the court where no direct sunlight enters the living areas during the day and cross-ventilation may be provided by a windcatcher across the high shaded summer room.

Diurnally in summer the family migrates from the deep, cool basements, where they eat and rest in the hot afternoon. In the mornings and the evenings they sit in the fresh shaded courtyard and at night they climb onto the roof to sleep beneath the stars.[6]

The rooms on the roof are much more closely coupled to the fluctuating temperatures of the sky while those sunk into the ground are coupled in temperature to the stable earth temperature, with a far lower rate of change, responding to the changes in seasonal mean temperatures rather than the minute-to-minute temperature changes that can be experienced in the open rooms of the roof of the Havelli in India, for example (see Figure 10.7).

Some basements in traditional Asian houses can be as deep as 9 m below ground level, providing a stable cool climate even when temperatures soar above 50°C in heatwaves. Some believe that as the temperature changes our best means of survival in extreme climates will be to migrate farther and farther underground as the challenge of controlling high energy use in hot climates begins to bite.[7]

As climate change begins to take hold designers will have to look very closely at the available heat and cold in and around a site, and learn how to manage and move the resource from where it exists to where it is needed and how to protect inhabitants from it when it provides no benefit. The ability to understand the available heat, coolth and moisture resource, the need for it and

(a)

(b)

10.8.

(a) Axonometric showing the variation in temperatures around a Yazdi house, Iran, demonstrating the advantages of intramural migration in achieving a comfortable indoor environment on a hot summer afternoon. 1. Roof, where the family sleeps at night; 2. talar – summer room; 3. basement room with pool for summer afternoons; 4. windcatcher; 5. hot west-facing wall with no rooms; 6. living room; 7. guest courtyard; 8. store; 9. well; 10. water tank; 11. kitchen; 12. stable; 13. ganat – underground canal; 14. trellis; 15. garden pond; 16. deep basement for mid-summer afternoons. (*Source:* Sue Roaf in *Living with the Desert*[7]) (b) By day the windcatchers protrude above the general skyline bringing air down into the building and at night acting as a vent for the heat which has built up during the day. *Source:* Sue Roaf.

the means of passively managing and moving that resource lies at the heart of the skills of the twenty-first century designer of buildings and cities.

MOVING COOLTH: THE TWENTY-FIRST CENTURY CHALLENGE

In a warming world the ability to stay cool is vital. Today we associate coolth with switching on an air conditioner but 2000 years before this modern miracle existed people feasted on ice-cream in the scorching Assyrian summers.

Even in Yazd, if it became too hot in summer a boy could be sent out to get the family an iced sherbet, made with ice from one of the great ice-houses of the city. Just as heat and coolth are stored in the earth and the fabric of buildings, so it can be stored in ice, for years. A very well-kept secret today is that, since the dawn of recorded history, we have been able to store the cold of the winter months to reuse it in the heat of summer in the form of ice. Our forefathers cooled their drinks, food, brows and rooms by cutting the ice off ponds and rivers, or scraping it from mountain sides, in winter and storing it in underground ice-houses through the spring. The ice-houses were opened in summer to provide ice for the kitchen, the invalid, the ambassador's salon, the greenhouse and the dining table.[8]

Let them unseal the ice of Qatara. The Goddess, you and [your sister] Belassunna drink regularly, and make sure the ice is guarded[9]

wrote a provincial Governor of Northern Assyria in a letter to his wife, Iltani, in 1800 BC. This, the first written record we have of the storage of ice in an ice-house, comes to us from nearly 4000 years ago from the plains of northern Iraq.

Ice-houses were built on every continent on the planet, except Australia, and were used extensively by the Greeks, Romans, Chinese and even the Latin Americans. Ice was cut from the Andes and lowered on ropes by Indians who then transported it some 90 miles on mule back at a brisk trot (where roads permitted) to Lima, a city that used between 50 and 55 cwt a day (a hundredweight being about 50 kilos). Tschudi, travelling in 1840,[10] claimed that the trade was so important that its interruption might '*excite popular ferment*' and consequently '*in all revolutions*' care was taken to avoid commandeering the mules used in the transport of ice.

Right up until the 1980s there are reports of natural ice being stored in winter for use in the 'salad days' of summer. Ice-pits in the Kurdish mountains of northern Mesopotamia were still being filled in the 1980s, apparently because certain local tribal chiefs prefer to drink their Johnny Walker Black Label whisky with natural ice as it was said to improve its taste. If only the British troops in Iraq had known they might have been able to fly in Kurdish ice to cool their tents and the citizens of Basra in the scorching summer of 2003 when the inhabitants of that beleaguered city had no electricity to cool their homes in temperatures over 50°C, and rioting broke out in the streets, demonstrating, again, the political importance of coolth.

Perhaps we will see a re-emergence of the global ice trade, one of the most remarkable in history, which resulted, in large part, from the simple invention in 1827 on Lake Wenham near Boston, Massachusetts, of the ice-plough by Nathaniel Wyeth. The plough was drawn behind horses and enabled large quantities of blocks of clear, pure ice to be cut from the lakes, stored in huge above-ground ice-sheds and then transported by train to the coast where they were loaded onto wooden sailing barques and transported to Latin American, Europe, India and as far as China, where ice allegedly was sold for the price of its weight in silver.

Imported ice became most popular in Britain in the 1840s and the last delivery of imported ice to the Royal ice-houses was as late as 1936. Originally from Lake Wenham, this 'arctic crystal' was widely used in Britain, where those selling it boasted that they could get a delivery of Wenham ice to any house in Britain within 24 hours. It was gradually replaced by 'Wenham' ice from Norway, from where over 300 000 tons a year were imported by the 1890s. The reason why it was preferred to British ice was that it was clear and clean, whereas the British ice was often muddy and thus not pellucid.

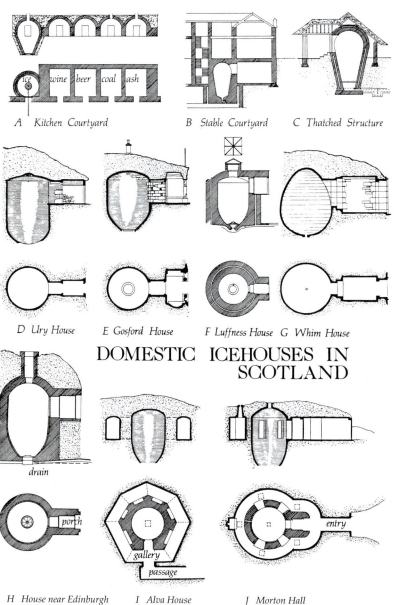

10.9.
Diagrams showing a range of different ice plans and sections in Britain.
Source: Beamon and Roaf,[8] p. 57.

10.10.
Ice harvesting in 1845 at Rockland Lake, New York State, USA, by the Knickerboker Ice Co.
Source: Library of Congress, Washington DC.

The end of the ice-houses of Britain

Three factors are cited as being responsible for end of the ice-houses, and the ice trade, in Britain:

- The First World War took the young men who harvested the ice off the land, and made the seas dangerous for those shipping it.
- The increasing use of the refrigerator obviated the need for the laborious process of ice collection and storage.
- The third reason for the demise of the ice-house was much less obvious. It was because the climate had changed. By the end of the nineteenth century the mean global temperature was rising steadily, heralding the end of the 'Little Ice Age'.

Four periods stand out in the recent history of world climates, as shown in Figure 10.2:

- A warm post-glacial period reaching a peak in 5000–3000 BC; a colder epoch culminating in 900–450 BC.
- A warm period around AD 100–1200, during the early part of which the Romans established extensive vineyards in Britain.
- The 'Little Ice Age', when the British climate was considerable colder, between 1480 and 1850. It was during this period that the ice-houses of Britain flourished. In the sixteenth century the Thames froze over on four recorded occasions, in the seventeenth century eight times, in the eighteenth century six times and in the nineteenth century four times. The last great freeze in Britain was 1878/79, when the Thames and other rivers froze over twice, much to the delight of many as the freezing of the river heralded the great ice fairs where bonfires were lit on the river and the gentlemen of Berwick on Tweed would traditionally celebrate by dining in a great tent on the river.
- The current warm period, in which the global temperature has been increasing since around 1870.

10.11.
Windcatchers on the skyline of Yazd.
Source: Sue Roaf.

The significant thermal factor for the ice-house was that although the mean increase in global temperature was relatively small, getting on for *c.*1°C between 1860 and 2008, this increase in temperature meant that over time there were no longer sufficient cold winters in Britain to regularly stock the ice-houses. So the key factor here for a particular 'thermal' technology is not how much warmer it gets, but whether the increase in temperature experienced crosses a critical threshold of performance for that particular technology.

THE IMPORTANCE OF THERMAL THRESHOLDS FOR THE SURVIVAL OF THERMAL TECHNOLOGIES

Because of climate change, the ice-house is now a climatically obsolete technology in Britain. Is this important lesson applicable to other forms of traditional buildings and technologies? What happens to a traditional house type that becomes climatically obsolete?

Let us investigate this a little further, because if thermal thresholds are important in the performance of, for instance, housing, will a warming climate in already extremely hot regions push indoor temperatures over thresholds of acceptability, and if so, what will be the consequences of that?

We saw this in Basra in the summer of 2003 when the buildings were too hot to occupy and riots broke out. We saw this in the summer of 2003 in France when some 15 000 people died unnecessarily because their buildings could no longer provide adequate protection from the summer heat, and an angry public caused the resignation of at least one minister in the government. What happens if whole regions become regularly too hot to occupy?

Windcatchers: a litmus paper technology

The windcatchers' function is to passively provide comfort in extremely hot desert regions. Many different forms of windcatcher are found in the Middle East. They work basically in three ways:

- They ventilate basements to remove smells from a heavily used area with few or no windows. In Baghdad, where the air temperature in summer gets up to 50°C and is too hot to provide 'cooling', windcatchers provide a source of conditioned, fresh air by passing it through high, narrow shafts before entering the basement.
- They cool people by convective cooling where the air temperature is below skin temperature at around 35°C, and evaporative cooling at higher temperatures where the humidity is not too high.
- They cool the internal structure of the house, the walls and floors at night, removing heat from the building, making it cooler internally during the day.

In the Yazd region, studied in the 1970s, the air temperatures on summer afternoons were over 45°C outside and 38°C in the ground floor rooms. Being downwind of orchards, groves and fields can reduce the mean outdoor air temperature by 2–5°C, and the towers here faced into the wind. Where the house was at the edge of the hot open desert the windcatchers faced away from the unpleasant wind and were used to draw the cooler air from the courtyard with its trees and planting through the summer rooms to exhaust it from the top of the tower. Small changes in the design of the building can have a large impact on its occupiability, even though only small temperature differences have resulted from the changes. This is because these change cross a critical threshold of performance for the occupants.

Below skin temperature (c.32–35°C) a person can be cooled by convection; above it, they cannot because the ambient air is then heating the body, not cooling it. Above this temperature the body can only be cooled by evaporation of sweat off the skin, which is why hot dry climates are more comfortable than hot wet ones because it is easy to lose moisture to the air when it is not saturated. So skin temperature represents a critical temperature range, or threshold.

Many of the villages of the Dasht-e-Kavir, the Great Central Desert, have no cool basements to resort to on the hottest afternoons and measured summer living room temperatures were up above 40°C in the 1970s, the upper end of physiological limits of survivability in this region.

With climate change, even relatively small increases in *mean* global or regional temperatures will push *absolute* maximum temperatures indoors up towards 50°C, and over the thermal threshold of habitable room temperatures. People will die, even those adapted to living in very high ambient temperatures.

If we look at the predicted mean global temperature increases over the next 50–100 years we can see predicted mean regional temperature increases in central Iran reaching 4–8°C. In this case it is inevitable that the already highly adapted traditional buildings of the region will cease to be occupiable at all without air conditioning. At what temperature does this occur? Such rural populations, like many others around the world facing the same predicament, cannot afford air conditioning, and will have only one option, to migrate to other habitats, that is, to change their ecological niches, to areas where either they:

- Do not need air conditioning to survive, or
- Can work to earn enough money to afford the air conditioning they need to survive.

However, in many less extreme climates of the world it may be possible to passively adapt the buildings and the lifestyles of the occupants to far harsher future climates. After all, the process of the evolution of buildings has been going on since those first small villages were built in the Zagros 9000 years ago.

HOW FAR CAN BUILDINGS EVOLVE? A CASE STUDY OF NAPLES

The extent to which buildings can and do evolve their ability to control the climate is well demonstrated in the buildings of the Naples region, looking at the evolution of buildings over two millennia to see whether they really did evolve to perform better in the bay area, famous for its architecture.

The Mediterranean is a region that will be badly affected by climate change. For this reason we looked at the palette of environmental strategies used in cooling a range of buildings through time in the region of Naples. These included the first century AD Villa Julio Polibio in Pompeii, the sixteenth century Pallazzo Gravina in Naples, the eighteenth century Villa Campolieto in Herculaneum, the twentieth century Modern Movement icon building of Villa Mala Parte on Capri, a 1950s' vernacular villa on Capri and the 1980s' 'bioclimatic' building of the Instituto Motori in Naples. What we found was that the simple Roman building evolved, over the following two millennia, into extremely sophisticated and efficient passive building types, but surprisingly the most sophisticated was that of the Baroque period in the late eighteenth century, since when the passive design skills of the master builders of the region appear to be in decline.

This case study highlights the interesting fact that vernacular architectures of the world appeared only to have discovered the climatic benefits of commonly building homes into the ground after AD 1000, be it in the Mediterranean or in the Middle East.

Villa Julio Polibio

The Villa Julio Polibio, Pompeii, was destroyed in AD 73 with the eruption of Mount Vesuvius. The house was built in several phases with four rows of rooms, around three courtyards: the semi-roofed impluvium, the kitchen court and the garden courtyard. The ground floor rooms were very open to these courts, while the first floor rooms were more sheltered from them.

The most southerly rows, right on the street, have seven small rooms around two larger double-height spaces with a stair leading up to a bank of rooms with south-facing windows onto the road. The passive solar gain here is far higher than in the rest of the house and these rooms onto the road would have been warmest in winter.

The second bank is centred around an open kitchen courtyard with a central pool and a double-height atrium open at the apex with an impluvium, or pool room, beneath to catch the rain. This pool was on a direct axis from the street to the inner garden, which could be left open for effective cross-ventilation over the surface of the pool to encourage evaporative cooling of the adjacent spaces. There is a second floor across this bank and in summer the upper rooms would have contained much of the incoming heat gain, leaving the rooms below to remain cool. The kitchen is on the west side of the building and would have been hotter in summer than the eastern atrium. The coolest rooms in the house were ground floor rooms facing north onto the garden.

The third bank includes the garden and a colonnaded walkway around it to the north, east and west. Note that the main route through the house is to the east of the building and not the west. A good climatic reason for this would be that in designing it this way the walls of the courtyard rooms are never heated and in particular the very hot western sun never touches and heats up the eastern wall. Plants may not have survived so well on an eastern wall as the western wall owing to the additional heat contained in the afternoon sun. The garden was well planted with six trees, including a fig, and a row of ornamental bushes against the west wall. The trees would have almost entirely shaded the courtyard, lending coolth to the house.

The openness of the ground floor rooms and the high thermal mass of the thick masonry walls would keep the temperature in many of the rooms at the mean temperature between maximum and minimum external air temperature. In the very hottest times of the year the inhabitants may well have splashed water on the floors of the more open spaces to cool them and retreated into a ground floor north-facing room and closed the door or hung curtains to keep out the heat of the daytime air temperatures while they took their afternoon nap. It is probable that the family migrated around the house using different rooms at different times of year and day to select the optimum temperatures available in the house.

Pallazzo Gravina

Pallazzo Gravina is a courtyard-style renaissance palace dating to the sixteenth century with introverted planning. In the building the resident family was separated from the servants in a system of complex vertical and horizontal planning in which three zones can be identified.

The double-height ground floor includes stables, guards and storage rooms, and steps down to cellars. The colonnaded walkway lends shade to the lower walls of the building and floor of part of the court. A single tree in the court harks back to former gardens. The piano nobile, or first floor, is where the family had its living and dining areas and bedrooms. The second floor housed the staff and more family, and the top floor housed store rooms and servants, linked to the ground floor by a separate stairwell not used by the family.

(a)

10.12.
(a) View, (b) plan and
(c) temperature readings taken
in March 1996 for the Villa Julio
Polibio in Pompeii.
Source: Sue Roaf and Mary
Hancock.

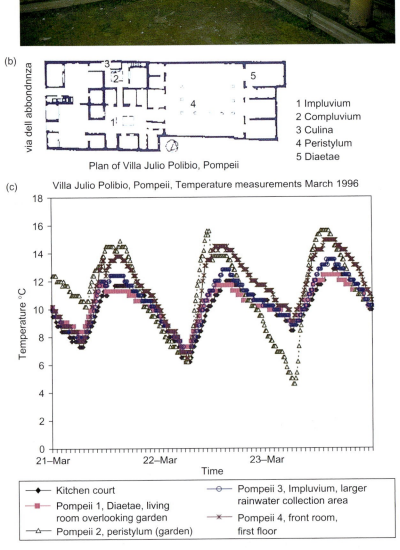

(b)

via dell abbondnnza

3
2
1
4
5

1 Impluvium
2 Compluvium
3 Culina
4 Peristylum
5 Diaetae

Plan of Villa Julio Polibio, Pompeii

(c)

Villa Julio Polibio, Pompeii, Temperature measurements March 1996

Temperature °C

Time

—◆— Kitchen court

—■— Pompeii 1, Diaetae, living
room overlooking garden

—△— Pompeii 2, peristylum (garden)

—○— Pompeii 3, Impluvium, larger
rainwater collection area

—✳— Pompeii 4, front room,
first floor

10.13.
View of the Pallazzo Gravina.
Source: Sue Roaf.

The whole building is constructed of tufa, or volcanic stone, which is highly aerated and provides excellent insulation and thermal mass. There are five key climatic strategies used in the building. Massive walls create interseasonal heat and coolth stores. Windowed galleria provided a thermal buffer for the family living rooms from the direct penetration of sun and hot air when closed in mid-summer into the family living room complexes, but enabled them to be nocturnally ventilated. Windows were carefully sized to prevent excessive solar gain. A complex ventilation system dependent on two stack systems in the staircases created the churn to drive cross-ventilation in the interconnected chambers, particularly in the main north-facing summer rooms on the south of the building facing the street. In winter the double-depth winter living rooms are not so connected. The stack would have drawn cool air from the colonnaded and planted courtyard below during the day, being driven by temperature difference up through the stack, and at night this churn would have been enhanced by the warmer air rising from the courtyard floor.

Villa Campolieto

This villa in Herculaneum, built between 1755 and 1775, is laid out in a square with the four corner blocks of apartments divided on the piano nobile, on the third floor, by a huge cross axis of double-height rooms capped by a large raised rotunda in the centre with windows on four sides creating a venturi tower. Beneath the ground floor are two further basement levels including water cisterns and an ice storage room. This villa has far larger windows than the previous buildings and the family quarters include south-, west- and north-facing living and dining rooms and bedrooms on the north of the building. The walls are massive, providing interseasonal heat and coolth storage capacity, with a plastered tufa construction. Daylight levels are high in the living areas and for summer cooling the ventilation system would have created perfect thermal comfort. The house is situated about half a mile from the sea.

The genius of this building is its ventilation systems. In warm weather the whole building could be opened up to catch the wind. In very hot weather the external doors and windows could be and the venturi tower of the rotunda above the stairway would draw cooler air up from the basements through the transverse ventilation system. In extreme heat ice from the ice store could have been brought up in boxes to cool individual rooms. In conditions of dire heat basement living areas would have remained cool and we have evidence of their use in summer. It should also be noted that the gardens have been landscaped to enhance coolth with the use of shade, ponds, fountains and a sunken date grove.

Each corner block has its own independent cross, transverse and stack-driven systems based around vertical stairways with venturi towers above each. These operate independently of the main rooms of the piano nobile of which the three main rooms, the drawing room, the dining room and the music room, have double-height ceilings with a buffer void above to prevent direct penetration of heat into them via the roof. The villa also includes a hidden system of ducts, vents and grills drawing cool air into rooms and expelling warm air from them. The success of the ventilation is that the shore-side location precluded the need for lateral buffering of spaces against the heat, as we found in the previous two buildings. This strongly suggests the movement around the building at different times of day.

The importance of thermal mass, or heavy-weight materials in buildings, increases in 'passive cooling systems', in which the design of the building itself, rather than the machines in it, is used to create acceptable internal climates. In a well-designed, heavy-weight building the indoor temperature can track the mean of the outdoor temperatures, levelling the diurnal, and even the monthly, swings in temperature to provide safer indoor climates in extreme weather.[11]

Villa Mala Parte

Built in the 1930s on a rock jutting out into the sea from the southern coast of Capri Island, this building is vertically zoned. The ground floor comprises kitchens and store rooms. The first floor has bedrooms and servants' quarters and the second floor houses the living and dining rooms and the main living apartment. The construction is fairly massive, with 600 mm wide walls of brick. The roof is of uninsulated concrete so potentially forming a heat source. In the lower rooms the central corridor restricts the effectiveness of the cross-ventilation and the rooms have limited window openings so preventing excessive solar gain. These remain cool. The upper floor has large areas of unshaded glass, which lead to high solar gain levels in summer. They slide open to provide direct cross-ventilation, but not easily, and the very exposed site means that winds can get very strong around the house. On sunny afternoons with a strong cold wind the comfort levels of occupants on this floor would be interesting to record. High-level open vents just under the concrete ceiling were designed, presumably, to remove heat from and ventilate the room in such conditions. In fact, the building owner's favourite room was the first floor east-facing study with a Kakkleoven for winter warmth and he preferred a first floor bedroom to sleeping in the main bedroom apartment. The windows whistle, apparently.

Villa Ranzo

Built by the Ranzo family in the mid-1950s, this typical neovernacular villa is located on the cool side of Capri in the shade of the central land mass so in summer it is cool but in winter the building becomes very cold. The basement rooms are stores and servants' quarters, the first floor the living and kitchen area, and the top floor has five bedrooms and four bathrooms. Direct cross-ventilation and lateral ventilation via windows and French doors is used in all main rooms and

(a)

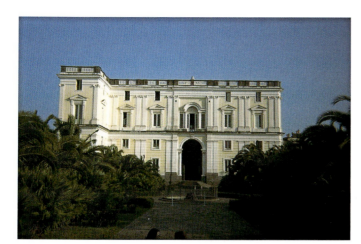

10.14.
Villa Campolieto: (a) view and (b) internal temperature readings taken in March 1996.
Source: Sue Roaf and Mary Hancock.

(b)

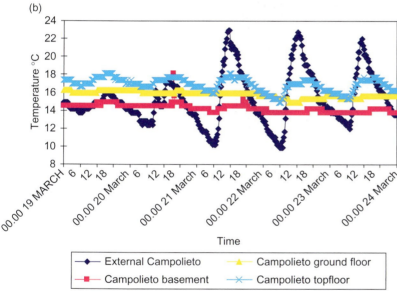

on the west-facing walls a veranda at first floor level shades ground floor rooms. The walls are of massive stone and render construction, and the roof is of concrete. The stairwell provides an effective stack moving air between floors.

Instituto Motori

Completed in 1992, the modern headquarters of this research institute is a well-publicized modern bioclimatic building. Covering over 6900 m^2 and housing a range of functions including offices, a library, a conference hall, a café, a museum and laboratories, the building is rectangular on a northeast to southwest axis. The basement level has a store and conference hall, and the first, second and third floors consist of offices and laboratories opening off a central hall open in the centre for three floors, above which is the museum on the roof. The flanking offices block off light from the central circulation zone and we found that all laboratories and offices typically had their doors shut. The windows of the building are 'smart', being reversible

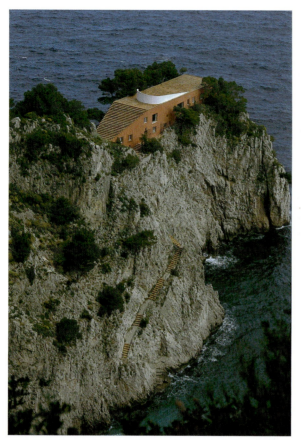

10.15.
(a) Exterior and (b) interior views
of Villa Mala Parte, Capri.
Source: Sue Roaf.

(b)

10.16.
View of Villa Ranzo, Capri.
Source: Sue Roaf.

so that the timber louvres can be put on the outside of the building, but many were broken and their ventilation value in a closed office was limited. The lightweight structure holds little thermal storage potential and provides poor insulation against the heat and cold. All thermal storage capacity would be held in the concrete floors, which were fairly universally carpeted, so reducing their effectiveness. There are no thermal buffering zones against the heat either horizontally or vertically, and no apparent zoning of activities according to location in the building in relation to its micro-climate.

Buildings of Naples: summary

In Chapter 9 we introduced the idea that buildings with 'adaptive opportunities' are more likely to be comfortable because the occupants are able to adjust the indoor climate to suit themselves. Table 10.1 shows that, despite the best intentions of the designers, the modern 'bioclimatic' building has the fewest passive opportunities for modifying indoor climate, followed by the Modern Movement icon building of the Villa Mala Parte. The traditional buildings employed a wide range of effective adaptive strategies to raise or lower indoor temperatures without using

10.17.
View of Instituto Motori, Naples.
Source: Sue Roaf.

fossil fuel energy. The temperature records show that while the indoor climate in the Roman house tracked the outdoor climate, in the Rococo Baroque Villa of Campolieto built in the eighteenth century the indoor climate, using a wide range of passive techniques, could, in places, be decoupled from the outdoor climate, potentially providing a cool environment even in the scorching heat of the future.

CONCLUSIONS

We have much to learn from the buildings and technologies of the past, and from the lifestyles and adaptive behaviour and opportunities created by their occupants. In times of climate stress people will increasingly resort to a wide range of survival strategies. They will:

- Migrate away from regions under climate stress if it threatens their health and ability to remain safe and comfortable.
- Build social resilience extending the ecological niches occupied by that group.
- Become adept at managing their indoor, outdoor and underground micro-climates, and range of adaptive opportunities to provide affordable comfort at different times of day and year.
- Migrate around the spaces in buildings and cities to take advantage of the potential comfort benefits of different areas in their territory.
- Evolve their buildings and industries to provide and take advantage of a changing range of adaptive opportunities to ameliorate indoor and adjacent outdoor micro-climates to combat increasingly extreme weather.
- Develop conscious processes to rapidly and passively evolve their buildings in non-intuitive ways, replacing the traditional, too slow, intuitive evolution processes.
- Learn again to look at buildings as sources and sinks of energy, and the available yields of and the opportunities for movement of heat and coolth around buildings.

Table 10.1. Range of adaptive opportunities available to building users to ameliorate their own internal climate using passive and active systems

Design strategy	Pom	Grav	Cam	MP	Ran	Mot
Cold site					1	
Cool site				1		
Solar orientation	1	1	1			
Sea breezes			1	1	1	
Summer use only			1		1	
Morning/afternoon use	1	1	1		1	
Summer/winter rooms	1	1	1			
Horizontal buffer zones	1	1	1		1	
Vertical buffer zones	1	1	1			
Verandahs/colonnades	1	1	1		1	
Planting	1	1	1		1	
Pools/evaporation	1		1			
Earth sheltering		1	1	1	1	1
Thermal mass	1	1	1	1	1	
Interseasonal storage		1	1		1	
Basement coolth use		1	1	1	1	
Hypercausts	1					
Shaded from west sun	1			1		
Cross-ventilation	1	1	1	1		
Stack cooling		1	1			
Lateral ventilation	1	1	1	1		
Venturi ventilation			1			
Ventilation ducts			1	1		
Door ventilation control	1	1	1		1	
Stack warming	1	1	1			
Insulated roof			1			1
False ceiling insulation			1			1
External shade	1				1	1
High rooms	1	1	1		1	
Small windows	1	1				1
Smart windows						1
Shutters				1	1	
Low-energy lighting	1	1	1		1	
Rainwater storage	1	1	1	1	1	
Ice for cooling			1			
Total	20	20	27	11	17	6

Source: Roaf and Handcock (1998).[12]
Pom: Pompeii; Grav: Gravina; Cam: Campolieto; MP: Mala Parte; Ran: Ranzo; Mot: Motori.

Unfortunately, as with the modern offices of Naples, exactly the opposite is happening as cheap fossil fuel energy and increasingly deskilled designers have unthinkingly drifted into a generation of modern buildings that are not adapted for the climates they occupy, let alone future climates; they are too often incapable of being affordably adapted for our rapidly changing climate and soaring energy prices. In Chapter 11 we look at some of the problems with these increasingly passé 'modern' buildings.

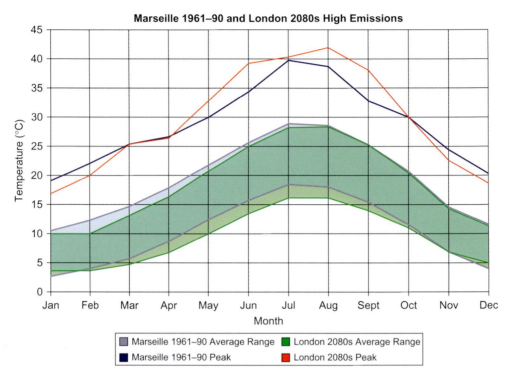

Marseille 1961–90 and London 2080s High Emissions

Legend:
- Marseille 1961–90 Average Range
- London 2080s Average Range
- Marseille 1961–90 Peak
- London 2080s Peak

10.18.

We know enough about future climates to be able to modify our designs today to accommodate them. The temperature in London in the 2080s is predicted to be very like that in Marseille today. Just as it is perfectly possible to stay comfortable in such Mediterranean climates today in good passive buildings so should be designing such buildings in London today if we want them to retain their value in a changing climate.

Source: Hacker, J. (2005) *Beating the Heat.* Oxford: UK Climate Impacts Programme.

NOTES AND REFERENCES

1   For a good simple outline of adaptive human responses see <http://www.bio.usyd.edu.au/summer/Human/HA_lectures/HA_lect/LECTURE2.pdf>.

2   For a good source book on the evolution of the early settlements and empires in Mesopotamia, the cradle of civilization. see M. Roaf, Cultural Atlas of Mesopotamia, Andromeda, Oxford, 1990.

3   S. Roaf, A Study of the Architecture of the Black Tents of the Lurs. Technical Thesis for the Architectural Association Part II exam, 1979.

4   For the best book available on the vernacular buildings, see P. Oliver (Ed.), Encyclopaedia of Vernacular Architecture of the World, in three volumes. Cambridge University Press, Cambridge, 1997.

5   J. Black-Michaud, Sheep and Land. The Economics of Power in a Tribal Society, Cambridge University Press, Cambridge, 1986 and Paris: Maison des Sciences de l'Homme.

6   S. Roaf, The Windcatchers of Yazd. PhD thesis, Oxford Polytechnic, 1989, For a further outline of the processes involved see S. Roaf, M. Fuentes, S. Thomas, Ecohouse2: A Design Guide, Architectural Press, Oxford, 2003.

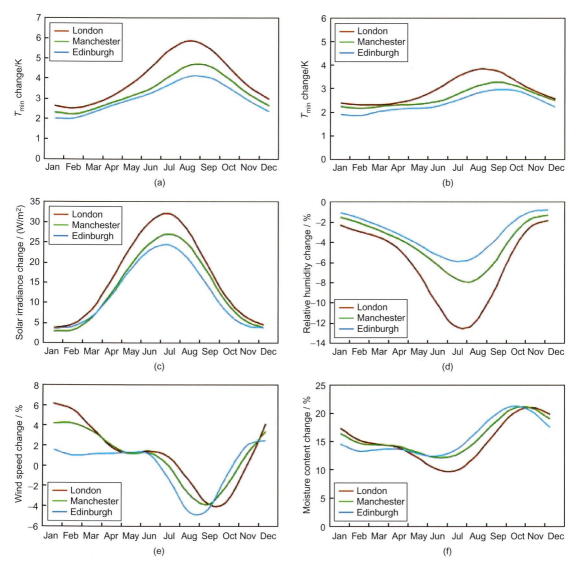

10.19.
The monthly changes in maximum and minimum temperatures, solar irradiation and wind speed, relative humidity and moisture content in the climates of London, Manchester and Edinburgh by the 2080s for Business as Usual model.
Source: Hacker, J. (2005) *CIBSE TM36. Climate Change and the Indoor Environment: Impacts and Adaptation.* London: Chartered Institution of Building Services Engineers.

7   Two excellent papers that touch on this challenge for Kuwait are: A. Al-Temeemi, D. Harris, A guideline for assessing the suitability of earth-sheltered mass-housing in hot–arid climates. Energy and Buildings, 36 (2004) 251–260; and A. Al-Mumin, O. Khattab, G. Sridhar, Occupants' behavior and activity patterns influencing the energy consumption in the Kuwaiti residences. Energy and Buildings, 35 (2003) 549–559.

8   For a complete history of the ice-houses and ice trade of the world see S. Beamon, S. Roaf, The Ice-Houses of Britain, Routledge, London, 1990, and for the desert buildings of the

Central Persian Desert see E. Beazley, M. Harverson (Eds.), Living with the Desert, Aris and Philips, Warminster, 1982.

9   S. Page, Ice, offerings and deities in the Old Babylonian texts from Tell el-Rimah, Actes de la XV11e, Rencontre d'Assylriologie (1969) Brussels, p. 181.

10   J.J. Tschudi, Travels in Peru during the Years 1838–1842 (1847) London, pp. 136–137.

11   Baruch Givoni, the doyen of passive design, presents thresholds for the operation of different types of such passive cooling systems. For the following ventilation strategies: comfort ventilation: ventilation to produce immediate human comfort, mainly during the day, and nocturnal convective cooling: ventilation to cool the thermal mass of building during the night in order to improve comfort during the day, the threshold value of the maximum ambient air temperature for the viability of comfort ventilation he gives as 28–32°C at indoor air speeds of 1.5–2.0 m/s, depending on the comfort requirements. This is based on the observation that the indoor air temperature approaches the outdoor air temperature as the ventilation rate increases. For comparison, the upper limit of the extended ASHRAE comfort zone (see Chapter 9) is 28°C at 0.8 m/s air speed. In offices, or similar environments, a combination of higher internal loads and restrictive expectations concerning dress would produce a reduction in the threshold that depends on the particular situation but which may amount to several degrees centigrade.

Givoni's rule of thumb for nocturnal convective cooling is that the indoor maximum temperature is less than the outdoor maximum temperature by nearly half the diurnal range in outdoor temperature, providing the envelope and internal gains are modest and the thermal capacity is high. Nocturnal convective cooling is applicable if the maximum ambient temperature is too high for comfort ventilation and the diurnal range is sufficiently large to bring the indoor maximum temperature down into the comfort range. For example, if the minimum outdoor temperature is 24°C, the threshold value of the maximum outdoor temperature is 40°C if the indoor temperature is not to exceed 32°C.

If building occupants retreat to a deep basement they can occupy a temperature that may be closer to the mean of the annual mean maximum and minimum temperatures providing an even safer temperature in extreme weather. The indoor temperatures in passive buildings are then determined primarily by the outdoor temperatures, the form and fabric of the building and the way it is used, and it is possible, therefore, to define threshold values for the outdoor temperatures, in relation to what passive systems would be effective in current and future climates for different regions. In buildings where the loads are significant compared to the heat that can be stored in the thermal mass with the available temperature swings, the threshold for viability depends on the loads and the effective thermal mass as well as the outdoor temperatures and may require complex, validated, simulation to predict performance in a range of climates.

See Givoni, B. (1991) Performance and applicability of passive and low-energy cooling systems. Energy and Buildings, 17, 177–99, and a range of his other books on the subject. The importance of the 'adaptation' of local populations in such calculations is clarified in Chapter 9 of the present text.

12   S. Roaf, P. Haves, J. Orr, Climate change and passive cooling in Europe. Proceedings of PLEA Conference, James & James Science, Lisbon, 1998, 463–436. S. Roaf, M. Handcock, Future-proofing buildings against climate change using traditional buildings technologies in the Mediterranean region. Proceedings of the Eurosolar Conference, Slovenia, PortoRos, 1998.

11 THE FAILURE OF 'MODERN BUILDINGS'

INTRODUCTION

At the heart of the global economic crash of 2008 lay a black hole of worthless assets into which the markets imploded. The leading 'real' asset owned by many financial institutions, along with gold, is buildings. Yet the long-term value of those buildings was never really questioned. Banks and insurance companies unquestioningly assumed a face value of these investments based on the short-term costs of selling and buying them on a rising bull market.

Well into 2007 markets were awash with cheap money apparently indiscriminately available to individuals and institutions alike to keep buying, selling, leasing and renting these assets for whatever they could get for them or get them for, in line with the market models and drivers taught relentlessly in business schools around the world. Buildings ceased to be seen as much-loved homes or well-liked and respected foundation stones for durable businesses, but rather as commodities that could be traded on eventually for profit.

The problem was that too little attention was paid to the durability of them as investments or their actual shelf-lives. *Durabilité* is the French term for sustainability and it is a very good word. Investors too often had a disastrously unrealistic understanding of the economic sustainability of the assets they were happy to pay so much money for. Very often it was not their own money and frequently decision-making individuals would be financially rewarded for the value of the portfolios they were trading in and were not accountable for losses incurred as a result of such decisions. Sound familiar? So what is the problem? The problem is that many of these buildings are 'investment nightmares'.

In the 2003 manuscript for the first edition of this book, published in early 2005, the poor quality of many modern buildings was pointed out. Many modern office blocks are built without proper walls, as described in the Building Regulations. These require that walls should have a 'transmittance' to heat (or U-value) of around 0.25. Many of the glass-box buildings in cities have double-glazed envelopes with 10 times that U-value. Increasingly in such buildings the bulk of the construction costs are used not on the fabric of the building, its walls, floors, windows, mass and insulation to protect and shelter occupants, but on machines to deal with the problem of overheating and cooling created by putting people into buildings that are little more than glass boxes with fixed windows. The result is buildings that are hugely costly to heat and cool, the machines have to be replaced every 10 or 20 years and very often such buildings do not provide high levels of comfort or breed 'affection' amongst their occupants. One of the common characteristics of 'sick buildings' which make occupants literally feel ill is these complex mechanical systems. People often become fond of buildings, leading to a 'forgiveness factor' that puts people in sympathy with their building and the work they do in it. The opposite can also be true as people dread going to work in sick or isolating buildings. Fewer and fewer modern buildings can claim such affection. Chronic problems in the indoor air quality have been reported in many of the new generation of Private Finance Initiative (PFI) schools, academies and hospitals, with the most high-profile event being the walk-out of teaching staff from new London academies owing to soaring indoor temperatures in April 2007. One solution often used is to throw more money into the air conditioning systems, but therein lies another problem, soaring energy prices.

Many of us ask ourselves, how do the lightweight glass-box buildings get through Building Regulations? Are local authority Building Control officers universally convinced by complex calculations presented by top engineering firms that ostensibly demonstrated that the buildings complied with the spirit of the regulations, if not the letter of its law? But worse than the questionable compliance issue is that of how in the world these buildings came to be seen as desirable or fashionable or even sensible. The situation is made clearer when we see that this building type is not only espoused by many fashionable architectural designers but also, with a stroke of genius, sold to investors as 'leading edge green buildings'. The bottom line is that many of these buildings are 'junk buildings', just like the junk bonds in which so many of our pensions are invested. They risk rapidly becoming worthless in an evolving market where soaring energy prices and tighter economic conditions ensure that *all* organizations are finding it increasingly difficult to cover staff, mortgage, rent or lease costs, and soaring energy costs as well.

Gensler, a leading international architectural firm, clearly detailed this problem in a seminal report called 'Faulty Towers' in 2005.[1] In it the managing principal of the London office, Chris Johnson, pointed out that:

Property fund managers are effectively sitting on an *investment timebomb*. The introduction of energy performance certificates will shorten the lifespan of commercial buildings constructed before the new regulations, and we expect the capital value of inefficient buildings to fall as a result.

The report also reveals that nearly three-quarters (72%) of company property directors believe that business is picking up the bill for badly designed, inefficient buildings and more than a quarter (26%) state that bad office stock is actually damaging UK productivity. What the chronic failure of the Building Regulations systems has meant is that many of the new buildings built after the new regulations were introduced perform even worse than those before them. To make the point further, the insurance industry charges a premium on homes built after 1971 because they are more likely to fail than those built before that date. So how did the building industry come to this pass? To start with, how did the idea of modern buildings arise?

In this chapter we deal briefly with the history of the emergency of high-energy 'modern' buildings, and the air conditioning machines with which they symbiotically co-evolved. The following chapter on 'tall buildings' deals with the extraordinary condition that drives people to build the 'tallest building' in a city, or the world, and the hubris behind it. In Chapter 13 we cover the impact of cheap energy on the built environment and explain why 'the party is over', covering issues of growing energy scarcity and the failures of supply that are beginning to inform and to drive the design paradigms. In Chapter 15 the issues of the vested interests in the current construction models are covered in terms of the players in the built environment who each have a hand in shaping the 'investment timebombs' that are proving so damaging to many UK businesses and families alike. In Chapter 16 we revisit the challenge of adapting our built environment for comfortable survival in the twenty-first century and offer some solutions to building designers, owners, regulators and investors alike on how they may be able to future-proof their lives against the twin challenges of climate change and fossil fuel depletion. At the heart of the building changes that have shaped the predicament we are in today is the miracle of air conditioning and emergence of the dream of energy 'too cheap to meter'.

MODERN BUILDINGS

Le Corbusier, arguably the greatest of the Modern Movement architects, published his influential book *Vers une Architecture* in 1928.[2] In this he expounds his theories of a new spirit, for traditional architecture that was 'stifled by custom'. In his writings in search of '*l'esthétique de la vie moderne*', the modern aesthetic, he had already developed in 1926 his ideas based on what would become known as 'The Five Points Towards a New Architecture':

1. The piloti is elevating the mass off the ground. This was seen by Corbusier as freeing up leisure space at ground level, but it has the side effect of decoupling buildings from the influence of stable ground temperatures.
2. The free plan, achieved through the separation of the load-bearing columns from the walls subdividing the space (creating an architecture of planes from which the thin tight-skinned building evolved).
3. The free façade, the corollary of the free plan in the vertical plane (signalling the demise of walls and windows in buildings).
4. The long horizontal sliding window (eliminating centuries of the evolution of the complex ventilation and shading strategies that are central to the effective performance of vernacular buildings in different climates).
5. The roof garden, restoring the area of ground covered by the house (the elimination of gardens for households, cutting the link between man and nature and creating a soulless rejecting language for streets, where the street becomes nothing more than an often hostile transport route cut off completely from the lives of those within the adjacent buildings).

Of those five points only the roof garden can improve the thermal performance of a building in some, notably temperate, climates. To raise a building off the ground is to decouple it from the stable temperatures of the ground and expose the sixth face of the building to the unstable climate of the air. This may be beneficial in the moderate temperatures of the tropics but can have devastating effects on the energy demand of a building in temperate, cold or hot climates and at various times of year.

The deep plan building makes mechanical air conditioning a necessity as only relatively shallow plan buildings can be naturally ventilated. The free façade has turned traditionally robust walls with sensibly sized windows into sheets of glass or thin cladding, which increase the vulnerability of the building occupants to any external climate by an order of magnitude, and impose huge energy penalties onto building owners as they try to stabilize internal climates into a controlled 'comfort' zone. The long horizontal sliding window, as we saw in Villa Mala Parte, almost eliminates any easily usable connection between the inside and outside climates and has led to the virtual elimination of usable windows from modern buildings, be it houses or offices. Yet these tenets by Le Corbusier continue to inspire generations of young and old architects who appear never to have questioned their applicability to the very different societal or environmental conditions of the late twentieth, let alone the twenty-first, century.

In *Vers une Architecture*, Le Corbusier wanted to make it clear why

'the engineer's aesthetic' is far more successful than architecture. Engineering takes advantage of the latest and most innovative building types, technologies and construction systems, based on mass-production, standardization and industrialization.

He omitted to say 'cheap energy' but it is implied. Architecture in the twentieth century, if it wanted to embrace the 'new spirit', needed to embrace these modern methods of technology and progress away from the static 'safe' traditional architecture. Le Corbusier encouraged economy (minimalism) and mechanical precision in architecture, as this was the driving force in the success of engineering.[3] Unfortunately, the engineer's triumph here tolled the death knell of much traditional climate design wisdom. Le Corbusier himself acknowledged the increased 'risk' of modern buildings, referring to traditional buildings as 'safer'. The extent to which he recognized that they increased the vulnerability of occupants to the external climate is not clear; however, he did not use his European design models when he built in Chandigarh in India, in Buenos Aires or in other colonial buildings he designed.

His famous statement that 'a house is a machine for living in' he justified by stating that a house requires efficiency, economy, simplicity, elegance and, most of all, a form that is clear with regard to the function. He skirts any mention of the need for comfort in all seasons, a sense of safety, quietness, and low energy and maintenance bills. His idea of economy and simplicity related to his demonstrated search for a 'minimalistic appearance' inside and out, rather than to efficient heating and cooling systems and structures. It was probably the limitations of previous building technology and the 'liberating' use of reinforced concrete which made access to light the overriding concern of much early modern architecture. Unfortunately, this romance with concrete meant that the buildings were riddled with cold bridges and the love of light encouraged overglazed façades. If the architects' grasp on the physics of buildings had been greater then perhaps twentieth century architecture would have been different. The power of Le Corbusier's vision of the 'modern' building is still in evidence at the Royal Institute of British Architects' (RIBA's) major million pound exhibition for the Liverpool City of Culture celebrations in 2008, at which the emphasis was on the iconic designers of the Modern Movement, who have little relevance to the way we solve the enormous challenges we face today of providing the radical buildings we will need in the low carbon economies of the very near future.

The Modern Movement architects really came into their own after the Second World War with the post-war rebuilding programme, the scale of which exceeded anything built before, as whole cities were 'replanned' and rolled out. Increasing numbers of buildings were built using new methods of construction and materials, which were often innovative, untried and apparently unquestioned. Because modern construction methods enable very rapid and large-scale projects, the impact on our cities was immediate and often devastating as the old hearts of cities were torn out and replaced by concrete and steel prefabricated structures, of which many have already been demolished, less than 40 or 50 years after they were built.

Le Corbusier dreamed that he could build anywhere in the world with '*une respiration exacte*', that is to say a controlled indoor climate, air conditioning with precise controls. But he and his co-workers did not always have the luxury of being able to air condition their buildings and their lack of understanding of many of the basic principles is evident in buildings such as those in Chandigarh, in India where extensive shading and natural ventilation were the norm. The growth of the 'modern building' paradigm with both commercial and residential buildings with lightweight partitions and glass cladding was initially dogged by overheating,[4] but was eventually made possible only because of the advent of air conditioning, fuelled by cheap fossil fuel energy, and based, until perhaps now, on the belief in the availability of limitless energy to power the machines that keep the buildings going. It also meant that buildings could be constructed at maximum speed and for minimum cost, which suited the post-war building boom.

Rod Hackney wrote of his homecoming to Manchester in 1968:

It was a changed Britain to which I returned: in just four years many towns and cities had been transformed. The guts had been torn out of them, and new buildings had been carried out at an alarming rate … Whole areas were unrecognisable – acres of terraces had been razed and replaced by new tower block estates. In the city centres, where I remembered rows of individual, small old shops, there was now a concrete slab precinct. All sense of scale and perspective had been lost.

It was not only the look of these places that had changed. People's attitudes had too. They had begun to protest against their new homes and environments. In Denmark I had grown used to informed dialogue between the public, the architects and the state. In Britain there were two simultaneous monologues – the public in opposition to official policy. Faith in the state machine had been badly shaken.[5]

In Manchester today, where the concrete modernist tower blocks of the Hulme development stood in 1968, which have been subsequently torn down and re-replaced by terraced streets of housing, there rises a new generation of speculative residential towers. These privately developed apartment blocks, often empty during the property slump of 2007–2008, have several differences from the Hulme blocks. Whereas the 1960s' tower blocks were built to last forever as first class social housing built by idealists in the city council, the modern towers are cheap investment vehicles and many, to be at all comfortable in mid-summer or winter, have to have air conditioning. High above them all, in a statement of architectural supremacy, is the Betham Tower of

11.1.
Flats in Singapore on a new residential estate without air conditioning in 1963. Today almost every dwelling on the island is air conditioned.
Source: Sue Roaf.

flats, which must be excruciatingly uncomfortable at many times of year, during high winds or on hot days, and exorbitantly expensive to power. Do rich people get disgruntled? Or can they afford not to be? At what point will they sue the designer for unacceptable internal climatic conditions? Will it happen in an extreme heatwave and when the lights fail? Will it happen at all? What duty of care does a designer have to ensure that a building is fit for purpose and should the law be clearer on what that purpose is in a rapidly changing climate?

THE MIRACLE OF AIR CONDITIONING

In 1939 S.F. Markham published his book *Climate and the Energy of Nations*, in which he pointed out to a Britain unfamiliar with air conditioning, the miracle of this new technology.[6] It was a miracle because it enabled people, adapted to the colder climates of Europe, to colonize the warmer parts of the world. Indigenous people already populated most parts of the globe, as we saw in Chapter 10, from the Arctic to the equator, from the high valleys of the Himalayas to the great below-sea-level basins of the Dead Sea and the Turfan Oasis in China. Intrepid European entrepreneurs and imperial armies had penetrated most of the far-flung corners of the globe by the end of the nineteenth century. What Markham saw was that for Westerners to actually live

11.2.
The Bentham Tower in Manchester under construction with flats and a hotel below.
Source: Sue Roaf.

all year in cool buildings, regardless of the climate outside, they could truly export their 'civilization', and their god, on a massive scale to 'heathen' lands, exploit economically untapped regions and capitalize on the wealth of even the most uncomfortable nations on the planet. And this is exactly what has happened, for better or worse.

The question is now asked: If air conditioning could be used to enable people to be comfortable in hotter regions than they are adapted to, surely it can be used to keep people comfortable in a hotter future?

AIR CONDITIONING HAS BEEN WITH US FOR OVER 150 YEARS

Air conditioning was first used on a large scale at the turn of the nineteenth/twentieth century to cool food, but as early as 1748 William Cullen at Glasgow University experimented with evaporating ether under a partial vacuum. It was not until 1805 that Oliver Evans, an American, caused water to freeze using a similar process, and the possibility of cheap coolth appeared. At that time many were also experimenting with freezing mixtures and the great natural ice trade was at its peak. In 1834 a closed cycle system was patented by Jacob Perkins, an American working in England, and in the mid-1840s the use of room coolers was pioneered independently in the USA by physician John Gorrie, who used ice to cool air in hospital wards in Florida, and Charles Piazzi Smyth, a Scot. Gorrie was not able to capitalize on his idea, being thought a crank by many, and he died a pauper, never dreaming that his invention would one day dictate the forms of buildings around the world.[7]

In 1862, at an International Exhibition in London, crowds were amazed to see hot-looking steam apparatus churning out miniature icebergs. One of these machines, made by Seibe (Ferdinand Carre produced the other ice-making machine at the exhibition), was bought by the Indian Government and sent to relieve the suffering of the troops in India. In the 1870s a few ice-production factories were set up in cities and provincial towns but they were expensive and took time to become established. In 1877 a breakthrough was made when meat from England was first exported to America in refrigerated ships, and in the 1960s many cities around the world still got their main ice supply from cold storage plants from which one bought blocks of ice. Fridges were not routinely designed into UK council houses until as late as the 1960s.

Early examples of air-conditioned office buildings were being experimented with in the UK and the USA in the 1890s, and by the 1930s large buildings in the USA were being more routinely air conditioned. Hotels had their main public rooms air conditioned by the early 1930s and by the 1940s every room in the best hotels had 'conditioned air'. What air conditioning did was to liberate architects and engineers to create 'modern buildings' in which the internal climate is completely disconnected from that outside. In modern buildings people are isolated in increasingly thin-skinned, fixed window, closed 'envelopes', rather than walls and windows.

Such modern buildings can only be occupied if the air conditioning system is operating, and are unoccupiable if the machines stop, making them extremely vulnerable to failure in an age when the lights are increasingly going off in cities around the world. The result too is a generation of 'James Bond' architects, who would never stay alive until the end of the film/building without being saved by some whizzy gadget. Name the greats like Rogers, Foster, Libeskind, Ghery and Hadid and they probably could not even design a larger building that would be usable without

11.3.
The evolution of buildings
changed dramatically with
the advent of air conditioning,
which significantly increased the
electricity demands of buildings.
Source: Sue Roaf, digitally
produced by Claire Palmer.

SUSTAINABLE SETTLEMENTS

HIGH ENERGY BUILDINGS

PASSIVE BUILDINGS

2000

1980

1950

1900

AIR CONDITIONING

REGIONALLY
APPROPRIATE
BUILDINGS

mechanical ventilation or air conditioning systems. They are the petrol heads of building design. Yet generations of young architects emulate them slavishly.

THE SIZE OF THE AIR CONDITIONING INDUSTRY

The air conditioning industry is one of the most powerful industries in the world, dwarfed only by the financial, insurance and motor industries. The US market for industrial air conditioning, refrigeration and heating machinery grew by 3.5% from 2001, to a value of US$28.1 billion in 2002 alone. The market for industrial air conditioning, refrigeration and heating machinery in the USA is relatively fragmented, with the top four players accounting for only 30.9% of sales in 2002.

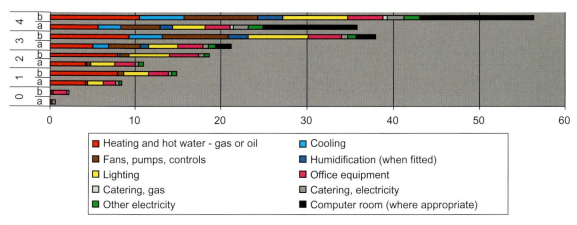

11.4.
Air-conditioned offices use significantly more energy to operate than naturally ventilated ones. This figure shows office building types and their annual carbon emissions (kg carbon/m^2 treated floor area) with (a) best practice and (b) typical. Type 1 is the traditional office building, shallow plan, naturally ventilated and typical of the traditional nineteenth and early-twentieth century buildings. Type 2 is open plan and naturally ventilated buildings, such as became increasingly used after the 1950s when the demand for urban office space grew rapidly. Type 3 is typically a deep or shallow plan, standard air-conditioned building and type 4 represents the typical 'prestige' or 'fashionable' air-conditioned, probably deep-plan office building of the type increasingly popular with 'modern' architects and developers. Type 0 has been added by us (with apologies to Bill Bordass) to represent what we hope twenty-first century, shallow plan, naturally ventilated or mixed mode (using air conditioning only at the hottest times of the year) buildings will look like, with type 0a operating on renewable energy where possible.
Source: Bill Bordass, 1990[9].

In 2002 the top four players in the market spent nearly US$1.5 billion on research and development. As the US market grows increasingly competitive and a lack of pricing power limits overall market value growth, many manufacturers have focused on overseas expansion to drive future sales, no doubt many looking to Iraq as a potentially fertile market for expansion, for instance. The US market more or less met expectations of growing by just over 26% during the 2003–2007 forecast period, reaching a value of US$37 billion by 2007.[8]

The UK is now following the USA and becoming alarmingly addicted to air conditioning. Today around one-third of all UK office blocks have air conditioning of one form or another, despite the fact that we know that air-conditioned prestige offices consume significantly more energy than traditional shallow plan, naturally ventilated buildings, as shown in Figure 11.4. Today is it easier to pass through the Building Regulations process in the UK with a high rating is a design if air conditioned, despite the fact that we may not need to cool well-designed passive buildings in northwest Europe for decades and despite the fact that heavier weight naturally ventilated buildings offer significantly more opportunities for the amelioration of indoor temperatures during heatwaves and cold snaps.[10]

The problem is that air conditioning is a key driver of climate change, the symptoms of which it was designed to address.[11] It has created a 'vicious circle' that we have to break if we are to meet the carbon emission targets of many cities and regions of the world. Buildings consume over 50% of all energy generated around the world and produce over half of all climate change emissions globally. In the USA alone air conditioning uses around 70% of all delivered electricity to air condition buildings! Around 20% of all energy used in the USA, including transport, is used to run air conditioners. The USA uses around 25% of all the world energy: that means that potentially around 5% of all the greenhouse gases in the world come from US air conditioning systems alone.

But the problem is greater than that. It is increasingly clear that we will not be able to supply the demands of air conditioning from conventional electricity generation sources. In New South Wales, Australia, it is estimated that by 2014, 20% of all electrical generating capacity will be needed for just 1% of the time during hot spells; today this figure is 10%.[12] The cost of maintaining that 20% of generation capacity on standby for 90% of the year is prohibitive. It will not happen. The lights and the machines will go out.

Over the past two decades there has been an exponential growth in European sales of air conditioning that has been in the double-digit percentage growth during most of this period. The market for packaged air conditioning in Europe grew by 20% in 1998 and 11% in 1999. The most rapidly growing European Union (EU) markets are in Greece, Spain and Italy.[13]

Two significant trends in the sale and design of air conditioning markets are:

- It is common for engineers to oversize air conditioning plant by 30–50% to ensure both that they do not fail in use and to future-proof buildings against climate change.
- Building usage patterns are changing in ever-shorter cycles, for example from office to apartment, shop to restaurant and power station to museum, requiring the market to develop more flexible, adaptable, systems with shorter payback periods to reflect shorter life cycles.[14]
- This trend for smaller systems, more often changed, also has a significant impact on the embodied energy of the systems, typically made with high embodied energy materials such as aluminium, tin and steel.

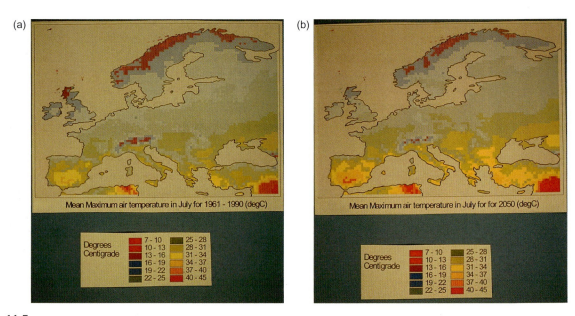

11.5.
The mean maximum temperatures for July in Europe (a) recorded for 1960–1990 and (b) predicted for 2050. This figure shows that Britain is predicted to remain with fairly moderate maximum temperatures well into this century and temperatures that mean, in a well-designed passive building, air conditioning will not be needed for the foreseeable future.
Source: Climate models by G. Kenny.

The air conditioning industry is fighting back through the means of their influence on Building Regulations, for instance in the UK, that favour air-conditioned buildings and in the USA through the promotion of Leading in Energy and Environmental Design (LEED) 'green building' ratings that again promote the use of large, centralized air conditioning systems (see Box 11.2).

It is perhaps not hard to understand why modern buildings have evolved in a form that requires expensive, often unnecessary, energy-profligate air conditioning systems. This is a very lucrative industry. Unfortunately, is has encouraged buildings to degenerate into being unoccupiable without machines. Architects were so concerned with producing ever more outré buildings they did not even notice that they had given away half their workload by deskilling themselves in building performance. They complain now their commissions have loosely halved from 10% to 5% and wonder why. This an almost lose–lose–lose situation for architects, building owners and occupiers and the environment, but architects did very little to stop it arising.[15]

As early as the 1950s architects and building services engineers were warned that the 'modern building' had serious design problems including their uncomfortable indoor conditions driving the need for air conditioning. They also highlighted the fact that, as early and later studies have shown, many people often do not actually like working in air-conditioned offices.

LIGHTWEIGHT, OVERGLAZED AND VULNERABLE BUILDINGS

It is important to deal with one of the key climatic design problems of 'modern' buildings, and that is the excessive use of glass in their external envelopes. We have known for nearly 50 years that there is a problem with overglazed façades, and these problems will be exacerbated in a warming climate.

Early uses of 'building performance appraisal' [16] techniques in offices in the UK were originally developed as diagnostic tools to understand the emerging problems of buildings that were changing from the traditional 'British' building to the larger, more complex 'modern' building type in the 'international style' that began to dominate the urban environment from the 1950s onwards.

In 1966, few air-conditioned buildings existed in London, and Flora Black and Elizabeth Milroy, working at the Building Research Station in Garston, completed a review and survey of the 'experience of air-conditioned buildings' in London.[17] Air conditioning was not then considered climatically necessary in the UK, and remains so in some buildings. Recent studies have shown that traditional passive buildings may be robust enough to provide comfort conditions for several decades to come, even with the changing climate, without year-round air conditioning.

Black and Milroy's 1966 study was designed to use feedback from office workers to optimize working conditions in future offices by understanding emerging performance problems as the paradigm changed. The results echo many, not dissimilar, studies done more recently,[18] namely that air-conditioned offices are perceived to be cleaner and quieter (the buildings studied were new with fixed windows), and in very hot weather were preferred to naturally ventilated buildings, but in 'less extreme weather, the thermal environment in the A/C buildings was in many ways less favoured than that in offices with opening windows'.

One reason suggested for this was the type of building, 'the heavier more conventional construction being more comfortable than the lightweight building with large areas of glazing'. This study was done to gauge the human impacts, and in turn the design imperatives, of the changing market in 'building types' with a view to informing regulations on the issue. Such early studies were, in effect, a 'kind of quality control writ large'.

A second study, published two years later, indicates how rapidly the office market was developing in the UK in the 1960s. The paper, by A.G. Loudon at the Building Research Establishment (BRE), resulted from the increasing problem of overheating in buildings due to excessive glazing.[19] In the 1960s the style of building was changing rapidly as more glass and lighter weight buildings replaced the traditional heavier type, and a survey by Gray and Corlett[20] showed that in pre-war offices the window areas averaged around 20% of the floor area and 85% of occupants wanted more sunshine in their offices, while only 9% were concerned that it should not be too hot. By 1961 a survey by Loudon and Keighley[21] in post-war offices had shown that as many as 40% of the occupants were sometimes too hot in summer and was widely published in professional as well as research circles.

The probable reasons for this increase were given as greater use of glass, with windows over 50% larger in the 1961 survey than in the 1948 survey. Moreover, 80% of the internal partitions on post-war buildings were lightweight, warming up quickly, and in the pre-war buildings they were heavy. The fact that there was more traffic noise in the later survey, making people keep their windows shut, was also thought significant, and more complaints about overheating were recorded near busy traffic routes.

(a)

(b)
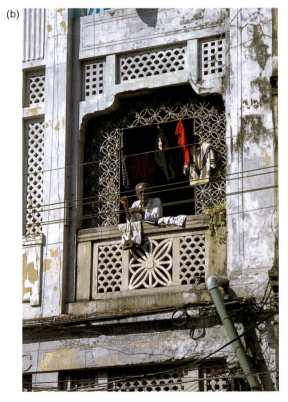

11.6.
(a) There are still cities in the hottest parts of the world where few buildings are air conditioned. View over down town Yangon, in Myanmar. (b) A man leans over a balcony in Yangon: windows are an important link between people and life inside buildings and the community outside. To close the window is to cut that link and alienate people both in and outside the buildings.
Source: Sue Roaf.

This study concluded that buildings of heavy construction could have up to 50% of the external wall glazed, but that unless sun controls were provided, glass areas in buildings with lightweight internal walls and ceiling should be restricted to 20% of the wall area, if they face south and are not shaded. If temperatures of 27°C were considered acceptable then this area could be extended to 30% of the wall area in noisy areas and 50% in quiet ones for lightweight buildings. If more glass was required for reasons of introducing sunlight or the view then excess heat could be removed by air conditioning; however, this was expensive and should be considered as a last choice after proper building design and the use of external shading. This study was one of the building blocks from which the 'admittance method' was developed.[4]

The performance of passive and low-energy cooling systems is, by their very nature, much more sensitive to climate than is the performance of refrigeration-based systems, and the low-energy cooling systems require higher levels of internal thermal mass in buildings and will never be successfully applied in lightweight, overglazed buildings that get too hot to handle without throwing vast amounts of energy at them to cool them on hot days. What the admittance method shows is that mass is essential to sensible, passive building design.

A clear symptom of overglazing in modern office buildings is that the blinds are so often closed, resulting in higher lighting energy use and not reducing the overheating problem. Once solar radiation has passed through glass, it is absorbed and re-emitted at a different wavelength at which it can no longer travel back out through the glass. This phenomenon is the basis for the greenhouse effect, and means that even with the blinds down, the building overheats.

That glass buildings with little or no shading cause severe overheating is an even more severe problem in hotter climates. From the Gulf, where the inside temperatures recorded on glass walls often reach over 60–80°C, to many fashionable modern buildings where internal temperatures soar on hot days, even with the air conditioning on, it appears as if, for some architects, the penny has not dropped that it is extremely difficult to live comfortably in a 'greenhouse'. That is without the added problems of the hotter climate and the rising energy costs of trying to keep such buildings cool.

11.7.
Downtown Buenos Aires, Argentina: like many cities in the world, the evolution of the high-energy building is obvious from the street. The early nineteenth century building have sensibly sized windows, shade, blinds and shutters and awnings. They gave way over the decades to the thin, tight-skinned, highly glazed buildings most commonly built today. There is little density change in the number of people occupying adjacent buildings but the modern buildings may well use four or five times more energy to keep occupants no more comfortable for many months of the year.
Source: Sue Roaf.

Despite the known problems with overglazed buildings, glass continues to be used more and more widely today. Apart from the issues of thermal comfort which are the main concern of Chapter 9, other user problems with overglazed buildings include:

- Loss of privacy: fellow workers can see untidiness, wall charts or flip boards that are being discussed in heated meetings.
- The difficulty of arranging furniture against glazed walls; for instance, desks placed against glass are impossible to use by women who wear skirts. This caused a famous engineering firm to replace the lower half of the glass windows on their new HQ building with frosted glass – no one had thought about this at the design stage!
- The excessive daylight and glare make it difficult to read computer monitors. Engineers cite the fact that some monitors are now so bright they can be seen in full daylight, but at what cost in energy and eye strain? Glare is also the reason why so many highly glazed buildings have their blinds full down and all the lights on, making the indoor conditions poor and energy use in them expensive.

These types of ostensibly trivial gripes are the sorts of factors that can make the difference between being happy at work and not.

Many attempts have been made to reduce internal temperatures of failing buildings such as the National Library in Paris, designed in the 1980s by architect Dominique Perrault. This grand monument eventually cost the French people US$1.3 billion, and an undue amount of trouble. The four glass towers contain more than one design flaw. For example, it was realized too late that a library built from transparent glass would provide little protection for the books from sunlight; and that in fact, excessive sunlight would actually overheat the towers (and pose a risk of turning them into blazing infernos!). To remedy this, the architect specified timber shutters to line the whole of the four towers to be made from top-grade mahogany from the Brazilian rainforests. In addition, the glass design failed to account for condensation, another threat to delicate books. These issues were remedied by the architect only after the construction had been started, and at considerable additional expense to the French public.[22] It is difficult to think of a modern 'monument' that does not suffer from similar problems, although the British Library, fortunately, was designed sensibly to avoid such foolish mistakes.

But there is a range of other well-known problems with 'shiny' and overglazed buildings, and some of these are illustrated in Boxes 11.1 and 11.2. These examples have been contributed by, among others, members of the American Society of Building Science Educators (SBSE), teachers of environmental science in US Schools of Architecture.[23] Collectively they show that tight, thin, lightweight and overglazed buildings are a chronic problem today – and air conditioning can never be a solution to all their problems.

INDOOR AIR QUALITY

Buildings are becoming increasingly 'sick'. In the USA the office worker on average takes a day a month off work suffering from 'sick building syndrome', a figure unimaginable in Europe where we are less dependent on air conditioning.

Indoor air quality can be worse in an air-conditioned building than in a comparable naturally ventilated one. Worryingly, researchers are finding that the filters, ducts and plant of air conditioning systems are often filthy, introducing air that is dirtier than if one simply opened the window, even in the city.[24] Ducts can harbour potentially killer chemicals and bugs, such as *Legionella*, moulds and particulates that are released back into the ducts from the filter. This happens particularly when the weather changes, for instance, on getting warmer and wetter in a warm front. Such changes happen every time a warm front moves across a region, only not in such a marked fashion.

Many internal ducts are not only seldom cleaned but also impossible to get at to clean, and to make matters worse actually give out toxic fumes from the plant, seals and ductwork. Often uncleaned filters and long dirty duct runs collect passing toxins and store them until ambient conditions become warmer and/or more humid. In addition, already dirty duct air is then mixed with the cocktail of volatile organic compounds, formaldehydes, moulds, fungi, dust mites and potentially toxic cleaning materials already inside rooms. This may be one good reason why in air-conditioned buildings many more people succumb to sick building syndrome.[25] Furnishings and finishes that are made of natural materials reduce the problem of excessive toxin levels in the room air.

Air conditioning units cannot filter out some of the most harmful of pollutants in the air, such as diesel and other particulates, polychlorinated biphenyls (PCBs) and any substances below approximately 9 Ångström in diameter. The poor location of air inlets often means that, in inner city locations in particular, the air circulated in air-conditioned buildings is of a lower air quality than if the occupants had simply opened a better placed window. The claim is often made that particular buildings such as laboratories, museums and hospitals should have air conditioning as a matter of course, but on the contrary, while there is a need for particular very clean spaces in such buildings studies have shown that office workers, artefacts and patients are happier, last longer and get better sooner in naturally ventilated spaces.

But there are also more serious concerns about air conditioning and the spread of pathogens. As Terry Wyatt pointed out in his inaugural lecture as President of the Chartered Institution of Building Services Engineers (CIBSE) in 2003, entitled *Adapt or Die*, even more worrying is growing evidence that hospitals, schools and doctors' surgeries are breeding grounds for disease owing to poor ventilation.[26] Brackman et al. have shown that up to 30% of the disease unwittingly caught by patients in hospital is due to airborne contamination. While the need for rigorous cleaning by hospital staff gets attention over the methicillin-resistant *Staphylococcus aureus* (MRSA) or 'superbugs' problem, air contamination is exacerbated by poor design and inadequate building standards in most parts of a hospital, clinic or school.[27]

Recent work by Rod Escomb at Imperial College has shown that for some types of infection, such as tuberculosis (TB), the use of mechanically ventilated or air-conditioned wards increases the rate of infection over naturally ventilated TB wards of traditional design. There was a great deal of sense in retreating to the cool, dry mountain air in the traditional sanatoria to fight such infections and perhaps there is a place for them again in the fight against certain deadly diseases. At a time when there is due to be a massive number of new hospitals and schools being built under PFI contracts, it is worrying that we may be storing up problems for the future.[27a]

WILL SYSTEM EFFICIENCY HELP?

There are several common-sense ways to ameliorate the negative impacts of air conditioning, including:

- Don't use it.
- Use it only when absolutely necessary at the hottest times of year in mixed mode buildings.

- Improve the performance of the walls, roof and floors of the building to minimize heating and cooling loads and discomfort.
- Make it run on renewable clean energies that do not lead to global warming.
- Make the controls more intelligent, so that they are not just set on one indoor temperature for the whole year (as happens in many systems) but can track outdoor temperatures and turn themselves off when unneeded, so saving up to 50–80% of their running costs.
- Make the delivered energy used in a building last longer by storing it in the thermal mass of the building.
- Zone the building so that areas of more extreme climate cannot be used during the hottest and coldest times of the year. Buffer zones may be built on the top floors (rising heat), west-facing walls (the hottest sun) or walls facing the coldest winds.

The importance of moving away from a dependence on fully, inefficiently, poorly controlled, air-conditioned buildings has been widely recognized. There have been experiments in different countries with methods of changing the traditional approach to air conditioning a building – with varying success:

- **Market forces**. The theory that environmentally friendly technologies will be increasingly used over more damaging ones does not seem to apply with air conditioning. Here, market forces appear to work in favour of 'prestige solutions'. In addition, the Green Buildings Movement, which claims to be moving forward towards low-carbon buildings, has to an extent been hijacked by the air conditioning industry. For instance, the US Green Building Council has developed the LEED rating system, which pushes designers towards the adoption of ***efficient** central air conditioning systems* in order to gain a LEED *platinum* rating. Central air conditioning systems are the least efficient method of air conditioning a building, coming a long way behind the use of split air conditioning systems[28] or the far lower water and energy use required for evaporative coolers that are particularly suited to hot dry climates. The firms that are supporting the US green building movement are listed on their website and we can leave the reader to judge where the vested interests of the funders of this rating product lie. The worrying trend is that many firms are trying to promote the market penetration of the LEED 'green' building rating system in other countries around the world. In so doing they promote the US type of building, those thin, tight-skinned, fully air-conditioned buildings that have been at the heart of the 'investment nightmare' of the property sector in 2007–2008 in western economies and increasingly in eastern and southern economies as well.
- **Standards**. There are several international standards that apply to the setting of indoor environments, from the International Organization for Standardization (ISO), Comité Européen de Normalization (CEN), the American Society of Heating, Refrigeration and Air conditioning Engineers (ASHRAE) and the American National Standards Institute (ANSI). These standards are aimed at setting indoor standards for temperature humidity and air movement. Standard ISO 7730 is based on the predicted mean vote index of Fanger (1970),[29] whose aim was to define comfort: 'Creating thermal comfort for man is a primary purpose of the heating and air conditioning industry, and this has had a radical influence … on the whole building industry' '… thermal comfort is the 'product' which is produced and sold to the customer …'.[29] So comfort is defined in a way that is relevant, not to the building but to its air conditioning system.[30] The latest version of ISO 7730 rates indoor environments according to how narrow is the range of environments they provide, encouraging the use of highly controlled, energy-profligate

buildings. CEN Standard 15251[31] and ASHRAE Standard 55-2004[32] are presented in similar terms, albeit with some allowance for greater freedom of indoor temperature in naturally ventilated buildings. Note that in the USA the standard is overseen by ASHRAE themselves.

*   **Guidance**. Guidance measures, however strong, appear to be useless. For example, in the UK for the engineering and architectural professions strong guidance not to use air conditioning systems has had minimal effect on the standards of environmental design of typical office buildings or their energy consumption. British Standard BS 8207:1985, the British Standard Code of Practice for Energy Efficiency in Buildings, Appendix B, has in Table 2 on the checklist for Design Teams Point 7: 'Only specify air conditioning where it is essential to do so.' The RIBA in 1989 in its policy guidelines advised its members against the unnecessary use of air conditioning and CIBSE has as Item 1 on its Code of Professional Conduct, devised to promote ethical practice: 'Avoid the use of refrigeration where natural and mechanical ventilation is a feasible alternative.' Negligible attention was paid to such guidance in the UK where this was superseded by legislation that encourages investors to go down the air-conditioned route.
*   **Legislation**. This works well. In the Canton of Zurich, Switzerland, a law was introduced practically overnight in the late 1980s, banning the use of air conditioning in buildings unless it could be proven to be absolutely necessary. Surprisingly, building designers adapted to the new challenge very rapidly.[27] The trouble is that legislation in the UK and in increasing numbers of states in the USA is pushing designers into building cheap, easy, air-conditioned buildings because that is what the law is promoting, in the UK via Building Regulations and in the USA via the requirement to meet LEED silver and platinum targets that typically produce worse energy buildings than those without these aspirational ratings.
*   **Political management of the problem**. A major drawback is that in most countries there is no single authority with jurisdiction over the control of energy use in, or CO_2 emissions from, buildings – neither the planning nor the Building Regulations departments – and hence there is no related authority to control the use and performance of air conditioning systems. With the increase in significance of CO_2 emissions from buildings, and their commoditization as an internationally tradable unit and legally controllable substance under international law, legislation for the control of energy use in buildings, and by countries, will inevitably be considered and eventually implemented in most countries. In the UK, despite the emergence of ever more imaginative ministries, the buck simply does not stop anywhere in the system. There is a lack of understanding of the problems at the highest level and just as we have a system that allows hundred of thousands of houses to be placed on flood plains in the UK, we have a political system that is overseeing the shift to high-carbon buildings. In fact, they add the extra fillip to the markets by commissioning many of them themselves.

THE FAILURE OF REGULATION

With so much riding on the need to change the direction of the trends in building performance the rather scandalous truth is that the increasingly poor energy performance in buildings around the world is actually being promoted by laws in the UK, the USA and other countries in a system where the powerful air conditioning industry all but writes the laws, the standards and the Building Regulations. How this arose should be investigated and why it is allowed to continue urgently reviewed. It is an example of how those who are supposed to be protecting the public from excessive environmental impacts in the building sector are actually adding to them.

11.8.
The non-air-conditioned buildings around the 'Padang' in central Kuala Lumpur light up for 'Merdeka', the independence day celebrations, in 1958.
Source: Sue Roaf.

In the UK a naturally ventilated office building will marginally fail the current Building Regulations emissions criteria, while an identical but air-conditioned design will pass. The UK Building Regulations now have increased their focus on summer overheating criteria but there are several methods of demonstrating compliance. An analysis of these methods was carried out by Paul Tuohy of Strathclyde University in 2008[10] and he identified issues that could lead to a risk of unnecessary air conditioning being deemed to be a requirement, either through implementation of air conditioning in a building that does not require it or through the creation of a building that performs poorly and has to be subsequently air conditioned. Key factors behind these risks are reviewed, including the use of the increasingly discredited fixed rather than adaptive comfort criteria and the lack of inclusion into the calculations of the impact of varying occupant behaviour in a building using, internal gains, fabric and climate. Fortunately, the energy rating for Energy Performance Certificates (EPCs) was designed to be based on the absolute emissions and to give a better rating to the building design that achieves the lowest carbon emissions, so taking into account the way in which people use and adapt the buildings they occupy.

The question has to be asked: Why has this systemic favouring of air-conditioned buildings occurred? It would be too cynical to suggest that regulations have evolved simply to promote the interests of those who write them. The reality is that this situation has been a long time coming and its evolution involves a complex web of payers.

Energy performance legislation in Europe

Energy Performance Certificates were born of the Energy Performance of Buildings Directive (EPBD), which was entered into on 4 January 2003 by the European Commission (EC). The EPBD is the main legislative instrument affecting the building sector in the EU, and reflects the very real ambition by the EU governments to tap the potential for energy savings from the buildings sector. The EC estimated that this sector has the highest potential EU energy savings, estimated at up to 28%.

Table 11.1 Buildings covered by the Energy Performance of Buildings Directive (EPBD)

(a) New
All to meet minimum energy performance requirements
For those with a floor area greater than 1000 m², alternative systems of heating and energy generation must be considered at the design stage
All for a requirement to introduce Energy Performance Certificates
(b) Existing
For those with a floor area greater than 1000 m² and undergoing a major renovation, the existing building's energy performance needs to be updated when technically, economically and functionally feasible
All for a requirement to introduce Energy Performance Certificates, when the whole building or apartments/units are sold or rented
(c) Buildings covered
- Central or local government offices
- NHS trusts
- Places of education
- Police buildings
- Courts and prisons
- Institutions providing public services, including museums, art galleries and swimming pools
- All homes on point of sale, lease or rent

Under the EPBD for larger public buildings Display Energy Certificates (DECs) are required to publicly display the actual energy use, carbon emissions and a rating on a scale from A to F for the building in use. This is effective where the *Operational Rating* is displayed, showing how a building actually works, but far less effective where the *Asset Rating* is displayed. The Asset Rating is based on the predicted performance of the building calculated using standard methods. Such models have been shown to be often extremely misleading to the extent that they can make a building appear to have a far better performance than in reality. Modelling is a key fudging tool, that can, along with black box composite 'sustainability' rating systems, be used to persuade a range of building clients into believing that the buildings they are purchasing will perform better in terms of greenhouse gas emissions than they do in reality. Table 11.2 shows clearly how a range of high-profile and apparently well-informed clients has been fobbed off with very poorly performing buildings sold to them as 'green' buildings by their architects and engineers, with their performance in reality being demonstrated using models that have patently failed to reflect their predicted design performance. There are no case-law precedents for clients to sue their architects over such breaches in trust, instruction and intention, but no doubt where negligence, or failure to meet the terms of the contract can be proven this will change. This may also be tested against chronic failure issues such as overheating and poor performance in other forms of extreme weather. Clients will increasingly build into their building briefs the requirement to remain occupiable for certain periods during blackouts and other system failures in an attempt to improve the performance resilience of buildings they own or lease.

Over 18 000 UK buildings, including town halls, museums, schools and job centres, are being tested to discover their ratings. By October 2008 one in four buildings measured had scored an

Table 11.2 DEC ratings for five high-profile modern buildings

Building	City	Date	Architect	Engineer	Rating
Eland House, DEFRA Head Office	London	1998			F
Imperial War Museum North	Salford		Daniel Libeskind		G
GLA London City Hall	London	2002	Norman Foster	Arups	E
HQ Department of the Environment					E
Welsh Assembly	Cardiff		Richard Rogers		G

F or a G and the average was D, showing that many so called 'green' and 'sustainable' buildings perform well below average. Only 22 buildings, 1% of those tested, recorded an A rating. Matt Bell, Director of Public Affairs at the London-based Commission for Architecture and the Built Environment (CABE), said when these figures came out, 'we review 350 significant new building projects a year at design stage and we hear a lot of greenwash. The knowledge that from now on this performance will be objectively measured should mark the end of that'.[7] The fear in the low-carbon buildings community is that ministers may be leant on to remove the requirement to display DEC in response to powerful construction industry pressure, but this would be a dereliction of their own duty under European law and may lay them open to court actions by involved non-governmental organizations (NGO)s.

Every house or flat in the UK now requires an EPC at the point of sale, lease or re-renting in the form of a visual representation, on a scale of A–G, of how energy efficient a home is. From April 2008 every new residential property or major refurbishment required an EPC by the Building Control Officer or Accredited Inspector to include:

- The energy efficiency of the dwelling.
- The carbon emissions figure.
- The cost of lighting, heating and hot water per annum.
- Recommendations on ways to improve the home's energy efficiency.

The genius of the EPBD was that it requires an actual measurement of the real energy use and CO_2 emissions of a building, and this simple requirement for performance to be demonstrated may well be the most effective weapon against plummeting performance standards in modern buildings. It is also an instrument that will have a huge effect on the money markets as companies whose business includes the ownership and management of portfolios of buildings will be able to see the actual worth of their building investments. We are entering an age when a buyer, given the choice of three buildings, being an A or a C or a G for roughly the same price (the modern prestige buildings in Table 11.2 were all considerably more expensive than their market competitors at their time of build) will inevitably choose the A from now onwards. The problem is for building owners, who will touch the Fs and Gs? This is exacerbated by the current requirement for the same tax to be paid on empty buildings as on those that are occupied. Where the growing number of buildings, usually 1960s' and 1970s' office buildings, were once left empty, stark evidence of the malaise of 'dead building syndrome', many are now being demolished; or at least they were, but this in itself is an expensive business and a drain on already troubled budgets.

IS AIR CONDITIONING HERE TO STAY?

In the USA it certainly is. The USA we see today would not be possible without the miracle of air conditioning. Some excellent books have been written about the importance of air conditioning to the American way of life and its economy. In particular, Gail Cooper points out:[33]

[the three different kinds of air conditioning in America] – the custom designed systems, the plug-in appliance, and the standardized installation for the tract home – illustrate the difficulties involved in integrating technical expertise into commercial products.

None of these systems fit [sic] perfectly the interests of the engineer, the company, and the aggregated groups known as the consumer … The customer-designed system produced the most technically rational design but surprisingly afforded the user little flexibility. The plug-in appliance privileged the consumer, but its complete divorce from the building compromised its performance. The standardized installation of the tract development provided affordability and performance, but in a buildings that was dependent upon its mechanical services and alarmingly inefficient in energy consumption.

The extent of the dependence of building users on inefficient air conditioning systems in poor buildings in the USA was also a conclusion drawn in another classic work on air conditioning America, by Marsha Ackermann, who concludes by mentioning that Lewis Mumford, who at the age of 75, wrote that air conditioning was deeply complicit in our society's authoritarian tendencies towards control. Ackermann adds:[34]

The counterpart of technologically enabled control is dependency, and the history of air conditioning provides it in full measure. Air conditioning has made it possible to erect structures that must be evacuated when the power fails, to make buildings in which people get sick. It gulps electricity; roars, wheezes, and whines; makes urban heat islands even hotter with the exhaust of a million air-conditioned cars and thousands of sealed buildings.

It has led to a human society that is increasingly unable to adapt to change, because of this dependency, but she adds:

For better and for worse, our world tomorrow will be air conditioned.

In Scotland over the 12 months between the summer of 2007 and 2008, soaring energy costs in the market pushed the number of vulnerable people in fuel poverty from 10% to 20% of householders. People are described as being fuel poor if they spend more than 10% of their income on energy. That definition scopes the breadth of fuel poverty but it does not touch on its depth. What about people who spend 20, 30 or 40% of their income on energy? We cite the classic dilemma in the UK of 'heat or eat'. In many parts of the USA, not least the areas of highest population growth and mortgage defaults such as Nevada and Arizona, this will translate into 'cool or eat'.

The cost of living the American dream is very high, with soaring insurance and medical costs on top of mortgage, transport and air conditioning costs. In April 2007 I prepared a list of approximate monthly costs for a single young professional in an inner city in Garfield, a downtown community in Phoenix, Arizona, and compared it to the monthly and annual bills of a person living in a new community of larger tract homes in Verrado, some 35 miles out of town (Table 11.3). A simple doubling of energy costs was then crudely included the table to show, as a simple ballpark figure, the difference in the cost of living with doubled energy and increased mortgage costs.

The impacts are profound and may go some way to explaining why the Arizona Valley is at the top of the list of US states for households defaulting on loans. The problem with the Arizona

Table 11.3 Double the energy prices and increased mortgage costs for Garfield community in downtown Phoenix, Arizona, and Verrado, 35 miles outside Phoenix, for a single young professional and the reasons for the sub-prime mortgage meltdown in that state become clear

Single person	Garfield 2007		Garfield + energy +Verraddo 2007 mortgage increases				Verrado + energy + mortgage increases	
	Per month	Per year	Per month	Per year	Per month	Per year	Per month	Per year
Mortgage	1400	14400.00	2000.00	24000	2000	24000.00	2800.00	33600
Property tax	500	6000.00	500.00	6000	500	6000.00	500.00	6000
Water + sewerage	80	960.00	160.00	1920	80	960.00	160.00	1920
Energy	200	2400.00	400.00	4800	300	3600.00	600.00	7200
Car purchase	300	3600.00	300.00	3600	300	3600.00	300.00	3600
Gas/petrol	100	1200.00	200.00	2400	250	3000.00	500.00	6000
House insurance	100	1200.00	100.00	1200	100	1200.00	100.00	1200
Car insurance	100	1200.00	100.00	1200	100	1200.00	100.00	1200
Telephone	100	1200.00	100.00	1200	100	1200.00	100.00	1200
Cable	50	600.00	50.00	600	50	600.00	50.00	600
Health insurance	200	2400.00	200.00	2400	200	2400.00	200.00	2400
Extras	100	1200.00	100.00	1200	100	1200.00	100.00	1200
Groceries	300	3600.00	300.00	3600	300	3600.00	300.00	3600
Credit cards	200	2400.00	200.00	2400	200	2400.00	200.00	2400
	3730	42360.00	4710.00	56520	4580	54960.00	6010.00	72120
& 30% tax		12708.00		16956		16488.00		21636
Annual salary?		55068.00		73476		71488.00		93756

Source: Sue Roaf.

Valley, which has been carpeted over the past two decades with wall-to-wall tract housing developments, is that it is one of the hottest places in the USA. When the outside air temperature is 120°F (60°C) and the house you live in has little or no insulation, and is made of little more than fibro (chip) board and matchsticks, you either keep the air conditioning on, visit the air-conditioned mall or possibly die. In 2001 in San Diego, when electricity costs nearly tripled because of corruption in the Enron Corporation, the elderly in some streets had to use one house to live in and share a refrigerator to ensure that they had access to coolth at all.

To make matters worse, the increasing heat islands in cities like Phoenix, fuelled by more bitumen surfaces, more hot air conditioning exhaust emissions, more people and higher temperatures with climate change, has been driving up temperatures year on year. It is the confluence of factors that has proved catastrophic and this case, where total dependence on air conditioning has meant that small changes in its cost to run and the amount needed because of hotter summers, may prove to be the final straw for families fighting to afford to keep their homes.

In such areas where dependence on air conditioning is complete other aspects of economic recession will have a major impact on the livability of regions. For instance, the death of the mall may be a factor in whether some poorer communities can continue to battle for survival in regions of extreme climate.

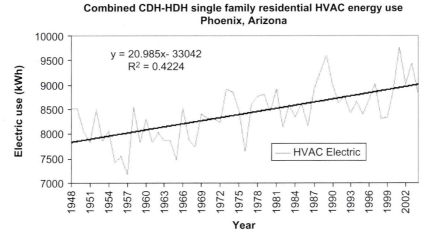

**Combined CDH-HDH single family residential HVAC energy use
Phoenix, Arizona**

$y = 20.985x - 33042$
$R^2 = 0.4224$

11.9.
Graph showing the 1948–2005 annual increase in the energy used to run the air conditioning system in the typical single family home in Phoenix, Arizona as a result solely of the increased of temperatures in the city resulting from the heat island effect. A key factor in this increase is that the night-time minimum temperatures remain high throughout the summer months requiring people to keep their air conditioners on for most of the night as well as during day-time.
Source: Harvey Bryan & ASU's SMART Program.

THE RISE AND FALL OF DINOSAUR BUILDINGS: THE MALL

The severity of the economic crisis in the USA in 2007–2008 manifested itself in many different ways on the faces of buildings across the country. One early symptom of its progress was the decline of the pre-eminent role of the mall in US settlements. Warning signs had been seen through 2006 when sudden hikes in the cost of petrol in April led to a dramatic drop in Wall Mart share prices, linked to oil price increases, as people stopped driving out to the mall for casual shopping. Out-of-town shopping centres not only occupy big tin sheds that are very expensive to heat and cool but they also require buyers to drive to them, so costing both the retailer and the shopper more money to use as energy prices rise. By May 2008 at least eight national retail chains in the USA had filed for Chapter 11 bankruptcy protection while an even greater number of companies had been forced to close branches and scale back expansion. The problem is that for many US towns, particularly in the Mid-West, life revolves around the mall, not least during the hottest months when malls provide a cool refuge for the increasing numbers of people who cannot afford to run their own air conditioning systems during the day and evening. The stores, restaurants and cinemas need hundreds of staff to operate, so when the mall stores start to close the jobs they provided also go. As more and more stores close the mall ceases to be the fun place it once was and people stay away. The travel costs of staff and shoppers start to become a factor in deciding whether to go there every day or once a week or visit a closer smaller store for daily needs. A vicious cycle begins. A fall in revenue of a mall then makes the banks wary of extending the credit that most retailers need to survive between the big spending seasons of Christmas, Easter and other holidays, and the whole show begins to unravel. Malls have closed all over the USA in the credit crunch that began in 2007.[35]

In Britain there is also 'trouble at t'mall'. By July 2008 many out-of-town retailers were beginning to get very worried. The cost of a trip to an out-of-town retail destination includes not only

(a)  (b)

11.10.
The Mataro Library, powered by Desiccant Solar Air Conditioning designed by ICAEN, the Catalonian Energy Institute.
Source: Rodrigo Leal, ICAEN, Barcelona.

the cost a few pounds in petrol but also a temptation to spend more than one can probably afford to, at a time when credit rates are rising and credit is getting harder to get. Numbers of people visiting out-of-town shopping centres declined at twice the rate of city centre malls, with the major drops in areas where people had to travel farther to a large centre. Fashion stores have been particularly badly hit and they account for 50–60% of floor space and 70% of sales in UK malls. With many people finding it increasingly difficult to pay their mortgages the first thing to go is the trip to the shops and the fashion purchases. The big winner has been on-line purchases, with a large jump in the number of purchases made via the Internet. However, the function of the shopping mall or precinct should also be seen in terms of the potential it provides for being a climate refuge in both hot and cold weather for the rapidly rising numbers of fuel poor globally.[36]

In Chapter 13 we look at the growing problems of oil and gas depletion that may, in the not so distant future, challenge this premise. Inevitably, we will all, sooner rather than later, have to 'restructure our expectations and our habits' to refocus our efforts and investments on the provision of our basic needs: shelter, health, real comfort, security and survival.

We need to extricate ourselves from a marketplace riddled with dinosaur buildings and settlement planning that was designed around them. We urgently need to redefine the 'normality' of what constitutes a good building for the twenty-first century, if we mean to ensure that the social, economic and environmental infrastructure of our built environment will see us through the difficult decades ahead.

Air conditioning may be with us for quite a while longer but changes in the industry will have to be even more radical than those in the motor industry at the beginning of the 1990s. The revamped motor industry itself may not survive. They got it wrong. They thought that 'efficiency' was the problem. In fact, it was the product, the paradigm, the understanding of the problem that they got wrong. Will General Motors survive? Certainly not in the form it took in 2008. If you thought the change in the early 1990s was radical, think again.

Similarly, the US air conditioning industry, with its monolithic structure and outdated, oversized and environmentally damaging product ranges, will teeter. It is not just the air conditioning, but the whole nature of the American type of building that will be unaffordable, with its cheap, thin, tight skin and lightweight structure. This model is probably no longer affordable by the Americans, let alone the rest of the world. Developing countries will have to be very wary in the future of having outmoded technologies and building paradigms dumped on them as the developed world learns that it can no longer build such wasteful products at home.

Rather than tinkering with small incremental improvements in the efficiency of air conditioning systems, we need a step change to new paradigms for cooling buildings. Just as with the cars, we need super-low-consumption, dual-fuel, eco-buildings that are naturally ventilated in spring, winter and autumn, and in summer are run on solar air conditioning when the sun is out, topped up by small amounts of grid electricity when it is not.

We have to move to a new generation of robust, heavier, shallow plan buildings with real walls and opening windows. To do this we need to wean ourselves from the 'path dependency' we have developed for ill-conceived, inadequate products in the place of what we really need, buildings that genuinely provide us with the attributes of affordable comfort, warmth, coolth and a healthy working and living environment. This is the way forward.

Box 11.1. Reflectance, glare and 'singing buildings'

Reflectance of light and heat from metal and glass finished buildings can often cause chronic problems, to motorists, pedestrians and adjacent buildings. The Hooker Building, built by Occidental Chemicals in 1980 in Niagara Falls, NY, was one of the first double-skin buildings in North America. It was designed with highly reflecting airfoil type movable shading devices on all sides that were supposed to reflect sunlight/daylight deeply into the interior. The reflection of the sun off these foils was so bright as to blind the motorists crossing the Rainbow Bridge from Canada to the USA. Within four months of the building being occupied they were refinished white to eliminate this problem.

The Ontario Hydro building in Toronto, on the corner of College and University Avenue, focuses the sun's rays onto the sidewalk in front. It has a concave curved front with reflective glass. The focusing effect of the sun at a particular time of year causes not only glare problems but intense solar heating. Luckily the front faces northeast so this occurs only for a short period during the summer in early morning, but it is obviously a generic problem that should be avoided. Curved buildings also have acoustic issues, as they can magnify sound as they reflect the sound waves within the curve.

This raises the issue of 'singing buildings'. The glass and steel TD Bank Tower designed by Mies Van der Rohe, with a black envelope, like the Seagram Tower in New York, was 55 storeys high and the first true skyscraper in Toronto. It was designed for thermal expansion on the south, east and west sides of the building to make allowance for the effects of the sun on those façades, particularly as black metal is highly affected by heat. When a new glass tower was built immediately to the north of the building it reflected so much heat back at the TD Bank Tower that its occupants were greatly alarmed by the loud creaking and groaning nioses that the building started to make owing to the unexpected solar thermal expansion on its northern façade. Steps were taken to control this unexpected movement in the building and the groans stopped, but at an enormous cost to the Bank.

The Hancock Tower in Boston was built in the early 1970s and won the 'most beautiful piece of architecture in Boston' award. It is also a textbook example of problems with glass in buildings. The 60-storey building framed in steel was totally clad, floor to ceiling, in two layers of reflective glass separated by a lead spacer soldered to the glass sheets. The inner surface of the outer glass light, or sheet, facing the cavity has a layer of silver reflective coating on it.[i]

Problems started from early on in the project and the first of four disasters struck. The foundations caused serious settlement of buildings in the surrounding streets. The second problem occurred when a windstorm hit Boston on 20 January 1973 and a number of glass panels being erected in the tower blew out. The falling panels caught in the air turbulence around the building hit and cracked a number of other panels, which had to be replaced. Experts who were called in identified the fact that the tower itself was not safe in windstorms and to remedy this the steel frame stiffness in the long direction was reinforced with 1650 tonnes of extra diagonal steel bracing. The final problem in construction, that of a number of glass panels cracking, was explained by the fact that the lead spacer had developed fatigue because the bond obtained between the melted lead spacer between the reflective coating and the outside light and that between the reflective coating and the lead sealer did not yield, and thus transmitted the motions from thermal expansion to the outer light, cracking it first. The seal was too strong. All the 10 344 identical panels of the Hancock Tower were replaced with single-thickness tempered glass. The cost of the building rose from US$75 million to $175 million and its opening was delayed from 1971 to 1976.[ii]

But the Tower's problems were not over. The building reflected so much heat into the adjacent Copley Square Hotel that the hotel sued the John Hancock building owners to pay for increased air conditioning equipment and operation costs. The owners of the Tower ended up purchasing the Copley Square Hotel to settle the issue, which was sold on recently for a sum of over $900 000.

External building elements can also cause temperature problems. The REJ building in Austin, Texas, was designed with attractive curvilinear, specular light shelves that would project light deep into the interior of the building. Unfortunately, this meant projecting light into hallways that were then impossible to walk down when the sun was shining just so. To fix this the building operator hung blinds permanently in front of the offending light shelves, making them into expensive plant shelves. Office furniture was also not installed as specified by the architects, further blocking the light shelves.[iii]

Many leading architects have predicted the need for more careful design of areas of glazing in buildings and the 'BetterBricks Daylighting Lab' in Washington has done a series of studies on the 'environmental' impacts of the new OMA-Koolhaus Central Seattle Library glass reflections. An

11.11.
Gehry's Walt Disney Concert Hall has had to be covered up owing to the excessive levels of glare experienced from its highly reflective metal surface.
Source: Bill Bordass.

extensive series of model studies was done on the nearly all-glass building. OMA spent a great deal of time and money working with Schott Glass in Germany in developing a multi-layered glass system to reduce solar gain, glare and, hopefully, reflected sun problems while admitting as much light as possible from the overcast sky. It will be for the building users and visitors to determine whether this has proved successful.[iv]

Another building to have major reflectance problems is the new Walt Disney Concert Hall, designed by Frank Gehry and owned by the County of Los Angeles, which has had to call in experts in an attempt to reduce the glare and thermal issues surrounding (literally) the building. There are convex and concave stainless steel surfaces, in some cases brushed, and in some cases polished. In late June 2003, when the builders peeled off the film used to cover the steel during construction, the owners of condo apartments opposite began to complain. In mid-afternoon the glare from the steel became so intense they had to leave their balconies, close the curtains and put on the air conditioning for three hours until the sun went off that face of the building. The temperatures in their apartments went up by up to 15°C because of the added glare off the building. Gehry blamed the builders. The county put a $6000 mesh over the steel as a stop-gap remedy, demonstrating a proactive approach to solving the problems to neighbours of heat and light pollution caused by a building they commissioned. Modifications to the external reflective surfaces have been completed in order to change the reflectance of some of the surfaces and more work will have to be undertaken, although this not a building that can be easily or lightly modified.[v]

[i]Levy, M. and Salvadori, M. (1992) *Why Buildings Fall Down.* New York: W.W. Norton, pp. 197–205
[ii]http://www.mit.edu/afs/athena/course/1/1.011/www/1.011-hancock-bostonglobe-290403A.pdf
[iii]A report on this can be found in Song, S., Haberl, J. and Turner, D. (2002) Sustainability assessment of the Robert E. Johnson State Office Building, submitted to the Texas State Energy Conservation Office, Energy Systems Laboratory Report No. ESL-TR-02/01-02, Texas A&M University, 139 pp. (April).
[iv]The report on this project can be found on: http://www.lightingdesignlab.com/daylighting/daylighting_studio.htm
[v]sbse.org/newsletter/issues.sbsenewssp04linked.pdf

Box 11.2. Is LEED leading us in the right direction?

The Green Architecture movement has grown amazingly in the USA, driven largely by the rapidly growing popularity of the LEED National Certification (NC) process. LEED stands for Leading in Energy and Environmental Design and was established by the US Green Building Council (USGBC) in 2005. It is now being exported as a Green building standard around the world. However, like the UK Building Regulations, the LEED rating system actually penalizes building that do not have air conditioning or mechanical systems, and in so doing pushes designers away from low-energy, naturally ventilated solutions towards higher energy alternatives.

Green Architecture, in the form of LEED and other rating systems, is sold as being a holistic process applied across all the building life cycle stages from the conceptual design stage through the advanced design stage, construction stage and building occupation, to demolition.

LEED deals with:

- Sustainable Site
- Water Efficiency
- Energy and Atmosphere
- Materials and Resources
- Indoor Environmental Quality
- Innovation and Design Process

LEED defines four rating grades:

Certified	26–32 points
Silver	33–38 points
Gold	39–51 points
Platinum	52–69 points

LEED Silver, with a minimum 33 points, is the most common goal, with the total possible points being 69.

Silver	Possible points	Prerequisites
Sustainable Site	14	1
Water Efficiency	5	–
Energy and Atmosphere	17	4
Materials and Resources	13	1
Environmental Quality	15	2
Innovation	5	–

The LEED NC rating system allocates 17 out of 69 points (25%) to Energy and Atmosphere, more than is allocated to other issues. However, in a recent conference paper Professor Edna Shaviv of the Israel Institute of Technology questioned whether LEED enhances energy-conscious building design, and concluded that it is not a priority in the system. LEED is a simple 'point-hunting' approach and until June 2007 it was possible to achieve LEED Silver without improving the energy performance of the building at all. After June 2007, a prerequisite of 2 points dedicated to optimizing energy performance was added as a requirement to achieve a reduction in energy consumption of 14% compared to the local standard. But that begs the question of 14% of what? A typical high-energy guzzling building? There are no actual per metre square energy targets included. An extraordinary step was taken to reduce the prerequisite for optimizing energy performance from 14% in 2008 to only 10% in 2009!

However LEED Gold does require a higher energy performance. To obtain LEED Gold or Platinum one must theoretically improve the energy performance of the building. However, to find the required 35% energy saving for LEED Gold in the Molecular Foundry building at the Lawrence Berkeley Laboratory in California, all that was required was that the mechanical and electrical systems were properly sized:

- The electrical system was reduced by using efficient bulbs with bi-level switching and occupancy-based controls.
- The heating, ventilation and air conditioning (HVAC) system was reduced by limiting the number of air handlers, downsizing the boilers and chillers.
- An energy-efficient elevator was used.

What was missing in part from the LEED Gold accredited Molecular Foundry Laboratory was an evaluation of the passive low-energy architecture (PLEA) features of the building. Potential passive design faults included:

- Minimal shading to protect the eastern and southern windows.
- No sunshades at all to protect the large west-facing windows in the main working cubical space.
- There are no special design elements to achieve passive cooling or heating.

This begs the question of how LEED deals with PLEA features in its points rating scheme. A prime case study here is of the San Francisco Federal Building, which did not get LEED accreditation, although it embraces the following PLEA strategies and technologies:

- It is a narrow building to allow daylight and cross-ventilation to all offices.
- The windows are operated by climate sensors, or manually by the users.

- Completely different, climate-appropriate façades: on the north side, vertical glass fins as brises-soleil; on the south side, perforated metal skin sunshades.
- Concrete floors and ceilings as thermal mass to reduce temperature swing in winter, and with natural night ventilation to cool the building in summer and, thus, no need for air conditioning.

So why is it that the San Francisco Federal Building, which consumes only about 33% of the power of a standard office tower, failed to receive the credit points for optimizing energy performance?

- This is because the systems used for environmental control are so innovative that they could not be assessed by the LEED grading system.
- Moreover, when you have no mechanical systems, you lose the option of getting the 10 credit points for minimizing energy performance. The LEED Performance Rating Method is based on Appendix G of ASHRAE 90.1-2004, which cannot be used for buildings without mechanical systems.

The USGBC claims that LEED is a work in progress, and agreed to take the next few months to re-evaluate the Federal Building. What this excellent PLEA building shows is that the Green Architecture movement has been developed to promote, and hence sell, efficient – or inefficient – machines that run the buildings.

LEED, like most of other Green Building Rating systems, is a simple 'point hunting' approach. One can achieve LEED Silver without improving the energy performance of the building. As all energy-saving features are put in one basket, this leads to the fact that energy efficiency in buildings may be achieved only by improving the mechanical, electrical and hot water systems and by adding photovoltaics. There is no requirement to improve the PLEA design in these rating systems. Moreover, using photovoltaics, solar panels for hot water, or buying Green Power, is awarded twice in LEED, once as it reduces the amount of total purchased energy and again as it contributes to the Green Power credit or to On Site Renewable Energy.

The use of the abundant free energy available in the form of passive solar energy is not considered as On Site Renewable Energy. Consequently, there is no incentive in LEED for PLEA. One should ask whether PLEA is still required when new and better materials and HVAC systems have become available. The answer is obviously yes. Green Building Codes must treat PLEA separately from HVAC and the hot water systems. The primary aim of a Deep Green building must be to run on as little fossil

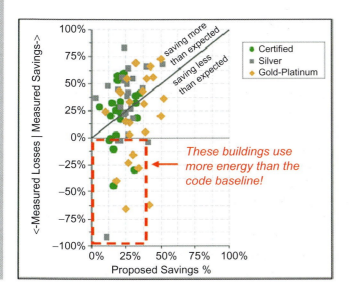

11.12.
Measured versus proposed savings percentages for LEED buildings. Energy performance of LEED for new construction buildings, Final Report, Vancouver, Washington. Presented at US Greenbuild conference, November 2007).
Source: New Buildings Institute, 2007.

fuel as possible, and be rewarded for doing so not least because the building itself is designed to last for at least 50 years, while the mechanical and hot water systems last less than half of it. It is much more important to get the building right first, so reducing the requirement for the secondary systems. Surely the LEED developers believe that?

LEED is becoming a very powerful tool for building improvement. In August 2008 the Mayor of San Francisco signed the green building ordinance that imposes the following requirement on all newly constructed commercial buildings over 5000 sq ft, all residential buildings over 75 feet in height and all renovations on buildings over 25 000 sq ft, that they must achieve 'LEED Certified' by 2008, 'LEED Silver' by 2009 and 'LEED Gold' by 2012. This will convert San Francisco into the city with the most stringent Green building requirements in the USA in terms of the LEED rating scheme, but will this make the buildings the lowest energy in the country? The answer is currently No. Cities such as San Francisco would be better off introducing an EPBD (European Building Directive) type rating system whereby buildings must hang, in a publicly visible position, a certificate stating whether that building has a A–G rating for its CO_2 emissions per metre square on actual annually recorded measurements. That would work to sort the energy sheep from the energy goats.

This box is based on Shaviv, E. (2008). Passive and Low Energy Architecture (PLEA) vs. Green Architecture (LEED), *Proceedings of the PLEA Conference*, Dublin.

11.13.
San Francisco Federal Building.

NOTES AND REFERENCES

1   <http://www.gensler.com/news/2006/07-31_sustainable.html>. See also many articles on building performance factors and 'the forgiveness factor' on the excellent site: <http://www.usablebuildings.co.uk>.

2   Le Corbusier, Towards a New Architecture, Dover Publications (Mineola, New York), London, 1986. This is a translated reprint of Corbusier's original book *Vers une architecture,* first published in 1928 in Paris.

3   <http://www.geocities.com/rr17bb/LeCorbusier5.html>.

4   F.J. Loudon, E. Danter, Investigations of summer overheating, Build. Sci. 1 (1965) 89–94.

5   R. Hackney, The Good, the Bad and the Ugly, Century Hutchinson, London, 1990, p. 37.

6   S.F. Markham, Climate and the Energy of Nations, Oxford University Press, Oxford, 1944.

7   R. Booth, Halls of shame: biggest CO_2 offenders unveiled, Guardian 11 October (2008) 11.

8   <http://www.hevac-heritage.org/papers/papers.htm>.

9   B. Bordass, Appropriate methods and technologies for new build and refurbishment: offices. Global Responsibilities of Architects, RIBA Publications, London, 1990, pp. 15–17.

10 P. Tuohy, Air conditioning: the impact of UK regulations, the risks of unnecessary air conditioning and a capability index for non-air-conditioned naturally ventilated buildings, Proceedings of Conference: Air Conditioning and the Low Carbon Cooling Challenge, 2008.

11 P. Haves, S. Roaf, J. Orr, Climate change and passive cooling in Europe, in: Proceedings of PLEA Conference, James & James Science, Lisbon, 1998.

12 R. de Dear, S. White, Residential air conditioning, thermal comfort and peak electricity demand management. Proceedings of Conference: Air Conditioning and the Low Carbon Cooling Challenge, Cumberland Lodge, Windsor, UK, July 2008, 27–29. For full paper see <http://nceub.org.uk>.

13 BSEE, Technology and market demands drive booming European air conditioning market, Build. Serv. Environ. Eng. 10 (December 2000).

14 <http://www.euromonitor.com/Industrial_air_conditioning_refrigeration_and_heating_machinery_in_USA_(mmp)>.

15 J. Nicol, S. Roaf, Adaptive thermal comfort and passive buildings, in: M. Santamouris (Ed.), Advances in Passive Cooling, Earthscan, 2007.

16 G. Baird, M. Donnne, F. Pool, W. Brander, C. Aun, This term was coined in the early 1970s, Energy Performance of Buildings, CRC Press, Boca Raton, FL, 1984, p. 7.

17 F. Black, E. Milroy, Experience of air conditioning in offices, Journal of the Institute of Heating and Ventilating Engineers, September (1966) 188–196.

18 A. Leaman, Post-occupancy evaluation, in: S. Roaf, A. Horsley, R. Gupta (Eds.), Closing the Loop: Benchmarks for Sustainable Buildings, RIBA Publications, London, 2004.

19 A.G. Loudon, Window design criteria to avoid overheating by excessive solar gains. Building Research Station Current Paper 4/68, published by the BRS, 1968.

20 P.G. Gray, T. Corlett, A survey of lighting in offices, Appendix 1 of Postwar Building Research No. 30. HMSO, London, 1952.

21 F.J. Loudon, E.C. Keighley, User research in office design, Archit. J. 139 (6) (1964) 333–339.

22 <http://www.pps.org/gps/one?public_place_id=350>.

23 <www.sbse.org/newsletter/issues/newsw03weblinked.pdf>.

24 G. Clausen, O. Olm, P.O. Fanger, The impact of air pollution from used ventilation filters on human comfort and health, Proceedings of the 9th International Conference on Indoor Air Quality and Climate, Monterey, vol. 1, 2002, pp. 338–43. <www.indoorair2002.org>.

25 M. Bjorkroth, V. Asikainen, O. Seppanen, J. Sateri, Cleanliness criteria and test procedures for cleanliness labelling of HVAC components, Proceedings of the 9th International Conference on Indoor Air Quality and Climate, vol. 1, Monterey, 2002, pp. 670–674.

26 T. Wyatt, Adapt or die: major challenges facing the building services industry, Inaugural Presidential Lecture for CIBSE, 2003.

27 J.V. Bennett, P.S. Brackman (Eds.), Hospital Infection, fourth edn., Philadelphia, Lippincott-Raven, PA, 1998.

27a A.R. Escombe, et al., Natural ventilation for the prevention of airborne contagion, PLoS Med. 4 (2) (2007) e68.

28 Jiang, Yi., ZhaoJian Li and Rong Qin, What are the major factors on energy consumption for cooling in Chinese residential buildings? Proceedings of Conference: Air Conditioning and the Low Carbon Cooling Challenge, Cumberland Lodge, Windsor, UK, July 2008, 27–29.

29 P.O. Fanger, Thermal Comfort, Danish Technical Press, Copenhagen, 1970.

30 The role of such standards and an suggestion of how they might be made more building-friendly is given in J.F. Nicol, M.A. Humphreys (2009). Standards, Categories and Energy Use Building Research and Information.

31 CEN, Standard EN15251. Indoor environmental input parameters for design and assessment of energy performance of buildings – addressing indoor air quality, thermal environment, lighting and acoustics, Comité Européen de Normalization, Brussels, 2007.

32 ASHRAE Standard 55, Thermal environment conditions for human occupancy, American Society of Heating Refrigeration and Air conditioning Engineers, Atlanta, GA, 2004.

33 G. Cooper, Air conditioning America: Engineers and the Controlled Environment, 1900–1960. Johns Hopkins Studies in the History of Technology, Johns Hopkins University Press, Baltimore, MD, 1998.

34 M. Ackermann, Cool Comfort: America's Romance with Air conditioning, Smithsonian Institution Press, Washington, DC, 2002.

35 Observer, Business, 2 April 2008, p. 3.

36 Guardian, 12 July 2008, p. 41.

12 THE END OF THE AGE OF TALL BUILDINGS

INTRODUCTION

The age of skyscrapers is at an end. It must now be considered an experimental building typology that has failed.[1]

With the arrival of the global economic slump in 2007/08, so began the end of the age of tall buildings. We wrote of its imminent demise in the first edition of this book and since then the prediction has come true. The reasons we gave in 2003 and what has happened since, are covered below in a review of the phenomena that must constitute the twentieth century's greatest 'follies de grandeur'.

Investors began to get cold feet about the mammoth investments required by 2005 and in January 2008 they started pulling investment from all new tall buildings on the books as property funds began their sharp fall. Shares in many property and development companies plunged in value. By February 2008 British Land, the second biggest developer in the UK, had lost £1.4 billion from the share value of its offices and out-of-town retail parks and the property markets continued on their freefall. British Land was particularly vulnerable to collapses in the property markets as it was heavily invested in two of the most price-vulnerable building types: the tall buildings and the mall buildings, which both became the fall buildings. For the tall building sector in the UK and elsewhere there are many reasons why mothballed projects will, and should be, permanently shelved.

SIZE MATTERS

Size matters, and always has mattered. It represents power, and dominance within a group. There are strong subliminal drivers for the idea that to be 'above' is better. In terms of defence the farther you can see, the sooner you know that the enemy approaches. In early warfare there were significant physical advantages to being 'above' when lobbing sling bullets, spears or cannon shot at the enemy, although this advantage is hardly relevant when the enemy is a disgruntled colleague, the hubris of the CEO of a large organization, or an anthrax spore.

In animal groups, dominant males strengthen the 'family line' through the idea of selective breeding, where the 'strongest' men, in a particular ecological niche, will win the fair hands of the strongest wives and so have the strongest children, so fortifying the line in perpetuity within that niche, be it because they can run faster, earn more or survive the cold. We also enjoy 'looking down on' people, from lofty 'heights', be they intellectual, financial or simply the seat of a great big SUV. In many settlements the best houses were raised above the unhealthy masses in the cleaner fresher air that wealth affords. We are also impressed by looking up at people, and their edifices, the ultimate symbol of great achievement. This tendency is reflected in a charming poem written in Cairo in the fourteenth century, about a windcatcher, which demonstrates that human nature changes little over centuries:

> A house resembling as-Samaw'al's castle has come to brag
> About one of its architectural features, saying:
> 'I see my windcatcher rise up high in the air,
> Being mightier and taller than those who go after it'.

(Ibn Abi Hajalah at-Tilimsani, 1325–1375)

The race to build the tallest skyscraper was first won in the late 1920s by the owners of the Empire State Building[2] at 381m and 102 storeys high over their rivals at the Chrysler Building, at 319m and 70 storeys. The title of the 'owner of the tallest building in the world' has been the ultimate goal of very powerful men since the tower of Babylon was built 3000 years ago. The Twin Towers of the World Trade Center held the title for a very long time.

The Burj Dubai is currently the tallest building in the world at 810m. The 101 Shanghai World Financial Center became the tallest building for a few months in 2008. Taipei 101 also led the field for a while, housing 12 000 people in the high block, and was designed to survive a 9/11-type attack. It has more escape stairs than the lower Petronas towers, not a small consideration, and can endure extreme winds and an earthquake above 7 on the Richter scale. Severe storms and tremors are common in Taiwan. It also has the world's fastest lifts, which travel at 37mph and take passengers to the 90th floor in 39 seconds – when the electricity is on, that is.[3]

The 88-storey Jinmao Tower, China's second tallest building, is located in Shanghai. London's tallest building, Canary Wharf, is someway behind in the stakes, at 235m high and 50 floors.[4] The 'Shard of Glass', which has recently been granted planning permission, designed by Renzo Piano at 305m high, is to be located in Southwark. The UK's highest residential building, the Bentham Tower, is 157m high, 47-storey glass tower, and was completed in Manchester in 2006. The height was dictated by the fact that Manchester airport sets a 160m height limit on buildings in the city. It is 30m taller than the Barbican Tower in London and cost over £150 million to build.

Some architects actively promote tall buildings

Richard Rogers is one who supports tall buildings, as was demonstrated by his attack on the UK Commission for Architecture and the Built Environment's (CABE's)[5] decision to oppose permission for the high-rise glass 'shard' building designed by Renzo Piano for London. Despite much opposition, by those who said that the building did not do enough to improve the public realm in the area, Richard Rogers, stated:

To stop a massive development because some people think the public domain is not as good as it should be is an absolute mistake ... It is completely throwing the baby out with the bathwater ... I don't believe that all tall buildings need public space.[6]

(a)

(b)

(d)

(c)
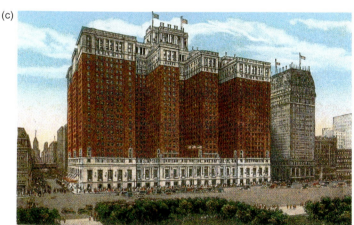

12.1.
Huge buildings in America were run with and without air conditioning in the 1930s and 1940s, still using careful climatic design, thermal mass, opening windows and shading. Here we see four: (a) the Hotel Lincoln in New York; (b) the Merchandise Mart in Chicago – an early 'mall' and the largest building in the world at that time; (c) the Stevens Hotel, Chicago, with circulating iced water in every room; and (d) the Chrysler Building in New York, with a pioneering air conditioning system.
Source: S. Ross, postcard collection.

In his evidence to the planning inquiry for the building he claimed that the building was:

a masterwork of architectural design, sited in the right place to maintain London's status as a world city. Its impact on London's protected skyline, as a part of a cluster of towers will be entirely positive, and will not harm statutorily protected views or harm the setting of St Paul's.[7]

A number of architects supported the tower, which was variously described as 'very special', 'audacious' and a 'true masterpiece', and declared that it would be embraced by Londoners for its 'meaning and elegance', though what that meaning was is still unclear. Those voicing strong opinions were notably those who make a living out of big buildings, one notably claiming that this building in particular 'sensitively reflects its local context', in contrast to CABE's concerns over its scale, form, detail, design references and the grain of the development. How do people justify such statements? What would sensitive mean in this context?[7]

In London, the then Mayor Ken Livingstone promoted the idea of high buildings to trumpet the international status of the city.[8] A number of new tower blocks had been proposed for London, including a 30-storey tower for the Southwark Estate and a number of other multi-storey developments in Greenwich,[9] Mill Harbour,[10] Docklands and the City.[11] One developer was even told to make his tower a number of floors higher, even though calculations showed that above 18 floors they would begin to lose money.

Many people think tall buildings are not a good idea

Several groups, such as English Heritage, have raised objections at the planning stage to these developments, while other groups have not only supported the building of these new tower blocks but also vilified the objectors. Livingstone famously likened English Heritage to the Taliban of British Architecture for its objection to the London Bridge scheme.[9]

Richard MacCormac and Sir Norman Foster have voiced their reservations about new tower buildings in the City of London, that can 'so easily become ghettos, just a series of fragments floating apart and looking after themselves'.[9] Sir Norman Foster sensibly called for 'less hysterical debate – The issues need to be discussed rationally.'[9] There is a number of people calling for a new look at the potential for 'ground scrapers', and low-rise, high- and medium-density developments.

And some cities resist them

Paris has one of the most untouched skylines of any city in the world, and is now considering lifting a 30-year ban on skyscrapers at the edges of the city. In 1974 they outlawed the building of any building above eight storeys over an area of 40 square miles. The move comes at a time when there is growing pressure on space, but plans are only being considered for new higher buildings in the city's outskirts, not in the historic centre, where the only high buildings are the Eiffel Tower built in 1889 to a height of 324 m[12] and the Montparnasse Tower, with 58 floors. It may be that major corporations that are now extremely concerned not to be situated in, or near 'target' buildings, may in future favour more 'secure' cities, free from such buildings.

SPACE PLANNING PROBLEMS

A high-rise building usually consists of a shaft and elevators surrounded by living units on each storey. The properties of openings in the south (sun: solar gain) and north (cold wind: infiltration) and the very limited opportunities for the floor plans, with restricted walk distances to fire exits and access shafts, drastically reduce the organizational possibilities of the plan.

Such are the conditions of a high-rise form that, because of its very height, it can severely disadvantage people who suffer from vertigo, a recognized condition in which individuals are psychologically frightened of being 'too high'. The enclosed access conditions for tall buildings may also

12.2.
Cities all around the world grew within a couple of decades to their soaring current forms. When the author was a girl in Sydney the highest building was the AMP building, at 28 storeys, and the radio weather programme would report occasionally that snow had been spotted on the top of this huge building! It can be seen behind the ferry by the wharf.
Source: Sue Roaf.

trigger agoraphobia, a condition that can be exacerbated by high temperatures. Many people cannot work in such buildings for this reason, which would be a problem if they were a key worker in an organization. It is unclear how employers can insist on employees only occupying 'high' offices, where their business is located, when this work condition would contravene employment law against the discrimination against individuals or 'minorities' with such conditions. How does a person climb the corporate ladder in a tall building when they suffer from vertigo?

The form also has climatic design limitations, magnified because they occur on every floor in a rigid plan form. It has been proven nigh on impossible, for instance, to prevent all south-facing apartments in high-rise buildings from overheating in summer and all north-facing ones being cold in winter due to radiant gains and losses. It is very difficult to attach solar shading to the outside of a sheer building face without increasing the risk of failure at the point where the shade connects to the buildings and controlling them in high winds where the wind pressure is significantly amplified with the height of the building. However, currently this problem is being looked at by some firms interested to try to achieve apartments that can have access to both façades.

The geometric properties of towers make it difficult to utilize solar hot water systems for occupants because of the low ratio of the external building surface area: unit/person. A rule of thumb for solar hot water system design is that there needs to be about $1\,m^2$ per person in the UK. This means that the tall building simply cannot generate sufficient solar hot water and/or solar electricity to heat and power its occupants, particularly in a deep plan building. However, the need, and challenge, of incorporating renewable energy into buildings is currently being explored by a number of practices who are experimenting with wind generators, transparent photovoltaics for window areas and geothermal pile foundations. Such work is increasingly important if one looks forward to a time when every building will have to be at least 10% (by 2010) to 100% (by 2050?) powered by new energy, or surprise sources, under conditions described in Chapter 14. Early calculations show that 50–60% of energy for recent designs could be generated on-site for high-rise buildings and it is maintained that the rest could come from off-site green sources.

Vertical circulation is also a problem that has traditionally been dealt with by using fast lifts. However, at times of crisis these lifts become a problem, with people becoming trapped in them being a major hazard when the power fails. Lifts are not used during fire events. Travel times in buildings are another issue arising from building height. For instance, the 'street door to destination' travel time for a visitor arriving at the building and then travelling up to say the 5th or the 100th floor will obviously exceed the travel time in a low- to medium-rise building of the same floor plan. This increases the stress associated with the visit and one consequence of this is the alienation of visitors, particularly in times of emergency evacuation, whether simulated or real. Similarly, increased travel times experienced by staff may increase the wasted time during the day experienced for everyday operation, and hence costs, for the business in question. Such travel times can be critical in buildings such as hotels and hospitals, and offices, as we now know from the Twin Towers, in times of emergency. It took people from the top floors some three hours to evacuate the building in 1993 when one of the towers at the World Trade Center was damaged by a bomb.

A related factor is that the high rise by its very nature piles floor upon floor, and people one on top of another. Hence when the building is catastrophically damaged causing collapse everything above the damaged floor falls, as we saw in New York. If the same space is arranged in a low-rise form, such as at the Pentagon, only a part of the building collapses. If the Pentagon had been a high-rise building most of the people in it would have died; because of its robust, low-rise form, far fewer occupants were affected when the structure was hit by a plane. In addition, the sheer amount of material generated by the collapse of the Twin Towers was exponentially higher than would have accompanied the collapse of say a 10-storey building of the same size due to the force of the collapse.

However, it was not only the main buildings of the Twin Towers that collapsed but six adjacent buildings also had to be demolished as part of the aftermath of the 9/11 attack. The decision to demolish the former Deutsche Bank building that overlooks the World Trade Center site was taken as late as June 2003. The 40-storey skyscraper became known as the 'widow' because of the black netting hung over it to prevent debris from falling onto passers-by. The building, constructed in the 1970s, was severely damaged, with a 24-storey-high gash rent in it by collapsing steel from the South Tower. Worse damage was inflicted by a mould infestation, caused by the sprinkler system going off and standing water going stagnant, making the building uninhabitable. The reason it had stood untouched for so long is that the insurers could not agree that it could not be salvaged. It was calculated to cost US$100 million alone to demolish, a sum that would cover the removal of asbestos and other contaminants from the building.[13]

Workplace Security and Business Continuity Planning experts also warn corporations, not surprisingly, to be wary of taking space next to 'high-risk' buildings in view of the impacts they may have on adjacent buildings if targeted in terrorist events, and the value of buildings adjacent to new high-profile 'target' buildings may be adversely affected by such trends in the business community.[14]

PSYCHOLOGICAL PROBLEMS

When high-rise buildings were first commonly built in the UK, studies were done evaluating and reporting on the often chronic problems amongst tower dwellers, including many psychological and social problems, such as slower motor development in children who are prevented from spending time outside without adult supervision; distress and alienation, especially amongst groups of certain ages or genders who spend many hours indoors – women, the elderly and children; dissolution of social connections; a higher crime rate relative to the same phenomena in lower buildings, particularly around lift shafts and stairways in poorer areas, where the lifts are often broken and irregularly maintained owing to the low priority of the task for already over-stretched budgets.[15,16]

There are now methodologies for including within the life-cycle costings for a building the increased costs to the UK National Health Service of different types and conditions of housing by postcode.[17] New studies could be instigated on the health costs of existing high-rise housing, so they can be incorporated in the cost planning on new towers for which they seek planning consent.

There is also, currently, real concern raised about the after-effects of the Twin Towers event in terms of psychological damage and the impact on the minds and even productivity of people who now occupy high-rise buildings around the world.

Voices raised against the skyscraper include that of the architect and urbanist Constantine Doxiades:[18]

My greatest crime was the construction of high-rise buildings. The most successful cities of the past were those where people and buildings were in a certain balance with nature. But high-rise buildings work against nature, or, in modern terms, against the environment. High-rise buildings work against man himself, because they isolate him from others, and this isolation is an important factor in the rising crime rate. Children suffer even more because they lose their direct contacts with nature, and with other children. High-rise buildings work against society because they prevent the units of social importance – the family … the neighbourhood, etc. – from functioning as naturally and as normally as before. High-rise buildings work against networks of transportation, communication, and of utilities, since they lead to higher densities, to overloaded roads, to more extensive water supply systems – and, more importantly, because they form vertical networks which create many additional problems – crime …

TOO EXPENSIVE TO BUILD, OPERATE AND MAINTAIN

In 2007, at the end of the global building boom, planning permission had been sought for a large number of high-rise buildings in the UK. In May 2008 CABE published a review of over 700 large public developments and concluded that fewer than 10 of them made sustainability a genuine priority. The report claims that there is an endemic 'piecemeal' approach to introducing sustainability into projects that concentrate too much on 'green gadgets'.

However, there does seem to be a virtuous circle that is operating that is making people aware that you simply cant have 'green towers' because they use too much of the Earth's rapidly dwindling raw materials, they cost too much, their impacts are too great for small areas and in most cases they don't retain their value as well as, or for as long as, lower less polluting buildings. The higher the building, the more it costs to build and operate, and the more costly and difficult it is to maintain.

The primary increase in build costs, per metre square, results from the increased structure and construction required to support the building, to earthquake-, fire- and weather-proof it, and the increased systems needed to operate it, including lifts, escalators, water pumping and electrical systems. These high costs can only pay back if higher than average prices are paid for the floor area, housing or offices than would be the case in a lower rise building. So, for instance, putting social housing up in the air is to ask the ordinary council tax payer to pay in perpetuity for the lift, concierge, policing, social worker, maintenance, refurbishment and demolition costs of the homes of a few people, who could just as well have been housed in low-rise, low-cost housing built for the same price.

Table 12.1 Results of a study of the embodied energy of buildings showing that the taller they are the more energy is embedded in them per metre square during construction. The case study buildings in Melbourne, Australia, show embodied energy results in GJ/m² gross floor area by element group

	Height in storeys				
	3	7	15	42	52
Structure group	5	7	9.9	11.7	11.6
Finishes group	0.6	0.4	0.5	0.4	0.7
Substructure	0.9	0.4	1.2	0.5	0.7
Roof	1	0.8	0.1	0.2	0.4
Windows	0.3	0.2	0[a]	0.2	0.1
Non-material group	2.9	3.2	4.4	4.9	5
Total	10.7	11.9	16.1	18	18.4

Taken from Treloar, G.J., Fay, R., Ilozor, B. and Love, P.E.D. (2001) An analysis of the embodied energy of office buildings by height. *Facilities*, 19(5/6), 204–14.

In addition, the higher the building, the more it costs to run because of the increased need to raise people (lifts), goods and services and also, importantly, because the more exposed the building is to the elements the more it costs to heat and cool. The higher the building, the higher the wind speeds around the building, the more difficult to keep the wind out, and the more the wind pressure on the envelope sucks heat from the structure, particularly as with many twentieth century tower blocks the envelope leaks. The higher the building, if standing alone, the more exposed to the sun it is and the more it can overheat. And hence the higher the building the more it costs to keep the internal environment comfortable.[19]

So in effect, by making the simple decision that those with less money will live in the air in social housing 'towers', their quality of life will be compromised: they will struggle to pay their utility bills and for the service charges for their lifts and for caretakers necessary to keep such buildings safe and clean. Local councils in the UK now have to charge homeowners what it costs them to run a building people live in. Previously such service charges were absorbed in the general council charges, so making all tenants and council tax payers pay to run the lifts in high-rise buildings that others occupied; now individual householders will have to foot the bills for the costs of their own homes. So individual council tax payers and tenants foot the bill for a politician's choice to go 'high'.

Lifts are very energy expensive and costly to run, maintain and replace. Lifts alone can account for at least 5–15% of the building running costs and the higher the building, the more it costs.[20]

The higher the building, the greater the annual maintenance costs to keep it clean, repaired and safe. The failure of a single building element can be catastrophic. For example, the silicone mastic used to weatherproof glazing panels was given in its early forms only a 15-year performance guarantee. If mastic fails, it can result in the need to remove and/or repair every single glazing panel in the surface of a building, which in a high-rise building would prove to be a crippling expense. Day-to-day maintenance of buildings can be similarly expensive and where building envelopes are problematic to access, they can have enormous annual cleaning costs. One famous tall building in the City of London has allegedly proved impossible to sell because of its astronomical maintenance and running costs, and even relatively lower rise buildings such as the Greater London Authority headquarters can run up annual window-cleaning bills in the region of £100000.

Many tower blocks have fallen into a very poor state of repair because their owners cannot afford their upkeep. The historical reality has proved that it is often cheaper to blow up tower blocks than repair them. 'Tower blocks are only for the rich', said Mike Holmes of Arup Associates, so why is anyone considering them for social housing at all, particularly when, with climate change, wind speeds, storms, flooding and solar intensity will increase significantly over the next decades, so speeding up their deterioration? Particularly vulnerable to a more extreme climate will be leaky envelopes, typical of concrete panel tower blocks; and glass and steel structures that suffer from very high levels of solar gain are very difficult to shade high up and have traditionally had extreme cold bridging problems through the structure. Tower blocks also typically have to have air conditioning, as they are of sealed envelope construction, a decision that can quadruple energy costs at a stroke, and in turn gives them a disproportionately high carbon emitter status, at a time when carbon taxes for homeowners are being spoken of. So on top of high running costs homeowners would have also to consider that they may have to pay far higher carbon taxes associated with high-rise buildings in the future.

OVERPOPULATION OF DISTRICTS

The concentration and compaction of high-rise buildings permits intensive land use but causes population overcrowding in localities, at certain times of the day or week. This can result in drastic affects on open areas, streets and parks, and places excessive strain on the existing infrastructure, such as parking, roads, transport, sewerage, water and energy. If one breeds bacteria in a test tube they can double and double in number many times with no noticeable impact on their population until the test tube is half full and when they double again the test tube becomes full. A single doubling incident becomes the point at which the habitat ceases to become viable as its capacity is exceeded.

Leon Krier has referred to this as 'urban hypertrophy', making the additional point that overloading any given urban centre tends to prevent the organic development of new healthy, mixed urban fabric anywhere beyond the centre.[21] Bear in mind, too, that some of the sturdiest and even aesthetically pleasing tall buildings of the early twentieth century are only now approaching the end of their so-called 'design life'. What is their destiny? The worst offender in this urban destruction is the monofunctional megatower, which paradoxically has become an icon of modernity and progress. This issue has also been dealt with in Chapter 7, in consideration of the effects on infrastructure and evacuation.

The sheer size of many megacities means that it can take four hours to get around, and people in cities such as Mexico or Buenos Aires may have to commute four or five hours a day to get to work. Where cities are high rise the problem is exacerbated by the fact that every building may have hundreds or thousands of occupants who need to get to work and back at the same time. In São Paulo, one of the great high-rise cities of the world, many parts of the city are impassable at various times of day. In response to this problem the rich have developed a new highway and have taken to the skies for their daily commute. The numbers of helicopters rose from 374 to 469 between 1999 and 2008, making it helicopter capital of the world ahead of New York or Hong Kong.[22] Below in the streets it is often gridlocked, so creating two worlds of the rich and the poor. With Brazil's booming oil economy this seems like a sensible development but what is one left with when even the rich cannot afford to fly? A dysfunctional city that will need major public transport developments to make it usable at all.

São Paulo:
6 million cars
820 helicopter pilots earning up to $100 000 each
420 helipads – 75% of all Brazil and 50% more than in the whole of the UK

SOLAR, WIND AND LIGHT ACCESS RIGHTS

There are real issues of solar rights with high-rise buildings that have to be addressed and agreed. The higher a building is the greater the shadow it casts on the buildings around it.[23] The shadow cast by a two-storey building is larger than the shadow of a one-storey building of identical floor plan by 2%. A building of 16 storeys casts a shadow 43% larger than a one-storey building, at noon on the winter solstice.[24] A high-rise building will cast a shadow over a huge area of a city, affecting the light and warmth and ability of the shadowed building to generate solar energy. Naturally, if the building is close to the high rise it will be shadowed for most of the year and if it is distant it will be shadowed perhaps for only a period in the day; however, this could be when the solar energy is most needed. Solar rights legislation is being passed in cities around the world and an excellent example is that of the Solar Law of Boulder, Colorado,[23] where legislation has been enforced to ensure that buildings do not steal the sunlight from adjacent properties. There is also a case to be made for wind rights to ensure that new buildings do not cut off the air flow around buildings that may be needed to power ventilation systems or generate electricity.

In a world where power failures will become more common, the use of non-grid-connected solar or wind generation systems for, for instance, fail-safe security and fire alarms and lighting, electric garage doors, uninterruptible power supplies systems for computer networks and emergency lighting, will increase, enhancing the need to protect the solar and wind rights of buildings. In the less energy-secure future we will have to rely increasingly on emerging energy generation technologies, such as wind, solar and hydrogen systems, to run our buildings for hot water, space heating and electricity.

The higher up one gets, the higher the wind speed, and so on the façades of high-rise buildings there will be huge potential for wind generators. There is much interesting work currently being done by Dr Derek Taylor at the Open University on how to power individual buildings using the wind. Again there will be optimal levels of building surface available in relation to building volume and occupancy to be explored here and optimal wind-driven building forms will emerge and be exploited. But again we come to the problem of stealing other buildings' energy, and if a series of wind generators is built on city buildings, and an adjacent tower block is erected in the direction of the prevailing wind, the wind energy of the first building is substantially reduced. There are also problems of generator vibration, passing through to the structure of a building, that will have to be solved in high buildings, and the necessary structural reinforcements would have to be factored into the system and running costs.

There are increasingly high-profile legal issues in allowing one building to steal the sun, light, wind and sound from one or many other buildings. Shanghai's Urban Planning Administrative Bureau has proposed curbing the height of tall buildings in the city.[25] Over the past decade the Chinese city has witnessed an extraordinary construction boom – the Chinese government's plan for Shanghai to replace Hong Kong as the financial hub of East Asia is thought to be on schedule.

But a consequence of the city's growing prominence has been a steep rise in land values, which in turn has contributed to the construction of a large number of tall buildings in the city. Now, with a growing number of civil court cases alleging that tall buildings can block light and raise the city's temperatures, it has been proposed that buildings should not exceed 30 storeys. The proposal is unlikely to please developers. Land prices have risen as high as US$1500 (RMB 12000) per square metre.[26] There are also concerns that the quality of some tall buildings is not high enough.

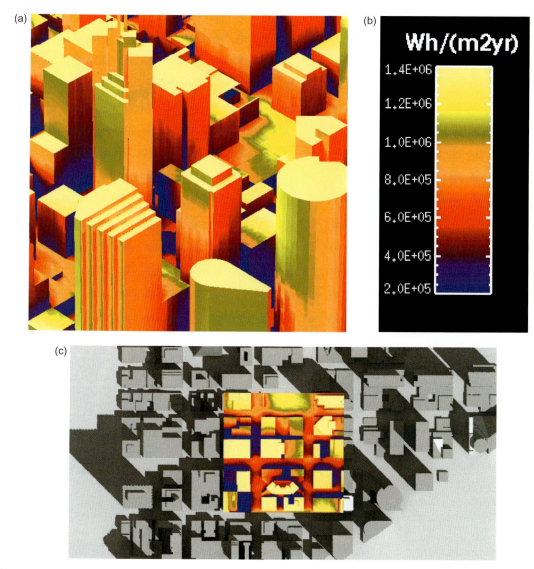

12.3.
Simulation of an aerial view of San Francisco showing the surfaces that get most solar gain over a year and the shadows that buildings of different shapes and heights cast across an area of the city. (a) Predicted total annual irradiation incident on building façades in San Francisco; (b) irradiation scale; (c) view from above of the 3D model of San Francisco with an overlay map of total annual irradiation for the study area.
Source: John Mardaljevic, Institute for Energy and Sustainable Development, De Montfort University; see www.iesd. dmu.ac.uk/

Two conditions conspire to make daylighting difficult in high-density buildings. One is how wide they are, from one external wall to another. Once the width of a building increases beyond about 12 m it is difficult to daylight it. Not withstanding the depth of a building, the amount of daylight reaching an interior is dependent on how much clear sky is visible from any particular window. The more sky can be seen from a window, the greater the amount of daylight that can enter a room. In a dense urban setting, it becomes clear that windows close to the ground will not provide significant daylight to interiors in high-rise districts.

WIND-PROOFING BUILDINGS

Peter Blake, in *Form Follows Fiasco*, condemned megatowers on several points. One was the disastrous wind shear that their surfaces created; another was fires that had burned out of control in two skyscrapers in Latin America. He warned the world that:

The first alternative to Modern Dogma should obviously be a moratorium on high-rise construction. It is outrageous that towers more than a hundred storeys high are being built at a time when no honest engineer and no honest architect, anywhere on earth, can say for certain what these structures will do to the environment – in terms of monumental congestion of services (including roads and mass-transit lines), in terms of wind currents at sidewalk level, in terms of surrounding water tables, in terms of fire hazards, in terms of various sorts of interior traumata, in terms of despoiling the neighborhoods ...[27]

Perhaps the worst climatic impacts that are associated with high-rise buildings result from the wind. The increasing height of a building results in two major factors:

- The speed of the wind increases the higher it is off the ground, resulting in higher air pressure experienced on the surface of the building.
- The higher the pressure at the top of the building the greater the difference in pressure between the top and the bottom of the building, increasing the speed of the wind between the apex and the base of the building.

The increasing high-level air pressure causes accelerated air speeds on the surface of the building, significantly increasing air penetration into the building, and out on the leeward side of the building through openings and cracks.[19] This can substantially increase the heating or the cooling load of an exposed high building over the loads of a low- to medium-rise building, often requiring expensive systems of climate control to even maintain a comfortable indoor climate the higher up the building one goes, but perhaps the potentially most severe impacts of wind discomfort occur in the outdoor spaces around high-rise buildings.[28] Many of us will experience such discomfort daily. In the city of London, for example, it is difficult not to notice the significantly increased wind speeds on an ordinary summer's day in say, Threadneedle Street, adjacent to a high-rise tower.

Wind becomes an annoyance at about 5 m/s, by causing clothes to flap and disturbance to the hair. At 10 m/s it becomes definitely disagreeable and dust and litter are picked up and by 20 m/s it is likely to be dangerous. In studies the Building Research Establishment (BRE) found that wind speeds of 5 m/s were exceeded less than 5% of the time in areas of low-rise developments but were exceeded over 20% of the time in areas with high-rise buildings.[29] With the increasingly deep low-pressure systems currently being associated with climate change and their associated increases in wind speeds, the ground-level turbulence and wind speeds in city streets may become increasingly less tolerable for the ordinary citizen in areas adjacent to tower blocks.

Higher wind speeds at street level are also associated with higher windchill factors, making the outdoors even more uncomfortable. Where today problems of outdoor air comfort may result from wind flow down and up from high-rise buildings, they may in future climates become the cause of increasingly dangerous street conditions as wind speeds increase.

There are several laboratories in the UK where the wind impacts of new city developments can be tested on models in wind tunnels or through simulation, as for instance at the Universities of Cardiff, Sheffield, Cambridge, UMIST and at the BRE and the National Physical Laboratory. Such wind testing is required by local authorities and by independent bodies, but for current climates only, and not future wind environments.

The highest percentage of the 85 UK construction-related deaths between 2001 and 2002 was caused by falls from height and a report on Health and Safety on sites concluded that 'designers are often abdicating their responsibility to reduce risk in relation to work at height by leaving it to the principal contractor without first considering how they could change the design in a way that would make it safer to build, clean or maintain'.[30] Increased wind speeds at height, with a windier climate, will significantly increase the risk of construction worker deaths to the point where building firms may become reluctant to put their workforces under such risks during certain seasons of the year.

SECURITY

There are at least five ways in which high-rise buildings will impact on the security of individuals, a business or a district. The first is obvious, being the security threat posed by occupying a 'target' building, occupied particularly by other target companies. In the anti-globalization atmosphere in current politics the larger the building the bigger the trophy. In New York it was the highest symbol of American Imperialism that was targeted by Islamic fundamentalist bombers. In London the Irish bombers chose again the district that represented the 'heart of the beast' to plant their largest bomb in the capital – Canary Wharf.

The second security issue is less obvious but may have more bearing on the everyday lives of people. It is the increasing wind speed at street level detailed above that has, and will increasingly have, the general effect that people avoid the streets. This impacts on street businesses as people begin to move out of doors less and less, leading to a general reduction in the quality of street life. American studies also show that lower numbers of people on the streets increase the levels of crime and violence, so reducing the security of whole districts.

In addition, studies of high-rise housing estates have shown that they are subject to higher levels of crime generally and can have disastrous impacts on society and culture. The problems of access and psychological alienation of high-rise housing have been well studied. Such was the scale of the problem in Hulme in South Manchester that the Chief Housing Office of the city quit his job in the 1970s to write a PhD on access in housing estates.

The third security issue is that of biological warfare. In buildings with fixed windows and extensive air circulation systems there is an increased hazard from biological agents. Ventilation ducts have proved to be a route of infection; at the Pentagon 31 anthrax spores were found in the air conditioning ducts of the building.[31] The problem here is the bigger the building, the bigger the risk. Many tall buildings have centralized circulation, servicing and air-handling units that make them very vulnerable to attack from many different sources.

A fourth issue we could add is nature's 'biological warfare' on us. For example, Hilton Hawaiian Village reopened in September 2003 after paying $55 million dollars in repairs that saw the building

12.4.
Just as financiers and pension holders alike have 'taken a bath' on the 'dog funds' that lost their value overnight, so many buildings may also say *Cave Canem* – 'Beware of the Dogs'. To avoid them look for signs of vulnerability to a range of hazards in a particular building.
Source: www.moloss.com

closed for 14 months, because a single tower block became infected with mould throughout its air-handling system, exacerbated by very high humidity within the building. The mould *Aspergillus eurotium* was said to be to blame, the same kind of mould seen on bread or cheese. It has no effect on most people, but some people get minor irritation of the nose when they are around it, the symptoms abating as soon as they move away, while a very few people have severe symptoms that in rare cases can be life-threatening. This is not confined to the tropics, and indeed a problem similar to that experienced by Hilton was found in hospitals across Canada in recent years.

Hilton has sued virtually every contractor that had anything to do with the construction of the Kalia Tower, including the architect, all the consulting engineers and other specialists on the project, and even the company that provided the lanai glass doors. It has argued that both the design and the construction of the building made it a 'greenhouse' for growing mould. The entire heating, ventilation and air conditioning (HVAC) system was rebuilt, mostly to ensure a more frequent turnover of drier air. The insurance industry has subsequently withdrawn 'mould coverage' from many policies and it is claimed that mould will be the 'new asbestos' in terms of payouts. The severity of the problem is reflected in the size of the payout to one family in a mould case, when a Texas jury awarded a family $32 million in a single toxic mould lawsuit against Farmers Insurance Group in June 2001.[32] Such outbreaks may become more prevalent with a warmer, wetter climate, which will make buildings more susceptible to systemic infestations of naturally occurring toxins within large-scale air-handling systems.

Urban piracy provides a strong fifth reason to avoid tall buildings. Just as the pirates off the coast of Africa with their small motor boats and hand-held rocket launchers can take hostage supertankers and cruise liners, so too can small, well-armed and determined bands of urban pirates take control of city neighbourhoods. Tens of thousands of people can be held hostage in their tower blocks, by a handful of people who control their one or two entrances and the roads around them, from street corner strongholds. Cities such as São Paulo are particularly vulnerable to the rule of the mob, not least because the city consists largely of tower buildings.

ENERGY SECURITY

The height of a building affects its internal climate. A building develops its own internal micro-climate, and heat from the lower floors will rise by natural buoyancy, making the higher floors hotter.

The higher the building the greater this problem of thermal stratification and the more energy that has to be thrown at cooling the upper floors.

In a high-rise building, where so many people are dependent on machinery for their very survival, there are severe repercussions from system failure. If a chiller breaks down and a part has to be obtained from Japan the systems of the whole building may be put at risk. In February 1998 in Auckland, New Zealand, all four main cables into the central city failed, cutting electricity to offices and more than 5000 apartments. Back-up cables also failed, due in part to the extreme summer temperatures[33] and for up to eight weeks there was chaos in the city buildings, where temperatures soared to over 50°C and allegedly in the top floors of tall buildings to over 80°C, making their habitation impossible. So taller means hotter at the top and more energy to heat and cool the building – a factor when floors are metered and lessees have to pay for the energy they use on their own floors. Businesses with all their eggs in one building basket will be very vulnerable to the impacts of energy outages, particularly in thin, tight-skinned buildings with no opening windows that have to be immediately evacuated because the air indoors becomes unfit to breathe once a blackout begins.

A 100-storey office block in the centre of London with a 50 m by 50 m floor plan would, if it was inefficient, use in the region of 1000 kWh/m^2 per annum of primary energy to run if it was of a business-as-usual design. This would translate to around 115 W/m^2 (1000/(24 × 365) W/m^2). Tall buildings, by their very nature of being tall, can use twice as much energy as equivalent low buildings – to raise people, goods, water, etc., throughout the building. Therefore peak demand from the building could be say 250 W/m^2 or 62.5 MW. A typical UK power station today has a rated output capacity of about 1 GW. So one more 1 MW power station would have to be built to cope with 16 new high-rise buildings in the City of London for instance, and this would be paid for from the bills of the ordinary electricity consumers of a region. 'Is this fair?', people may begin to ask, and especially when energy security is increasingly a core requirement of UK government policy.

Such buildings are a large part of the energy security problem in that they draw down so much of the energy in an area that they can jeopardize supplies to surrounding buildings, particularly where the power supply infrastructure is weak. The need to turn off or turn down buildings was seen in the case of the factories and shopping malls of Shanghai that had to be 'turned off' during brownouts (severe drops in voltage that cause the lights to dim).

Many towers are advertised as 'energy efficient' or 'green', and such claims could be taken with a pinch of salt. However, mitigating against reductions in air conditioning use with efficient technologies is the fact that standards of environmental design of building envelopes are decreasing continually, as evidenced by the fairly universal trend in office buildings in the 1990s, and increasingly in residential properties in the USA, towards thin, tight-skinned buildings, often with non-opening windows.[34] The lack of insulation in the external envelopes of such buildings, often coupled with poor thermal fabric storage internally, increases the heating and cooling loads of the buildings. With increasingly poor standards of environmental design, including widespread excessive use of glass in envelopes, and rapidly increasing levels of equipment use, and in particular of computers, air conditioning becomes more and more essential.[35]

FIRE

A designer of the Twin Towers stated on television the day after the event that if they had designed in sufficient escape stairs for the building then there would not have been enough office space left to make the building economically viable. It is increasingly recognized that in such cases, in tall buildings, everyone above the fire is likely to die. As a result of this open acknowledgement of the risks of occupying high-rise buildings, the BRE has been pressing UK ministers to tighten building regulations related to fire and has written to the Department of Transport, Local Government and the Regions raising the issues.[10] The current regulations do not take into account the provision for illegal acts, catastrophic fires or terrorism, nor was there sufficient provision in the guidelines for very tall buildings. The increasingly stringent costs of building in new standards for fire precautions may affect the financial viability of high-rise projects.

Statements were also made after the 9/11 event that no building could have withstood the forces of the two aircraft and the associated catastrophic fires after their crashes. What we know from the Pentagon impact, however, is that in a robust, securely designed, low-rise building fatalities can be reduced. After 9/11 the whole way in which fire engineers calculate survival risks in cases of fire has changed. Traditionally, they estimated on the notion of phased evacuation where the floor of the fire and the one above and one below are evacuate first. Today we know that in any fire event in a high-rise building people will think '9/11' and all scrabble to evacuate simultaneously. There would never be enough fire exits in any high rise to enable that to happen within the minutes that may be available. We also know now that the fire engineers' theories about 'pressurized' escape stairs are flawed and that it is impossible to maintain a pressurized escape when more than a few doors are opened into it at the same time.

The New York Fire Department says that a fully clothed fire-fighter can reach and operate effectively to around the tenth floor, but not higher up, so people who need attention on floors higher than this may never be reached.

We also know that in catastrophic fires, explosions and blackouts, sprinkler systems and fire lifts can fail. We now know that the increasingly hot summers will increase general fire risks out of and inside cities and that they are often associated with wide-scale power failures. And we know that fires can be caused for many reasons, and 'insecurity' will increase the risk of their being triggered. On 1 February 1974, in São Paulo, Brazil, a fire caused by electrical faults broke out in the upper storeys of a bank building and killed 189 people, many of whom leapt to their deaths. On 31 December 1986, in San Juan, Puerto Rico, fire in the Dupont Plaza Hotel set by three employees killed 96 people, largely due to occupants breaking windows at the point of 'flashover', when a fireball explodes, instantly killing many of the victims. On 23 February 1991 a fire broke out on the 22nd floor of the 38-storey building known as One Meridian Plaza in Philadelphia. The fire began in a pile of oil-soaked rags left by a contractor. It burned for 19 hours, eight floors were gutted and three fire-fighters lost their lives.[36] In the August 2003 blackout in New York the city fire brigade was called to numerous fires caused by candles used for light.

With all the improvements in systems since the 9/11 attack the problem of fire in tall buildings cannot be made to go away. On 19 August 2007 fire broke out in the Deutsche Bank tower in Manhattan next to Ground Zero. Two fire-fighters died. We know that tall buildings are not safe in the case of some fires. Is it only a matter of time before designers, developers and owners are sued by relatives of those who died in such fires as being culpable? What happens if an owner is told that negative pressure cannot be maintained in the fire escape after more than two doors are open, but the fire strategy relies on negative pressure to maintain safe evacuation conditions? Facilities managers will have to report such failures to owners or face liability themselves. Do the owners sell up and leave, or sue the engineer who designed a system that would not work, or the builders who built it so that it could not work?

CITIES ON THE EDGE OF A CLIFF

The tall building represents a building type that has such a huge environmental impact that in some cases tall buildings, imposed on a city or region that simply does not have the resource or infrastructural capacity to support them, may push the area over an 'environmental cliff'. The following are some regions that may be on the edge of such a cliff.

Las Vegas

Las Vegas is one of the most energy-hungry cities in the world. Not only is it located in a dry desert that is too hot and dry to support non-acclimatized 'Western' populations without huge energy implications, but the types of buildings on 'The Strip' are some of the most energy hungry in the world.

At a time of growing energy and water shortages the city now has over $30 billion of new developments on its books to be completed in the next 10 years, with the first one being the new City Centre development which should be complete by 2009. It is located on the imploded site of the old MGM lot and the new seven tower block development will cost c.$7 billion, cover 1.8 million m^2 and include hotels, casinos and residences. It will house 8000 new visitors and need an additional 12000 staff to service it. This is planned in a city with high levels of employment, soaring house prices, no free school places, and an electricity and water supply system in crisis.

Each new resident will need 20000 kWh of electricity a year. That will require an extra 400000 MW per annum generation capacity at a cost of $40 million a year, producing 160 million tonnes of carbon dioxide (CO_2) per annum.

In April 2005, when the ground was broken on this project, there was a global price spike for oil that went through the $60 a barrel mark, and the world began to wake up to the reality of Peak Oil. In April 2006 the price spike hit $80 dollars a barrel in the wake of the devastation wrought by Hurricane Katrina in the Gulf of Mexico, and short-term demand briefly exceeded the global capacity to produce and refine it. Federal Reserve Chairman Alan Greenspan said in 2005, 'Markets for oil and natural gas have been subject to a degree of strain over the past year not experienced for a generation', and things have got a lot worse since then.

Wall Street Goldman equity analyst Arjun N. Murti went farther in a report in early April 2005, saying there was the distinct possibility of $105-a-barrel for oil by 2007 and that the "Super Spike Period May Be Upon Us." Murti then cited the problem as being that Opec's 'space capacity [is] essentially gone' and global refinery capacity is 'now running full out' and suggested that by 2015 we may have the $300 barrel. If so, by 2015 the energy costs of that single new City Centre development could be as high as $200 million a year, at a time when many of the median-income visitors may well no longer be able to afford the air flights into the city. By July 2008 oil had shot up to $147 a barrel and talk of the $300 appeared even more credible, making the prospects of keeping the lights on in such towers even more of a challenge in an economy that would be reeling from soaring energy prices.

Then there is water. This single new MGM development will create additional demand for 2.3 billion gallons of water per year. This is taking a very conservative assumption of 10000 people in the development multiplied by the average Las Vegas Valley consumption of around 230000 gallons of water per year.

Nevada is already triggering a water war with neighbouring Utah as it tries to purloin its underground water reserves by drilling in areas in the north of the state like Snake Valley, and it seems that once again the lawyers will be the ones to cash in big time. In the face of this Las Vegas just gets more and more water and energy greedy.

From the Colorado River every year Arizona takes 2.8 million acre-feet, California takes 4.4 million acre-feet, Mexico takes 1.5 million acre-feet and Nevada a mere 300 000 acre-feet, from which the Las Vegas Valley draws 90% of all the water. One acre-foot equals approximately 326 000 gallons. Lake Mead behind the Hoover Dam today holds an optimistic 13 958 KAF (thousand acre-feet), not allowing for the considerable silting that is filling its bottom. This is 4 550 308 million gallons, around 54% of its potential capacity. Lake Mead may in 2005 have appeared to have enough water for 2000 years of this new City Centre development of 20 000 people, but will it be able to provide for the five more huge developments on the books plus the growing population of greater Las Vegas area, which is 1.6 million people and rising? Worse than that, Lake Mead is drying up.

The warming climate has caused a rapid decrease in the snow pack of the Rockies that feeds the Colorado River and its dams. In 2007 researchers Barnett and Pierce at Scripps Institution of Oceanography at the University of California at San Diego calculated that there is a 10% chance that Lake Mead will dry up by 2015 and a 50% chance that it will be gone by 2021.[37]

Kuwait

Kuwait is a city with many similarities to Las Vegas, with its desert location and lack of natural water sources. Kuwaities drive Humers, wear Rolexes and live like Las Vegans in air-conditioned palaces, glass-walled Utopias on borrowed time and money. Kuwait has been a state only since 1913, and has for decades subsidized the price of electricity, which is sold now for the unbelievably low price of around 0.05 pence a unit (kWh) to its citizens. This may have been acceptable over 10 years ago, when oil was around $10 dollars a barrel and there were fewer people in the region. In 1995 the population of Kuwait was 1.8 million, in 2005 it reached 2.4 million and it is predicted by the Kuwaiti government to rise to 4.2 million by 2025 and 6.4 million by 2050.

The Kuwaiti nationals live typically in large, air-conditioned houses. If they paid the UK going rate for energy it would cost around £12 000 a year just to pay the electricity bills for a medium-sized house, at 2008 prices. The average income for a teacher there is around £40 000–50 000 a year, and house costs are high. With globally rising energy prices that could double and triple in the coming years, the cost of cooling a house there could take up to a quarter of a household's income. As the power fails the water cannot be pumped, as a blogger on 22 August 2006 says: 'How can a country like Kuwait be suffering from shortages in electricity and water?? One of the richest countries in the world, going through the best economic periods with surpluses going through the roof … Why the hell are we living like Syria with electricity blackouts and water shortage right in the middle of the hottest time of the year, where the temperature is 50 degrees, no ACs are working, and at the same time people can't shower, so you can just imagine the beautiful aromas all around!'[38]

The Kuwaitis, who look so secure in their oil wealth, are perhaps some of the most vulnerable people in the world to the impact of the Peak Oil problem. People lower their voices when talking about the possibility of removing the subsidies for electricity, claiming that it would lead to revolution. Every summer blackouts are experienced in Kuwait, where temperatures rise to over 54°C, because the electricity generation capacity is being exceeded. Yet they are building more glass towers in the city, including the first tower block to be granted planning permission for more than 20 floors, a 100-storey all-glass tower. In 2008 civil unrest resulted in the replacement of the Kuwaiti prime minister who pushed through the reductions in the energy subsidies in the country. As in Dubai, if people have to pay a market price for their energy they may not stay in a country that requires so much energy to remain comfortable; and they may abandon the most energy-profligate building types, of which the glass towers are by far the worst.

London

The damage this is doing to our cities and businesses was dealt with in a London report, *Faulty Towers*,[8] published in July 2006 by the international architectural group Gensler. In it they issued a stark warning to commercial property investors that 75% of property developers believed that impending legislation to grade the energy efficiency of buildings (in response to the EU's Energy Performance of Buildings Directive) would have a negative impact on the value and transferability of inefficient buildings when certification was to be imposed from 2007. They claim that

Property fund managers are effectively sitting on an investment timebomb. The introduction of energy performance certificates will shorten the lifespan of commercial buildings constructed before the new regulations, and we expect the capital value of inefficient buildings to fall as a result. We expect to see a shake up in the market, with investors disposing of inefficient stock, upgrading those buildings which can be adapted and demanding much higher energy efficiency from new buildings. According to their research, more than 27% of companies' property-related energy consumption could be saved by making offices more sustainable, the equivalent of £155 million wasted every year. The report also reveals that 72% of company property directors believe that business is picking up the bill for badly designed, inefficient buildings and 26% state that bad office stock is actually damaging UK productivity. With spiraling energy costs pushing energy efficiency up the agenda, business is shown to welcome the grading of buildings and is aiming to reduce property related energy consumption by 12% over the next 5 years. However, there is a perception amongst developers that there is no demand for sustainable buildings. As a result, they lack the incentive to commission greener buildings. The research shows that this pessimism is misplaced and that business recognize the benefits of energy efficient buildings and is willing to pay 10% more in rent for more efficiently designed and constructed buildings.

In 2006 London had 25 new glass skyscrapers on the books to be built over the coming decade. The 2008 recession saw many of them shelved as developers realized that they could not afford to invest in a building type that had become albatrosses around the necks of so many major development and funding institutions. They knew it was coming. By summer 2008 Lehman Brothers, a leading Wall Street Bank, was preparing for a 28% drop in the value of their UK building portfolio, proving that the *Faulty Towers* Report had been timely and right. We knew, as the first edition of this book is testament to, what was coming.

Dubai

It is hardly necessary to describe the problems faced by Dubai. It is the world's greatest victim of the Ozymandias Syndrome (see poem at the end of this chapter). Just as in Kuwait, where energy scarcity and cost are an insurmountable problem, so too in Dubai the desire to develop the dream city is hindered by the simple fact that however much money one has today it is impossible to generate enough energy to meet the dream, and the exponential growth of the city is unsupportable with the current or planned infrastructure. The Burg Dubai alone requires around 500 MW of cooling and with other loads is getting on for being the first Gigawatt Building in the world. The energy requirements of Scotland are in the region of 6–7 GW. People will lose very large amounts of money and it will be interesting to see what form civil unrest takes when it involves the super-rich.

DEAD BUILDING SYNDROME

As you pass by the railway stations of cities around the world you will see from the carriage windows the growing numbers of dead buildings. You see them typically around the railway stations that were the hub of commercial life in towns and cities when rebuilding occurred after the Second World War, in the 1950s to 1970s. They are, as Gensler put it, 'Faulty Towers'. They perform very badly, they are often sick with their filthy inaccessible air-duct systems and they often look awful with their crumbling concrete and sad, single-glazed façades. The city centre has moved on but they just quietly died, empty, falling to pieces, and yet their sites were not worth the demolition and rebuilding costs they required. That is until the new site tax was brought in by the UK Government, which makes owners pay the same tax whether a site is occupied or empty. This will cause tremendous hardship for many building owners and investors. Even as I sit writing this on the train I leave behind a large dead building by the station at Crewe. We see another being built in the middle of two-storey Hemel Hempstead, like a symbol of the complete lack of understanding of the local council who passed it of the fact that this glass tower, now not even a gesture to having real walls, is a dead building waiting to happen in a decade or so, and they will be left with the bill for making it safe or pulling it down. What were the planning officers or members thinking? Let's make Manhatten in Hertfordshire? What do those poor people who have had the sun blotted out for them in perpetuity feel about it, and what mechanisms are in place to compensate them for the fact they can never warm their homes in winter or power them with free, clean energy ever again?

In cities of the rust belt of North America, where the industries that spawned prosperity decades ago, like iron and steel, cars, railways, canal building, typewriters, washing machines and agricultural machinery, have died or moved to Taiwan or China, even beautiful, fine, tall buildings of stone and brick lie empty. Of the 18 towers in Cleveland, Ohio, eight are completely empty and others only partially occupied, and some of these could be counted amongst the world's great buildings. They have simply lost their economic *raison d'être*.

Many cities today are building towers without a clear economic function. In Leeds, Manchester and Liverpool many of the recently built towers are partially or completely empty as the credit-starved buy-to-let markets evaporated, leaving many young and old people in chronic debt. This is happening everywhere developer greed knew no bounds when credit was cheap. The great new capital city of Astana in Kazakhstan is filling up an urban chessboard of tall glass tower buildings on the windblown Siberian steppes. Thousands of $200000–$1 million apartments exposed to freezing climate for a population where the average teacher earns around $15000 a year. Buildings with little economic future.

DO TALL BUILDINGS DESTROY THE AUTHENTICITY OF HISTORIC CITIES?

Every city has its own scale, form and history, written in the materials of which it is built, and the streets, and doors and windows, and places with which it has been woven into a landscape over time. Where a great town or city flowered in a particular era it makes sense to try and preserve the authenticity of its greatest age(s) to maintain for the city a unique selling point for visitors and preserve for posterity a living museum piece of that age. Thus, in half-timbered Chester the Tudor period can be visited, or in Bath that of the Georgian age. To spoil the unique historic feeling of such places would appear to be an act of vandalism not only for the visitors but also for the ordinary residents who may well have moved to a city for its particular historic setting and ambience.

This feeling is shared by Edinburgh which in 1995 gained world heritage status for its medieval historic Old Town and the eighteenth century neoclassical New Town.[39] 'The harmonious juxtaposition of these two contrasting historic areas, each with many important buildings', is deemed by the United Nations Educational, Scientific, and Cultural Organization (UNESCO), the world heritage organization, to be what gives the city its unique character. 'Edinburgh retains most of its significant buildings and spaces in better condition than most other historic cities of comparable value'. The director-general of UNESCO, Koïchiro Matsuura, called for a halt to Edinburgh's major developments in August 2008, while an investigation into the city's world heritage status was carried out. Matsuura warned that schemes such the £300 million Carltongate project master-planned by Allan Murray and designed by Gensler would damage Edinburgh's skyline, and should be put on hold while the organization carries out a review into whether the city should be placed on its 'at risk' list of endangered sites. UNESCO's findings are vital for the city as its world heritage status is of enormous importance to a city where around two-thirds of visitors come to see the historic city. The result is also vital to Scotland as a whole, in a country where the main industry is tourism. Here the final decisions on whether a greedy developer, trying to push a development too far and make it too big in the process, will prevail over the greater interests of the people and the authenticity of the place itself. The loss of the unique feel of such a historic centre would be a tragedy.

One Chinese city facing similar choices[40] has taken the bull market of extravagance and excess by the horns and begun to pull down its taller buildings to regain the historic feeling of the place. City officials in Hangzhou have implemented plans to lop floors off exclusive hotels, a television tower and other lakeside buildings in an attempt to win the coveted UNESCO world heritage status. The 2000-year-old city in Zhejiang, eastern China, is famed as one of the country's most beautiful places. China applied 12 years ago for the area around West Lake to be named as a heritage site to boost tourism. It is often packed with domestic visitors at peak season, but is less well known to foreign travellers. UNESCO requires historic sites to be kept intact, and the 40 million yuan (£4 million) resizing plan is the latest element in Hangzhou's attempts to beautify the site. Wang Chuanyue, a Professor of Architecture at Peking University, said that increasingly numerous tall buildings were making the lake look smaller, detracting from its beauty. Planners also intend to remove some smaller commercial buildings around the lake.

The *China Daily* newspaper said that all buildings more than 24 m tall on the lake's eastern shore would be shortened. A notice posted on the city government's website said that it would require taking floors off lakeside complexes, including the seven-storey east wing of the Shangri-La Hotel, where suites cost thousands of pounds a night. The gaining of world heritage site status would have a huge economic impact on the city and region, making it a focus for international tourists as well as Chinese visitors.

WHAT IS THE FUTURE FOR TALL BUILDINGS?

In an increasingly insecure world, do we really need to live in buildings in which the risk from climate change and the cost of energy increases year on year? What would common sense tell us about how high a building should be?

- High enough not to be a 'target' building – to nestle beneath the canopy of the city skyline to escape storm winds and not shade the buildings next door from the sun – this depends on the area of a particular city.

- High enough that a fire-fighter could run up, fully clothed, to people in a fire – so no more than 10 floors.
- High enough to be able to be evacuated by everybody within 15–30 minutes.
- High enough to be comfortably naturally ventilated – say 15 floors.
- High enough for occupants to be able to carry bags, and buckets of water, up and down the stairs safely if a blackout occurs – say three to six floors.

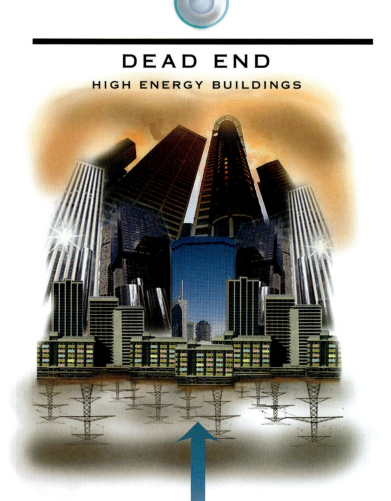

12.5.
Buildings with extremely high energy costs and exposure to extreme winds and solar gain may be one of the evolutionary types of buildings that die out first as the climate changes and the costs of energy rise over the next decades.
Source: Sue Roaf, digitally produced by Claire Palmer.

So, a compromise would be around six to eight storeys, but its anybody's choice and anybody's guess. A sensible choice may be found in the city of Paris, which has a canopy built to these heights. So, interestingly, the French, with their 'Beaux Arts' tradition and few notable low-energy buildings at all, may have a model for a low-risk city. What will the market benefits of that be over the coming decades? Each city must decide for itself what sort of place it is, what form it should have in the future and how tall it should be. It should not be developers who drive that discourse. It would be like allowing bankers to decide, unfettered by shareholder caution, how big their bonuses should be.

Perhaps the days in which size matters more than other considerations are over. Our building choices in the future may be dominated by the desire to ensure that what we build from now on has the smallest impacts and lasts the longest time, rather than making the biggest impression today. Whatever form of building we choose to live and work in, in the future, one thing must be sure: that the occupants can survive in it when the lights go out, because, in the last decades of the fossil fuel age, energy insecurity will drive many of our lifestyle choices. It is to this that we turn next.

Ozymandias
Percy Byssche Shelley, 1792–1822
I met a traveller from an antique land,
who said: two vast and trunkless legs of stone
stand in the desert. Near them, on the sand,
half sunk, a shattered visage lies, whose frown,
and wrinkled lip, and sneer of cold command,
tell that its sculptor well those passions read,
which yet survive, stamped on these lifeless things,
the hand that mocked them, and the heart that fed,
and on the pedestal these words appear:
'My name is Ozymandias, King of Kings:
Look upon my works, ye Mighty, and despair!'
Nothing beside remains. Round the decay
of that colossal wreck, boundless and bare,
the lone and level sands stretch far away.

Box 12.1 The impact of '9/11'

The thrill of tall buildings has, to a large extent, been dampened for New Yorkers, and many others around the world, by the events on and after 11 September 2001. Some 70 million square feet of office space was destroyed on 9/11. Two months afterwards the demand for office space in Lower Manhattan was almost negligible because commerce and industry had moved out of the area to what they consider to be safer premises, lower and less prestigious perhaps, outside the city centre.

The Empire State Building, one of the city's prime pieces of real estate, has become less prestigious and desirable.[i] Once again New York City's tallest structure, it has lost a number of its 880 tenants since September 2001, and others have said they are thinking about new locations. Many business owners who are staying in the Lower Manhattan area have numbers of employees, and their back-up information centres, located elsewhere owing to their fears of further terrorist attacks. Others found they were losing money because of their location.

In New York it is not only the big players in the property markets who suffer, but also the florists, the grocers and the restaurants, many of whom are also moving out having lost everything, to try to start again elsewhere. They have lost tens of thousands of well-heeled customers in the space of a couple of blocks due to the event and out-migration of workers and there is not enough business left in the area to keep many afloat. Economic migration is already happening in downtown New York.

'The attacks on the World Trade Center and the Pentagon changed everything – and have created immediate and intense visibility for Corporate Real Estate.' This quote from Cathy Guilbeault, Workplace Resource Director, Sun Microsystems Inc.,[ii] shows how importantly businesses are taking 'workplace security and business continuity planning' in light of 9/11 and 'planning for the survival of the enterprise' now includes obvious risk mitigation, such as:

- Shifts in preference from signature buildings in traditional business development plans to low-visibility facilities in dispersed or less popular locations.
- A shift from high-rise to low-rise buildings with a preference for lower level offices.
- Less visible external signage.
- Greater emphasis on building safety, with more pressure on corporate real estate to ensure that they have done everything possible to provide for the safety and security of employees.
- A shift to medium-sized cities (in the UK this would favour places such as Manchester, Birmingham, Bristol, Newcastle and Leeds).

In London, businesses are apparently also wary of occupying high-profile, high-rise buildings, because, in part, of the perceived terrorist risks. At Canary Wharf, rents fell steadily over 2003, with around 15% of the office space empty in the summer, and some of the tenants having deals letting them give back rented space without paying financial penalties, despite the fact that Middle East investors were shifting their attention from US markets to Britain and Europe.[iii] The half-empty Swiss Re tower building proved a problem for its owners when it became very difficult to let the other half of the 600 000 square feet of building at St Mary Axe in the heart of the City of London (Swiss Re had taken the bottom floors of the building). Many reasons were given for this, including that the shape of the space was difficult to use; no doubt fear of occupying a 'target' high-profile building did not help, nor what were then the highest rents in the city. At stake was half of the £2.5 million a year rental costs if no occupant for the top half of the building could be found. At that time around 20 million square feet of business space was available in central London, presumably a further disincentive to the building of major new high-rise developments.[iv]

Just like the 'dog' bonds that financiers cannot sell because they lost nearly all of their value overnight, we now look as if we may have a generation of 'dog' buildings. Here we see the issues, writ large, that it is not the micro-level considerations of how the building management system works or what the 'U' value of the walls is, but the fundamental market image of the building that drives sales. There is money to be made from this realization.

[i] http://www.newsday.com/business/local/newyork/ny-bzcov182469047nov18.story.
[ii] www.corenetglobal.org/pdf/learning/9_11_impact.pdf, loaded on 2 October 2002. This site shows how importantly businesses are taking 'workplace security and business continuity planning' in light of 9/11 and 'planning for the survival of the enterprise'. There are many websites, mainly US, that can offer valuable insight, including guidelines from the Federal Protective Service on How to Make Buildings Safe, etc., for instance on: www.gsa.gov.
[iii] *Observer*, Business, 24 August 2003, p. 4.
[iv] *Evening Standard*, 19 March 2003, p. 20.

Box 12.2 Ghettos in the sky

There is no industry-wide policy of not offering mortgages on high-rise flats and different lenders have their own policies as to what they will lend on. There are several issues that lenders will take into account when considering whether to lend on a flat. These will include whether the area, and the block, is predominantly owner-occupied, whether there is likely to be ongoing demand for the property and what the short- and long-term maintenance costs are likely to be.

Large maintenance bills can be a particular issue in tower block flats. Some borrowers have been faced with bills of £30 000 if major refurbishment is carried out on a block. If there were any possibility that a borrower would be faced with a bill of this order it would severely restrict their ability to pay their mortgage and affect the security of the loan, so older, poorly maintained blocks are not favoured by lenders.

The fact that a lender is not prepared to accept the property for mortgage purposes may have as much to do with the fact that there is little or no demand for such properties in a particular area as with an individual property's specific physical condition.

The type of construction is also an issue. Individual lenders will have their own policies on the types of construction they are prepared to lend on. Concrete panel construction has caused problems in the past, including cold bridging and air leakage problems through the envelope, and many lenders are reluctant to lend on this type of property. However, if the construction type is an unfamiliar one or there are doubts about its durability, the lender will often ask for a recent structural report. If the potential borrower is unwilling to pay for this then the mortgage will be refused even though the property may be acceptable. This associated risk is also amplified by the experience of large payouts from the insurance industry related to a single event, such as the gas explosion in a single flat at Ronan Point, London, resulting in the collapse, and subsequent demolition of, an entire tower block.

For low income people in Glasgow there is little chance of ever getting a mortgage in a tower block on a council estate. This is one reason why famous tower blocks that have dominated the Glasgow skyline for over 40 years are being demolished. This is doubly the case after the economic collapse of 2008–2009. The blocks had become synonymous with crime, poverty and urban decay in Britain's unhealthiest city and billions of pounds will be spent over 10 years to transform the bleak landscape of Scotland's biggest city, which has the highest concentration of public-owned housing in Europe. Most of the 250 blocks of flats will be knocked down to make way for thousands of new, purpose-built homes after the city's 94 000 flats are transferred from council control to community housing trusts. Under the plans, the Glasgow Housing Association is being given a £6 billion budget to deal with dilapidated housing stock, including the tower blocks.

Housing consultants estimate that the cost of refurbishing flats at Red Road, Glasgow, to a standard that would last for the next 30 years would amount to more than £70 000 per home. They say that it would be cheaper to get rid of them and start again.[i]

For the same reason many other cities across Britain are blowing up their tower blocks, including Birmingham, where all the 315 tower blocks are planned to be demolished. Officials confirmed that finance for the transfer is based on a programme to demolish 100 tower blocks in the next five years, and almost all of the remaining 215 blocks before 2018.[ii]

Although some lenders have a greater appetite (and capacity) to take on loans that are considered a greater risk than others, and will insure some tower flats, only a few will expose themselves in this market and this is why it is very important that tenants who are considering whether to exercise their right to buy should be advised of the additional risks involved in purchasing a tower block flat and the possible problems they may have if or when they come to sell it.

Some local authorities may be willing to buy back the property under the 'Buy Back Scheme' introduced on 1 April 1999, where local authorities are able to buy back homes from leaseholders or others who are in difficulty or are having problems selling their property. It allows local authorities to regain a property that can then be re-let, but it is doubtful whether many authorities would do this for such high-risk properties, which is one reason why Glasgow has chosen to demolish its tower stock. Alternatively, individuals could seek a cash buyer or someone who would see it as an investment property, as an investor may take a different view of the risks posed. Some tower blocks are being retained owing to very high demolition cost resulting from the asbestos content of their construction.

However, there are too few houses in southeast England, and thus forced high house prices, meaning that ordinary working families are unable to afford to live near their work and have to commute, sometimes for hours, to get to work. Local councils are increasingly asking for a higher percentage of 'social' or 'affordable' housing in all developments, up to 40–50% from some councils.

Developers reap less profit from social housing and are very reluctant to build more than the minimum they can get away with. In April 2003, the then London Mayor Ken Livingstone threatened to block Broadway Malyan's 50-storey apartment block in Vauxhall as its 25% affordable homes was insufficient.[iii] He has developed a formula, dubbed the 'Kenculator', that responds to a range of factors to arrive at a reasonable figure for what numbers of low-cost houses, up to 50%, should be included in every new development. Developers are reluctant to lose such a substantial percentage of their profits by providing low-cost housing that gives them lower profit levels, particularly in the current economic climate. Further, if a higher percentage of units were social housing then the mortage lenders may be less willing to provide loans to buy non-social housing units owing to their rules of thumb of the proportion of owner–occupiers they require in a block to agree to lend on it.

However, some of the 1960s' and 1970s' tower blocks have been refurbished. Two 15-storey tower blocks on Conway Street, Liverpool, were in such poor condition that they seemed fit only for demolition, but having successfully renovated two similar blocks on Manchester's Wythenshawe estate one developer saw an opportunity to provide affordable homes. He bought the two towers for £1 million each and is spending eight times that amount to transform the 1960s' towers into flats, with purchase prices starting at £49 500. The difference in the refurbishment costs estimated by Glasgow's consultants of £70 000 and the money spent on these blocks begs the question of how long the refurbishments here will hold and, once they fail, will these blocks just turn into ghettos again? In the current economic recession the high costs of such high-rise conversions are economically challenging to developers who are struggling to survive through a period of catastrophic house price collapse.

[i]http://society.guardian.co.uk/housing/story/0,7890,565387,00.html.
[ii]http://society.guardian.co.uk/housingtransfers/story/0,8150,632697,00.html.
[iii]*Building Design*, 17 April 2003, p. 6.

Box 12.3 Stealing sound and vision

In 1997 the House of Lords refused a claim by 700 residents of east London who claimed that their television reception had been severely affected by the building of Canary Wharf. While the court accepted that this did amount to quite severe interference to their enjoyment of their properties and could reduce their market value, there was still no legal basis to award compensation.[i] There is, however, hope for such residents who have suffered as the result of radio and television wave shadows in that the approach taken by the courts is regarded as unlikely to survive the introduction of the Human Rights Act.[ii] If the loss of television and sound quality from the erection of a tall building constitutes 'severe interference' to the enjoyment of properties then it does indeed constitute a 'material consideration' and councils are obliged by law to consult with those so affected in the planning process. So perhaps the residents affected could sue the councils for failing to meet their statutory obligation to consult with all those who will in future be affected by a development.

[i]All England Law Reports: 1992, p. 426; *Hunter* v. *Wharf*, available from: http://www.lib.nus.edu.sg/linus/96oct/llbcdnew.html.
[ii]*Guardian*, Money, 16 February 2002.

NOTES AND REFERENCES

1 J.H. Kunstler, N. Salingaros, (2001) The end of tall buildings. At: <http://www.peoplesgeography.org/tall.html>. See also N. Salingaros, Theory of the urban web. J. Urban Des. 3, (1998) 53–71. See <http://www.math.utsa.edu/sphere/salingar/urbanweb.html>.

2 The Empire State Building was the brainchild of John J. Raskob, the vice-president of General Motors, who wanted this new building to exceed the height of the Chrysler Building, still under construction, when the plans were released on 29 August 1929. The site had previously housed the 'twin hotel' of Waldorf–Astoria (Waldorf Hotel 1893, Astoria Hotel 1897, both by arch. Henry J. Hardenbergh), both built by the Astor family and eventually connected by a wide hall. After a fire the buildings were demolished, a new Waldorf–Astoria built farther uptown and the construction of the Empire State Building was started on the site. The excavations for the foundations were begun on January 1930, work on the steel framework in March of the same year, and the building was completed on 11 April 1931.

3 Guardian, 18 October 2003, p. 20.

4 Independent, 28 October 2003, p. 9.

5 CABE's stated aim is 'inspiring people to demand more from their buildings and spaces'. CABE's home page states:

'We believe that well designed homes, streets, parks, workplaces, schools and hospitals are the fundamental right of everyone. We use our skills and resources to work for a higher quality of life for people and communities across England, with particular concern for those living in deprived areas. We do this by making the case for change, gathering hard evidence, providing education opportunities and through direct help on individual programmes and projects.

'We motivate those responsible for providing our buildings and spaces to design and develop well. We demonstrate to those clients that investment in excellence will pay back many times over through a more productive workforce, more contented customers and a healthier bottom line.'

6 Building Design, 9 May 2003, p. 1.

7 Building Design, 25 April 2003, p. 4.

8 <http://www.london.gov.uk/view_press_release.jsp?releaseid5 210>.

9 Building Design, 6 July 2001.

10 Building Design, 5 October 2001.

11 Building Design, 22 July 2001.

12 Guardian, 3 November 2003, p. 16.

13 Guardian, 21 June 2003, p. 28.

14 <http://www.corenetglobal.org/pdf/learning/9_11_impact.pdf.>

15 O. Newman, Defensible Space, The Architectural Press, London, 1973.

16 C. Alexander, et al., A Pattern Language – Towns, Buildings, Construction, Oxford University Press, New York, 1977 pp. 114–19, 468–76.

17 J. Rudge, F. Nicol, Cutting the Cost of Cold: Affordable Warmth for Healthier Homes, E&FN Spon, London, 2000.

18 P. Blake, Form Follows Fiasco: Why Modern Architecture Hasn't Worked, Little, Brown, Boston, MA, 1974 See also an interesting discussion around the subject on: < http://www.geocities.com/Athens/2360/jm-eng.fff-hai.html>.

19 I. Meir, Y. Etzion, D. Faiman, Energy Aspects of Design in Arid Zones. J. Blaustein Institute for Desert Research, Ben-Gurion University of the Negev, 1998, p. 115.

20 L. Al-Sharif, Lift and escalator energy consumption. Proceedings of the CIBSE/ASHRAE Joint National Conference, Harrogate, 1996, pp. 231–239.

21 L. Krier, Houses, Palaces, Cities, St Martin's Press, New York, 1984.

22 Guardian, 20 June 2008, p. 27.

23 P. Littlefair, Solar access, passive cooling and micro-climate in the city: the polis project. Proceedings of EPIC 98, the 2nd European Conference on Energy Performance and Indoor Climate in Buildings, Lyons, (1998) p. 984. See also the solar ordinances of Boulder Colorado, 1991, on: <http://www.sustainable.doe.gov/municipal/codtoc.shtml>. The City of Boulder's solar access ordinance guarantees access to sunlight for homeowners and renters in the city. This is done by setting limits on the amount of permitted shading by new construction. A solar access permit is available to those who have installed or who plan to install a solar energy system and need more protection than is provided by the ordinance. For new developments, all units that are not planned to incorporate solar features must be sited to provide good solar access. They must also have roofs capable of supporting at least 75 square feet of solar collectors per dwelling unit. Non-residential buildings have similar requirements for siting. When applying for a building permit, a simple shadow analysis must be submitted to the City's Building Department.

24 Meir et al. Energy Aspects of Design in Arid Zones, p. 116.

25 A. Viljoen, K. Bohn, Urban intensification and the integration of productive landscape. Part One, in: Proceedings World Renewable Energy Congress VI, Elsevier Science, Oxford, 2000, pp. 483–488.

26 RIBAWorld, Issue 231–232, Friday 23 August 2002, 16:17:1010100 <http://www.RIBAWorld@inst.riba.org>.

27 Blake, Form follows Fiasco, p. 150. See also <http://www.peoplesgeography.org/tall.html>

28 T. Lawson, Building Aerodynamics, Imperial College Press, London, 2001.

29 See R. Geiger, The Climate Near the Ground. Harvard University Press, Cambridge, MA, 1965. T.R. Oke, Boundary Layer Climates. Methuen & Co, London, 1978. A. Penwarden, D. Wise, Air Flow around Buildings, Building Research Establishment Digest, Garston, Watford, 1975.

30 Building Design, 9 May 2003, p. 3.

31 Guardian, 18 October 2001.

32 More results from <http://www.bizjournals.com>.

33 <http://www.helio-international.org/Helio/anglais/reports/newzealand.html>.

34 G. Robertson, A case study of Atria, in: S. Roaf, M. Hancock (Eds.) Energy Efficient Building: A Design Guide, Blackwell Scientific, Oxford, 1992.

35 B. Bordass, Appropriate methods and technologies for new build and refurbishment: offices, in: Global Responsibilities of Architects, RIBA Publications, London, 1990.

36 For a detailed analysis of this event and its implications for the fire hazards posed by tall buildings see <http://www.iklimnet.com/hotelfires/meridienplaza/html>.

37 T.P. Barnett, D.W. Pierce, When will Lake Mead run dry? Water Resour. Res. 44 (2008) W03201.

38 Observer, Business, 2 April 2008, p. 3; Guardian, 12 July 2008, p. 41.

39 See <http://whc.unesco.org/en/list/728>.

40 Guardian, Chinese city to trim tall buildings, Friday 12 December 2008. See <http://www.guardian.co.uk/world/2008/dec/12/hangzhou-urban-development-china>.

13 THE FOSSIL FUEL CRISIS

INTRODUCTION

The year 2008 saw the global economic 'carnage' caused by the combination of personal greed, cheap debt and lack of trust between banks. Underpinning this chaos is the uncertainty surrounding current and future energy prices and the fear that we are at the end of the age of cheap energy. Every sub-prime matchbox MacMansion rolled out across the desert plains of Nevada or Arizona was made by energy-hungry machines and production lines, and every desert home is only inhabitable because of the cheap machines that pumps them full of coolth.

The point at which energy soared above the level the middle classes of America could afford to pay for it, was the point at which those buildings became unsellable, and in hot states this was speeded up by soaring air conditioning cost (Figure 13.1). This economic crisis is not just about debt. It is about bad buildings and the increasingly unaffordable energy costs of occupying them in a changing climate.

The affordable cost threshold of the energy needed to keep those building comfortable will, like the temperature threshold of passive technologies and buildings before them, dictate whether buildings and cities live or die. The end of the age of cheap energy also inevitably marks the end of energy-profligate building because we will simply, increasingly, no longer be able to afford to run them.

The challenge now is to restructure our entire lifestyles to wean ourselves off fossil fuel energy. In the UK buildings use around 46% of all the energy we produce simply to heat, light, cook and run equipment, without the energy costs of materials to build them and transport to get to them being taken into account.[1]

The huge structural cracks had already opened up in the fossil fuel supply lines by 2003 when the White Paper on Energy Policy published by the UK Department of Trade and Industry outlined the key energy aims of the UK government to:[2]

- Put the UK on a path to cut the its carbon dioxide (CO_2) emissions – the main contributor to global warming – by some 60% by about 2050 with real progress by 2020.
- Maintain the reliability of energy supplies.
- Promote competitive markets in the UK and beyond, helping to raise the rate of sustainable economic growth and to improve our productivity.
- Ensure that every home is adequately and affordably heated.

13.1.
Tract home settlement of the deserts of South Western USA is only possible because of air conditioning.
Source: Sue Roaf from Raf from Solar Cities 2006.

Since then, according to several pundits, we have passed the all-important point of 'Peak Oil' for conventional reserves on most continents, and global demand for fossil fuels is rapidly increasing with demand soaring in emerging economies like China and India. It is the growing gap between the fossil fuels we use, and the exponential rise in the demand for energy, that has already resulted in the volatile energy markets reflected in the oil prices soaring first through $100 a barrel in January 2008, then to $147 a barrel in July 2008 and back down to $60 a barrel in November 2008.

Petrol and diesel at the pump in the UK was around 75 pence a litre in 2003, when the first edition of this book was written, and by July 2008 diesel had soared to 127 pence a litre and petrol to 123 pence a litre. The rising oil prices have pushed petrol prices up at the pumps and in the UK alone an average two-car family paid £400 more a year for its petrol in 2008 than in 2007. Diesel cars, which tend to be more fuel efficient than their petrol equivalents (though more polluting with their high levels of particulate emissions) were particularly badly hit by rising prices and rather than being a cheaper fuel diesel rose to around 8 pence more expensive a litre than petrol. Drivers took to the streets in organized civil protests in July 2008 against unaffordable petrol. By November 2008 petrol was back down at 90 pence a litre.

The rising costs of energy have not only had huge impacts on road transport costs but also provided the first major barrier to a future of unconstrained air travel. Airline industries across the world have cancelled orders, parked and scrapped aeroplanes, and cancelled routes and flights across the board. In May 2008 alone American Airlines, the world's biggest airline, scrapped 75 planes, cancelled 12% of its flights and specified that a large number of its staff would be shed. British Airways anticipated a zero profit for 2008 and other airlines are reducing flying speeds and weights carried, down to developing lighter drinks trolleys!

By June 2008 American Airlines had laid off a fifth of its fleet, some 455 planes, and up to 1600 staff. Several airlines have folded, such as Maxjet, Eos, Aloha Airlines and ATA. In July 2007 Professor Sir David King branded the plans for a third runway at Heathrow airport as a white elephant, pointing out that at a time when we are decarbonizing our economy this must mean that alternative means of transport such as road and rail will be chosen over air transport. The cost choices he claimed of putting an additional price on carbon, a solution favoured by the British Government, together with the increased costs of fuels will drive people away from air travel and discourage investments in new runway capacity.[3] Despite this the British Government seems hell bent, just as it was putting so many people in new developments on the flood plains of the Thames, on building more runways against a growing quantity of very good advice.

Since the turn of this century, the fossil fuel crisis has already been reshaping the very structure of our economy and some of the reasons behind this are outlined below.

OIL

Current estimates of how much oil we have left range from 30 to 40 years, but the nature of oil reserves, exploitation and reporting is very complex.[4] Colin Campbell gives some insight into the complexity of the forces at play in the industry in his very interesting piece called 'The Heart of the Matter', and his many published works offer a fuller outline of the mechanics of the oil supply industry. He has been the founding father of the Peak Oil movement.[5]

Since the futurologists of the 1970s' oil crisis began to warn us of the 'end of oil' based on estimates from fairly crude field surveys, the industry has become highly proficient in identifying potential

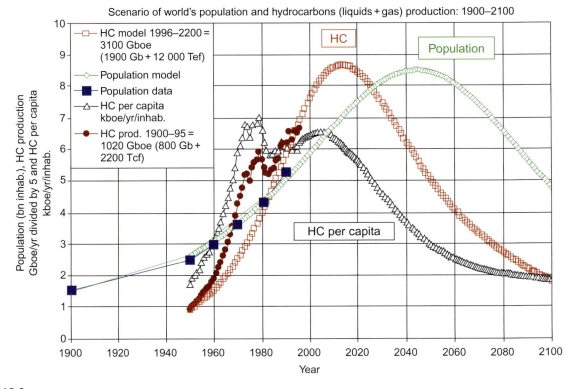

13.2.
Increases in the world population, coupled with the decrease from now on of fossil fuel availability, will cause energy prices to skyrocket. Gb = billion barrels; Gboe = billion barrels oil equivalent; Tcf = trillion cubic feet (5.5 Tcf = 1 Gboe); HC = hydrocarbons.
Source: www.energycrisis.com.

oil fields, locating, quantifying and exploiting them with extremely sophisticated equipment and technologies. The industry can now identify the 'needle in a haystack'[6] with emerging scanning and test drilling techniques including the new electromagnetic field mapping techniques to identify 'resistors' such as oil and gas fields to depths of over 3000 m. With marine drilling rigs now costing in the region of $700 000 a day to hire, high levels of confidence are needed to begin drilling as energy and its extraction become ever more expensive.

How much oil is there left?

There are two kinds of commonly defined sources of oil and gas:

- **Conventional** – which is considered, roughly, to be all the sources that are not:
- **Non-conventional:**
  - Oil from coal and 'shale' (immature source rock)
  - Bitumen and extra-heavy oil (< 100 API)
  - Heavy oil (10–17.5 API)
  - Polar oil and gas
  - Deep water oil and gas (500 m depth)[7]

There are some 22 000 conventional oil fields around the globe. Technical estimates of the size of a field are relatively constant although they evolve as knowledge grows. These confidential estimates are tested by drilling, and a plan for the exploitation of a field is then developed. Oil companies report estimated reserve sizes, but are prudent in typically underestimating them to ensure that investors are impressed by the rising outputs from a field. The process of reserve reporting is a

13.3.
Image from the cover of Colin Campbell's book *The Essence of Oil and Gas Depletion.*[5] Campbell was the first to highlight the global problem of 'Peak Oil' and alert the world to the coming energy crisis that he accurately predicted would occur as soon as 2008 and be associated with global recession.
Source: Bill Hughes, Multi-Science Publishing Co., Brentwood, Essex. *You see, it is all coming true.*

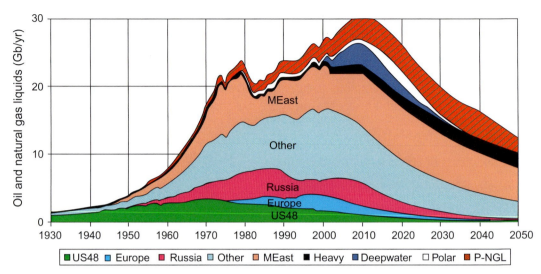

13.4.
Showing the available global fossil fuel reserves (2003) and indicating how badly off the USA and Europe are in relation to their dwindling stocks. Gb = billion barrels.
Source: www.peakoil.net.

finely balanced one, and one that is easy to get wrong, as both BP and Shell know to their detriment. In 2001 the then BP Chief Executive Lord Brown announced that output would be only 3% up on the previous year rather than the 5.5% growth promised. This was the third time he had slashed his estimates in a single year and he personally lost considerable market credibility in having to do so.[8] In January 2004 came the astounding news that Shell was downgrading its known reserves by 20%, a shocking admission that led to a rapid fall in its price on the markets. These events caused a severe loss of confidence in the mechanisms of oil reporting but are considered by many to be the tip of the iceberg of misreporting in the sector. No one really has a complete idea of what is out there and the credit crunch has meant that investors are increasingly wary of putting money into expensive drilling when they have no idea what price they will get for the oil once it reaches land.

In reality, the reserves in any field are finite and output from oil fields roughly follows a bell-shaped curve with a plateau that represents the peak output of that field. One of the great challenges over the past decades has been to develop technologies that were able to get as much of the available oil out of the ground as possible, and enormous advances in extraction methods have taken place. However, it is unrealistic to expect that new technologies will release vast amounts of new conventional oil.[9–11]

Soaring energy prices have now made the harder to reach reserves of oil economical to pump and have led to a boom in deep-water drilling off Brazil and in the Mexican Gulf and to the plundering of massive reserves of the Athabascan tar sands. These were deemed to be economical at barrel prices above $70 and are difficult and polluting to process, requiring excavation of the oil shales, crushing, and hot water extraction to create an oil slurry that is mixed with naphtha to remove remaining minerals and water. The bitumen is then heated and skimmed to produce lighter synthetic crudes ready to be sent to a conventional refinery. About 2 tonnes of tar sands produces a barrel of oil and during the process around one barrel of oil is required to provide the

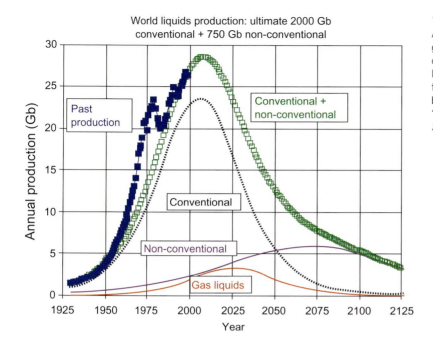

World liquids production: ultimate 2000 Gb
conventional + 750 Gb non-conventional

13.5.
Annual recorded and predicted global oil production of conventional and non-conventional liquid gas and oil liquids production from 1925 to 2125. Gb = billion barrels. Note when production 'peaks'.
Source: www.energycrisis.com/.

energy to produce a barrel and a half of oil. Somehow these figures are often omitted and the producers claim that the process produces only 15% more CO_2 than conventional oil production. However, in the Canadian tar sands process huge lakes of polluted liquids are a by-product and the costs of repairing the region or their long-term impact costs are not calculated in the production costs per barrel. How the Canadian Government is going to afford to make these regions habitable ever again is unclear. Much of the heart of Canada now looks like an environmental disaster zone but no one seems to be complaining! One wonders why? Are the Canadians happy to leave this legacy of destruction of a large part of their country to their children?

A further major problem arises because the majority of the remaining reserves of conventional oil are located in areas of the world where demand is not greatest, in parts of the Middle East, Eurasia, Africa and Latin America. Half of the remaining oil lies in five Middle Eastern countries: Abu Dhabi, Iran, Iraq, Kuwait and Saudi Arabia. At some point when the gap between supply and demand has ceased to be cushioned by these swing states' contributions, and the gap between what we can produce and what we need yawns, the market will react, probably in proportion to its preparedness for that transition.[11] The result may well come in the form of oil shocks, not in a gradual decline in supply, as Bartsch and Muller predicted way back in 2000:[12]

It is not that we will not have enough oil to take us to 2020 but that the road is likely to be bumpy and subject to a number of economic and political shocks.

Another real problem for Western users is the location of the oil reserves geopolitically. The USA in particular is having problems exerting sufficient influence to stabilize and secure the oil production and transport facilities it would ideally want. The civil and political forces in Latin America, Asia, the Middle East and Africa have proved difficult to overcome, even for a superpower. China has moved in to buy influence over vast reserves in Africa and Asia at what will inevitably be the expense of the oil-addicted populations of North America.

By 2008 the full extent of the growing fossil fuel crisis began to emerge as the dependence of the oil industry on market liquidity and stability to maintain a reasonable exploration and field development programmes came into focus. Despite record profits large oil firms began to pull out of more expensive operations and as Lord Ron Oxborough, Former Chairman of Shell, wrote in the introduction to a new report on energy security in the UK in October 2008,[13]

There isn't any shortage of oil, but there is a real shortage of the cheap oil that for too long we have taken for granted.

Even the deeply conservative International Energy Agency has warned of an Oil Crunch by 2013. The authors of an October 2008 report on the Oil Crunch outlined three possible scenarios:

1 In a '*plateau*' scenario, like the one Shell foresees, global production will flatten around 2015 and remain on a plateau into the 2020s, propped up by expanding volumes of unconventional oil production because of the decline of conventional oil production. (This means much more expensive energy.)
2 In a '*descent*' scenario, global production falls steadily as oilfield flows from newer projects fail to replace capacity declines from depletion in older existing fields.
3 In a '*collapse*' scenario, the steady fall of the 'descent' scenario is steepened appreciably by a serial collapse of production in some – possibly many – of the aged supergiant and giant fields that provide so much global production today.

On balance, the expert team, headed by Jeremy Leggett, considered that the 'descent' scenario is a highly probable global outcome. They also feared that a 'collapse' scenario is possible. Collapse, like runaway climate change, is now inevitable in the oil and gas industry just as it is for climate change. We had better learn to adapt pretty quickly to an age when the oil will run out. Although very impressive technologies are already available for squeezing the last drop out of old oil fields, these are expensive and what they can produce is really only a drop in the barrel of the growing gap between supply and demand. Like the question of who will pay for the emerging carbon capture and storage technologies, we need answers to the question of who is able and willing to afford the rising costs of these technologies? From where we stand now the loud answer appears to be – no one.

GAS: 'THE NEW OIL?'

Reserves of natural gas are far more abundant than those of oil but it is a far more mobile substance, which means it leaks from its traps. More of it is recoverable from reserves than oil, around 75%, and its depletion profile gives a constant supply over a long period before coming to an abrupt end, when production plummets and prices soar.

It is also much more difficult to model gas depletion, because its profile is dictated more by market forces than by the immutable physics of the reservoir. The middle point in production is estimated by Campbell to come at around 2020. The USA, and in the not too distant future, Canada, are facing chronic gas shortfalls. Europe faces the same general future but has the advantage of being ably to tap, by pipeline, into the reserves of the Middle East, the former Soviet Union and North Africa, politics permitting.

Britain no longer has enough gas supply left to meet its own total demands. In November 2003 the first flow of gas *into* the UK via the gas interconnector pipe from Belgium occurred, accompanied by a sharp hike in the cost of UK gas (by up to 10% higher than the weeks before), making prices for natural gas in the UK some of the highest in the developed world. Before that the interconnector had been supplying gas *to* the Continent, at a time when UK prices were, even then, more than a third higher than the equivalent elsewhere in Europe.[14]

Gas is a 'cleaner' fuel, emitting less CO_2 per unit of 'delivered' energy produced, and hence politically a more popular fuel for the generation of electricity than coal or oil. It is also mainly located in politically interesting territories.

In November 2003 Shell signed a historic deal to explore a region of Saudi Arabia for gas. Shell's stated belief is that gas will overtake oil as the primary source of energy in the world, and already gas is playing an increasing role in meeting the world demand for energy. It will overtake oil some time after 2020 as the 'preferred' fuel,[15] although no doubt through necessity rather than actual preference.

However, gas supplies are decreasingly secure as UK imports of gas grow to meet growing demands and dwindling supplies from UK sources. A £5.8 billion plan to develop Norway's Ormen Lange gas field, to be operated by Shell, will, the UK Government claims, 'secure' the UK's long term supplies via a 1200 km pipeline to Easington in Yorkshire.[16] This field is structurally difficult and expensive to tap and extract,[16] with questions over the reservoir quality of the gas, according to Norsk Hydro, who are developing the field.[17] Putting lots of British eggs in this particular gas basket is not a risk-free stratagem for the UK Government.

There is also growing concern about the fact that Russia is controlling more and more of Europe's gas and oil supplies. In March 2007 Russia signed a deal to build a 157 mile, £619 million

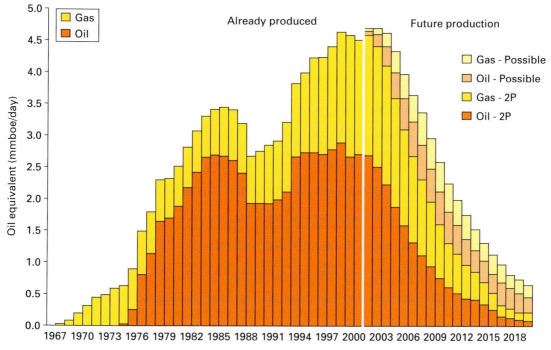

13.6.
Produced and predicted oil and gas reserves for the UK. mmboe = million barrels oil equivalent.
Source: UK Department of Trade and Industry, via www.peakoil.net.

oil pipeline across Bulgaria and Greece. Russia provides around 33% of Europe's oil and 40% of its gas but it is increasingly difficult to diversify supply away from Russia's hold as India and the Far East are dominating purchases from many non-traditional European suppliers like Angola and Ethiopia. In January 2007 a major row blew up as Russia threatened to cut a vital gas pipeline across Belarussian territory, cutting a major supply line to Germany, Poland and Ukraine, exacerbating concerns that Russia had Europe at its mercy in terms of both gas and oil supplies.

Liquid natural gas (LNG) is seen as an efficient way of importing gas into the UK and the government has invested huge amounts in building the infrastructure to import it. However, in 2008 imports of it dwindled almost to a halt despite rising prices of gas from the European interconnector. Not only is much of the global LNG going to the Asian markets but the UK energy industry has shifted its emphasis away from gas with bigger fish to fry. A gas power station takes around two years to build, a coal one four to eight and a nuclear power station over 10 years to build and commission. However, in a bid to build energy security the UK has now relaxed its opposition to dirtier coal-powered stations, so encouraging energy providers to plan building not only a new generation of nuclear stations but also new coal-powered stations.[18]

There are a number of new developments in the area of reducing pollution from related generation. Although CO_2 sequestration technologies are coming on line that will reduce the greenhouse gas emissions from gas plants, particularly CO_2, they will actually require 10–20% more energy to produce the same amount of electricity as a result, so here we have the question of whether it is more acceptable to reduce climate change emissions and use our dwindling reserves of fossil fuels more rapidly, or the reverse.

ENERGY WILL COST MORE

In 2003 we predicted that an inevitable result of such factors will be increasing prices for consumers of oil and gas. In December 2003 came the news that British Gas was going to raise gas and electricity prices for its 15 million consumers by 5.9% from 10 January 2004. In fact between 2003 and 2008 the price of gas rose by 72% and electricity bills by 64.%.[19] In one year alone, in 2003, unprecedented wholesale gas prices rose by 15% and electricity rose by 15% with further dire warnings of rises. Opponents of the rises then criticized the hikes saying that the significant reductions in wholesale prices over the past few years had not been passed on to the consumers.[20] But in a market of rapidly rising market prices for oil and gas in 2008 gas prices rose for British Gas customers by a further 54% and electricity by over 20% for many firms.

Price hikes most affect the numbers of people in fuel poverty, those who spend more than 10% of their net income on energy. Almost 70 000 homes in the UK were disconnected in 2001, 2002 and 2003. The numbers in fuel poverty halved between 1996 and 2001 from 5 million to 2.5 million, 1 million of which could be attributed to falling prices. But it does not take a great increase in prices to switch someone back into fuel poverty, and what has happened since 2001 is that the almost doubling of energy costs between then and 2008 have put those same people back into fuel poverty. In the UK as a whole in 2008 around 20% of all households are fuel poor, with the cost of delivered energy still rising. The Labour Government had a policy to end fuel poverty by 2010 for the vulnerable and by 2016 for all. This target has already slipped well out of reach. If it was really serious about this it would tackle the scandal of the poorest paying significantly more for the their energy in pre-paid energy meters than the rich who can do it on-line (up to £400 difference per household) and face up to the fact that the big six companies who monopolize energy supply in the UK and are hell bent on snuffing out the type of competition that might provide serious cost competition or alternative sources of free renewable energy to households (once installed) such as the micro-renewables industry. As with the transport industry, which is also dependent on fuel costs for pricing regimes, in the long term the government will have no option but to introduce major legislation to control the energy supply companies and their costs as fossil fuel energy becomes scarcer. The alternative, which is already being fairly widely discussed, is renationalize these industries. It is only a matter of time before the numbers of fuel poor rise to unacceptable levels (40–50%?) and it is understood that they cannot pay for both the energy they need to sustain an acceptable lifestyle and shareholder profits for utility companies.

Price increases are also being driven by the need to maintain and modernize power distribution networks to enable more renewables to be included in supplies and to prevent the power outages that have become increasingly common over the past years. The infrastructure of the privatized and publicly owned energy industries around the world is weakening as plant comes to the end of its life and maintenance practices slip.

The impact of such neglect was demonstrated in 1998 when an explosion ripped through Esso's natural gas plant in the southern Australian state of Victoria, killing two workers, injuring eight others and shutting off energy supplies throughout the state for at least a week. One union official confirmed that the number of maintenance workers at the 30-year-old plant had been halved over the past six years, and cited this as a possible contributory factor to the explosion.[21] Such accidents could cripple whole regions for long periods.

The pan-European industry lobby, Eurelectric, claimed in February 2008 that Europe will need a further 520 MW of generating capacity by 2030 to meet rising demand and around £1 trillion to upgrade energy supply networks around Europe by that time.[22] Please note that in the UK it is predicted that the 2012 Olympics will require the introduction of over 400 MW of extra power alone, so it is difficult to see how these figures add up. How such ambitious expenditure fits with the meeting of increasingly stringent European Union (EU) emissions reductions target is unclear. There are vast sums at stake in who controls the European energy markets and fierce competition exists at all levels to secure the available investment. The question of whether to invest in big coal and nuclear power stations or put more money towards renewables is a particularly tricky political issue.

COAL

There are sufficient global reserves of coal left to last for over 200 years. Coal currently provides only 26% of the world's primary energy consumption, very much less than in 1950 when this figure was 59%. There are abundant reserves of coal in the ground, estimated to be capable of lasting over 200 years. Over 50% of the reserves are in the USA, China and Russia. The coal industry has the problems of poor working conditions in some mines and the high costs of transport for the fuel. In France nearly all coal mines closed by 2005.

The main problem with coal now is that it is a dirty fuel and contributes 38% of CO_2 emissions from commercial fuels. It is also a major source of sulphur dioxide and nitrous oxide emissions as well as particulates and other emissions. The UK Government has struggled to find ways of accommodating the EU's Directive on sulphur emissions, which threatened the future of Britain's coal industry. Other European sources of coal have a lower sulphur content (Britain's coal is dirtier) and therefore could comply with the Directive.

Under the Directive the UK would have to reduce sulphur dioxide emissions by 575 000 tonnes per annum, the bulk of which would come from the electricity industry. The impact of these savings was seen to be to close much of the UK coal industry, posing a further real threat to the security of energy supply. The solution discussed was to further tighten up on emissions control from power station chimneys, but the government's only public comment on the issue was to state that they would go for the lowest cost option for industry to solve the problem, implying that national security of supply to them was not high on the list of priorities when making such decisions.[23]

The current UK Government appears now to be seriously considering a new generation of coal-fired power stations but this development appears to have temporarily disappeared at the same time as access to cheap credit and this may give time for more serious reflection in the face of the increasing pace with which climate change, and most obviously, melting ice caps reinforce the need for real action on global leadership for emission reductions. Talk is one thing that we have a sufficiency of.

NUCLEAR POWER

Nuclear energy at present provides around 25% of the electricity supplied in the UK and is claimed not to contribute to atmospheric CO_2, although such claims do not take into account the energy costs of the buildings and transport associated with the industry.

The ageing and fragile nuclear power industry is on its way out in Britain and has, worryingly, been sold off in part to American buyers.[24] The UK plants are leaking and poorly maintained and the problem of what to do with the radioactive waste from the plants has not been solved.

Another major problem with nuclear power is that it is too expensive to produce. The UK Government, or more accurately the people of Britain, have been bankrolling the industry for decades, to the tune of billions of pounds over that time. In September 2003, British Energy, the nuclear power generator, close to bankruptcy having been bailed out to the tune of £650 million by the government, suffered further heavy financial losses due to shutdowns at two power stations. The company produces 20% of UK electricity. A problem at Sizewell B in Suffolk in 2003 resulted from leakages from two welds in the generator. The other shutdown was at Heysham 1 plant in Lancashire, caused by a failure in a sea-water cooling pipe in the plant's turbine hall,[25] and lasted for well over a month. Friends of the Earth said at the time, 'This is a classic example of why a future based on nuclear power is a bad idea'. The huge power supply outage would have to be replaced by dirty coal as gas prices are already too high to compete with the coal-powered stations.[26]

Nuclear energy suffered another major setback when British Nuclear Fuels announced that it was to close its Sellafield's Thermal Oxide Reprocessing Plant (THORP) on 25 August 2003. It was estimated that there would be around £3 billion worth of cleaning up to be completed to make the site safe. It was opened in 1994 and was expected to close in 2010, two years before the proposed closure of a much older reprocessing works, built in the 1950s by the Ministry of Defence to separate plutonium for nuclear weapons. This latter plant will stay open until 2012, when all the old Magnox nuclear power stations, which currently produce 8% of the UK's electricity, are closed. All these stations are currently running at a loss but are needed to keep the lights on.[27] The

Sellafield site was condemned as 'unsafe' to occupy in August of 2003, owing to the poor condition of buildings and the leaking of highly polluted water and radioactivity from the structures.[28]

Although it was claimed that the widespread blackouts around the world in the summer of 2003 meant that the UK Government was forced to reconsider the role of nuclear energy in terms of provision of high levels of energy supply, limited greenhouse gas emissions and the need to keep lights on,[29] climate change has already proved to be threatening the proper operation of the French nuclear power stations because of a lack of cooling water for the plants.

In France in August 2003 the scorching temperatures caused the nuclear plants to overheat and then have to be shut down. In a plant in Fessenheim, near Strasbourg, staff were forced to hose down the building to cool it as temperatures rose to 48.5°C, only 2°C below the point at which an emergency shutdown would be triggered.

As temperatures across France continued at 40°C for the second week running French nuclear plants were granted permission late in August to pump their cooling water into the nearby rivers at higher temperatures than usual to allow them to continue generating electricity. Demand for electricity soared as people turned up the air conditioning and fridges and rushed out to buy fans. In some regions river water levels dropped so low that the vital cooling processes in the stations had become impossible, while water temperatures downstream of the cooling process exceeded environmental safety levels.

That the UK cannot rely on French supplies to tide it over in difficult periods was then demonstrated during the heat of August, 2003 when, in an attempt to conserve energy for the nation, France, Europe's largest energy exporter, cut its power exports by more than half on 12 August 2003, causing a shortfall in supplies to the UK.[30] This is another indication that cross-border dependency on fuel leads to insecurity of power supplies.

It is difficult to see nuclear power playing the role of the fairy godmother for our extravagant lifestyles, although it may well plug the energy gaps as we grow used to doing more with less and as new solutions come online. Already, the UK Government has delayed the decommissioning of some older stations by five years, to give them more time to achieve their targets on greenhouse gas emissions, but no new UK stations are planned. This is part of a global trend, with Germany having committed to phasing out its nuclear industry within 20–30 years. However, with the approaching oil crisis the UK Government may well have to review this policy. It is difficult to see how we will cope without nuclear power, but selling off the nuclear industry to the highest bidder could cause problems in the future when the high costs of the plant have to be recouped. Cutting corners can have catastrophic impacts in this industry. On 15 April 2003, Tokyo's main power company, Tokyo Electric Power Co (Tepco), shut down the last of its 17 nuclear reactors for safety checks after a series of accidents and scandals concerning lax safety procedures. Tepco was ordered to suspend operations for a safety review after it was found to be hiding structural problems in the plants and obstructing government inspections.[31] The shutdown caused serious problems because Tepco produces around 40% of the power used in the Tokyo area, and about 30% of Japanese energy overall is nuclear.

Countries that have abandoned nuclear power include Italy, Denmark, Ireland, Greece, Luxembourg and Portugal. Construction of nuclear plants has stopped in Spain. However, most of the world's big industrial powers still rely, to a greater or lesser extent, on electricity generated by nuclear reactors, including the USA, Russia, Britain, Japan and France. Whether this is a judicious move or not is open to question and Sweden, which made great play of the fact that it was going to close down its nuclear plants, soon found out that it would have to import electricity from dirty coal plants in Denmark and has subsequently reversed its policy.

In 2007/2008 British nuclear power stations suffered a series of chronic breakdowns causing a real threat that the entire grid may be brought down. Contrary to many people's impression, nuclear energy, which is supposed to create, clean reliable energy, has proved to be a dangerous element in the mix in terms of the energy security it provides to the population. The problem is that the power nuclear stations are such an important part of the UK energy mix that when they fail they really provide cause for concern. In November 2007 the government was forced to publish a 'no cause for concern' message to the public after the National Grid issued a 'transmission system warning' calling for an immediate extra 300 MW of energy to cover any unexpected surge in demand. This was a bald statement of the fact that they had run out of extra capacity, and this was a result of the shutting down at one time of no fewer than five of the nuclear reactors by British Energy, because of 'safety concerns'. This came also at a time of an unexpected decline in North Sea gas output and a 30% surge in gas and electricity prices.

In addition, 2008 proved a difficult year for the French nuclear industry owing to a major spate of leakages. In July it was reported that over 100 staff at the Tricastin plant near Avignon, owned by EDF (Electricte de France), had been irradiated with low levels of radiation, a uranium spill occurred polluting two nearby rivers and citizens continued to drink contaminated water through the next day because they were not informed of the event. Later that month 120 people were evacuated from the plant when the alarm sounded. Areva, a rival bidder for the £1 billion a year contract to manage the Sellafield complex (Britain's largest), was also under fire from regulators over the uranium leakages.

In recent years the cost of cleaning up the existing UK nuclear plants has been rising at around £10 billion a year and is predicted to end up at over the £70 billion mark for 2009 alone.

The British nuclear industry has never been able to convince successive governments of the wisdom of investing in nuclear because it is a cost-efficient method of generating energy. It has always been by far the most expensive way of producing electricity.[32] But somewhere in the backrooms of Whitehall politicians, not all of whom are renowned for their grasp of science and statistics, have been persuaded of its value to the defence industry and to the 'security of supply' for Britain. It is currently being promoted as the technology that will 'keep the lights on'. It is in fact perhaps the most failure prone of all energy supplies and the problem with putting all one's eggs in the nuclear basket is that when the supply does fail, as it will, then the whole system collapses, as it did in heatwaves in France in 2003, or Chicago in 1995, when tens of thousands of people died when the lights went out. In France many more may have lived if the nuclear power stations were not turned off because they overheated in 2003. Instead, should we not be building a new generation of resilient buildings and communities in which most of the lights can go off some of the time without great loss of life, while the really important ones can stay on?

RENEWABLE ENERGY

The advantage of renewable energy is that it is infinite. Add to that the clean energy it produces, and the fact that people now want it. In July 2009 the Scottish Government agreed targets for the production of 50% of energy from renewables by 2050, and to achieve these targets will require integrated solar and wind generators on buildings, as well as locating them in the countryside. This means a revolution in the way we supply energy in the UK, because if we are to do this then it will be necessary to re-engineer the UK energy supply network to accept contributions from millions of small power stations instead of 100 large ones. The only solution is to rewire Britain.

Table 13.1. Renewable energy (RE) generation 2005 and targets for 2020

EU Renewable Energy League	% Generated from RE 2005	New target % by 2020
Top		
Sweden	39.8	49
Latvia	34.9	42
Finland	28.5	38
Austria	23.3	34
Portugal	20.5	31
Bottom		
Cyprus	2.9	13
Netherlands	2.4	14
Ireland	3.1	16
Belgium	2.2	13
UK	1.3	15

In January 2007 the EU White Paper on energy policy proposed the setting of a reduction target of 20% CO_2 emissions by 2020, with 15% of all energy to be produced by renewable energy by 2020 and 30% by 2050, of which wind power would account for around one-fifth. By 2020 Britain is aiming to have an ambitious 35% of its energy from renewables, up from a mere 5% today. The move to micro-renewables for the UK is being actively promoted by the government after a series of reports that showed that with little difficulty embedded and local generation could reduce energy demands from conventional power stations by up to 5%.

In November 2008 the French Government announced that it is to build at least one major photovoltaic (PV) generation centre in every region by 2011, with a new minimum generation capacity of 300 MW, and higher capacities installed in sunnier areas. By June 2008, the installed PV capacity in metropolitan France was around 18 MW, in fourth place in Europe behind Germany, Spain and Italy. Currently there are already 12 000 planning applications in place in France for a further 400 MW peak in total for connection to the grid, in a PV market that is currently increasing at a rate of around 130% annually.

Such rapid developments demonstrate one of the strong advantages of a wholly state-owned electricity industry that can work quickly to actively promote new technologies for the benefit of its customers and voters. It may also reflect the growing understanding of one of the major limitations of nuclear energy, that when the energy is most needed, as electricity for cooling during heatwaves, is just when the nuclear power plants overheat and fail, as they did in 2003. This failure contributed to the deaths of around 15 000 people, mostly old, in that single heatwave event. PVs, on the other hand, work best during those peak summer demands and may be used to reinforce the national grid during summer days. This niche generation slot in the annual jigsaw puzzle of supply and demand provides a high-value use for this solar technology, during summer days, and one that offers currently unavailable security of energy supply during critical heatwave conditions. Similarly, wind may fit a vital supply slot during winter mornings and evenings in the UK. Thus renewable energy contributions can develop tailor-made energy supply solutions for helping to provide security of supply in a rapidly changing climate.

The growing understanding of the importance of renewable energy in the fuel supply mix was acknowledged in an influential report commissioned by the UK Department of Business, Enterprise and Regulatory Reform and published at the beginning of June 2008. The report clearly

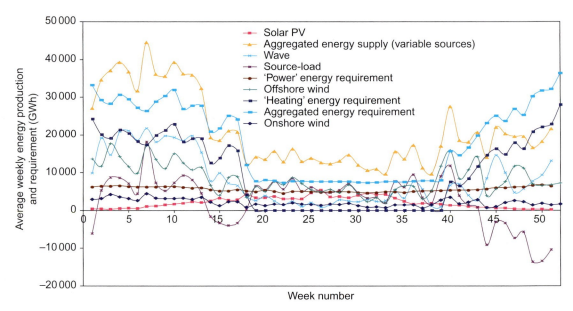

13.7.
A study done by researchers in the CREST centre for renewable energy shows that regionally we may well be able to meet most of our annual demand from a cocktail of renewable energy sources over time.
Source: Catherine Streater, by courtesy of David Infield, CREST, Loughborough University.

states that buildings equipped with solar panels, mini-wind turbines and other renewable energy sources could generate as much electricity a year as five nuclear power stations. A large-scale switch to micro-renewables energy units could save 30 million tonnes of CO_2, equivalent to 5% of all emissions produced by UK electricity production. It is estimated that there are nearly 100 000 micro-renewable units in the UK, including 90 000 solar hot water systems, PVs and others including biomass boilers. If no action is taken at all the report claimed that Britain could see around 500 000 micro-generators installed by 2015 and 2–3 million by 2020. With the right incentives one in five, or 5 million of 25 million UK homes, could be fitted with them by that time. Incentives could take the form of 50% grants for their installation, feed-in tariffs and soft loans. Some people have called for an ambitious target of 50% of all homes to have solar systems by 2020 and there is no reason why this could not be achieved. For a cost of £1 billion a year, the amount of money the six big utilities make every year from the EU Emissions Trading Scheme, the government could partner the public, paying the other 50% of installation costs to install a million solar hot water systems a year, each saving an average of around 1000 kWh a year of gas currently used to heat water and reducing emissions by an additional 1 million tonnes of CO_2 a year. In 12 years we would have 50% of UK homes with solar hot water systems and be saving around 4% of the total UK emissions by this single strategy alone. Micro-renewables may appear to be a no-brainer but the big disadvantage is that it offers no opportunity for large utility companies to make profits in perpetuity from selling the energy, which goes some way to explaining their reluctance to invest in this solution and their preference for the highly polluting coal generation options.[33]

By July 2008 the renewable energy sector was being hailed as the new Klondike, with a green rush to finance and be part of the renewable energy projects. The value of shares in the sector soared over the summer of 2008. In 2007 alone wind projects attracted over $50 billion of investments and around $29 billion went into new solar projects. China raised $2.5 billion on EU and US markets for solar projects and India raised the same for wind in 2007.[34]

Hydro power

Hydro power is currently the world's largest renewable source of electricity, accounting for 6% of worldwide energy supply or about 15% of the world's electricity. In Canada, hydroelectric power is abundant and supplies 60% of the electricity needs. Traditionally thought of as a cheap and clean source of electricity, most large hydroelectric schemes being planned today are coming up against a great deal of opposition from environmental groups and native people. Over the long term, silting of large dams has also been a significant problem for larger schemes.

Hydro power is particularly susceptible to climate change, both to unprecedented spells of drought and to flooding. In March 2001 Brazil faced wide-scale blackouts after two years of drought because the reservoirs that fed the hydro plants were less than one-third full. Brazil generates about 70 000 MW of electricity annually, and consumes all but an estimated 5% of total output. Ninety per cent of Brazil's electricity comes from hydro power and although there was some ability to import extra energy from Argentina the country had no option but to ration energy and accept a rolling programme of blackouts.[35] Similar situations have arisen in the hydro-dependent economies of Tasmania and New Zealand.

Solar energy

Solar energy has many advantages as an energy source of choice for buildings, being the easiest to integrate onto buildings and cities. PV systems provide clean electricity while producing no CO_2. It is estimated that for every kilowatt hour (kWh) of PV electricity that is produced 0.6 kg of CO_2 is saved, with this figure rising to 1 kg/kWh when the PV replaces off-grid diesel. In ordinary UK houses, for instance, it has been shown to be possible to reduce CO_2 emissions by up to 60% with energy efficiency measures, but using PVs, solar hot water and passive solar systems, 90% reductions in emissions can be achieved, enough, in the view of the Royal Commission on Environmental Pollution, to stabilize climate change,[36] if such reductions were achieved across the buildings board.

PV energy supply is located at the point of demand so there are few or no losses incurred in transporting the electricity, and therefore enhancing security in the supply. PVs can supply electricity to locations remote from a traditional grid. The PV electricity supply can be isolated from the grid supply and so provide a reliable back-up at periods of grid failure. This factor is already important because over 3 billion people today are connected to conventional electricity supply systems and PVs offer the opportunity for them to have such back-ups when the power fails, although the connection mechanisms are not well developed to achieve this yet. Thus solar energy will become increasingly important as conventional grid supplies become less reliable.

In many parts of the world brownouts (reductions in voltage that dim the lights) and blackouts already occur at the times of day when power is most needed. An example of this is in hot countries when the surge of demand on hot summer afternoons means that blackouts shut down air conditioning systems. In sensible low-energy buildings cooling may be achieved with PV-powered ceiling fans or passive cooling, so making buildings, in many climates, comfortable again. Although PV systems cannot run large air conditioning systems, great advances have been made in the field of solar cooling. Solar systems are quiet, robust and require little maintenance or repair. They often form part of the building skin itself, so reducing the cost of installation. When properly integrated into a building, solar systems can also perform other functions, such as rain screen cladding, roofing, sun shades, covered walkways, brises-soleil, roof tiling systems or solar slates, and PV generation systems on motorway barriers. PVs often have few or no moving parts, and so are potentially very durable systems. There are many knock-on effects that may be important in a changing climate, such as the fact that a solar roof is 'slippier' than one of conventional construction so may not have to be so steeply pitched in areas vulnerable to heavy snowfall, making large construction savings. Also, because each PV module is attached to the roof with firm fixings, it is less vulnerable to storm damage than some common roofing systems.

Photovoltaic systems actually become less efficient as temperatures rise above their test condition temperature of 25°C and so although they generate more power with more solar radiation they do not perform well during heatwaves.

Recent work has shown that in fact Britain is very well suited for solar technologies and will increasingly be so because of the predicted rise in solar availability and intensity with climate change. Domestic solar PV systems could save half the annual energy needs for an individual home, for an average saving of £100 a year, says the UK Energy Saving Trust. PV systems can generate up to 25% of a home's total energy requirements over winter months.[37]

Solar markets have expanded rapidly, often being driven by local authority edicts, but none more so than that of the German town of Marburg. The Green Mayor and councillors passed a law in June 2008 forcing every home to install at least $1\,m^2$ of PV panels for every $20\,m^2$ of roof for owners of both new and old homes. The cost would be at least 5000 euro but should be paid back over 15 years to the homeowner.[38]

At the other end of the supply spectrum Portugal is leading the way in renewable capacity in Europe. In an ambitious plan initiated in 2004 the Portuguese Government decided to reduce the country's dependence on oil and gas and 'go for' renewables. They hope to have 31% of all their energy generated by renewables by 2020, with 60% of all their electricity generated from wind, hydro, ocean and solar energy. As part of their programme they have built on the Alenjeto Plain a £250 million, 45 MW solar PV array that will provide enough power for 30 000 homes.

Wind power

Wind energy has become a major player in the energy generation field and will become even more so with a planned increase in wind markets over the coming years. On 18 December 2003, the Department of Trade and Industry and the Crown Estate announced that 12 successful developers have been offered 15 site leases, with a potential combined capacity of 5.4–7.2 GW of offshore wind energy.[39] New wind farms should provide enough power for about one in six British households by 2010, and will help to meet the target of 10% of UK energy from renewables by that date. The government hoped then that Britain would get 20% of its electricity from renewables by 2020 and not only are the power companies enthusiastic about the boost for wind power but also the government predicts that local communities will benefit as it is estimated that the manufacturing of the wind turbines, and the construction and maintenance of the offshore wind farms would employ about 20 000 people.

Large firms with little experience in energy generation are also getting in on the market. British Telecom (BT) is considering plans to build wind turbines on its own land and invest in other renewable energy schemes in an attempt to meet its own targets for reducing greenhouse gases. The company believes that unless something drastic is done the (self-imposed) target of

10% from renewables by 2010 will not be met; action is needed promptly to counter the shortage of capacity in production of renewable energy.[40] The government needs a huge shake-up in the way it approaches the renewable energy sector, including more public finance, according to a Report in October 2003, commissioned by BT from Forum for the Future, a sustainable development charity.[41] The Forum recommended that BT commission a detailed audit of its buildings and land to see where it would be feasible to install its own on-site renewable energy generating facilities, and urged BT to investigate the potential for investment in the renewable technology sector, one that has grown at a rate of 20–30% per annum over the past decade. This is an example of a major company actually delivering on its own corporate social responsibility commitments and using renewable energy as a high-profile, and cost-effective, means of doing so.[42]

Since then wind power has become the mainstay of UK government attempts to meet its current EU target of 15% renewable energy by 2020. To achieve this 35% of all electricity will have to be generated by renewables, which is a considerable challenge. The plan is that 45% of all new wind energy will come from Scotland, 18% from Wales and 10% from Northern Ireland, leaving 32% from English farms.[43] One planned wind farm alone on the Isle of Lewis would have had 154 turbines and generate some 550 MW of energy, around 10% of Scottish energy needs. It was refused at planning in April 2008 but the scheme gives an idea of the scale of thinking by the rapidly growing energy wind sector today. The Portuguese built the world's biggest wind farm in 2007 with 130 turbines along the Spanish border, only to be overtaken by the construction of a 140 turbine wind farm in Renfrewshire, powering 100 000 homes. The Spanish Government has itself a huge wind and solar programme, in contrast to other Mediterranean countries such as France, Greece and Italy, which are well behind in the renewable generation stakes. A series of vast offshore wind farms in the UK will be built between now and 2020 in what the UK Government sees as the equivalent of a new North Sea oil boom.[44] The scale of the renewable energy ambitions is remarkable and points the way to building real fuel security in the decades ahead, led by wind.

Wave power

The UK has an incredibly long coastline. Just one Scottish county, Argyll and Bute, has a longer coastline than the whole of France. While wave power is weather dependent (though less subject to

13.8.
One of the six metre turbines owned and extensively tested by the company OpenHydro at the European Marine Energy Centre test site in Orkney. This model will be used to generate between 1 and 3 GW of electricity in the coastal waters of Alderney, one of the Channel Islands. *Source:* Richard Northwick, Alderney.

the short-term vagaries of weather than are wind and solar), it could provide an important source of energy in the future, although the technology still has some way to go. Existing policy and economic constraints have done little to foster this industry but that is all changing as the cost of conventional energy soars.

Portugal, with its ambitious renewable energy programme, has commissioned the Edinburgh firm Pelarmis to build for them the world's first large wave farm near Porto, funded to the tune of £1 billion by the Portuguese firm Energus. The generators will provide energy for 450 000 homes.

One of the first major wave power generation fields is currently being trialled in the strong marine tides around the Island of Aldernay. Aldernay Renewable Energy company was granted a Master Power Generating Licence (MPGL) in 2008, giving it exclusive access to 50% of Alderney's waters for a minimum of 50 years, and within years it is hoped that up to 3 GW of energy will be generated and exported to France, providing an income source that will be used to future-proof the island's inhabitants against soaring energy prices.

Tidal power

Following the oil price crisis in 1976, the government set up the Severn Barrage Committee to assess the feasibility of a tidal barrage across the river Severn. According to evidence from this Committee to the Parliamentary Select Committee on Climate Change in March 1999, just this one barrage could make a significant contribution. It would cost around £10 billion to build, but it would produce 6% of the annual electricity demand of England and Wales, and reduce annual greenhouse gas emissions by 16 million tonnes. A more ambitious scheme could generate even more power.

A tidal barrage would create more benign conditions in the Severn estuary and one recent proposal for the Severn estimated that a barrage could lead to 40 000 new jobs in the area. Such a barrage could be operational within 15 years of getting the funding to proceed. A tidal barrage across the Severn could reduce the tidal flood risk upstream, although measures might be needed to prevent excessive siltation, provide for disposal of effluent from Bristol and Cardiff, and safeguard wetland wildlife.

The biggest stumbling block to such a project is the length of time it would take to pay back the large capital costs, but as pressure grows for more 'clean energy' sources, the project becomes increasingly attractive.

Combined heat and power

Large-scale combined heat and power (CHP) plants are usually sized according to the base load heat demand of the buildings or area they are supplying. Their overall efficiency and commercial success depend on the combination of heat transfer efficiency and electrical generation efficiency, and the demand cycles for electricity and heat. Thus, CHP is not necessarily more efficient than the alternative of stand-alone heat and grid-supplied electricity. CHP is most attractive when the price of grid electricity is high and fuel for the plant, e.g. gas, is low.

In a fairly revolutionary development the world's first commercially available domestic CHP plant, the 'WhisperGen', has been developed jointly by Whisper Tech in New Zealand and Powergen in the UK. It fits under the worktop in a kitchen, like a dishwasher, and provides hot water like a normal boiler. However, it contains a generator powered by a Stirling engine, which produces electricity from the same gas supply. Any surplus electricity will be fed back into the

National Grid and bought back from consumers by Powergen.[45] Some estimate that micro-CHP systems will power up to 20% of all homes by 2020. Developments in this field have not been as rapid as originally anticipated.

Biofuels

In the first edition of this book, written in late 2003, we stated that 'with current technology, for the UK, biomass energy crops arguably have the greatest potential of all non-nuclear renewable energy. As less and less farmland is needed for growing food crops, or rearing livestock, more is available for growing biomass. In addition, British Biomass have calculated that there is more than enough land currently not suitable for conventional agriculture but which could be used to grow biomass crops'.

Biomass for heating buildings includes wood, especially willow, or other plants, which can be harvested for energy. Forestry and agricultural residues can also be used. This is an area where UK expertise is world class. Although biomass burning releases CO_2, a greenhouse gas, no more is released than is absorbed during growth, or would be released if the material was allowed to rot naturally, so the energy is virtually CO_2 neutral. Experiments by the Forestry Commission on 'short rotation coppicing' have shown that biomass can provide a continuous supply of fuel for small-scale local power stations. Biomass is much less weather dependent than, say, wind or solar power and, in the short term, biomass planting could give governments a further breathing space by acting as a CO_2 sink for the purposes of the Kyoto Protocol. However, the use of biomass boilers in new buildings included to help meet stringent local government targets for renewable energy contributions has been so rapid that, for instance, in the Edinburgh region, where the city council has 10–20% renewable energy target and biomass delivered to a building costs only around £40 a tonne, designers are already expressing concern that limitations of future supplies would drive this price up to uneconomical levels.

It is difficult to cover this field in which so much conflicting evidence is constantly being presented. The answers appear to depend very much on which crop is being considered and from which location. It is an emerging field that we will cover in more depth in the third edition of this book.

One aspect of the increase in the use of biomass for domestic dwellings has been the potential rise in local pollution. The *Guardian* noted on 12 November 2008 that on 27 and 28 October 2008 in Salford, nitrogen dioxide levels exceeded government limits, with a rise in particulate pollution. This coincided with a cold snap and people increasing their use of solid fuel fires in the area. Coal in particular is a dirty fuel but this type of occurrence provides a reminder of the potential for a return to the smogs for which British cities were once so famous.

Ethanol and biodiesel

The importance of ethanol (alcohol) is that it can be used to power petrol and diesel engine vehicles with minimal modification – just a computer chip in the fuel system and a fuel line made out of slightly different materials. It is a relatively clean fuel with a higher octane rating than petrol, but is less of a fire risk, and it can be produced anywhere plants can be grown. The burning of ethanol results in release of the carbon trapped by the plant, but this is far better than releasing the carbon formerly trapped in fossil fuels for millions of years because it is a truly renewable form of energy, which can be regrown rapidly year on year, rather than being a finite resource like oil and gas.

But since the first edition of this book a biomass revolution has occurred and the international rush to the use of biomass for transport has increasingly been blamed in part for the soaring food prices in 2008. From April 2008 all UK petrol had to have at least 2.5% biofuel content as a stepping stone to the UK 5% target for 2010. Europe is currently considering a 10% biofuels target for 2010.

First generation biofuels used crops such as corn, rapeseed, palm and soya. Second generation biofuels use fibrous non-food plants that can be grown on more marginal lands, thus providing less of a threat to food production. However, the problem of fuel production displacing food production was so great that by July 2008, according to the International Monetary Fund (IMF), it was responsible for 20–30% of the rise in food prices at that time, leading to a call to the UN's Food and Agriculture Organization (FAO) to produce a set of International Standards to ensure that plant-derived ethanol or biodiesel did not harm the food supply.

ENERGY FUTURES: THE AGE OF DARK CITIES

In the transition from the fossil fuel age to whatever comes after it, energy prices will rise and the hardest hit buildings will be those built in the last half century when energy was abundant and the size of a building and its energy profligacy were a sign of its success. The era of Big is Beautiful has already passed, and as we saw in Chapter 12, the smart money is already moving out of tall buildings and out of the hearts of dense cities.

You cannot occupy a tall building when the power fails. You cannot power a tall building on solar energy, but you can power a robust, well-designed, sensibly sized building using renewable energy in Britain. Similarly, you cannot run a HVAC system in a thin, tight-skinned building in a hot country from PVs. You can run ceiling fans from PVs in well-designed, naturally ventilated passive buildings in the same climate. We are entering a new era in which fossil fuel and nuclear energy will become increasingly unaffordable, and in which the burgeoning renewable energy industries will begin to dominate the energy generation markets. This is a good time to invest in the right technologies.

In the annual publication of the International Energy Agency's *World Energy Outlook*[46] in November 2008 it was predicted that global energy demand will increase by 45% by 2030 and oil prices will rise to $200 a barrel by then. They claim that the July 2008 surge in prices to just shy of $150 has highlighted the ultimately finite nature of oil and gas reserves. They called for an energy revolution and a 'major decarbonization' of global fuel sources as the world confronts tighter supplies caused by shrinking investments. It adds, 'The need to address climate change will require a massive switch to high-efficiency, low carbon energy technologies'. More important than technologies are buildings.

We have to rapidly implement the step changes needed to create a new twenty-first century paradigm of deeply passive buildings that can be run largely on renewable energy supplies, because in settlements around the world the lights are already going out. Some say we are, even now, at the threshold of a new Age of Dark Cities. We are certainly approaching the beginning of the end of the Fossil Fuel Age.

NOTES AND REFERENCES

1   C.H. Pout, F. McKenzie, R. Bettle, Carbon Dioxide Emissions from Non-domestic Buildings: 2000 and Beyond, Building Research Establishment and Department for Environment, Food and Rural Affairs, Garston, Watford, 2002 p. 10.

2   <http://www.dti.gov.uk/energy/whitepaper/index.shtml/>; see also <http://eeru.open.ac.uk/ natta/renewonline/rol46/9.htm/> for information on UK energy consumption and policies.

3   Guardian, 30 July 2007, p. 13; Guardian, 5 June 2008, p. 27.

4   <http://www.energycrisis.com/campbell/TheHeartOfTheMatter.pdf>.

5   See the following classic works on the subject: C.J. Campbell, The peak of oil: an economic and political turning point for the world, in: N. Low, B. Gleeson (Eds.), Making Urban Transport Sustainable, Palgrave Macmillan, Basingstoke, 2003, pp. 42–67; C.J. Campbell, The Essence of Oil and Gas Depletion. Multi-Science Publishing, Brentwood, 2002; C.J. Campbell, The Coming Oil Crisis, Multi-Science Publishing, Brentwood, 1997; See also W. Youngquist, Geodestinies: The Inevitable Control of Earth Resources Over Nations and Individuals, National Publishers, OG Portland, 1997; K. Deffeyes, Hubbert's Peak: The Impending World Oil Shortage, Princeton University Press, Princeton, NJ, 2001; P. Hoffman, Tomorrow's Energy: Hydrogen, Fuel Cells and the Prospect for a Cleaner Planet. MIT Press, Cambridge, MA, 2001.

6   Campbell, The Peak of Oil, p. 44.

7   Campbell, The Peak of Oil, p. 45. API stands for American Petroleum Institute; degrees API is an oil-industry term used as a measure of density. See also D. Strachan, The Last Oil Shock: A Survival Guide to the Imminent Extinction of Petroleum Man, published by John Murray, 2007.

8   Observer, Business, 3 November 2002, p. 3.

9   <http://www.hubbertpeak.com/deffeyes/>. See Deffeyes, Hubbert's Peak.

10 Campbell, The Peak of Oil.

11 See also <www.opec.org/>.

12 U. Bartsch, B. Muller, Fossil Fuels in a Changing Climate, Oxford University Press, Oxford, 2000.

13 The Oil Crunch: Securing the UK's Energy Future, First Report of the UK Industry Taskforce on Peak Oil & Energy Security (ITPOES), October 2008. Taskforce member companies included: Arup, FirstGroup, Foster and Partners, Scottish and Southern Energy, Solarcentury, Stagecoach Group, Virgin Group, Yahoo!

14 See <http://peakoil.solarcentury.com/wp-content/uploads/2008/10/oil-report-final.pdf/>.

15 Guardian, 17 November 2003, p. 25.

16 Guardian, 5 December 2003, p. 23.

17 <http://www.hydro.com/en/press_room/news/archive/2002_09/ormen_iland_en.html>.

18 <http://aapg.confex.com/aapg/barcelona/techprogram/paper_83493.htm>.

19 Guardian, 28 April 2008, p. 25; see also R. Singh, Costing carbon. European Power News, London, July 2003, pp. 23–24.

20 Independent, Home, 7 January 2008, p. 9.

21 Guardian, 9 December 2003, p. 17; Guardian, 5 December 2003, p. 23.

22 <http://www.wsws.org/news/1998/sep1998/gas-s29.shtml>.

23 Guardian, 7 February, 2008, p.29.

24 Guardian, 17 November 2003, p. 25.

25 <http://www.guardian.co.uk/nuclear/0,2759,181325,00.html>.

26 Guardian, 27 November 2003, p. 22.

27 Guardian, 31 October 2003, p. 32.

28 Guardian, 26 August 2003, p. 1.

29 Guardian, 26 August 2003, p. 4.

30 Guardian, 22 October 2003, p. 22; see also Guardian 5 August 2003, p. 3.

31 Guardian, 13 August 2003, p. 13.

32 Two important reports on the UK nuclear industry show how it evolved serendipitously and how it is currently unlikely to build major new plants for many non-technical reasons. W. Patterson, Going Critical: an unofficial history of British Nuclear Power. See <http://www.foe.co.uk/resource/reports/going_critical.pdf/> and a Report presented to the Parliamentary Committee on 26 November 2006, called: Nuclear Power: Unnecessary, Dangerous and Expensive. See <www.nuclearpowernothanks.co.uk/>.

33 Guardian, 16 April 2003, p. 13.

34 Guardian, 3 June 2008, p. 9.

35 Guardian 2 July 2008, p. 27.

36 <http://www.iclei.org/EFACTS/HYDROELE.HTM/> and <http://eces.org/archive/ec/np_articles/static/98575920040789.shtml/>.

37 <http://www.re-focus.net/news_archive/index.html>.

38 <http://www.re-focus.net/> See also S. Roaf, R. Gupta (2007). Optimising the value of domestic solar roofs: drivers and barriers in the UK. in: D. Elliot (Ed.), Sustainable Energy; Opportunities and Limitations: An Introductory Review of the Issue and Choices. Macmillan.

39 Guardian, 23 June 2008, p. 20.

40 <http://www.rcep.org.uk/newenergy.html> and <http://www.dti.gov.uk/energy/renewables/technologies/offshore_wind.shtml>.

41 <http://www.enn.com/news/2003-07-15/s_6554.asp>.

42 S. Roaf, Corporate Social Responsibility Chapter 4 in Closing the Loop: Benchmarks for Sustainable Buildings, RIBA Publications, London, 2004.

43 Guardian, 21 June 2008, p. 8.

44 See <http://www.offshorewindfarms.co.uk/> for a full outline of sites and programmes of development for offshore wind farms.

45 <http://www.whispergen.com/>.

46 See also <http://www.peakoiltaskforce.net>.

14 FUEL SECURITY: WHEN WILL THE LIGHTS GO OUT?

INTRODUCTION

A key challenge in the current energy markets is to provide fuel security to populations, to ensure that the lights stay on even in the most extreme conditions. It is this increasingly difficult challenge that is ostensibly driving governments around the world back into the arms of the toxic, expensive, nuclear industry and to the drawing boards with a new generation of polluting coal-fired power stations. However, many are deeply concerned that the plans being promoted by governments are simply not stacking up. This was the conclusion of the Oxford University task force report in June 2007. Chaired by Lord Patten of Barnes, the report claimed that the UK policy was a hotchpotch of measures that would not deliver on security, would not deliver on climate change and would not serve the poorest in our societies.[1]

In January 2007 the European Commission published its White Paper on energy policy in which it was pointed out that by 2030 84% of European Union (EU) gas and 93% of EU oil will come from overseas. Its promotion of nuclear energy for the production of hydrogen was controversial as an EU-wide poll showed that only 20% of people supported nuclear energy. The Commission also proposed measures to break up the monopolistic stranglehold of huge energy groups such as France's EDF and Germany's Eon on the markets. However, conversely, many are now questioning, from experience, the efficacy of relying on poorly regulated energy markets to enhance national fuel security.

In many developing countries it is accepted that 'brownouts' and blackouts will and do occur. This typically happens during periods of peak electricity demand, which in hot countries are usually in mid-afternoon to coincide with peak air conditioning demand at the hottest times of day and year, and in cold climates in the evening and mornings, before and after work. What is now happening is that in all countries blackouts are increasingly happening for a wide variety of reasons and the challenge of keeping the lights on is proving too much for many economies and administrations.

WEATHER-CAUSED OUTAGES

The worst blackouts of recent years occurred over the hot summer of 2003. The UK had 'insufficient systems margins' seven times, that is inadequate reserve capacity to provide a cushion for expectant demand surges, and each time generators stepped in to provide extra power.[2]

Suppliers paid as much as £1000 per megawatt-hour one day, on peak tariffs, in the 2003 winter as opposed to normal wholesale prices of £17 because the UK energy supply system simply does not have the capacity to cope with severe weather.

A report commissioned by Brian Wilson, the then Minister at the Department of Trade and Industry, from the independent consultants British Power International in May 2002, warned that several UK companies might not be able to cope with a widespread storm, because a number relied on the same pool of contractors to provide mobile generators, engineers for overhead lines and the technology to handle surges in calls. The contractors would only be able to respond to one call at a time and would thus have to leave some areas uncovered if the devastation caused by some storms was widespread.[3] This report came in the wake of the storms which left more than 20000 customers of 24Seven, the utility that covered parts of London and East Anglia, without power for more than a week, as a result of staff cuts and bad management, although they claimed that the continuing failures were due to stronger winds in their region. 24Seven ended up paying over £2 million in compensation to its customers but some of the blame for cuts was also passed on to the Regulator, who in 1998 placed an energy price cap on firms making it necessary to introduce cuts for staff and tree maintenance programmes.

Weather-related blackouts are a major cause of outages. Hurricane Isobel in late September 2003 plunged 4.5 million people in the Washington area into darkness as trees fell onto cables around the city.[4]

Italy experienced power cuts in mid-August 2003[5] caused by massive surges in demand due to very hot weather and the unprecedented use of air conditioning systems.[6] The weather was also responsible for the later Italian blackouts of 2003, when 57 million people were plunged into darkness on 28 September. The problem started when a tree, uprooted in a storm, tumbled onto a power line in Switzerland, cutting out 3000–4000 MW of supply and setting off a cascade effect of failures throughout the Italian grid. The impacts were catastrophic:[7]

- Planes were grounded.
- Some 110 trains were halted, some for over 12 hours, with 30000 travellers on board.
- Lifts stuck.
- Stores and underground car parks were unable to open their security gates.
- Electric turnstiles failing trapped people in buildings.
- Traffic lights failed, causing numerous accidents.
- Mobile phones failed.
- Hundreds of elderly people were hospitalized after falling over in the dark.
- Sales of coffees, food and ice-creams worth 50 million euro were lost.
- Frozen food worth 70 million euro spoiled in freezers.
- Hospitals ran out of fuel for their emergency generators.
- Water pumping systems stopped, causing water supply problems in cities.
- Sewage plants stopped operating, causing effluent build-ups.

On a smaller scale, the impacts of a local blackout can be just as disruptive, as this anecdotal story shows. When the power failed one morning in a school in Scotland, no one in the building knew what to do because the emergency plan and all the emergency contact numbers, parents' telephone numbers, etc., were on the computer, so the children could not be sent home. The school could not supply lunch but the children had used their lunch money to top up their magnetic swipe cards, which they would normally use to buy lunch, so they could not even go to the

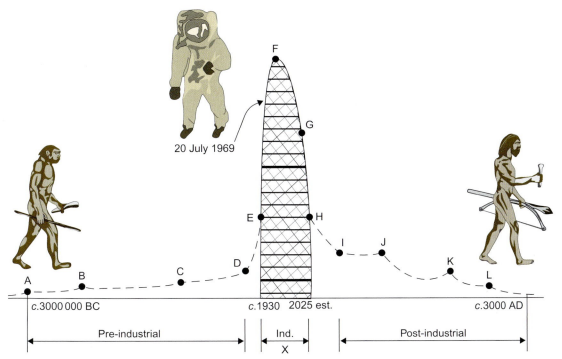

20 July 1969

1. Pre-Industrial Phase (*c.*3000 000 BC to 1765)
   A   Tool making (*c.*3000 000 BC)
   B   Fire used (*c.*1000 000 BC)
   C   Neolithic agricultural revolution (*c.*8000 BC)
   D   Watt's steam engine of 1765
2. Industrial Phase (1930 to 2025, estimated)
   E   Per capita energy use 37% of peak value
   F   Peak energy use
   G   Present energy use
   H   Per capita energy use 37% of peak value
3. Post-Industrial Phase (*c.*2100 and beyond)
   I, J, K, and L = Recurring future attempts at industrialization fail

   Other scenarios are possible.

14.1.
Time for lights out. An image that represents the concerns of many of the public politicians around the world: the impact of per capita consumption patterns over the coming decades.
Source: www.dieoff.org.

shops for a sandwich. They all had to leave the school buildings because the fire alarm had no battery back-up, and so they stayed in the playground for hours until the electricity was fixed. Here the weather was good but imagine what would have happened in a storm! Our dependence on electricity is so pervasive that nothing seems to function if the power fails nowadays.

EXTREME EVENTS

On 28 February 2008 fire broke out in a water treatment plant, causing the shutdown of a large part of Britain's largest gas terminal at Bacton in Norfolk. This terminal alone imports 13% of

UK gas from the continent and the fire sent UK oil prices soaring over concerns about energy supply. Major terminal and storage depot fires are not uncommon and can have catastrophic consequences.[8]

In December 2005 the skies over Buncefield Oil Storage Depot, Hemel Hempstead, Hertfordshire, were rocked by an enormous explosion and filled with plumes of toxic black smoke that blanked out the sun over most of southern England.[9] On 30 January 2008 the Health and Safety Executive (HSE) published the societal risk consultation outcome from the extensive investigation that took place after the event. Criminal proceedings have been commenced against Total UK Ltd, Hertfordshire Oil Storage Ltd, British Pipeline Agency Ltd, TAV Engineering Ltd and Motherwell Control Systems 2003 Ltd following a thorough and complex criminal investigation conducted by the HSE and the Environment Agency (EA). The result of this event was that a legal precendent had been set to ensure that societal risk should be taken into account when assessing safety measures at onshore major hazard installations and for planning applications on the use of land for development in areas around such sites. The severity of this event set a benchmark and demonstrated that due to criminal negligence and human failure major disruptions to energy supply on land were not only possible but to be expected.

A wake-up call was delivered to the energy supply industry during the summer floods of 2007. Significant flooding was experienced in Worcestershire and Gloucestershire between 20 July and 2 August 2007 and Central Networks, which distribute electricity to 5 million domestic, commercial and industrial customers in central England, played a key part in the protection of the energy supply and distribution networks at that time. It is the second largest electricity distribution company in the UK. The regional network was rapidly expanded in the 1950s and many of its assets are over 50 years old. The overhead networks are particularly susceptible to damage by extreme weather, especially from high winds, snow, ice and lightning. Flooding presents an additional, and traditionally considered secondary risk to the resilience of the network. However, all this changed in July 2007 when some 50 000 people lost power for up to two days from 23 July onwards.

It is not considered to be practicable to protect every substation at potential risk of flooding, particularly when the premises supplied by them are not themselves protected. Therefore, the primary focus of such a network is to protect the major strategic sites supplying a high number of customers (typically more than 10 000). However, flood protection is increasingly considered an essential part in the design of new facilities. An example of this is the new substation at Port Ham in Gloucester, which has been constructed on stilts. In that region alone 113 substation sites have been identified as being potentially at risk of flooding on the basis of a one in 1000-year event. Of these, 81 sites are within the one in 100/200-year flood risk areas. Flood-induced energy outages must now be considered part of everyday life in some regions of the country as utilities learn how to protect and future-proof the systems against ever more extreme weather events.[10]

SYSTEM FAILURE

Electricity production is responsible for nearly 40% of all UK carbon emissions in a system in which a number of large power stations, generally far from centres of demand, generate the electricity that is then transported via an extended grid network to where it is needed. The heat produced when energy is generated represents a wastage of more than 60% of the total energy content of the fossil fuels. Further losses occur as the electricity travels along the transmission wires and distribution system. The move towards decentralized energy supply systems where generation and supply are co-located and waste heat can be reused in buildings potentially offers carbon and cost savings. In addition, because local demand is met by local supply, load on the large grid is significantly reduced. Thus expense on upgrading the grid can also be reduced. The big grid approach is not only a wasteful system but also one that is very vulnerable to failure.

The UK's biggest power cut in 25 years hit large parts of London in the early evening of 28 August 2003. The 37 minute blackout was caused by the failure of a single piece of sophisticated equipment that shut down when power surged through it. There was also a problem with a transformer in Kent and further blame for the severity of the blackout – which involved the loss of 20% of the capital's power – was levelled at the slow response time of France's EDF electricity grid company in responding to the surge in demand.[11] This in turn was caused by the high demand experienced in France due to very hot weather and the poor performance of the nuclear reactors in the extreme heat.

The effects on London during the evening rush hour were dire. The Underground and rail networks were paralysed. The problem for people trying to find other ways home was exacerbated by the fact that automated cash machines were down, preventing them from getting access to the additional cash they needed to, for instance, pay for taxis. Pubs benefited in the city though, as many commuters avoided the grid-locked streets and overcrowded buses with the pleasure of a slow pint on their long way home.[12]

On Thursday 14 August in 2003, in the USA, where US Energy Secretary Abraham said:

Reliable electric power is the lifeblood of the economy for both the United States and Canada. ... It's more than just a personal convenience – it's essential to the health and safety of the two countries' citizens[13]

50 million people were hit by America's and Canada's worst power failure. The effects of the blackouts were particularly felt in cities like New York, Cleveland (Ohio), Detroit (Michigan) and Erie (Pennsylvania), as well as in many Canadian cities such as Toronto, Ottawa and Niagara Falls.

New York City suffered badly when office buildings were evacuated shortly after 4 pm. The events of 11 September 2001 were on people's minds. Many were convinced, wrongly, that terrorists had struck again. On the Thursday night, thousands of stranded commuters slept on the streets and in bus and train stations rather than venture on long walks home. In hotels guests had to sleep outside on the pavement because there was no electricity to operate the electronic room keys and knock-on effects also included:[14]

- During the night from Thursday to Friday New York suffered 60 serious fires, mostly caused by people lighting candles in the dark.
- Nine nuclear reactors in four US states were taken off-line, contributing here to the problem of fuel insecurity rather than solving it.
- The US Federal Administration halted flights into six airports – three in the New York area, one in Cleveland and two in Canada.
- Sporadic looting was reported in at least four areas of the Canadian capital, Ottawa, and 26 people were arrested for looting in Brooklyn, New York.
- The blackout closed the Detroit–Windsor Tunnel, which links the USA and Canada and is used by 27 000 vehicles daily.
- In the Canadian mining town of Sudbury some 100 miners were trapped underground until power could be restored.
- Detroit's 15 major car plants closed down until Monday 18 August 2003.

14.2.
The lights go out in New York in August 2003 and in cities around the world, at a time of unprecedented global heatwaves.
Source: Associated Press.

A US–Canadian government investigation of the massive power outage in the northeast singled out a series of operator mistakes, computer failures, violations of grid rules and inadequate maintenance by FirstEnergy Corp., the Akron-based utility serving northern Ohio, as the primary causes of the largest blackout in North American history.[15]

In July 2007 major power cuts in Barcelona in Spain that plunged around 350 000 homes into darkness during the hottest time of the year also had a range of dangerous impacts:

- The metro system collapsed.
- Operations were cancelled.
- There was traffic gridlock.
- Cash machines failed.
- Looting was reported.
- 'More light – less police' saucepan lid protest took place in the city centre.
- A major substation fire broke out.
- There was a mobile phone blackout.

The backlash was enormous, not least because the city that is medium rise in its form with good passive building has recently allowed a rash of new highly glazed office and residential towers to sprout up around its edges, towers that fail catastrophically in the heat in such blackouts. The Catalan government was so incensed by the power failure, which lasted for 56 hours and 42 minutes, that a year later, in July 2008, they proposed a £17 million fine for the two largest Spanish utilities who were held responsible for the event, some £8.5 million each. The utilities companies called this excessive and appealed.

One of the consequences of grid failures in an all-electric world grown dependent on electric cooling is that buildings and vehicles begin to overheat. Buildings can be evacuated but as early as the 1960s Fergus Nicol had conducted a study for British Rail on how long it takes for a train carriage to overheat on a hot day, once it is stranded, and like buildings this could be anything from half an hour to two hours before it becomes a lethal environment, according to how many people may be in it and how hot it is outside. It is no doubt time to look again at manual opening window provision in all buildings and public transport as standard for just such instances.

POOR MANAGEMENT OF SUPPLIES

California is perhaps the prime example of a region where mismanagement of energy supplies has caused widespread hardship, and death. In California, the supplies across the whole state have been affected by rolling blackouts in recent years, due in part to poorly managed privatization of the electricity industry and an inflexible legislative system. Very high energy demand from buildings, for instance in the heatwave of 2000, caused a surge in demand and private companies, once a price cap was lifted in June, raised their prices by up to three times in a matter of months. Poor management, in part by the Enron Corporation and the state, resulted in outages in many cities and settlements. Reasons given for these failures included:

- Excessive energy demand at peak period consumption, related in a large part to high air conditioning use in very hot weather.
- Lack of energy conservation measures in buildings and equipment.
- Poorly managed energy tariff systems.
- Lack of coordination of plant outages on an emergency basis.
- Lack of back-up generating capacity.
- Poor state management of the sector.
- Corrupt private utilities.

By contrast, in New England in the USA the electricity supply problems are different. The plans to increase the percentage of electricity generated by gas-powered stations from 16% in 1999 to 45% by 2005 proved unrealistic, not only because of the soaring cost of gas in the USA but also because:

- During peak demand some advanced gas turbine plants would not be able to switch quickly enough to their back-up oil supplies to avoid temporary outages.
- The existing gas pipeline capacity in the region would potentially be insufficient to supply the demand of the 45% increase in gas-generating plants at peak periods, a fact that has caused gas supply problems since 2003.
- The pipeline construction and power generation companies are not one and the same.

There is concern that the New England power supply system, like that of California but for different reasons, will not be able to meet demand within a matter of years. The Boston area is particularly vulnerable as the ageing grid in the area is considered, as in many other areas of the USA, to be on the brink of failure. The competitive market is also failing as suppliers are pulling out of the market rather than jumping in. The problem was highlighted in spring 2000 when an unexpected heatwave forced the power companies to call Boston customers to cut down on electricity use in order to prevent blackouts. Other cities have similar problems, such as New York where 2000 residents lost power in 1999 prompting the city to plan to install 10 mini-power plants as back-up to its main lines – a seemingly pointless gesture in the face of the scale of the 2003 blackouts.

It would appear that to improve its fuel security, what America needs, as well as better energy infrastructure, is to use less energy.[16]

We are moving into an era in which we can no longer, in any country in the world, presume 100% security of delivered energy supplies. In the UK the old research facilities of the Electricity Industry at Capenhurst, where work on the optimization of power supply and demand was undertaken, have been closed and such research is no longer being undertaken in a coordinated fashion by the UK Government. This results in a lack of long-term, in-depth, knowledge, skills and planning on such subjects, which will manifest itself as our supply and demand systems are increasingly placed under pressure from new developments, climate change and energy scarcity.

The UK Government's move to privatize 100% of the UK energy supply market has exacerbated our energy insecurity. For instance, part-privatization of the London Underground was blamed for exacerbating the August 2003 failure that brought the transport system to a standstill and affected tens of thousands of tube passengers who were stuck in tunnels as trains stopped. In 2002 London Underground's 97-year-old independent power station, Lot's Road, was shut, and responsibility for powering the tubes was handed over to a new consortium, Seeboard Powerlink, in a private finance deal under which the tube now gets all its power from the National Grid. Seeboard provided a back-up power station at Greenwich, south London, for use in emergency, but the arrangements failed, leaving dozens of trains stranded, raising again with the unions, and many others, the question of the advisability of handing over to private finance contractors the responsibility of key public services. Senior Seeboard executives had decided not to start up the Greenwich generator when the 28 August blackout began at around 6.30 pm at the height of the rush hour, hoping to switch supply from other parts of the grid that were still working. Questions were later asked as to why it had been felt necessary to change a system that had kept the Underground working all through the Blitz.

The move away from state-owned generating companies had sent prices tumbling around the world over the past decade until 2007, when soaring oil and gas prices drove energy prices at the plug up two and three times in as many years. Privately owned utilities had not been investing in new plant or infrastructure because they saw their profit margins being squeezed, and continued shutting down what they saw as excess capacity to maintain their profits. However, when soaring oil and gas prices precipitated a new energy cost crisis, plans for new generations of nuclear and coal-powered stations soon appeared on the tables of Whitehall. The Government in 2007 to 2008 was now much more amenable to the building of these polluting and potentially highly toxic plants simply to keep the lights on in Britain. The crisis has been anticipated but the response was surprising, as the solution in terms of coal would prevent the UK from meeting its emission reduction targets and drive the increases in the unpredictability of weather that cause the difficult-to-manage surges in power demand. Rather than solving the problem the move to coal-powered generation was fuelling it.

The summer 2003 crisis in Italy highlighted the country's chronic dependency on foreign sources of energy. GRTN, Italy's grid manager, draws in power not just from France and Switzerland, but also from Austria, Slovenia and even Greece via an underwater cable. Sixteen per cent of Italy's requirements are met from outside the country. At that time a bill to increase Italy's generating power by a quarter had been stalled in parliament for months and calls were being made to restart the nuclear programme that had been abandoned after a referendum in 1987. Its four remaining nuclear plants are currently being dismantled. More than 75% of electricity generated in Italy comes from oil, gas and coal and producing it accounts for 25% of Italy's greenhouse gas emissions. The need for energy efficiency measures to damp the summer air conditioning peak was clear in this instance.[17]

Massive power cuts in Denmark in late September 2003 were said to be caused by damage to the power transmission lines linking Sweden and Denmark, from where Denmark obtains much of its power. Some even claimed that the lines had been sabotaged by terrorists.[18] This transboundary dependency for energy is increasing the risk of political as well as physical and economic insecurity.

Public concern also acts as a restraint on the operations of the privatized utilities in their efforts to ensure supplies. President Bush's plans to exploit the Alaskan oil fields were thwarted by a 52 to 48 vote in the US Senate on 20 March 2003, when Democrats and eight Republicans voted to block, for at least a year, drilling for oil over a 600 000 hectare area of the wilderness refuge of Alaska. The USA uses around 7 billion barrels of oil a year and the government estimated that as many as 16 billion barrels could be found in Alaska.[19] In the face of mounting oil shortages in the USA it is only a matter of time before the interests of environmentalists will, inevitably, have to give way to the need of Americans to feed their growing dependence on oil, and in turn, electricity, an issue that has already led to civil unrest on the streets.

Shanghai, a city with a booming population soaring above 20 million people and the leading city in the Chinese economic revolution, is now facing an energy crisis. As the population flocks from the country to the city to cash in on the £2900 average annual income available to workers, more and more tall buildings have emerged to house the population and provide them with workplaces. However, the energy infrastructure is unable to meet the rapidly growing demands for power and in December 2003 the municipal authorities ordered many factories to move to night shifts because energy supplies were unable to meet the soaring daytime demand for electricity.[20]

Tens of thousands of factory workers were affected and ordered to work nights because of power shortages caused by the rapid growth of China's economy. Shanghai also urged shop owners to turn down thermostats and conserve electricity. Such moves not only embarrassed government officials but also presaged a battle for energy supplies in Asia. Car ownership in the city is rising at 25% a year. It has the world's first commercial magnetic levitation train. But on the 4th December 2003 the city announced that unless it took drastic action to overcome the energy problems the trains might not run and the street lamps and skyscrapers may be blacked out.

As mid-winter approached the city authorities calculated that the city was 2 million kilowatts short of the 11.6 million it needed to meet peak demand. Although the city buys electricity from the new Three Gorges Dam, and plans to buy an extra 1 million kilowatts from there, it was still facing major problems. The city planned to shut its most energy-intensive small factories and change work shifts to midnight to 8.00 am in energy-intensive industries. Many of the population can now afford electric heaters in winter, and one of the main problems has been identified as the gleaming new shopping malls, where 0.4 million watts could be saved by lowering the temperature in them alone. Power pricing is changing to encourage people to use less during the day (highlighting the need to use thermal storage in buildings).

China's general power consumption rose by 15% to 1.88 trillion kilowatts in 2003. More than half of China's provinces have been hit by shortages and the government has warned that the energy shortfall could hinder growth, despite more plant being brought on-line, and shortages would remain chronic until at least 2006. China was an energy exporter for three decades but is now one of the world's biggest oil importers.

Such necessities of reducing consumption, rapidly, and on a large scale, also exist in the UK. In the face of the blackouts in August 2003, the National Grid company Transco denied that there was any risk that inadequate generating capacity in the power stations would lead to power shortages in the winter, although it did admit that it had written to some of its largest industrial customers to offer inducements for lower usage contracts in August 2003. The suggestions, sent to major manufacturing plants, as owned by Rio Tinto and the aluminium manufacturer Alcon, and other heavy power users, include inducements for accepting 'interruptible' contracts where the grid can reduce supply at 24 hours' notice to enable the Grid to free up capacity to meet regional peaks in demand. The contracts can be worth as much as £56 000 an hour, a bonus at a time when electricity prices are expected to rise by as much as 30% over the next year for the renewal of such contracts.

Australia is a country that is particularly vulnerable to peak surges in demand. South Australia has the peakiest demand in Australia, and is one of the highest in the world. Peak demand is more than double the average which means that more than 50% of the infrastructure is unused for 90% of the time. South Australia also has 90% penetration of air conditioning in the residential sector. This leads to huge volatility in the spot market price for energy and in South Australia the average demand for electricity is in the region of 1400 MW but peak demand can exceed 3000 MW. Prices range from $10 to $10 000 per MWh in a single day and less than 1% of the energy traded is worth over 20% of the market value. This pattern is repeated throughout the Australian states to a lesser extent although the Sydney region is set to exceed South Australia in the terms of its peak electricity demands.[21]

There seems to be a lack of political will to solve such growing problems. Intelligent management of the regional grids could see, for instance, an excellent integration of building-scale and large-scale photovoltaics used to reduce afternoon air conditioning peak loads on conventional generation supplies, and the use of energy storage, particularly in buildings, can be very effectively used to shift and shave loads in smart distributed grid systems. There are potentially large financial opportunities for companies to reduce costs and actually make money, for example by HVAC plant operators selling demand response capabilities to retailers. Too many energy experts are still crudely pricing renewable energy supplies at their base rate costs rather than understanding the potential to reconfigure regional energy demand and supply profiles, integrating renewables in highly managed and well-behaved stable independent power zones or micro-grids. To ignore this potential will inevitably lead to the large-scale failure of conventional power supplies as warmer weather drives up those air conditioning peaks.

UNCONTROLLED DEMAND

The UK Government appears to have no convincing handle on the relationship between excessive energy demand and the scale of emission reductions needed to meet their statutory reductions target obligations. Why else would they condone a new generation of coal-fired power stations? Why else would they be interested in building new airport capacity?

This gap between fantasy and reality is further exemplified by the UK Government's inability to understand the implications of how buildings actually work in terms of energy consumption. If they are serious about even trying to honour international targets they need to understand the relationship between the wrong types of buildings and settlements and their ability to meet targets. A classic example is that of the carbon implications of the 2012 Olympics. The business heart of the City of London, with its shining, eternally light glass towers, is the single most energy-profligate place in Britain. The new city district has a power demand of over 1000 MW that is expected to rise by over 80% in the next three to five years. The Docklands alone has a power demand of over 250 MW that is expected to rise by over 90% in the same time, driven not least by the huge energy needs of the information technology services they provide.

An average tower building in these areas requires around 5–6 MW of energy to keep its lights on,[22] which is the output of a major power station such at Didcot B in Oxfordshire. According to industry rumours the 2012 Olympics will require a further 400 MW of power which will require a further 100 km of electric cabling and the building of over 100 substations. One problem here, just as with the development of the nuclear programme, is that there are simply not enough qualified engineers to make this happen in time.

Because running data centres and their computers is so energy expensive, EDF, the French company that supplies much of London's energy, has now said that for energy reasons there can be no more data centres in Docklands or the City, but this apparently does not apply to Telehouse, the company that ran the Beijing computer systems and will supply the 9000 new server spaces needed for the 2012 Olympics.[23]

When set against such figures the claims by the government that they intend to meet international targets seem ludicrous. Uncontrolled energy demand is driving energy insecurity and when huge new demand draws are placed onto a creaking energy supply infrastructure they will inevitably increase the propensity of the system to fail in the future.

ECONOMIC DOWNTURN

On 21 November 2006 LogicaCMG, on behalf of the Department for Trade and Industry (DTI), launched a new report called 'Mind the gap – the black hole at the heart of the UK's energy supply',[24] one report of a long line, warning of impending gas and electricity shortages for the UK over the coming years. The UK 'energy gap', it claimed, would come sooner and be more severe than expected owing to a looming energy crisis in the UK. They were right and they outlined some of the symptoms that defined the 2008 recession: domestic energy prices had risen 93% in two years (how much more so now), UK had become a consistent net gas importer for the first time in 30 years and in March 2006 the National Grid issued its first ever 'balancing alert', to warn industry that it may need to shut off their gas supplies. This crisis is primarily caused by the decline in our indigenous fuel and the ageing of our generation capacity. There is now a significant risk of an 'energy gap', where the supply of energy is no longer sufficient to cope with the levels of demand, leading to voltage reductions (brownouts) and power cuts (blackouts). In particular, the LogicaCMG report runs through various scenarios, what it calls 'Optimistic' and 'Conservative' for the years 2010, 2015 and 2020. The problems could be severe by 2010. The summary of the very realistic and very close 2010 scenarios states:

'In 2010 we foresee a risk of a 5–15% (allowing for contingency) gap at peak times. A likely scenario is that this would be managed by asking energy intensive users to curtail production. These users, from industries such as aluminium, steel, glass, refineries, bricks, lime and cement, Chlor-alkali, paper and manufacturing use 5–6% of UK gas. Diverting from these users could free up gas for homes and gas power stations to maintain electricity supplies. The report states that the UK could be importing 80% of its gas by 2014, six years earlier than the usual quoted year of 2020.'

The writing has been on the wall for a long time, begging the question of where the politicians have been and, as some imply, whether they were being ill-advised by people who had very different interests.

OTHER CAUSES OF POWER OUTAGES

There are two further major threats to the security of supplies. The first is terrorism. The blowing up of power lines and plants is such an obviously effective means of bringing a region to its knees and inflicting major economic damage that it significantly influences the thinking of politicians on the subject of future fuel mixes. The second, and it has happened already, is when a country simply can no longer afford to pay for the oil and gas to run its plants. We are at the brink of a period in which we may see cities and whole countries go bankrupt. Will that mean that for whole regions of the world the lights will go out? It has happened for short periods where energy resources and infrastructure have failed for two to three weeks as in Brasilia, Auckland, Vladivostok, and has been threatened in some of the former Russian states, but in periods of economic chaos, when bills simply cannot be paid and new equipment bought, could that become months or years?

EMBEDDED GENERATION

The electricity blackouts around the world in 2003 demonstrated clearly that many countries have become absolutely dependent, for the ordinary functioning of society, on a constant, and high-quality, supply of electricity. Quality of supply can be considered to have three elements:[25]

- Reliability – long- and short-term interruptions of power supply.
- Power quality – frequency and voltage stability, waveform abnormalities.
- Service – response time and restoration time.

Not only do we need a constant supply of electricity for basic functions like street and domestic lighting, that can operate under quite varied voltage conditions, but the advanced electronic equipment found in modern working environments often requires a high level of reliability from the incoming electricity supply.

For example, today's complex manufacturing processes rely heavily on microcomputers, variable-speed drives and robotics devices to achieve high levels of product throughput and product quality. This leads to higher expectations of electricity end-consumers, who place increasing demands on electricity suppliers to meet the demand for quality of supply. Evidence for this is given by the large market for power quality measurement and analysis systems.

National regulations dictate the minimum quality of electricity and, if these are complied with, the needs of most consumers will be met. In the case of consumers with special requirements, or in areas where quality measurements give rise to concerns, there are methods of ameliorating shortcomings in the electricity supply. However, some of these methods can themselves have an effect on the supply network.

The winds of change?

There are new factors that raise several issues with regard to the current distribution regulatory arrangements, which were not considered 20 years ago. The industry is changing, with greater emphasis on:

- Quality of supply.
- Security of supplies.
- Improving the environment.

In recent decades, Great Britain has relied almost exclusively upon electricity generated by large, traditional power stations that are connected to the higher voltage national transmission system. In line with this, distribution networks, the lower voltage part of the system, have largely been concerned with delivering electricity in one direction, from the transmission network to customers' homes. However, structural changes are ahead, including the anticipated growth of 'distributed' generation – that is, small, local power generators, particularly of renewable energy – to underpin the 'rewiring of Britain'.

What is embedded generation?

Embedded generation (also known as distributed, embedded or dispersed generation) is electricity generation connected to a distribution network rather than the high-voltage transmission network. Distributed generators are mostly – though not exclusively – those generating power from environmentally friendly renewable energy sources (including small hydro, wind and solar power) or from combined heat and power (CHP) plants.

Historically, distribution networks have been designed to take electricity from the high-voltage transmission system and to deliver it to customers. The management of this one-way flow of energy has been termed 'passive'. In order for the networks to accommodate increased levels of distributed generation energy flow in both directions will have to be managed – both to the customer and from the distributed generator. This is termed 'active' management. This move from passive to active management is a major challenge.

The nature of distribution networks today means that many smaller generators find it difficult and expensive to connect to networks that were not designed to accommodate them. The output from photovoltaics (PVs) from a single house into the grid is little more than noise on the line, but when the whole street has solar hot water systems and PV arrays then the solar contribution to powering houses down the street becomes significant, especially if the householders are out all day at work during the week but at home during the weekend. Matching the load profiles to the electricity supply becomes a real challenge.

Naturally, the large distribution companies involved find it much easier to deal with the outputs from a handful of major generators, but in the changing climate, with resource pressures developing year on year, a strong theme of the UK Government's White Paper on Energy is the need for energy security, and it is widely felt that the sole reliance on the mega-grid for the supply of future energy would be a very high-risk strategy to follow.[26]

Future grid scenarios also need to be built to cover the potential for 'renewable energy cities, suburbs and streets' within which a relatively high proportion of, for instance, the domestic load is locally generated, during spring, summer and autumn, from building-integrated solar hot water, micro-wind, CHP systems and PV systems that supply unpredictable energy, depending on the weather of the day and the month. For such small-scale embedded generators, work is focusing on 'micro-grid' systems where power demand and supply are controlled within a local grid, separated from the main grid by a power gate that can be shut off in times of power supply emergencies to ensure security of supplies within the main grid system.

Within such micro-grids, it is envisaged that a cocktail of different generating sources could be located, from a range of solar, wind, hydrogen fuel-cells, CHP plants, hydro plants and other sources. Such systems can work well at the level of the 'campus', where a single owner is responsible for the plant inside the power gate and the management and control of energy supply and quality within the mini-grid. One example of such a campus site that has a two-way power gate into the national grid is that at the Centre for Alternative Technology at Machynlleth, Wales, which has a range of embedded generators including wind and solar within its micro-grid. As part of its active energy management system the site has a bank of batteries to provide energy storage, and a buffer against fluctuating supply and load situations.

The design of distribution networks is becoming increasingly complex as the grid begins to absorb a wider range of inputs from a far greater variety of sources. The output of a PV roof may create a very small stochastic input into a local grid while if a whole group of houses or a village is wired up into a micro-grid or a registered power zone (RPZ) behind a single power gate the excess generation will be absorbed by a building next door and the total effect may not be any export from the RPZ at all but simply a significantly reduced load on the grid from that group of buildings. Similarly, an entire industry, such as the Alcan aluminium smelting plant at Fort William, may generate most of the power requirement for its processes and buildings from its own hydro-electric plant's power station, presenting the grid simply with a lower energy demand. However, a large amount of research is currently being undertaken on the implications for micro- and macro-grid control systems, transformers with tap changers that can control voltage locally and absorb a variety of supplies. If the cost burden that different sources of generation impose on networks is not recognized early on by the charging arrangements, then the most efficient network/generator configurations are unlikely to be implemented and charges to customers will be higher than need be in the long term as oil and gas prices rise. Insufficient investment at the right time may cause future supply systems to be even less secure.

Energy storage

The generating capacity available must be able to meet the peak demand and, as demand is below peak for most of the time, a significant amount of generating capacity is under-utilized. It has been estimated that the average utilization of generating capacity is around 50%. One way of improving generator utilization is to use 'off-peak' electricity in energy storage schemes.[27]

There are some very large schemes, for example, the Dinorwic pumped hydro scheme, in Wales, where electricity generated at off-peak times can be pumped back up to the reservoir and used to generate again at peak periods. Despite there being suitable technology available, for example regenerative fuel cells, as yet there is little storage in the current supply chain.

It is often considered that renewable generation is of two types, despatchable and stochastic. **Despatchable generation**, such as conventional hydro or that powered by biofuels, can be made to provide electricity in a manner that is related to demand. **Stochastic generation**, such as that powered by wind or wave, fluctuates in a manner that is unrelated to demand. However, stochastic generators can provide electricity that contributes coherently to the demand cycle if they are associated with appropriate energy storage systems.

The trading system for Great Britain was designed to enable competitive markets to develop, but critics claim that it is extremely complex to implement, creating problems for users.[28]

The main technical problem to be overcome in moving to embedded generation from the traditional grid system is that of providing constant, high-quality, electricity from unpredictable sources. The lack of back-up energy storage facilities in the UK systems will be exacerbated by the increased use of generators powered by fluctuating (stochastic) renewable energy sources, such as wind and tide. Many of the proposed technical solutions will also mean significantly increased costs of energy to the consumer.[29] As fossil fuel prices rise, the marginal costs of this storage capacity will decrease relative to the cost of the 'delivered' energy, that enters a building through the meter.

For many power generators, downtime, when power outages occur in plant, including its hidden costs, can represent 5–10% of annual revenue and potentially 30–40% of annual profits, and outage optimization regimes are increasingly central to the management of the energy supply system to make sure that neither mechanical nor human error causes unnecessary blackouts.[30]

A NEW POWER PARADIGM IS NEEDED

We face a future in which we will no longer be able to rely on a constant, reliable, high-quality supply of energy; and 2003 gave us a taste of what is to come. Key issues are:

- **Quality of supply**. How important is quality if there is no supply? How will the inevitable 'rewiring of Britain' to accept renewables affect the quality of supply? Will we have to adapt to using lower quality energy, as well as to using less of it?
- **Security of supply**. This will be increasingly challenged by the end of the fossil fuel age; the rise of embedded generation, micro-grids, privatization, deregulation, lack of investment in the industry, geopolitical insecurity, extreme weather, and a plethora of other forces are gathering to test our ingenuity in keeping the lights on for as long as possible.
- **Environment**. This must be the driver: energy use is dependent on weather and our warmer and more extreme weather has proved to be the wild card that carries the poker game. The blackouts in August 2003 were caused in large part by high demand in a hot summer, the sort of hot summer we will increasingly expect every year or two in the future. The other critical factor is that of the global environmental impacts of energy generation, the burning of fossil fuels that is driving the climate to change. Those who maintain that the problems of a changing climate can be solved simply by throwing more energy at them – that energy-profligate buildings will provide bastions of comfort for those who can afford it – are mistaken.

The Institution of Civil Engineers (ICE), in their State of the Nation Report 2003,[31] pointed out the chronic structural problems the UK faces:

- Over 95% of the country's present generation mix is made up of coal, nuclear and gas supplies.
- Emissions constraints meant that the remaining UK coal plants were to have closed within 15 years.
- Only one nuclear power station will remain open after 2020.

They asked for:

- Increasing investment in infrastructure (including – I would add – the knowledge infrastructure).
- Investment in developing the full range of fuels.

Add to this the need for more long-term storage of fuels in reserves. France, Germany and Italy have storage of more than 20% of annual consumption – more than 70 days' worth. The UK has less than two weeks' worth.

Add to this the need for stringent demand-side management policies to make consumers use less.

Add to this the need to store more energy in the thermal mass of buildings, where the thermal capacity of a building offers the potential for providing a significant reservoir for heat or coolth.

Add to this the urgent need to rewire Britain to accept emerging energy technologies.

And finally add to this the imperative to design buildings in which we can survive when the lights do go out, and we can see that a new power paradigm is urgently needed.

ENERGY INSECURITY ESCALATES

Soaring energy prices

Markets for energy around the world are see-sawing at an astounding rate. On 11 July 2008 a barrel of oil reached $147 and within a month had plunged to $112 a barrel. While spot prices fluctuate wildly energy prices at the plug do not and the inexorable rise in the cost of gas and electricity has meant that the average energy costs for a household have more than doubled in five years and unprecedented hikes in energy costs have become commonplace. British Gas announced a further 40% increase in bills in July 2008 and other companies followed with further rises. As world energy prices then plummeted commensurate falls in energy prices for building owners did not always follow as the markets hoarded profits where they could be gained. Whether energy prices catch up on falling market prices as fast as they do on rising ones remains to be seen.

Fuel poverty and energy security

Keeping the lights on has proved to be not only a technical challenge but also a social and economic one at a time of economic crisis. Soaring oil and gas prices have hit the 1.5 million people who have no access to gas and rely on deliveries of heating oil particularly badly. Prices between winter 2007 and 2008 increased by more than a third but the soaring prices of gas also meant that the numbers of fuel poor, who spend more than 10% of their income on energy, nearly doubled. One in five homes in Scotland could not pay their energy bills by the winter of 2008. The September 2008 pledge by the six largest energy generators in the UK to put £1 billion into helping the poorest pay their bills was greeted with derision by a public who cannot understand why the poorest 20% of households, who have to pay their energy bills via a domestic meter, are made to pay up to 20% more than other customers for their energy by the same big six companies.

Evidence from the 2002 Scottish House Condition Survey showed that an estimated 286 000 households (13%) were fuel poor. Of these, 24% (69 000) are in extreme fuel poverty (i.e. would have to spend more than 20% of their income on fuel to maintain the standard heating regime). Most of the extremely fuel poor are single-person households. The Scottish Government's review of fuel poverty published in July 2008 showed that the 2002 figures had almost doubled by 2008 to a figure of 543 000 Scottish households, in which nearly one million people live, being classed as fuel poor.[32] Rising levels of fuel poverty are associated with having to pay bills for increasingly expensive fossil fuel and nuclear energy, bills issued in the UK largely by a monopoly of the big six energy supply companies.

Very low-energy solutions to the powering of individual homes can be achieved through a partnership between good passive buildings and micro-renewable energy supplies. The Oxford

14.3.
Scenes from Low Carbon Wolvercote, a village on the outskirts of Oxford. The emergence of such communities links energy security and growing social resilience.

Ecohouse, owned by the author, proves this to be the case. The annual electricity bill for the six-bedroom home with a 4 kW photovoltaic (solar electric) roof was for 2006–2007 *negative* £20. The building itself can provide a high proportion of the required heat through good design and detailing.[33] Simple changes like cooking on an electric induction hob powered by the PV roof work well, and the next step is to introduce the zero-carbon fridge that chills mainly during the day and stores the coolth overnight in the insulated mass of the fridge itself. In the search for zero-carbon housing a number of existing and new communities are exploring the idea of becoming energy-independent entities. From the individual almost self-sufficient home it is a small step to the almost self-sufficient community and the registered power zone.

In an extraordinarily rapid development villages, towns and cities are moving to build their own resilience against both climate change and Peak Oil problems by joining a range of renewable energy movements. At one end there are villages like carbon-neutral Ashton Hayes[34] and the increasing number of other Carbon Reduction (CRed) Communities.[35] Low Carbon Wolvercote[36] in Oxford is one such village where the added benefits of an increasingly strong community spirit built around the climate change and solar communities agenda were demonstrated when the village all but flooded in the summer of 2007 and everyone pulled together to ensure that the most vulnerable were safe. Strong, low-carbon communities are resilient communities.

Perhaps the fastest growing of these movements is that of the Transition Towns, where a community works together to look Peak Oil and Climate Change 'squarely in the eye' and address this big question: 'for all those aspects of life that this community needs in order to sustain itself and thrive, how do we significantly increase resilience (to mitigate the effects of Peak Oil) and drastically reduce carbon emissions (to mitigate the effects of Climate Change)?' The Transition Town philosophy also recognizes two crucial points:[37]

- The need to use the scale of creativity, ingenuity and adaptability employed on the way up the fossil fuel energy supply slope, to manage the descent down the other side.
- The need to collectively plan and act early enough to create a way of living that is significantly more connected, more vibrant and more in touch with the environment than the oil-addicted treadmill that we find ourselves on today.

Communities as far apart as Totnes[38], Lampeter[39] and Stroud[40] have all risen to the clarion call of the movement and with some remarkable results. In Stroud working groups have been set up in the town dealing with a wide range of issues including the arts, energy, building and water, food, lifestyle and livelihoods, 'connections', events, bright ideas, health and well-being, transport, textiles, business and government and information technology in what amounts to almost an alternative council for the town, working bottom–up from the strengths of the few to build capacity and grow resilience for the many. And these are just the first wave of the great power demand and supply shift that will characterize the decades ahead.

Are new coal plants the solution?

In January 2008 Medway Council in Kent gave permission for the building of the first new coal-fired power station in Britain for more than 30 years, the first of five proposed. The £1 billion Kingsnorth plant was proposed by the German-owned gas and electricity provider Eon, which argues that the new generation of cleaner plant would replace the dirty older model. ICE claimed that Medway Council had made a sensible decision. Green campaigners who protested outside the site in August 2008 claimed that if John Hutton, the UK Business Minister who has the final say on the station, gave permission for the plant he would be chronically undermining the government's ability to meet its legally binding emission reduction targets. They also pointed out that if £1 billion were invested in co-funding with the public the installation of a million solar hot water systems on UK roofs, each replacing 1000 kW of heat energy a year for UK homes, then the equivalent of 1000 MW of generation would be saved. The difference between the two models is that with the renewable energy solution the utility does not get the opportunity in perpetuity to charge for the energy generated. The call at Kingsnorth to nationalize the utilities in Britain to ensure that investments around the issue of the UK generation and fuel mix were driven by social and environmental reasoning rather than the need to optimize shareholder profit were loud and clear at the event.

UK Government opts for the nuclear option

In January 2008 Gordon Brown's government gave the go-ahead for the building a new generation of nuclear power stations, 'short-circuiting' obstacles to the building of 10 such stations, designed to produce 20% of the UK energy and replace ageing current capacity.

Those bidding to build the stations were keen to ensure that negotiated conditions provided a safe investment environment before they would move forward. In particular they wanted:

- Fixed prices for carbon that ensured that gas and oil fired stations were penalized for their carbon emissions, making their energy outputs more expensive and so favouring nuclear energy.
- A ceiling on the costs private companies would have to pay to dismantle reactors, so capping the liability of private companies and exposing the tax payers to unlimited liability for nuclear clean-up in perpetuity.

The cost of building the new stations, and the fact that there is a chronic shortage of skilled labour to build the plants add to the reasons why no firm plans have been made for when and where the first new station will be built. Added to this, nuclear power is extremely expensive to build, there are real concerns about the availability of uranium over time, there is growing concern about selling our energy security to foreign companies like EDF, which is largely owned by the French Government, and it is difficult to see exactly when they will actually be built. Alex Salmond, the First Minister of Scotland, has said that Scotland will not need or be building any new nuclear capacity and will rely instead on renewables to meet the growing demand in energy.

CIVIL UNREST

The rapid rise in petrol prices in 2007 and 2008 led to a range of protests by drivers on the streets. In Britain another impact of soaring energy prices was the systematic stealing of petrol and farm diesel. Eddie Cowpe woke up one morning on his Lancashire farm to find that thieves had stolen the 100 000 litres of diesel stored in his farm tank, leaving him with a fuel and clean-up bill for over £70 000. Many other farmers have suffered similar thefts around the country and a parallel rising problem at fuel stations is the problem of 'drive-offs'. The number of people who drove off from a petrol station without paying rose by 13.5% from 2007 to 2008 at a cost to suppliers of over £32.5 million. Yet another widely reported problem has been the theft of heating oil from tanks in gardens.

Just as with water, when resources become scarce or expensive they will increasingly become the target of illegal or violent protest or action. When the number of fuel poor in Scotland rises from 20% to 40% or 50% then questions will be asked about whether people are still willing to pay not only for the energy but also for the shareholders' profit. What is happening now is that local communities are putting local renewable energy systems in place to reduce their need for energy from the big six generators. Local renewable cooperatives or ESCOs (local energy companies) are now being assisted by local authorities to set up their own community supplies, as is happening in Scotland.[41]

These developments by civil society pose a real challenge to Big Energy. Why would a community choose to pay for shareholder profits when they have the choice to simply pay for the energy they need? The companies' question the role of such new developments for their business. Their real fear should be in the long term of being nationalized to solve the growing fuel poverty problem. In reality the emerging micro-grid market has huge potential for new market models in which they can play a rewarding role. Utilities simply have to invest in the research to pioneer them and in so doing will be contributing to increasing energy security in the UK.

THE CASCADING GRID SOLUTION

The UK Government is wrong to see the major linchpins of an energy security strategy as the building of new coal and nuclear plants. These two so-called solutions would reinforce the current business-as-usual model that takes us down the road towards unaffordable energy and civil insecurity, big grids that fail during extreme events and expenditure of our vital economic resources on tying the British people into being hostages who will have to pay not only for the energy they need but also for shareholder profit.

The reality is that a billion pounds spent on new coal generation to build X megawatts for coal-powered stations belonging to Big Energy, would equally pay for the same X megawatts of energy, negative demand, in the form of energy efficiency and demand reduction measures and embedded renewable energy systems belonging to the community and building owners. The difference is that in the first model the homeowner has to pay what Big Energy demands in perpetuity for every unit of delivered energy, whereas in the second mode the homeowners get their energy free forever. The difference is that the billion pounds is currently in the hands of Big Energy and their friends', Big Government. Energy experts do not get elevated to the Lords because they run a local energy cooperative, but they do get there by being chairman of a very big company. Many of the staff of the energy regulators come originally from Big Energy. Many politicians believe that the views of Big Energy are vital to the economic health of the country. However, the time has come for a fundamental rethink on the question of how we design for energy security.

One idea is to go back to the old municipal grid model, linked by a supportive grid. The individual linked micro-grids would become part of the chainmail armour built to protect the country against large-scale grid failure. A cascading grid model, in which one or more of these micro-grid links could be sacrificed to ensure the integrity of the whole, may provide a far more resilient solution than the type of monolithic grid solution that failed so catastrophically on the eastern seaboard of America in August 2003. The cascading grid model is based on a number of tenets:

- **Reinforced grid**. Taking the existing grid and dealing with weak supply lines by shoring them up with larger renewable energy capacity in their extremities to bolster the strength of the supply. As branch lines reduce in size the size of the renewable supply can be smaller. Vast amounts of money will be saved by not having to substantially rebuild the national grid.

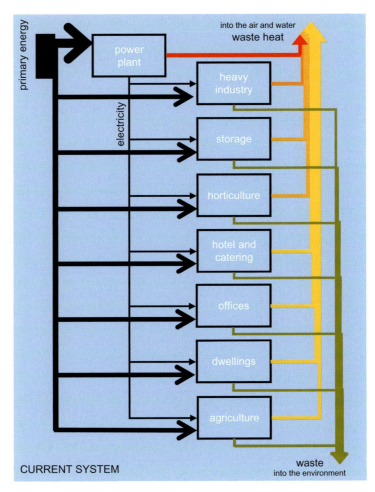

14.4.
The energy cycle: the current energy system.
Source: van den Dobbelsteen, A., Gommans, L. and Roggema, R. (2008)[42].

- **Cascading grid**. Disaggregating the grid into a jigsaw puzzle of smaller, integrated grids that can be taken on- and off-line as required and be left off-line during local grid failures. Agreements could be drawn up as to how long a micro-grid can be sacrificed during outages. Some grids, e.g. homes, could be sacrificed more often, while other buildings, e.g. hospitals, might be last-resort blackouts. A grid that can be turned on and off in parts, in extremis, and in a managed order is a resilient grid. A cascading grid will source energies of different quality within a region and use them optimally to fulfil required functions with minimal CO_2 emissions or fossil fuel use.[42]
- **Knowledge grid**. Reopen the electricity research facilities at Capenhurst and spend large amounts of government money on building knowledge of how to design, construct, operate and manage a cascading grid. Money saved on not rebuilding larger power lines could be spent here.
- **Fair grid**. Put an equal proportion of people representing small energy and renewable energy industries onto the boards of energy quangos and regulatory bodies to those who are now

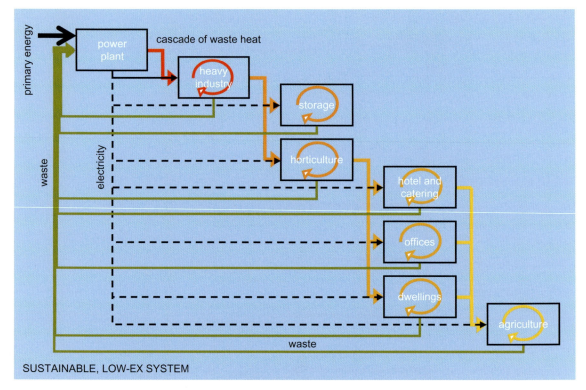

14.5.
A more sustainable low exergy energy system in which cascading grades of energy are used appropriately in an optimized energy supply and demand system.
Source: van den Dobbelsteen, A., Gommans, L. and Roggema, R. (2008)[42].

occupied by Big Energy, and get them into the Lords and the corridors of power where the deals are done.

Finally, energy security is not just about the technology of power, it is about the very nature of our society and our economy and the relationship between the three. The future of the energy demand and supply in Britain will be very different from that of the twentieth century as we move to build social resilience in the face of the enormous changes happening all around us. A touchstone of social resilience is energy equity and the new power systems on which it is founded.

NOTES AND REFERENCES

1   Guardian, 4 June 2007, p. 25.

2   Guardian, 13 August 2003, p. 16.

3   Guardian, 15 November 2002, p. 9.

4   Guardian, 20 September 2003, p. 16.

5   Guardian, 13 August 2003, p. 16.

6 Guardian, 29 September 2003, p. 3.

7 Guardian, 29 September 2003, p. 3.

8 Bacton

9 <http://www.buncefield-oil-fire-hemel-hempstead.wingedfeet.co.uk/> <http://www.bunce-fieldinvestigation.gov.uk/press/news.htm>.

10 <http://www.publications.parliament.uk/pa/cm200708/cmselect/cmenvfru/49/8020402.htm>.

11 Guardian, 11 September 2003, p. 2; Guardian, 29 September 2003, p. 3.

12 Guardian, 29 August 2003, p. 7.

13 <http://www.citymayors.com/news/power_blackout.html>.

14 <http://news.bbc.co.uk/1/hi/world/americas/3152985.stm>.

15 <http://www.washingtonpost.com/wp-dyn/articles/A62280-2003Nov19.html>.

16 IPG, International Power Generation, DMG World Media, UK, March 2001.

17 Guardian, 30 September 2003, p. 15; Daily Telegraph, 29 September 2003, pp. 1, 3 and 21.

18 Guardian, 29 September 2003, p. 3.

19 Guardian, 21 March 2003, p. 18.

20 Guardian, 6 December 2003, p. 21.

21 Dr J.K. Ward, CSIRO Energy Technology, Outside the Box – HVAC Management Techniques That Consider the World Around Them, Lecture given on 22 October 2007 for the Annual Conference of the Syracuse Center of Excellence in Environmental and Energy Systems.

22 N. Kalita, S. Watts, of David Langdon and Everest, Tall Buildings – Cost Model, April 2007. See <http://www.building.co.uk/story.asp?sectioncode=113&storycode=3085522&c=1>.

23 Guardian, 29 May 2008, p.3. Story by Pete Warren.

24 On 21 November 2006 LogicaCMG, on behalf of the DTI, launched a new report called 'Mind the gap – the black hole at the heart of the UK's energy supply'. The UK has become a consistent net gas importer for the first time in 30 years and in March 2006 the National Grid issued its first ever 'balancing alert', to warn industry that it may need to shut off their gas supplies. See Sixth Report of the Joint Energy Security of Supply Working Group (JESS), April 2006, p. 14. <http://www.dti.gov.uk/files/file28800.pdf>.

25 Sixth Report of the Joint Energy Security of Supply Working Group (JESS), April 2006, p. 14. <http://www.dti.gov.uk/files/file28800.pdf>.

26 The following sections come largely from the IEE Policy Statement on the issue. For a full text on the subject see <http://www.iee.org/Policy/Areas/EnvEnergy/embedgen.pdf> and <http://www.dti.gov.uk/energy/whitepaper/index.shtml>.

27 <http://www.ofgem.gov.uk/elarch/retadocs/golive_explained.pdf>.

28 <http://www.ofgem.gov.uk/ofgem/shared/template2.jsp?id54221>.

29 <http://www.ofgem.gov.uk/ofgem/index.jsp>.

30 International Power Generation, November/December 2002, p. 17.

31 ICE, The State of the Nation: An assessment of the state of the UK's infrastructure by the Institution of Civil Engineers, 2003. See text on: <http://www.ice.org.uk>.

32   S. Roaf, K. Baker, A. Peacock, Evidence on Scottish Hard to Treat Homes, Report to the Scottish Government, August 2008.

33   S. Roaf, M. Fuentes, S. Thomas, Ecohouse: A Design Guide, third ed., Architectural Press, Oxford, 2007.

34   See <http://www.goingcarbonneutral.co.uk/> .

35   See <http://www.cred-uk.org/index.aspx> .

36   See <http://climatex.org/wolvercote/>.

37   See <http://www.transitiontowns.org/>.

38   See <http://totnes.transitionnetwork.org/>.

39   See <http://transitionculture.org/>.

40   See <http://transitiontowns.org/Stroud/Stroud>.

41   Renew Scotland: <http://www.renewenergy.coop>.

42   A. van den Dobbelsteen, L. Gommans, R. Roggema, Smart Vernacular Planning – sustainable regional design based on local potentials and optimal deployment of the energy chain, in: Proceedings of the Sustainable Buildings 2008 Conference, Melbourne, 2008. The authors are from the Faculty of Architecture, Climate Design and Sustainability at the Technical University of Delft.

15 THE PLAYERS

INTRODUCTION

Buildings are in the front line of the battle against climate change. They are on the front line of humanity's struggle to survive. Either they change fast and radically or we lose the war. We must, with all speed, use buildings for:

- Mitigation: radically reducing the production of greenhouse gases to reduce the hazard.
- Adaptation of our buildings and cities to minimize the exposure of communities to the impacts of a changing climate.
- Protection of the most vulnerable individuals and communities against the plethora of related social, economic and environmental hazards we face together.

Without equity of opportunity to survive with decency there can be no security for anyone. In every country on Earth,[1] regardless of class, creed or wealth, buildings must be made more resilient to the changes ahead because ultimately no one can buy their way out of the impacts of a cyclone.

Many learned books and reports on the subject of adapting buildings to climate change try to fudge the problems concerning buildings because of the daunting scale of the necessary changes ahead. They are easily fudged. Analysts often dwell on particular unidimensional aspects of the problem: how a micro-grid or building control system, or wall construction or glass type works under particular conditions.[2] They offer small incremental changes but do not challenge the very nature of the beast, the fundamental paradigms of the buildings that our cities, designers, industry and the marketplace accept 'how we do things today'. However, conventional twentieth century wisdom must now change rapidly in the face of the catastrophic events happening all around us.

CAVEAT EMPTOR: BUYER BEWARE

The market mantra of 'you get what you want' is but a hair's breadth away from the chilling 'you get what you deserve', and 'buyer beware', take the consequences of your own poor decisions. The time has come for building buyers and occupiers to educate themselves about, and future-proof themselves against, climate change. Who really wants to buy a house that will flood? Or work in a building one cannot get out of when it does? Or have a bedroom that is too hot to sleep in or for which one cannot pay the energy bills? Or live under a flyover where the air will become polluted in a heatwave? Or live where the drains in the street spill out raw sewage every time there is heavy rain?

To change the conventional wisdom of building will require a revolution in itself, because of the deeply entrenched positions of the key players in the built environment. The need exists to fundamentally restructure the political, professional, business, industrial, academic and media roles in our built environment, as touched on below. This is already changing faster than any of us anticipated when the first edition of this book was written because of the events that have hit the fan of history since then. But the rank and file of the markets and the regulators and the industry still do not seem to 'get it'.

The smart high-end movers and shakers have, however, already moved on, left town, become more efficient, reduced their impacts and reinvested in quality, leaving many of the good old boys to hawk their new 'modern' ideas and dated products to their cronies, to the ill-informed, and not least to the developing world. The building industry has responded just like the American car industry, buildings SUVs when the Japanese manufacturers were sensible enough to move into the small, efficient car market, leaving two of the three great US makers dead in the water. The same is true of the US air conditioning industry that was still churning out monolithic inefficient central air-handling systems when the market for them was evaporating as rapidly as the SUV markets. The problem with the construction industry, as in the American car and computer industries, was not just that there was toxic ignorance at the top, but also it was all too easy to turn a buck, and they just got sloppy.[3,4]

THE INTERNATIONAL COMMUNITY

The Kyoto process has theoretically been extremely influential in creating targets for emission reductions, and Europe is leading the world in the imposition of targets for greenhouse gas emissions. On 9 December 2008, in Poznan at the 12th COP meeting, European Union (EU) leaders agreed to combat climate change by ordering that one-fifth of Europe's energy mix should come from renewable sources within 12 years. The Agreement was hailed as a 'landmark' deal and a breakthrough by politicians and the green lobby alike.

The agreement reached in December 2008 paved the way for a law obliging all EU countries to meet national targets for renewable energy.[5] The problem for governments is how to turn the requirement to reduce impacts into a requirement to deliver target reductions. The faster, cheaper mentality, characteristic of the height of the fossil fuel era, favoured privatization. But that idea is evaporating as water and fuel become scarcer and corporate profit requirements are paid for by unacceptable financial impacts for the person in the street. In Scotland, 35% of homes were classified as being in fuel poverty by the end of 2008.

The 'rate' of change required to meet such targets may also work against success. In 1950s' and 1960s' Britain the momentum for urban reform resulted in the destruction of the hearts of many well-loved towns and cities beneath a carpet of brutal concrete and bitumen. Labour's current declared policy of building new towns in the green belt has been widely challenged by, among others, Richard Rogers, who said that the agenda to 'go fast' in building new towns was wrong, and that we have made the same mistake before and had to pull the lot down. New developments, he argued, should be concentrated in places like Birmingham and Milton Keynes, echoing the trend amongst leading global businesses to move to provincial centres and away from 'target' buildings in major capitals like London.[6] As John Prescott, former deputy Prime Minister, a famously muddled communicator, said, 'The Green Belt is one of the great success stories of the Labour Party and we intend building on it.'

One of the immediate actions that EU governments can take now is to work to tighten up and extend the Energy Performance of Buildings Directive (EPBD).[7] This legislation could be used to provide performance certificates to demonstrate exactly how well or badly a building works in reality. The clear, simple Display Energy Certificates (DECs) of the original EPBD enable investors to choose to spend their money on a good, medium or poor building. The far-sighted intentions of those who drafted the original EPBD are currently being successfully undermined by the lobbying efforts of the European construction and development industries. You have seen throughout this book that the majority of 'modern' buildings are typically performing worse, decade on decade, in terms of their energy consumption, carbon emissions and resilience to extreme weather conditions. The genius of the EPBD was originally to create a legislative framework that would stop that happening. Currently, in England and Wales every public building must put in full view a DEC that rates the building on how much carbon dioxide (CO_2) it emits per square metre per annum.[8] Scotland, by contrast, only requires Energy Performance Certificates (EPCs) that provide information on the theoretical performance of a building, based on building models that can be 30%, 50% or even 100% wrong. EPCs are also more costly to produce as they require a full model of the building rather than a simple reading of its energy meters, resulting in significant extra costs for the building owner.

On 13 November 2008 the European Commission published EPBD2, which has been modified so that in future only EPCs will be required. This retrograde step puts the vested interests of lobbyists for those who develop, build and sell buildings before those who use and buy them. This is a further reflection of the fact that society at large is poorly represented in the heart of decision-making machines around the world. Rather than the UK Government adopting EPBD2, they should not only insist that the real performance of buildings is on display in DECs rather than EPCs, but they should also roll out the requirement for DECs to be displayed in all commercial buildings. The designers, developers and building owners will argue that they will be disadvantaged if people know how the buildings they deal with actually work because many of their buildings will perform badly. However, the downside of allowing the 'greenwashing' of the UK building stock to occur with the systematic theoretical rating of buildings using already biased rating schemes is that the ordinary people in the street will have to make the most important spending decisions of their lives without reliable information on how the building works. Just as ultra-smart bankers were fooled with complex packages of derivatives, society at large and some of the smartest operators in it will be left with a package of rubbish buildings, having exchanged the family silver of solid, resilient structures built with robust cavity walls and strong roofs for a throwaway generation of offices and homes constructed with chipboard and plasterboard, matchsticks, Lego, glass and plastic. The most effective thing that the EU and UK Governments could do would be to reinforce the original EPBD and insist on DECs.

THE HEADLONG DRIVE TO PRIVATIZE THE UTILITIES

Chapter 14 touched on the impact that privatization has had in destabilizing the security of the energy markets. In the USA, in particular, privatization has undermined the reliable provision of, for instance, energy in California, spurred on by corporate greed and corruption, famously flag-shipped by the Enron scandal. The trend of governments everywhere to rush headlong to priva-tize core industries pervades many different aspects of the way we design and manage our built environment.

One example is the loss of long-term theoretical research from the public to the private sec-tor. Formerly publicly funded research establishments, such as the UK's Building Research Establishment, and the research centres of British Rail and the Electricity and Gas industries, have been sold to the highest bidder or the attached industries, so losing for the nation an invalu-able powerhouse of expertise that would be essential in future-proofing Britain against the exi-gencies of the coming decades. In their place we have a 'product-oriented' research community dependent on short-term research contracts handed out by a government increasingly interested in getting 'added value' for their research investments by favouring research that is co-funded by industry. That means that instead of investigating theoretical or generic issues, priority is given to testing products, in a manner that promotes the agendas of the funders, that is, industry. Gone are the researchers with decades of experience on the 'big issues', replaced by a hustling research marketplace, dealing in diminishing research funds, with large tranches of taxpayers' money being paid directly to the privatized service industries to do with as they like to. By con-trast, the monolithic, multinational Électricité de France (EDF) is excellently placed to research and develop new energy supply systems, as it is doing now.

The conflicts of interest among the industry, the regulators and the research community must be dealt with and delineated, and contraventions of the bond of trust placed in these bodies staunchly defended through the courts.

GOVERNMENTS

We saw in Chapter 11 how no act of governance has been successful in controlling the onwards march of poor modern building performance, neither market forces nor professional guidance nor regulations.

The Royal Institute of British Architects (RIBA) may urge its members against the unnecessary use of air conditioning and the Chartered Institute of Building Service Engineers (CIBSE) includes in its Code of Professional Conduct the admonition to 'Avoid the use of refrigeration where natu-ral and mechanical ventilation is a feasible alternative', but both professions continue to move indiscriminately to almost universal use of air conditioning in their larger buildings. The RIBA Gold Medals for design typically go to energy-profligate, highly serviced buildings without so much as a nod to the challenge of making them low impact in reality as well.

However, it is hoped that other new initiatives will prove more successful. Many local councils recognize that they have to play a larger part in tackling climate change. The Local Government Association has teamed up with the Energy Saving Trust to fund a senior project officer to work at the Greater London Authority on sustainable energy and climate change, and to update the Association's policy on such matters, in light of climate change developments and the govern-ment's White Paper on energy that required a 60% CO_2 emissions reduction by 2050.[9] It may well be that people will come to recognize the urgency of acting promptly and move on from the tenets of corporate social responsibility that were prevalent in the boom years when many cor-porations espoused the wisdom of 'doing well by doing good'.[10] Some large corporations were talking up sustainability, but lower down the food chain developers were rarely so keen to make gestures towards the need for carbon reductions. In the time of bust will everyone forget sustainability or, out of the ashes of the twentieth century house building industry, will a new market for smaller, very low-energy and affordable homes rise?

What is difficult to justify is that the Building Regulations in Britain promote the use of air conditioning in poorly performing, high-risk buildings over low-energy, naturally ventilated, resilient buildings (see p. 222). The same Regulations have enabled a generation of glass tower buildings that should never have been allowed to be built because of their patently poor building performance and profligate energy use to rise over our cities. Whoever they are written to protect, it is not the citizens of the world or of Britain, or the environment. The lobbyists have succeeded.

The same can be said for the silent hand of vested interests in the planning profession. John Prescott was very successful in bullying through the new developments on the Thames flood plains in the Thames Gateway communities. It appears that the UK Government favours the interests of the developers over those of their voting populations. Similarly, many of us were aghast when civil servant, and lackey to the government, Sir Michael Pitt produced his planning review of the 2007 floods that was published on 25 June 2008 telling us that we simply had to continue to develop on the flood plains because we could not afford, as a nation, to do otherwise (see p. 86). Yet this conflicts with the findings of the Stern Review, which clearly lays out the economic imperative of investing early in reducing the exposure and vulnerability of populations to climate change.

What Sir Michael Pitt, in his detailed review did not really answer was the key question: Where does the buck stop in the decision-making process that leads to new developments on the flood plain when they consequently flood?

Qui Bono: Who benefits? And more importantly, who pays?

The buck in the UK Government apparently does not stop anywhere. There is no demonstrable accountability in the system. If the Thames Gateway floods in a storm surge, neither the developers nor the planners nor John Prescott himself are currently in line to be held directly responsible, least of all the former Deputy Prime Minister. Who actually makes the choices to build huge new energy-profligate buildings or developments in regions meaning not only that emissions rise but also that every home will pay more for their energy to cover the costs? Such mega-buildings may require new generating capacity to be paid for by existing households or overstretch the existing generating capacity and increase the risks of the lights going out locally in extremely cold or hot weather. If the Londoner has to pay to have extra generating capacity of 5MW installed, so putting up their own bills, to cope with the peak load of a single new tower block development in the city, this is not taken into account at the planning stage, nor is the impact of the new water demand on the availability of drinking water in the region during drought periods, an already chronic problem. Such new developments are typically seen only as a sign of the economic success of a region!

When homes flood in new developments of care homes and social housing in the flood plains, we know that heads should roll, but we do not know whose. There is no central UK Government fund to pay for the victims of flooding, even though it is their current policies that put people in care homes, schools, hospitals and social housing on the flood plains. It will be the local authorities who pick up the tab for the poor and the uninsured who flood, so why do they tolerate moves to expose more buildings to future costs they will have to cover themselves?

Not until we have lines of accountability for decisions made by government, lines that identify who is responsible and who pays for mistakes in political judgement and leadership, will we have a government that deals with the human as well as the financial costs of climate change responsibly, and acts in the interests of the person on the street rather than those of the political lobbyists.

PLANNERS

The front line of our battle against climate change should be the planning profession. Unfortunately, planners, although many are very proactive on such issues, are all too often simply not equipped with the knowledge, or the statutory teeth, to deal with 'unsustainable' developments. At worst planners, and the voting councillors they serve, are responsible for major mistakes that could blight the lives of hundreds of thousands of people. At best enlightened planners are leading the way forward in building low-carbon, low-impact and low-risk communities in a rapidly changing climate.

First, however, we must deal with the important issues of why planners do not understand the dangers posed by developments in the flood plains. It could be a combination of factors:

- Planning policy in England allows flood plain development in certain circumstances, namely if there is nowhere more suitable.
- Many parts of the southeast of England are short of land for development and what land there is often in an area of prime agricultural land, a Site of Special Scientific Interest, a Conservation Area or green belt or similar. As such it is protected against development by powerful interest groups with legal backing.
- Planning officers do not have to worry about the hassle of designing or financing flood defence schemes, as they do in Scotland. Instead, they pass this on to the Environment Agency.
- Planning officers are under pressure from property developers who often have undue influence over local or national political parties. Perhaps it is coincidental that developers are often found to be major contributors to the funds of political parties.
- Planning officers are also under pressure from local elected members who want to see more development in their councils to bring in more income and wealth.
- Planning officers almost never consult with key stakeholders like the insurance industry, landowners, residents' associations, flood survivor groups or others over flood risks as they do in Scotland, so they get an entirely one-sided view of the problem.
- Many planning officers and members of committees on local councils simply do not understand the issues involved because they are not presented with adequate information and do not to talk to key stakeholders such as insurance companies who could help them to understand the implications for local communities. By contrast, local authorities in Scotland regularly take advice from the insurance industry and in return the industry helps to resolve possible local difficulties of availability and affordability of insurance.

However, as a result of the scale of the recent flooding events in the UK, the insurance industry is taking a much harder line on developments in the flood plain. Because the new EU Directive on Flooding now defines a flood as the 'temporary covering of land by water that is not normally covered by water' (relating it not to how it got there but to the fact that it is there) the insurance industry is now moving to use legal precedents such as *Tate Gallery v Duffy Construction Ltd*, 2007, to explore the possibility of excluding flood cover from standard building insurance policies, making owners take on extra insurance to cover floods and satisfy mortgage lenders.

In 2003 the government launched its 'Sustainable Communities' plan, accelerating the provision of housing, largely in new green-field developments in areas like the Thames Gateway, London–Stansted–Cambridge corridor, Ashford, and Milton Keynes–South Midlands, many of which are on flood plains. Are such politicians really blind to the risks they are creating with such developments?

The Environment Agency, our supposed bastion against the onslaught of vested interests and poor political judgement, appears to be developing stronger legal teeth. In the case of the *Administrative Court in R (Environment Agency) v Tonbridge & Malling District Council*, the Council's decision to allow sheltered housing to be built on a flood plain was struck down as failing to take policy guidance sufficiently into account. The case *Bloor v Swindon Borough Council* also considered the relevance of flood plain policy to overall development planning policy, and in 2007 the Environment Agency won in the High Court against a local council that wanted to put a new development for 63 sheltered housing apartments on the flood plain on a site that had been recently severely affected by flooding. The Council was shown not to have followed the sequential test laid down under planning policy guidance. In cities like Leeds, Sheffield and Manchester, where planners have encouraged new high-rise residential blocks on flood plains, it may be only a matter of time before a class action law suit is filed by the tenants who can no longer get insurance for their homes. Victims of flooding could use the legal precedent set by *Ryeford Homes v Sevenoaks District Council*, where a claim was made for damages against the planning authority in respect of flooding caused by allowing overdevelopment, implying that it should be possible to take a council or a developer of the homes to court for damage.[10]

Planners lack training in the numerical understanding of infrastructural system capacity limits for new developments and in the basics of how buildings work. Time and time again areas of cities that cannot cope with extreme events such as urban flooding are given permission for more and more development, as we have seen in Leeds, Sheffield, Coventry and Blackburn. During the 2007 floods the sewage systems in many parts of these cities overflowed into the streets, filling them with toxic swilling raw sewage because the drainage infrastructure was not sufficiently large to pump it away quickly enough. Yet at the point of recommending whether a new development would be given planning permission, these issues were not taken into account. Neither were the capacities of the public transport systems, school places, hospital bed availability, electricity generating capacity or water availability of the city taken into account.

In the current planning process, there is generally no detailed statement on the thermal or environmental performance of a proposed building given to councillors for consideration before it is granted planning permission. So the planning officer who decides whether to promote the building, or a planning council member who will vote on it, may have no idea of the potential environmental impacts of the building on greenhouse gas emissions or water usage in the building. Planning officers and the elected councillors will judge a building by what it looks like, and what image of their own area or city they would like to promote. Committees can give approval for fashionable, unshaded, all glass and steel buildings with huge air conditioning systems, and remain blissfully ignorant of the task they have passed on, in the process, to the Building Control Officer to try to conform to UK Building Regulations. Councils will promote the use of thin, tight, shiny, poorly performing cladding systems over robust traditional construction as a matter of course because they want their city to look 'modern', regardless of the performance implications.

If the government intends to meet the reductions targets of the EU Directive it is difficult to see how this will be achieved without key decision-making roles, like planners, councillors or the Environment Agency, being better educated in the issues and having more statutory teeth.

Buildings will have to meet the required standard *before* they are given planning permission, not afterwards. As the climate changes buildings will have to incrementally upgrade their defences against the sun and wind, with awnings, shades, solar systems, shuttering features and even wind turbines, and it will be necessary for the planning organizations to decide the rules for their generic application, and to retrain planning officers in relation to their applications. Every planning department must have a trained sustainability officer to deal with the technical issues.

There is also a clear need for a new generation of planning tools that can be used to systematically assess issues of infrastructural system capacity at the settlement level.[11] A range of tools is now being widely used for the assessment of carbon emissions from settlements and particularly where these have planner- and public-friendly outputs, in the form of maps. One such model is the DECoRuM model, which provides a bottom–up tool for mapping building energy use and emissions. Using such tools councils will eventually be able to insist on developments reducing carbon emissions locally by the required amount to compensate for the emissions increase caused by the new development.[12]

It should also be compulsory for developers to provide a report on the future costs for the eventual refurbishment and demolition of developments. As it stands the refurbishment of problematic building types such as tower blocks generally ends up with the council, which has received little previous benefit. Refurbishment can be hugely expensive. In addition, some buildings are incapable of cost-effective demolition and should never have been built. Buildings should be designed such that they can be demolished effectively and planners should be trained to understand the demolition implications of buildings before they give permission for them to be built.

The disaster mitigation services in England and Wales also need urgent revision to deal with emerging climate-related events (the system in Scotland has already been revised). Neither the Emergency Powers Act 1920 nor the Civil Defence Act of 1948, both affected through the planning system, has been updated in England and Wales since the end of the Cold War.

Under the Civil Contingencies Bill, local councils in England and Wales, including planning departments, will form core 'Local Resilience Forums', tasked with emergency planning, providing information to the public, risk management advice and ensuring that businesses continue to operate. For the first time councils in England and Wales will have a statutory duty with respect to emergency planning as 'First Tier Responders', although many see this Bill as potentially impinging on civil liberties.[13]

County, metropolitan, unitary and London borough councils, unlike districts, receive direct funding in the form of a civil defence grant but its value, even in the face of climate change, has been falling year on year. In 2000 it rose from £5 million a year to £19 million, and has stayed at this level ever since. Studies have shown that the actual expenditure on emergencies in England and Wales is over twice this, and flood-prone regions are disproportionately penalized, particularly by flooding. These sums cover facilities such as the serious casualty access teams, chemical spills and mobile decontamination centres, the latter developed for nuclear industry leakages. Some counties, at the hub of transport networks, also bear an undue burden of emergency planning costs.

THE INTERNET AND THE MEDIA

The Internet is the most amazing source of future-proofing ideas, opportunities, strategies and experiences in the world. It is so fast-moving and all-pervasive that new ideas become universally available instantaneously. It can also peddle agendas and well-disguised lies, in the form of apparently 'high-end' information and guidance that effectively promotes the interests of the funding organization of a site. This problem also applies to the truth, in that a search engine such as Google sorts information according to patterns of its use, a system that can be manipulated by clever webmasters. With determined interrogation, however, that is, looking through all the pages on a subject, many sides of a discussion will be aired and a broad perspective on a subject can be enjoyed in the comfort of one's own home.

The press is also very important in educating the public with key messages, such as the fact that when watering gardens, one sprinkler uses in an hour what a family of four consumes over a week. Such information could change habits. That in heatwaves city fountains can be used to reduce heat stress. That in the 2003 heatwave Parisian train drivers had strict speed limits imposed to reduce the levels of ozone. That a facilities manager had taken the decision to shut down the Treasury building in London and send everyone home because it was too hot to work in summer 2003. We all learn from such stored incidents and so increase our own range of adaptive opportunities to which we can resort in extremes.

Many of the references in this book come from papers, journals and the Internet. That is because:

- Change is happening so rapidly. Many of the developments in the field are so fast that books and journals are out of date by the time they get to press.
- Truth is stranger than fiction. Many of the small and apparently disconnected facts fall outwith the reductionist and focused purview of researchers who may not notice them as viable adaptive tools for that simple reason. They may, however, be very important.

However, the downside is that the 'opinion-forming' journalists need to be very well versed in the issues, and to provide first class copy on those issues if they are to help turn the zeitgeist of the general public, and the ship of government, in more sustainable and effective directions.

We have been pretty poorly served by the range of architectural correspondents in our major organs of the press. Many are not even architects, being often trained in related disciplines such as philosophy, art history and history, or even architects who have little grasp of how buildings 'work'. It is not uncommon to read articles in which buildings are described solely by how they look, on the 'philosophy' or 'symbolism' of a building, as seen by the journalist. This opinion-based reportage reflects the way in which assessment of work goes on in schools of architecture, as staff and students proffer opinions on design. Many serious publications in the architectural press are now making an effort to provide serious and informed reporting on issues of sustainability in the built environment, but a major emphasis in all reporting should be on how buildings perform and are appreciated by real people.

However, yet again, the vested interests of architecture have gone a long way to ensuring that the voice of the common person is not too loud. At least one, well-known, British architectural journalist was effectively banned from candid commenting on buildings by her editor, because a 'great man' of architecture slapped a writ on his desk the morning after she had dared to voice a criticism of his latest masterpiece. A number of leading designers are notoriously litigious. Stephen Brand, author of the excellent book *How Buildings Learn,* had to scrap a whole print run of this book for the UK market because he pointed out that the buildings of one famous British architect were often very expensive to maintain. Brand was threatened with legal action and withdrew the book, which then had to be altered before reprinting despite the fact that the American publication was published with the full text. The libel laws in Britain enable the interests of powerful people in any sector to effectively silence the press over such issues and thus suppress intelligent discussion in public about how buildings actually work in reality. The UK libel laws prevent building designers, their clients and the public alike from learning from their own and others' mistakes because of that lack of discussion.

QUANGOS

There are several building-related quangos that operate in the UK. The government in 2003 put major funding into the Commission for Architecture in the Built Environment (CABE).[14] In February 2003 its funds were increased from £4.4 million to £10 million a year. It was also given a series of new responsibilities to ensure that the 200 000 new homes in the Communities plan would meet a high design standard. This includes the massive £466 million investment planned in the Thames Gateway area and the £164 million for Milton Keynes, Ashford and the M11 corridor. Tony Blair had promised to personally oversee the Thames Gateway development. By accepting the money, CABE was accepting that it was safe to develop in the Thames Gateway. Can one be too concerned about long-term performance if one thinks the development will flood in the near future? Was this issue ever even discussed? If not, is this part of the systematic and self-interested infrastructure of denial?

CABE now has its fingers in many architectural pies, and in November 2003 it became involved in the Building Listing Process, by which buildings are protected under the law from demolition because of their architectural merit. The growing power of CABE in this process was questioned by the traditional defenders of the British landscape, English Heritage and RIBA. The President of RIBA, George Ferguson, rejected the idea, saying:

The RIBA believes that the sole criteria for listing should be those of architectural, cultural and historic importance.

He maintained that CABE's proposal to take a lead role would 'corrupt' the listings system and distract English Heritage from its main role in assessing the historic significance of any building.[14] But CABE has proved itself useful in many roles and has acted as a funnel for funds into improving quality in the built environment and education on it. Unfortunately, its view of what constitutes 'good design' is based on the opinions of its members' panels, of whom many are London-based 'modern' architects who may represent a biased opinion. Any quango is potentially open to the influence of vested interests and in March 2004 one senior member of CABE was investigated for a conflict of interest, after people raised concerns that developments proffered by his own company for review by CABE design quality panels always came out with high marks for excellence, unlike a number of other developments. CABE is ultimately a high-profile government quango, led by individuals who control money and therefore have power. But they inevitably dance to the government's tune.

It is pertinent to ask whether the money thus spent could be better used to understand what, in the eyes of real building users, constitutes good design. The most effective nemesis of poor buildings to date has been the EPBD. This has proved an effective sorter of the building sheep from the dogs, and of those architects who have been in the habit of routine greenwashing of their own buildings to an unsuspecting public. If every building client, owner, occupier and designer were able to continually revisit the performance of their buildings then not only would building performance be radically improved but the same mistakes would not go on being repeated. If CABE spent most of its money on the instigation of routine post-occupancy evaluation for every building they would improve building standards much more effectively – but they may be less good at promoting the government line on what constitutes good buildings.

ARCHITECTS

What ethical and moral responsibilities does the profession have to provide good buildings? In his book *Streets for People*, in 1969, Bernard Rudofsky wrote, no doubt in part as a response to the brutal redevelopment of many city centres at that time:[15]

Unlike physicians, today's architects are not concerned with the general welfare; they are untroubled by scruples about strangling the cities and the misery that this entails. Architects never felt the urge to establish ethical precepts for the performance of their profession, as did the medical fraternity. No equivalent of the Hippocratic oath exists for them. Hippocrates' promise that 'the regiment I adopt shall be for the benefit of my patients according to my ability and judgement, and not for their hurt or for any wrong' has no counterpart in their book. Criticism within the profession – the only conceivable way to spread a sense of responsibility among its members – is tabooed by their own codified standards of practice. To bolster their egos, architects hold their own beauty contests, award each other prizes, decorate each other with gold medals, and make light of the damning fact that they do not amount to any moral force.

Since this was written the Architect's Registration Board (ARB), the body with the statutory responsibility of registering UK architects, as opposed to RIBA which is really a professional club, included in its Code of Conduct an implied professional duty of care relating to their wider social responsibilities,[16] stating that:

In carrying out or agreeing to carry out professional work, Architects should pay due regard to the interests of anyone who may reasonably be expected to use or enjoy the products of their own work.

... Whilst Architects' primary responsibility is to their clients, they should nevertheless have due regard to their wider responsibility to conserve and enhance the quality of the environment and its natural resources.

What teeth such matters have in law is unclear, although architects do have a tried and tested legal duty of care, under the laws, to avoid injuring someone, damaging their property or causing financial loss due to inadequate expert advice.

Design at what cost? A moral issue

We have seen in the previous chapters that modern prestige buildings often carry a very high environmental cost, in terms of the energy they use and, in many, the risks they pose to their occupants and owners, including the financial penalties of being landed with very high cleaning and maintenance costs. This disregard for the 'cost' of a building to its owners is reflected in the growing tendency for buildings to come in well over time and over cost on building budgets. This disregard for the client's welfare first shocked the British public when they were forced to pay for what turned out to be the billion-pound 'Millennium Dome' fiasco. Hackles have been kept raised by the sheer audacity of the insouciance of architects to the implications of what such costs may mean.[17]

The £750 million design of the new Wembley Stadium will ultimately be reflected in the ticket price fans have to pay for a seat in the stadium.[18] The University of Birmingham had to cancel its landmark library following a dramatic rise in the estimated budget from the original £100 million to £170 million in September 2003. Is it ultimately the Birmingham University students through their fees who will in future have to cover the cost of expensive designs that are then scrapped? It is the people of Wales who paid for the hugely inflated costs of the Welsh National Assembly in Cardiff, where uncontrolled spending led to a ban on regular monthly payments to designers? The Audit Commission had to investigate why the original cost of £12 million had risen to over £30 million and attempt to stop the practice of what some saw as the signing of blank cheques for those firms involved in the construction of the project.[19]

The most publicized overspend to date was for the new Scottish Parliament building at Holyrood, designed by the Catalan architect, the late Enric Miralles. The cost of this building rose from £37 million to an astronomical £375 million, that is, around £150 for every home in Scotland.[20] The fact that the designer knew nothing about the British climate, people and building industry of Scotland must surely have added to these ridiculous costs and also to the risk of future building failure. Miralles designed many complex windows that stand proud from the face of the building, and which will at every joint potentially fail. In addition, future maintenance and cleaning bills on the structure are huge, and each of those outstanding windows forms a cold bridge out into the chill winds of the windy city, and will rapidly deteriorate, particularly in the increasingly wet and windy, and scorching, future climates we expect. A wrong decision on the wrong building will be made worse by a changing climate.

Competitions and exhibitions

Many have questioned the role of the 'design competition' in these overspends. For example, in May 2003 the European Commission received a 20 page complaint about the Scottish Parliament building claiming that the competition that was won by Miralles disadvantaged some entrants unlawfully; so suggesting that there were breaches in EU regulations on the letting of contracts and secrecy and political bias over the selection of the site.[21] Some believe that it was solely on the preference of the then Scottish leader, the late Donald Dewar, that the project was given to the late Enric Miralles.

What we do have is a system in which the judges of fashionable competitions often include many fashionable architects whose life's work has been devoted to a particular type of prestige architecture. Reflections of their own style convictions become apparent in their choices of competition winners, setting a benchmark standards of what are 'architectural masterpieces'. Typically, the greater the 'icon', the greater its environmental impact. Issues of environmental performance rarely figure in the requirements of such competitions and too often the resulting buildings, subsequently evaluated for their performance after construction, prove to be 'nightmare' buildings.

In October 2003 the Laban Dance Centre in Deptford, southeast London, won the £20 000 Stirling Prize for Architecture. The judges were Julian Barnes, novelist, Justine Frischmass, singer from the band Elastica, and others. Technical competence to evaluate the performance of the buildings was obviously not a core requirement of the judging panel. Designed by the Swiss team of Hertzog and de Meuron, it was a popular win. The sealed-envelope, fully air-conditioned building on a waterside site could easily, and very pleasantly, have been naturally ventilated, in parts at least. No consideration of its environmental performance was made in the judging and the current and long-term running costs of the building were never discussed by the press or the judges of the competition.[22]

Well-known architects get high-profile exhibitions at the best venues. It is a fact of life that because certain designers dominate the architectural press, the competitions and the zeitgeist of the late twentieth century public consider them to be the 'maestros' of architecture. The fact that famous people often sit on the panels that choose the designs of famous offices for display is merely an indication of their global excellence. Is this tending towards being a closed shop?

ARCHITECTURAL EDUCATION

Engineers are crucial to the solution of these [climate change] problems, but it might be that they could be avoided in the first place if the education and training of engineers was to include a bit more about the globe's essential life-support systems. It is after all these systems which ensure the habitability of our planet as it spins in the vast spaces of the universe.

HRH Prince Philip, writing in the January 2000 edition of the magazine Ingenia,
the Journal of the Royal Academy of Engineering

In 2008 an international Oxford Conference on architectural education was convened, 50 years after the first Oxford Conference on the subject chaired by Sir Leslie Martin.[23] The presentations are available on the Internet. There appeared to be there a strong consensus that the schools of architecture in the UK and around the world need to make a serious and concerted effort to reconnect with the marketplace for buildings. As Sunand Prasad, President of the RIBA, and many others said, schools of architecture are too often no longer producing architects who know how to design buildings that are fit for purpose in the twenty-first century. After five years of education they should be setting the agenda for leading-edge building design and yet often they know little or nothing about the design, detailing and construction of real buildings. There was a call for much more use of post-occupancy evaluation of buildings during teaching, where students go out to record and report on the strengths and weaknesses of real buildings. There was real debate about the overdependence on studio teaching, where the design tastes of the studio leader so often dominate what is produced rather than the particular strengths of an individual student. There was real concern about their understanding of their 'wider responsibility to conserve and enhance the quality of the environment and its natural resources' or even the interests of their clients.

Many students in schools of architecture around the world are poorly taught on issues of building performance. In her doctoral thesis, Marianne Ryghaug did a detailed study of how architects in Norway view environmental issues such as energy efficiency and found that it has a very low status in the teaching of the subject. Architects were perceived as more 'artistic' than engineers and more preoccupied with design and form. She put the blame for this partly on architectural education, where in many schools energy and environmental courses were optional. The 1990s was a decade of extensive demonstration building funded by the EU. She also identified the need for stricter regulations and funding for demonstration buildings, although perhaps more funding for post-occupancy evaluations of the actual, not the predicted, performance of buildings would be money better spent.[24]

A report funded by the Centre for Education in the Built Environment (CEBE) found that sustainability is rarely considered in the design curriculum and, when it is, the subject is treated as a one-off project or tagged to an existing brief. Many schools have just one or two lone individuals who teach students to use sustainable design features, but the RIBA and ARB, the validating bodies for the schools, it argued, should insist that the subject is demonstrated on all design projects. One head of school said that he thought it was a matter of opinion whether sustainability should be the driving force for architectural education, and his view reflects those of many heads of architecture schools in Britain.[25]

Technical teaching has often been downgraded in schools of architecture so where a school had several individuals teaching lighting, services, construction and structures they may now have one or two generalists, who will often teach by case studies rather than getting students to grips with the basic principles of building physics and performance. The environment is not an issue to most design teachers in schools of architecture. Perhaps this is because they really do not have a firm grip on the basics themselves or because the 'lighter touch' approach complements the studio teaching style prevalent in many schools.

One result of poor teaching is that students are often not well versed in their statutory responsibilities. Architects are currently poorly educated in their duties under the law with regard to Health and Safety. A study by the Health and Safety Executive (HSE), published in May 2003,[26] looked at designers' compliance with the Construction Design and Management (CDM) Regulations of 1994 and found architects' awareness of their duties to be woefully inadequate. The highest percentage of the 85 construction-related deaths between 2001 and 2002 was caused by falls from a height, and the report concluded that 'designers are often abdicating their responsibility to reduce risk in relation to work at height by leaving it to the principal contractor without first considering how they could change the design in a way that would make it safer to build, clean or maintain a building'.[27]

So what do they teach in schools of architecture?

Some of the best teaching on environmental issues takes place in the American schools of architecture,[28] often not greatly encouraged by some heads of school. This was the impression given by an extraordinary website (which has recently been pulled) that showed how distressed students at the Department of Architecture at the University of California at Los Angeles were losing their rights to pragmatic teaching in favour of a 'highly' theoretical approach to design of the kind that has resulted in the type of buildings known as the 'pointy', the 'falling over' and the 'blob'.

Many of the counter-intuitive forms of such buildings have been largely influenced by 'deconstructionism'. The following section on deconstructionism was inspired by an important recent paper on the subject by Nikos Salingaros.[29]

Deconstruction is a method of analysing texts based on the idea that language is inherently unstable and shifting and that the reader rather than the author is central in determining meaning. It was introduced by the French philosopher Jacques Derrida in the late 1960s.[30]

Deconstructionism disaggregates a specific text or building and then reassembles the components in a manner that makes the viewer look at the building not in terms of its formal function but asks the question why the architect designed it in that particular way. It is about the 'signature' of the designer.

Deconstructionism's most visible manifestation is in architecture, in a building style characterized by broken, jagged and lopsided forms, evoking physical destruction.[31] Salingaros states that architectural theory has embraced deconstructionism in order to reverse architecture's main *raison d'être*: to provide shelter. Architecture's goals happen to be precisely what Derrida rejects: aesthetics, beauty, usefulness, functionality, living and dwelling. The randomness of the buildings this approach produces[32,33] is the antithesis of nature's organized complexity housing buildings such as scientific departments, university buildings and museums, whose function is to enhance and complement the order of the universe, in chaotic jumbles of form – an often unnoticed irony.

Otherwise knowledgeable clients, including academics, have been seduced to commission tortuous buildings in the deconstructionist style, applauded by fellow architects and considered ugly, odd and useless by ordinary people. Daniel Libeskind's new Research Centre at London Metropolitan University caused a stir when the police cordoned off Holloway Road after a passer-by had phoned-in saying the new building had fallen down! Salingaros builds up a careful picture of how forces combine to make such buildings apparently 'acceptable' to those commissioning buildings, including its incomprehensibility, the silliness of people who do not want to appear not to understand it, the desire of architects to ride a wave of stylistic fashion for fame and profit, the desire to reject the 'context' of a building, and the desire of some architects to be seen as 'leading edge' and 'innovative', hiding behind phrases such as fractals, complexity, emergence, chaos as well as their more conventional and perhaps more potentially questionable late modernistic terms, such as transparency.

After their initial infatuation with deconstruction, some architects have turned to other wider influences for design inspiration, such as 'blobs' or 'folding', a reflection of the fact that deconstruction is not a style that can be adapted or evolve to meet changing needs and as such is already *passé*.

Cities around the world are now seeing the next generation of 'blobs'. In the UK the first famous blobs were the four silver metal blobs of the National Centre for Popular Music in Sheffield, which were inappropriate for the surrounding brick terraced streets.[34] A decade on, the buildings remain,

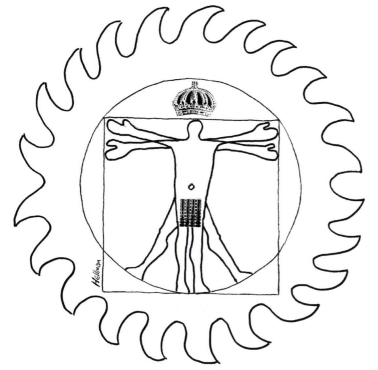

15.1.
'The Emperor has no clothes!' (© Louis Hellman, 2004).

getting dirtier and dirtier as local groups cannot afford the high cleaning costs. The Centre folded, although people have tried to use these funny building forms for different activities subsequently, none very satisfactorily. Like the Dome, the shapes are not quite right for anything.

The largest UK blob is four storeys high and wrapped in a skin decorated with 15000 spun aluminium discs painted blue. It is the new Sainsbury's supermarket in the Bull Ring redevelopment in Birmingham, designed by Future Systems and opened in the summer of 2003. It was described as 'Top of the Blobs' by Jonathan Glancy of the *Guardian*, and it makes no gesture at all to fit in to its context of surrounding buildings. It was hailed by Glancy as 'architectural entertainment'.[35]

Any end-of-year show at an architecture school will be dominated by blobs and shards, not least because many of the teaching staff are skilled at teaching blob design, which relates largely to digital simulation skills. The computer images of blobs look stunning and many schemes are marked in schools by the quality of the digital presentation, rather than whether they illustrate a building that would work, could be used or would be liked by its clients, let alone what its impacts would be on the local, regional and global environment. More than a few teachers in schools of architecture would not consider it necessary, desirable or conscionable to mention the actual construction or performance of a building, its buildability or functionality, during the studio tutorials, and in some cases students can pass though five years of architectural education being virtually illiterate on performance-based subjects. They then emerge into the offices of unsuspecting practitioners who are expected to educate them in the boring realities of how buildings work and are built, while paying them for the privilege.

Peter Cook, head of the Bartlett School of Architecture, and a blob designer himself, was very worried about the increasing obscurity of his students' work:

Some of Britain's brightest students are producing work that not even their experienced tutors can understand, never mind clients, planners and the public … During last year's summer exhibition I was often

15.2.
The National Centre for Popular Music in Sheffield.
Source: Steve Sharples.

puzzled and bemused by the obscurity of intention, of brief or nature of the pursuit … lovely stuff that you had to play guessing games with … we are in danger of collective headiness sustained within a 'bubble' of arcaneness.

Cook said that he would in future personally check that work is better declared and described.[36]

In the UK, however, this could be changing as the RIBA and the ARB have got together to ensure that teaching standards across the board are of an adequate standard, and if not they withdraw their recognition from that school in an effective system of policing standards in education.

One of the most effective 'exclusionary' techniques used by 'theoretical' teachers and deconstuctionists alike is to brand traditional architecture as bad, retrograde, non-innovative and an impediment to progress, eliminating solid traditional buildings from consideration in the teaching studio or the marketplace.

Leon Krier expressed the view that architects like Rogers and Foster, arch proponents of the great British 'glass box' tradition, in particular, 'have too much power', and in agreeing with him Robert Adam said it was 'offensive that they are so dogmatic … They believe the future is theirs and there is no other way. You are a traitor to the future if you disagree with them. It is intolerant'.[37] Unfortunately, adaptability and flexibility are two of our survival mechanisms, and we end up with white elephant buildings. Our changing environment will result in white elephant architects as well.

We return here to the notion of conventional wisdom, represented by the established theoretical 'design'-driven teachers in schools of architecture:[38]

Maynard Keynes noted that we are ruled by ideas and by very little else … But the rule of ideas is only powerful in a world that does not change. Ideas are inherently conservative. They yield not to attack of other ideas but to the massive onslaught of circumstances with which they cannot contend.

The economic and environmental context, around the glass houses, the shards and the blobs, is changing rapidly, and it is this need to respond to these changes that will drive society back to demanding robust buildings rather than 'architectural entertainment', because the former are capable of adapting to those changes while the latter are not.

In light of the importance of future-proofing our buildings and cities against climate change the time may well have come to split architectural education into two distinct arms, one for those primarily interested in learning graphic and digital skills and another for those interested in becoming more pragmatic building designers who are specialist in, for example, designing low-energy and low-impact buildings. Then it would be clear to students, who will increasingly have to pay for five years of their university education themselves, exactly what they are getting for their money.

POWER IN THE BUILDING INDUSTRY

Powerful firms have dominated the agendas in the pre-2008 building markets with a firm grip on government, clients, the press, the professional bodies, the quangos and the opinion of the chattering classes. Key people in key positions of political influence. No people were more powerful as architects than Norman Foster and Richard Rogers in their prime. Rogers, former Chair of the Government's Urban Task Force, was also London Mayor Ken Livingstone's Chief Adviser on Architecture and Urbanism and the Chairman of Richard Rogers Partnership (RRP). He was originally appointed to this post as a consultant in April 2001, supported by a small group in the Architecture and Urbanism Unit (A1UU). Unfortunately, there arose during his time there a range of 'conflicts of interest', including the weight given to his deliberations on the future of tall buildings in the capital. Other minuted conflicts of interest arose over his bids for work in a range of projects, although particular care was taken to ensure that he 'stepped outside' when such conflicts arose during meetings.[39] No one should underestimate the power of such individuals in the market to impress on the general assembly their notions of 'correct' design.

Real concern about too much design work going to a few large firms was also voiced by the Office of Fair Trading, which was asked by the Better Regulation Task Force in May 2003 to launch an inquiry into the government's procurement policy because they claimed that small and medium-sized design and construction firms were being excluded from government construction contracts.[40] This monopoly of influence led, in part, to the generation of glass box architecture that has done so much to stifle the development of truly resilient, low-impact building, and leaves behind it a swath of dead buildings that will be almost worthless when the energy performance labels are put in their lobbies.

BUILDING SERVICES ENGINEERS

It is not surprising that in the age of 'machines for living in' engineers dominate the building process. Architects, who seem to be happy to pass on as much design liability as possible to anyone who will take it, often transfer their challenging designs to engineers and rely on them to 'make them work'.

The engineers who had to try to make the original design of the GLA headquarters building work had their work cut out for them. They had to design out much of the glass on the roof, and try to control the indoor air temperatures with the sun beating down through the envelope into the building from above – a task that can only be done by using not insignificant amounts of energy to remove the heat once in the building. The question must be raised over who must bear responsibility for the F or G rating for the building's performance: the architect or the engineer?

Some consolation for engineers during the twentieth century when issues over energy were almost non-existent was that as 'modern' offices started to overheat in the 1950s, engineers were increasingly paid according to how much plant and duct work they could get into a building. The more environmentally 'innovative' the project, the more they got paid – effectively to rectify the basic design mistakes of the architect.

If we are ever to get green buildings we must ensure that this contractual arrangement is promptly changed to ensure that engineers are fairly paid to reduce energy consumption, not encouraged through their contracts to increase it. Engineers should work side by side with the architect, from the first days of the brief, to ensure that the form and the fabric of the building itself is used to minimize its costs and impacts, not expensive machines.

Terry Wyatt, former President of CIBSE, in his inaugural speech in 2003/04,[41] entitled 'Adapt or Die', outlined the exciting possibilities for engineers who will have to retool for a business climate in which the traditional work of building services engineers is shrinking while they will have to bear the brunt of pressures to reduce waste in the construction industry by 30%. He identifies that work such as calculations, sizing, positioning and coordination, specification, costing, manufacturing and the construction and fitting out of the building with traditional air conditioning systems will diminish. This work he regards as the 'filling in a sandwich' between one 'slice of bread'

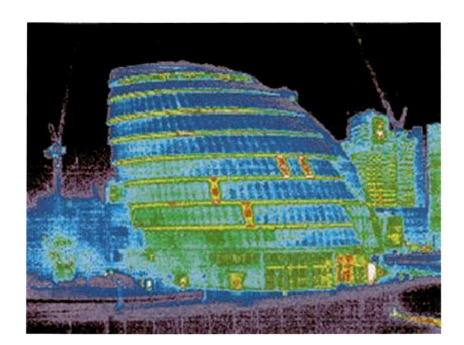

15.3.
The engineers who had to try to make the original design of the GLA headquarters building work, had their work cut out for them. They had to design out much of the glass on the roof, and try to control the indoor air temperatures with the sun beating down through the envelope into the building from above – a task that can only be done by using not insignificant amounts of energy to remove the heat once in the building. The question must be raised over who must bear responsibility for the F or G rating for the building's performance – the architect or the engineer?

that involves the briefing, footprint design, concepts and budgets for the building and the other slice that includes operation and maintenance work to keep the building functioning well and to make future change possible.

He represents the industry that makes buildings work, and this design knowledge will be increasingly important in the building design process. Engineering work could thus become more central rather than less so in this process. He demonstrated how far-sighted companies are increasingly well positioned in the marketplace, such as Colt in solar shading, Nuaire in efficient air-systems equipment and Thermomax in solar thermal collectors, as engineers become key players in increasing building efficiency.

The biggest opportunity he saw as actually being offered by climate change was government efforts to reduce carbon emissions by 60% by 2050, accompanied by targets for energy efficiency and renewable energy over the next 20 years. He describes the 2003 Energy White Paper as throwing down the gauntlet. Carbon management offers huge opportunities for services consultants and the wider industry, and the building services industry has a major opportunity to be at the forefront of carbon management within buildings. He suggested that engineers would grow into the role of building-related renewable energy specialists using wind, solar, biomass and water power.

CIBSE has intelligently sought to educate its members with high-quality annual conferences and a wide range of specialist groups who meet to inform the membership of developments, and act quickly and effectively to pre-empt the changes happening all around. One of these is the need to begin to calculate the climatic performance of buildings for future climates, and their climate change group has been developing a dataset for future climates so that decisions made today about buildings that will hopefully stand for 100 years, can be tested against future climates.

Another problem for the forward-looking environmental engineer or architect is the current state of the international standards for defining the environment in buildings. These tend to favour closely controlled, energy-intensive buildings. This even applies to European Standards aimed at underpinning the EPBD. Traditional thinking supposes that close definition of the environment is necessary, but what is needed are low-carbon buildings with steady, predictable indoor conditions which, as shown in Chapter 11, people will happily accept (Table 15.1)

BUILDING OWNERS, OCCUPIERS AND EMPLOYERS

Organizations have a range of strategies to hand to future-proof their own interests against the exigencies of climate change and fuel insecurity. All businesses should now have a continuity planning strategy to include emergency procedures for all events. The global corporate real estate network has a range of strategies they promote, including, to list but a few:[42]

- Shift from high rise to low rise with a preference for lower level offices.
- Less visible external signage.
- Careful lobby design.
- Parking strategies.
- Designs for evacuation including location and design of stairwells.
- Security in terminology in leases and insurance policies.

Extreme climate events and blackouts over the summer of 2003 reinforced the need for businesses and building owners to make preparations for the repetition of such events.

Under UK legislation employers may face investigation and prosecution by the HSE if they fail to devise suitable contingency plans for emergencies. It is envisaged that claims could arise from workplace accidents caused by the sudden loss of lights, power to lifts or failure of air conditioning systems in hot weather. Panic-induced trampling could occur, particularly if personnel are not promptly informed about the cause of the failure. Stress claims could be brought, particularly if staff suspect a terrorist attack. While many employers have strategies for incidents of fire or terrorist attack it is now considered necessary, by legal experts in the field, that they should also have an appropriate response to deal with total sudden power loss, under the 1999 Health and Safety Regulations,[43] which require employers to undertake a 'suitable and sufficient assessment' of workplace risks. Extreme weather events were involved in most of the summer 2003 blackouts and so this issue should be factored into business planning for blackouts in the future.

There are certainly identifiable dangers associated with swift and protracted power failure at work. Further widespread electricity failures are foreseeable. Secondary lighting sources, generators and evacuation procedures were cited as primary options, but what it is not possible to do is to provide air conditioning over a long period for a high-energy building with back-up generators alone. Accidents during darkness, complete or partial, could lead to prosecution. Health and Safety prosecutions are worrying because liability is absolute save for the defence of reasonable practicability and employers might argue that they had done everything that was reasonably practicable if they followed the HSE advice. There is a possibility that if an employer follows the HSE guidance to the letter but there is still a bad accident the employer might seek redress from those liabilities from the HSE.

Table 15.1. (a–c) Building categories in the existing International (ISO), European (EN) and American (ASHRAE) Standards for indoor climate. These are designed for the concerns of the HVAC industry and encourage the use of highly serviced (and energy-intensive) air-conditioned solutions. (d) A proposed category system which would encourage radical reductions in carbon emissions from buildings rather than rewarding high levels of energy use in air conditioning systems (*Source*: Fergus Nicol).

(a) ISO 7730 (recommended for ASHRAE 55)

Category	PPD/DR Local disc	PMV
A	<6%/<10% <3–10%	−0.2 <PMV <+0.2
B	<10%/20%	−0.5 <PMV <+0.5
	<5–10%	
C	<15%/<30% <10–15%	−0.7 <PMV <+0.7

(b) EN15251: Mechanically cooled

Category	Applicability/level of expectancy	PMV range
I	High: Buildings with high expectancy for sensitive occupants	± 0.2
II	Normal: New buildings	± 0.5
III	Acceptable: Existing buildings	± 0.7
IV	Low expectancy only for short periods	± >0.7

(c) EN15251: Free running

Category	Applicability/level of expectancy	FR Temp. range
I	High: Buildings with high expectancy for sensitive occupants	± 2K
II	Normal: New buildings	± 3K
III	Acceptable: Existing buildings	± 4K
IV	Low expectancy only for short periods	± >4K

(d) Twenty-first century comfort standards

Category	Possible description
A	Buildings which are comfortable with no/little use of energy for heating and cooling
B	Buildings which are comfortable but only use energy part of the year for heating and cooling
C	Buildings which are comfortable but use energy all year for heating and cooling

Lawyers have commented on another dimension of the issue. Under the Building Regulations, fire safety regulations apply to those who build a building in the first place, or modify one. For many years this has meant having an 'appropriate means of escape in case of fire', that is, one that is capable of being safely and effectively used at all material times. But emergency lighting is not mentioned, although it would be hard to argue that an escape route that cannot be safely used when the power fails is 'appropriate'.[44]

Employers also have a duty of care under the Fire Precautions (Workplace) Regulations 1997 to provide emergency lighting. Regulatory breach is an offence but does not give rise to civil liability. The quality of the emergency lighting may depend on the property's age, and of course the diligence of the employers in ensuring that the regulations and legislation are complied with. Deep plan offices, with less available natural daylight, require more emergency lighting than offices with a shallower floor plan. Regular maintenance of battery systems is also important. QC Graham Eklund warns that legislation has enabled electricity supply companies 'to restrict their liability for economic loss caused by negligence disrupting the supply', so it is likely that 'economic losses consequent on a negligently caused blackout or failure of the electricity supply' will not be coverable.[45] In New York in the August 2003 blackouts it should be noted that both simple and sophisticated systems for emergency lighting failed alike in some buildings.

Questions will arise in the law as to where liability lies where buildings also have to be abandoned in extreme weather events, such as the emptying of the Treasury building in the heatwave of August 2003. We have known since the 1960s that certain building types, those with excessive glazing in particular, overheat in hot weather. It could, and no doubt will be, argued that because of the quantity of related information in the public realm on the subject, designers could be held liable for buildings that provide unnecessarily uncomfortable temperatures during hot spells. This has yet to be tested in the courts but a good case could be made. Similarly, where loss of life occurs during flood events due to insufficient attention being given to the problem at the design stage then designers could again be held culpable.

BUSINESS

It has been an eye opener to see how vulnerable global markets are to the exigencies of the catastrophic changing of circumstances around them. Governments around the world have favoured not only the banks but also the 'traditional' energy-based industries such as the automobile or aviation industries (leave alone the oil industry) on the basis that existing jobs (and industries) must be saved. At the same time there is increasing pressure for 'green Keynesianism' calling for the development of new low-carbon industries to get the economy going out of recession. If building workers are facing unemployment why not put them to work installing insulation or secondary glazing in hard-to-heat older buildings? Why not put redundant car makers to work building wind turbines, as was done during the Second World War to manufacture jeeps and tanks? The government response is to build Olympic facilities and more prestige buildings; they are by no means a firm hand at the tiller.

Trade unions also have a part to play, not only in ensuring that their members' interests are safeguarded in newly emerging green industries but also to ensure that they are well served by the buildings they work in. Metal sheds that overheat in summer and freeze or use excess energy in winter are neither healthy nor safe. Offices that rely too heavily on energy supplies to keep them comfortable and safe potentially fail on both counts if the energy supply is no longer reliable. Every unionized workplace should have an environmental officer who is responsible for pressuring the management to take climate change and energy instability seriously.

Industry, in a changing climate, appears to do one thing well, to respond to the marketplace. In simple terms this means that in warmer winters Marks & Spencer sells fewer overcoats. In Milan in the heatwave of 2003 consumption of water soared to 50% more than normal[46] in the same week that Tesco predicted a 100% increase in the sales of ice-creams in the heat, taking out 500 lorries to keep stocks supplied around the country. The heatwave of 2003 in the UK led to a dramatic increase of 11% in the sales of bottled water on the year before, reaching a record retail value for the marker of over £1 billion a year. Many industries like the water supply industry are already prepared with their 50-year plans. For smaller bottled water provision companies the five-year plan with seasonal provision, based on good climate-related data, will need careful thought. For major product distribution services, including those in the building industry, the need to plan for extreme climate events may tend manufacturers towards on-site provision of products, like on-site ice-cream-making facilities at large supermarkets, if gridlock on the roads hampers delivery during periods of peak demand.

Industry, including the building industry, will have to plan carefully over the short, medium and long term to be capable of responding to, and profiting from, demand. The problem is that it is very difficult to predict the weather, so access to the best information, predictions and scenarios by industry will be an increasingly vital cog in the wheel of maintaining profits in a rapidly changing marketplace.

INSURERS

Insurers know what the problems are; they pay out on them. In relation to flooding they are particularly well prepared. A system has been developed for capturing flood and storm damage data. It has been tested on a number of flood events on a pilot basis, and evaluated and refined by loss adjusters, architects and academics. The system was also used to assist in establishing a national flood claims database for the UK.[47]

The system is called FASTER (Flood And STorm Event Reporting). The FASTER system not only streamlines the inspection of damaged property but also provides all the data needed to build a vulnerability database, and has been endorsed by all the key insurance industry bodies.

There is significant reluctance within the claims side of the industry, however, to change existing systems, because the main benefits would be to loss adjusters, consumers and technical underwriters responsible for rate setting, while the benefits to individual insurers' claims departments are less obvious.

The UK insurance industry could perhaps follow the example of the National House Building Council in the UK and the Institute of Business and Home Safety in the USA, by employing their own inspectors, or training government inspectors. In Australia, insurers and mortgage lenders have gone even farther, by drawing up their own set of standards for certain types of buildings. The standards are called the 'Blue Book' and have in effect made the official standards redundant because all builders know that unless they follow the Blue Book, the building will not be insurable and the bank will not lend money on it.

Another approach would be to classify new housing according to the build quality and specification, which would allow insurers to charge different rates according to vulnerability to windstorm, subsidence and flood. This would be similar in some ways to the different groupings used by motor insurers: it would reflect the risk better, and could lead to public pressure for improved standards.

But in effect the insurance industry stands to be a major loser in the face of a changing climate, not only because of the escalating payouts for which they are responsible but also because a significant proportion of their funds is already invested in what could be surmised to be high-risk buildings. Many of the more glamorous buildings in major cities are owned by the insurance industry, which holds significant stocks in 'prestige' developments. These are what is increasingly being recognized as the high-risk end of the property markets. There is an Achilles' heel in the system. Insurance companies charge similar rates for office space by postcode, regardless of the risk an individual building or space within a building poses. Similar insurance premiums are charged for offices at the top of a very tall 'target type' tower as may be charged to a low-rise robust office in a medium-sized city. So people in resilient buildings may be subsidizing the risk of the target buildings, the buildings that are perhaps most vulnerable to extreme climate events. This unfair situation will only last until the government decides to legislate that buildings should pay according to the risks they present, or until the first clever insurance company divests itself of its 'white elephant' and high-risk buildings so that it is itself sufficiently unencumbered by a portfolio of high-risk buildings to offer fair, lower premiums to low-risk building owners, according to their actual risk *vis-à-vis* claims related to perhaps extreme climate or power outage events.

Architects, in the wake of 9/11, were actually told by the insurance industry in March 2003 to stop offering clients advice on ways of protecting buildings against terrorist attacks and of providing escape routes because the service has recently been excluded from professional indemnity insurance policies and it is felt by the industry that architects would be stepping out of their area of expertise by doing so. Most insurers have now dropped clauses in their building insurance policies that cover terrorism because insurers feel that it is not something that is insurable without specialist coverage.[48]

In the maelstrom of the 2008 economic meltdown very careful steps were taken by the Association of British Insurers (ABI) to shed risk and in November 2008 came a significant reduction in the extent of the properties that the ABI members would be obliged to insure on flood plains. Increasingly, insurers will retreat from risk as their survival, in difficult financial times, becomes more precarious. So those wishing to build on risky sites must understand that they may not be covered if they do. Unfortunately, postcodes are not allotted until after buildings are built and many people buy off-plan. This in itself provides an opportunity for misunderstanding that building buyers should be aware of.

REAL ESTATE MANAGERS

The blame for the property 'bubble' can be laid partly at the doors of real estate and property portfolio managers. But perhaps 'the higher you rise the harder you fall'. The larger companies that have accumulated portfolios of high-end prestige buildings have already been faced with plummeting prices. In October 2008 alone commercial property prices fell by 4.3%, taking the market's total decline from its June 2007 peak to nearly 30%. The October Investment Property Databank's monthly index showed that prices for shops, offices and industries fell by the largest amount in its 22-year history. Retail property fell in capital value in that month by 4.7%. Many real estate agencies have closed and others were down to skeleton staff by the end of 2008. In the new markets of the post-bust era, when building performance will play a crucial role in sales, this profession, like that of architecture, will need to pay significantly more heed to issues like energy use, building resilience, durability and long-term investments as evidenced by the current rush to quality in the property markets.[49] It is strange that estate agents pushed clients into more and more prestige offices and when the credit crunch came it was these offices that so many could not afford to occupy. How many companies, and how many families, were tipped over into the financial abyss because they chose to occupy buildings they could not afford, and to what extent was the real estate industry, paid a percentage of the price of the property, responsible for pushing people into irresponsible investments?

CONCLUSIONS

The sad truth is that today the buildings we design and occupy are year on year becoming more and more energy profligate. Just ask the facilities manager of your local hospital, office or school whether they agree. Yet we have the technology to build almost zero-energy buildings.[50] Is this a comedy of errors rather than a tragedy of self-interested endeavours by people who could simply not see the wood for the trees? The big picture is very complex and interconnected. But the writing is now clearly on the wall, and circumstances are changing catastrophically around us. The time for radical change has come.

- This change must start with government who alone have the legislative power to bring about fast and **radical** change (as they did during the Second World War).
- It must be seen by everyone – individuals and corporations, architects and engineers – as **necessary**, otherwise government efforts will be bypassed and ignored rather than complied with and achieved.
- In order for this to happen it must be also be seen as **fair** (like rationing during the war) or people will not cooperate.

In this process the building industry is centrally placed and all the players have their parts to play. Table 15.2 makes some suggestions for actions which each of the players could make. The time has come to act.

Poem by Omar Khayyam
Born: 31 May 1048 in Nishapur, Iran; Died: 4 December 1131

The Moving Finger writes; and, having writ,
Moves on:
nor all your Piety nor Wit
Shall lure it back to cancel half a Line,
Nor all your Tears wash out a Word of it.

Table 15.2. Suggested actions for the players in the built environment that could inform the radical change needed to build truly twenty-first century buildings

Players		Actions
Government	1	A clear map of where responsibility lies for political decisions that impact on populations in a changing climate and the mechanisms for ascribing accountability.
	2	A clear outline of how costs will be met to pay for damage incurred in the event of climate-related events.
	3	A National Planning Body to be established to look at the national planning implications of climate change, and develop plans for say 2020, 2050 and 2080.
	4	Government Monopolies Commission to review power bases in construction to avoid conflicts of interest and monopolies.
	5	A fair share of seats on decision-making bodies to be given to a wider range of stakeholders in the construction process including local community groups and NGOs.
	6	Revision of the Building Regulations to make naturally ventilated buildings mandatory, to ban air conditioning in the UK except where absolutely necessary, to make all building have a demolition plan and a plan for extreme weather events, blackouts and evacuation.
	7	Promote new standards for buildings which encourage low-energy solutions by making low or zero energy a top priority (Table 15.1)
Planners	1	All planners to receive training on building types and performance.
	2	All planning departments to have access to a staff member who is competent in the fields of building performance, energy performance of buildings, carbon accounting, system capacity (energy, sewage, fresh and storm water, schools, hospitals, transport systems), accounting and renewable energy.
	3	Every building at the early planning application phase should be presented with an EPBD building performance rating before it is given planning permission.
	4	Systematic checking of predicted performance against real performance should be made for recently erected buildings.
	5	Every building should be submitted with a refurbishment and demolition plan.
	6	Every building should be able to be naturally ventilated to obtain planning permission.
	7	Every building should submit an emergency response plan for flooding, blackouts and extreme hot and cold spells, and a full evacuation plan at the planning stage.
	8	Every development in the flood plain should have a plan for the predicted future flooding repair costs and an agreement on who is responsible for them.
	9	Every building site should be allocated a postcode before it is submitted for planning and the projected insurance costs for the building should be submitted as part of the planning application.
	10	New tools to be developed for planners to assess infrastructural system capacity in current and future climates.

(Continued)

Table 15.2. Continued

Players		Actions
Internet and media	1	The press to champion twenty-first century buildings and employ correspondents who understand and can write interestingly on the performance of buildings in conditions of climate change.
	2	Fight for freedom of speech on building performance. Where buildings that perform poorly are promoted in the press, exhibitions and awards, this should be reported on honestly without fear of repercussions from over-powerful designers.
CABE	1	Spend a large proportion of the CABE income on capacity building design professions and owners to implement post-occupancy evaluations.
Architects	1	All EPBD ratings on all buildings to be published on the RIBA website in sortable categories by rating, by architect and by building type.
	2	Every building designed must be capable of being naturally ventilated and provide adequate shelter during extreme climate events and blackouts.
	3	All competitions to have a requirement that the performance of a building is an important component in the judge's brief.
	4	Mixed panels of rural and urban judges for all exhibitions and competitions including the Summer Exhibition at the Royal Academy.
Architectural education	1	All schools to include mandatory real building projects in their studios with live constraints and clients.
	2	All teaching staff to undergo minimum basic training in issues of buildings performance and sustainability paid for by the school.
	3	All students to be required to understand thermal comfort, occupant satisfaction, energy use in buildings and how to do post-occupancy evaluations of buildings.
	4	Schools should use live projects for real useful building types, e.g. schools, offices and health service buildings, during their training.
	5	All students to work on at least one low-carbon building design studio.
	6	All students should be taught how to proportion a façade for opening windows, how to naturally ventilate buildings and design buildings to be resilient to extreme climate events and energy outages.
Building engineers	1	Instigate mandatory contracts to pay building service engineers according to the performance of the building systems instead the amount of HVAC equipment in them.
	2	Future climate data to be made freely available to designers so that buildings today can be built to provide shelter in future climates.
	3	Instead of only being taught how to fill buildings full of potentially unnecessary machines, building services students should be routinely taught about passive architectural engineering, including the use of natural ventilation, thermal mass to attenuate indoor temperatures and store free energy, and embedded renewable energy systems and low-carbon built forms.

(Continued)

Table 15.2. Continued

Players		Actions
Building owners and businesses	1	Demand and move to low-energy, low-carbon and comfortable buildings that are resilient during extreme climate conditions and blackouts. Pay more up front to build and life-cycle cost the long-term benefits of occupying better buildings.
	2	Invest in, and promote, the development of new low-energy products.
	3	Trades unions take the dangers of climate change seriously to safeguard their members at work.
Insurers	1	Develop a central system for planning departments of every local authority to know the insurance availability and exposure rating of every site, and ensure that this is clearly included in the reports on every planning application they deal with and put before the public.
Real estate agents	1	Use the EPBD as an opportunity to inform the movement to low-carbon buildings and understand and promote their value.
Construction industry	1	Change the profit model. Dash to value. Invest in capacity building in refurbishment services.
	2	Routinely use carbon accounting and life-cycle costing on every project.
	3	Work at the community scale.
	4	Re-employ redundant workers in refurbishment to reduce energy use by buildings.

NOTES AND REFERENCES

1   The notion that there is a developed and an undeveloped world is dated in our 'global' society. In most countries there are groups of people who live the 'fossil fuel life' and live in big comfortable houses, drive big cars, and are globally 'connected' by cheap flights, cyberspace and growing trends in obesity. There are in most countries, including the USA, pockets of extreme deprivation, where the lack of food to eat could be seen as part, also, of a global problem. The global economy has done nothing to break down the internationally ubiquitous wealth-based class systems, and is widely claimed to be exacerbating the gaps between the rich and the poor.

   By 2005 we passed the point at which 50% of the world's populations live in urban areas. Squatter settlements in the USA and the UK may provide models of what will develop within or around our cities in the future as cities become a dumping ground for people working in unskilled, unprotected and low-wage industries and trades and '…the slums of the developing (and developed) world swell' (<http://www.unhabitat.org/global_report.asp>).

2   P. Ekins, Projects and Policies For Step Changes in the Energy System: Developing An Agenda for Social Science Research, Report of the ESRC Energy Research Conference, 2003. Text Available on: <http://www.psi.org.uk/docs/2003/esrc-energy-conference-report.doc>.

   Jim Skea, in summing up, 'emphasized the context of the Energy White Paper: the importance of the international dimension, and the need to secure international cooperation on the reduction of carbon emissions; and the importance of assessing energy developments in a broader framework of sustainable development, which includes issues of affordability, reliability and competitiveness, as well as carbon reduction.

'Addressing such an agenda requires a wide disciplinary perspective, in which engineering–economy modelling had an important, but not exclusive, role to play. An emphasis on evidence was particularly important in this field: much good research in a variety of relevant areas had been carried out in the past, and this needed to be brought together through systematic reviews and through research into the effectiveness of different policy approaches and into the evaluations of policy initiatives that had already been implemented. There were many issues that still needed further work, including assessment of the geopolitical situation, the need to invest in strengthening the electricity distribution network, the whole relationship between supply chains and the different interests of the actors they comprised, and the nature and role of public engagement. It should not be forgotten that a lot was already known about these issues. It might be that in this situation an investment in networking existing knowledge might be more cost effective than new projects which sought to add to it. It would be good if the new Research Council programmes could bear this in mind.'

3 See <http://dir.salon.com/tech/feature/2000/12/06/bad_computers/index.html>.

4 Terry Wyatt, in his 2003 Presidential Speech titled 'Adapt or Die' for CIBSE, put forward the idea that the building industry needs to radically change the products it offers in order to survive. See <http://www.cibse.org/pdfs/terrywyattaddress.pdf>.

5 For current news on climate change issues see the Guardian website on <http://www.guardian.co.uk>.

6 Building Design, 16 May 2003, p. 2.

7 For coverage of post-occupancy evaluations and building performance evaluations see two recent books. S. Roaf, with A. Horsley, R. Gupta, Closing the Loop: Benchmarks for Sustainable Buildings, RIBA Publications, London, 2004, and W. Prieser, J. Vischer, Assessing Building Performance, Butterworth-Heinemann, Oxford, 2004.

8 See <http://www.eurisol.com/pages/EPDirective.html> and <http://www.defra.gov.uk/environment/energy/internat/ecbuildings.htm>.

9 See <http://www.lga.gov.uk> or ring 0207 664 3131 for more details.

10 <http://www.benfieldhrc.org/activities/misc_papers/AXA_Climate_Change.pdf>. For legal references see Tate v Duffy, EWHC 361TCC; Ryeford v Sevenoaks, 46 Building Law Reports 34 or 16 Construction Law Reports 75 or 1990 Journal of Planning and Environment Law 36 or 1990 6 Construction Law Journal 170; R v Tonbridge, 2001 49 EG 118. <http://www.benfieldhrc.org/activities/misc_papers/AXA_Climate_Change.pdf>.

11 See <www.carboncounting.co.uk>.

12 See <http://www.decorum.co.uk>.

13 <http://www.cityoflondon.gov.uk/our_services/law_order/security_planning/civil_contingencies_bill.htm>.

14 Building Design, 7 November 2003, p. 2. See <www.cabe.org.uk> and Building Design, 7 February 2003, p. 1.

15 B. Rudofsky, Streets for People, Doubleday & Co., New York, 1969.

16 <http://www.arb.org.uk/regulation/code-of-conduct/conduct-and-competence.shtml>.

17 Overbudget projects are listed on: <http://news.bbc.co.uk/1/hi/uk/911317.stm>. See also other follies on <www.follies.btinternet.co.uk/dome.html>.

18 The Professional Footballers Association questioned the wisdom of spending £750 million on a new national stadium at Wembley following news that football chiefs and the government are set to declare that contracts for the controversial project had finally been rubber-stamped, two years after a major game was last played at the famous ground. The £750 million cost of the project included £352 million to build the stadium, £120 million to buy land, £50 million for improving infrastructure, £23 million for demolition, £40 million for development costs and £80 million in financing costs. At a time when so many Football League clubs were facing financial crises, Gordon Taylor, Director of the Association, expressed his fears that 'the new stadium could become a "white elephant", and was not convinced it was the best use of government (taxpayers') and FA money at such a time. Wembley had been overtaken by events, such as the collapse of football broadcaster ITV Digital and the serious financial problems of one of the FA's flagship leagues. Cardiff, Manchester and literally dozens of other magnificent stadiums have been created for a lot less and are being used by regular occupants. The fact that money is being borrowed from Germany rather than in this country makes one wonder at the future viability of the scheme. <http://www.givemefootball.com/pfa.html>.

19 Building Design, 12 September 2003, p. 2.

20 The cost of the new Scottish Parliament building at Holyrood rose from £37 million to £375 million, while running badly over time. The consultants' fees alone were thought to exceed £60 million. £18.5 million was spent on windows that 'don't quite fit' and £14.35 million was spent on extra fees to architects, engineers and cost consultants and for site running and construction management. Building Design, 13 June 2003, p. 1.

21 Building Design, 30 May 2003, p. 2. In May 2003 the European Commission received a 20 page complaint about the Scottish Parliament building claiming that the competition disadvantaged some entrants unlawfully, also suggesting that there were breaches in EU regulations on the letting of contracts and secrecy and political bias over the selection of the site.

22 Guardian, 13 October 2003, p. 10.

23 See <http://www.oxfordconference2008.co.uk>.

24 CADDET InfoPoint, Issue 2/03, p. 7. See <http://www.caddetre.org/newsletter/back_issues. php>.

25 <http://www.cebe.heacademy.ac.uk/>.

26 <http://www.hse.gov.uk/construction/designers/index.htm>.

27 Building Design, 9 May 2003, p. 3. Only 8% of designers surveyed had been trained how to comply with the CDM Regulations. See also <http://www.hse.gov.uk/statistics>.

28 See the Excellent Website of the American Society of Building Science Educators (SBSE) on <http://www.sbse.org/>.

29 I am indebted to Nikos Salingaros, the American architect, philosopher and mathematician, for much of the following section on deconstructionism. The full text of his important and thoughtful paper on the subject is published in: N. Salingaros, The derrida virus, Telos Winter (126) (2003) 66–82. Also available online on: <http://www.math.utsa.edu/sphere/salingar/ derrida.html>.

30 See Encarta World English Dictionary, St Martin's Press, New York, 1999.

31 Architects designing in a deconstructionist manner include Peter Eisenman, Frank Gehry and Daniel Libeskind.

32 R. Scruton, An Intelligent Person's Guide to Modern Culture, St Augustine's Press, South Bend, IN, 2000 pp. 141–142.

33 D. Lehman, Signs of the Times: Deconstruction and the Fall of Paul de Man, Poseidon Press, New York, 1991 p. 55.

34 Apart from the alienating design, the architect chose a very rapidly deteriorating surface to clad the blobs. Sheffield is a very 'dirty' city owing to the cold air inversion in the valley and the blobs looked awful within months. One very energetic group in Sheffield put forward a clean-up bid, as reported here: 'A bid to clean the grimy shell of the failed National Centre for Popular Music has been given the brush off. Campaigners wanting to see the tarnished stainless steel drums restored to their gleaming former self have failed to persuade regeneration agency Yorkshire Forward to underwrite a clean up. The group called Pride in Sheffield had lined up a £3000 bargain contract with local firm Stealth Access to restore the glitter to the building – wrong material – wrong shape.' See <http://www.freelists.org/archives/ncpm/102002/msg00017.html>. If such inappropriate materials are used in a dirty city their deterioration in a changing climate will be hastened. The importance of local knowledge is emphasized here, including the fact that this building was located in what is not a rich neighbourhood and that the £3000 required was a great deal of money for them. It is a pittance when compared to the tens of thousands of pounds that the Greater London Authority pays simply to clean the windows of its new headquarters blob building every year.

35 Guardian, G2, 1 September 2003, p. 13.

36 Building Design, 1 February 2002, p. 1.

37 Building Design, 1 February 2002, p. 1.

38 J.K. Galbraith, The Affluent Society, Mentor Books, Canada, 1963.

39 <http://www.sd-commission.gov.uk/>.

40 <http://www.london.gov.uk/assembly/stndsmtgs/2003/stdoct16/stdoct 16item05.pdf>.

41 <http://www.bsee.co.uk/news/fullstory.php/aid/2733/CIBSE%92s_new_president_highlights_the_pressing_need_for_a_future_of_change.html>.

42 Guardian, Society, 27 November 2002, p. 8.

43 <http://www.corenetglobal.org/pdf/learning/9_11_impact.pdf>. See also the business continuity section PAS 56 on <http://www.thebci.org>.

44 <http://www.hmso.gov.uk/si/si1999/19993242.htm>.

45 When the lights go out, Independent Review, 16 December 2003, p. 12. For an interesting case see AE Beckett & Sons (Lyndons) Ltd and Others v Midlands Electricity Plc <http://www.lawreports.co.uk/civdec0.4.htm>.

46 Observer, 13 July 2003, p. 5.

47 A. Black, S. Evans, Flood Damage in the UK: New Insights for the Insurance Industry, University of Dundee, Scotland, 1999 (ISBN 0 903674 37 8).

48 Building Design, 28 March 2003, p. 1.

49 For current information on property markets see <http://www.rics.co.uk>.

50 See S. Roaf, M. Fuentes, S. Thomas, Ecohouse: A Design Guide, Architectural Press, 2007. The Oxford Ecohouse and other cases studied in the book produce a fraction of the CO_2 of normal homes.

16 DESIGNING BUILDINGS AND CITIES FOR 3°C OF CLIMATE CHANGE

INTRODUCTION

We can now see clearly the growing scale of the devastation wrought on our ecosystems, societies and economies by climate change. Ours is a world in which more people[1] consume more resources,[2] pollute more and are increasingly addicted to the rapidly vanishing fossil fuel resource. Oil and gas are vital to the way we generate energy, grow, fertilize and refine food, make materials, move goods and people, keep ourselves warm or cool and do most of the work of our increasingly unequal and energy-hungry societies. As oil prices soared towards $150 a barrel in July 2008 food and energy costs rocketed and house prices collapsed. We are witnessing the beginning of the decline and fall of the Oil Empire, a transnational phenomenon that has placed the likes of you and me on the pinnacle of Maslow's triangle (Figure 16.1) and will see us, eventually, fall from it. This final chapter is about how, in the light of all that has been covered in this book, we might start re-engineering our aspirations, infrastructures and lifestyles for a softer landing in a hotter, post-fossil world.

In October 2008 Ross Garnaut published his influential report on the impacts of climate change on the Australian economy, as Stern had done for the UK in 2005. Garnaut warned the world that it must wake up to reality, understand the level of warming we are facing and strive to reach agreement on decisive action or else risk a failure that 'would haunt humanity until the end of time'.[3]

In parallel with such credible reports and exhortations the world is acting but, even in the best of works on how we should transition towards viable models of twenty-first century societies and economies,[4] building designers and developers, for some inexplicable reason, have been able to get away with producing ever more exposed, vulnerable and energy-profligate buildings. They have done this despite a common understanding that buildings themselves are the greatest source of greenhouse gases on the planet and are our first and greatest defence against the elements.

High-energy buildings are taken for granted and promoted as 'green', even in our latest building regulations and building rating systems. New developments are actively encouraged in areas that will flood because 'we cannot afford not to develop on flood plains'. We give design awards to a generation of 'sustainable' buildings decked out with 'efficient, green' machines where machines may not have been necessary if a proper building, with solid walls and good windows, had been built in the first place.

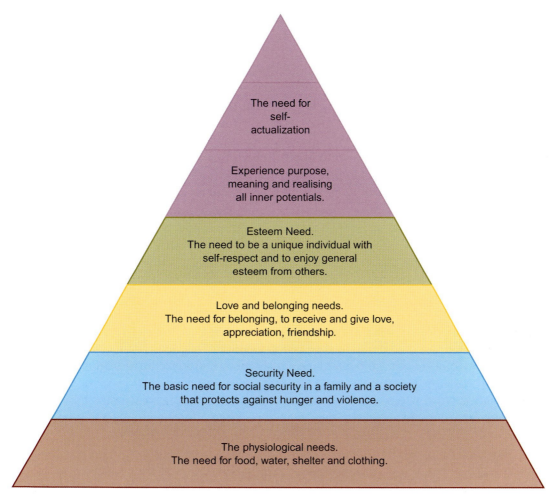

The need for
self-
actualization

Experience purpose,
meaning and realising
all inner potentials.

Esteem Need.
The need to be a unique individual with
self-respect and to enjoy general
esteem from others.

Love and belonging needs.
The need for belonging, to receive and give love,
appreciation, friendship.

Security Need.
The basic need for social security in a family and a society
that protects against hunger and violence.

The physiological needs.
The need for food, water, shelter and clothing.

16.1.
Maslow's triangle.

What has been slower in coming are new visions of a future with simpler, robust, low-key, low-carbon buildings that work in reality as they say they will do on the tin. We are beginning to realize we have too often been seduced by our models of building performance that can be 10–50%, or more, wrong in their predictions of energy consumption and resulting carbon emissions from buildings. These models tend to operate in such a way that people are seen as a problem in the prediction of the proper operation and performance of buildings. Yet passive buildings[5] need those individuals, and their learning and adapting behaviour, to understand how they work and sail them like ships in the wind. You would not consider sailing a boat or a plane without pilots, why should a complex building be capable of being run by machines alone? Buildings are not machines for living in, they are one part of the complex three-way relationship among themselves, people and the environment (including climate), as are boats or planes. Nor are people machines for living in buildings.

Rajat Gupta estimates that for as little as £200–250 billion every home in Britain could be upgraded to reduce fossil fuel energy use and carbon emissions by over 60%.[6] This would result in the growth of durable low-carbon industries and increased social and economic well-being for the majority. If the costs were shared between government and public investment then for a sum of around £12 billion a year from the UK Government for 10 years we could build the resilience of every citizen in the UK to climate change and fossil fuel depletion and create the promise of a safer and more durable world for our children and grandchildren. To put this is context: £15 billion is what American banks paid top bankers in performance bonuses in 2008 alone, a year that saw the plunging value, and in some cases failure, of those same institutions; £1.1 trillion is the cost of the Iraq War to the USA by the end of 2008, according to Nobel Prize winning author Joseph Stiglitz; £46 billion is the amount of UK taxpayers' money poured into UK banks in 2008 to fill the black holes left by reckless investment, without expectation of repayment in some cases – this figure is predicted to rise to over £75 billion in the future; £20 billion was lost by small investors in UK property funds in 2008 alone; and £80–£100 billion is the sum that the UK Nuclear Decommissioning Authority (NDA) is required to pay to clean up the existing nuclear power stations, with much of that being spent at Dounreay in Scotland and Sellafield in Cumbria. The NDA is currently being funded at the level of around £70 billion for 2009 alone just for the clean-up of those stations. And they promised us that nuclear energy would be too cheap to meter! The budget put aside for the next generation of nuclear power stations is around £10 billion per station. The benefits of the millions of pounds a year of UK taxpayers' money spent on lobbying a 'listening' legislature in both houses can be clearly seen. Our generation may be the last that can afford such sums of money to make safe a toxic industry, but where in the future will such sums be found to clean up the next generation of failing stations? This does not even touch on our failure to find a way to deal with the huge stockpile of waste fuel from these stations, let alone pay for its long-term storage.

So how can we make better decisions on ways forward to a truly sustainable future? We have to understand where we want to be in the future and devise effective strategies for getting there.

WHAT TARGET SHOULD WE LOCK ON TO?

We believe that it is the predicted rate and scale of climate change that should now determine the effort and investment we put into redesigning our buildings and cities for a very different future. It is obvious from the often cavalier way in which the built environment is being developed that very few people, from the decision makers in government to ordinary families in their own homes, understand the urgent imperative to prepare to survive in a rapidly changing climate change and a post-fossil fuel world.

To clarify this need for urgency we have redrawn the diagram of some of the environmental impacts we might expect from the 2007 Stern Report (see p. 347). Figure 16.2 simply plots choices we face in our buildings, communities, regions and nations, and emphasizes the short period of opportunity we have to act now to build resilience against climate change. It highlights the potential for catastrophic impacts arising from the widening of the cracks already emerging in dysfunctional communities into chasms into which we all may fall.

We can also crudely, for the sake of argument, put dates on the rate of warming we face if we use the temperature increase trajectory for the Business as Usual greenhouse gas emissions models that we are currently following and exceeding, taken from the 4th Assessment Report of the Intergovernmental Panel on Climate Change (IPCC), modelled using the A2 Medium/High Emissions scenario (see Figure 16.3 and p. 348). What is so shocking in this simple exercise is

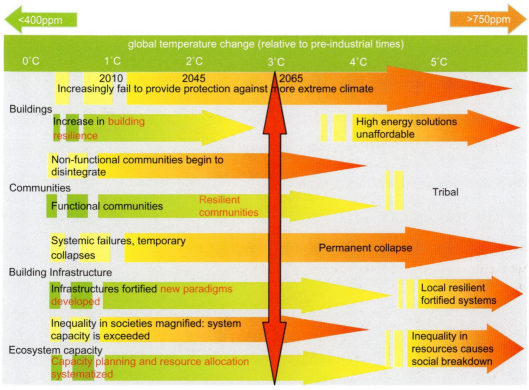

16.2.
Rapidly rising risk in the built environment: alternative paths forward in a warming climate for buildings, communities, infrastructure and ecosystem under resource constraints. The figure shows the projected impacts of climate change over multi-dimensions aggregated across several studies. The arrows indicate the approximate temperature at which we may start to see these impacts, where the darkening shade shows the increasing risk and intensity of impacts as temperatures rise. Already committed to 0.5–1°C of temperature change above pre-industrial, BAU gives serious risks of exceeding 5°C.
Source: Sue Roaf after Nicholas Stern.

that the mean global temperature, today already at around 1°C warmer than the 1860–1990 average, will rise to 2°C warmer as soon as 2045. It took around 150 years for the temperature to rise 1°C, yet it will take only three or so decades from now until we enter the predicted two decades of more than 2°C of warming. It then takes, on this trajectory, only until 2065, a mere 20 years, until the increasingly disturbed climate surges through the +3°C of warming mark. If that possibility, even if it is only a possibility, does not focus the attention of decision makers, nothing will.

Now there are a number of ways in which we can build a target to aim for as we go about planning the future. One is *forecasting* (Chapter 2), where we project trends forward and build a game plan on the wisdom accrued through our experience to date of the range and scale of impacts already experienced as we pass the 1°C warmer world mark. A second method is *backcasting*, for which we pick a future date and, using inputs from as wide a range of disciplines as possible, build a credible image of the conditions that will exist at that future date. We ask the reader, for the sake of the discussion below, to join us in choosing the target dates of 2045 to represent the approximate period when we pass through the 2°C hotter mark, and 2065 to loosely represent a date for passing through 3°C of warming. Using the 2°C and 3°C warmer marks we propose

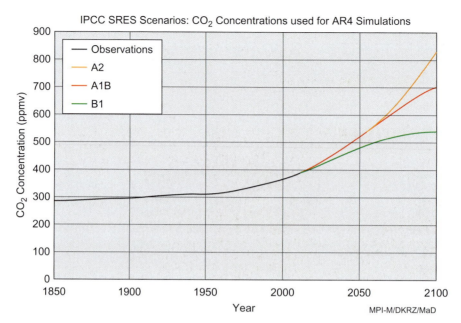

16.3.
Crude approximation of when we reach mean global temperatures 1°C, 2°C and 3°C warmer than the 1860–1990 average, following the SRES A2 scenario in the AR4 IPCC Report.
Source: Sue Roaf and www.ipcc.ch/SPM6avr07.pdf.

two step changes for which we urgently need to plan if we intend to build true resilience into our buildings, cities and societies over the coming decades. While the science of climate modelling is good, it is by no means infallible and cannot predict major climate events like volcanoes, earthquakes or landslides. But the climate models here can give us a rough approximation of temperature increases on which we can devise adaptation strategies for survival.

We saw in Chapters 9–11 how remarkable humanity has been at adapting lifestyles and buildings to the extreme climates of the planet and how these highly evolved design skills are too often being lost in our machine-dominated, fossil fuel-dependent, 'modern' world. We have also seen that people are basically animals, physiologically limited to a range of temperatures in which they can survive. Those limits can vary considerably but once a thermal threshold has been crossed for an individual, or a locally adapted population, then heat stress, hyperthermia and death become a possibility.

It is the lot of our 'transition' generation to have to relearn, to value and to enhance the traditional passive design skills we use to provide ourselves with shelter. Our challenge is to combine the best of the emerging low-impact technologies in a truly twenty-first century vernacular of locally appropriate buildings and cities.[7] Because of the predicted magnitude and proximity of the temperature changes ahead we need to have path to follow, a routemap to follow, to minimize and deal with the damage inflicted by the changing climate. We are not currently on track to do anything but increase the greenhouse gas emissions to the extent that when our children and grandchildren are our age we will have left them nothing but a legacy of climate chaos.

Even now some members of the building services industry are rubbing their hands in Enron-like glee at the prospect of soaring sales of air conditioning systems from which they will profit,

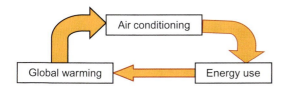

16.4.
The devastating feedback loop between air conditioning, greenhouse gas emissions and climate change.
Source: Fergus Nicol.

16.5.
A great Moais, on Rapa Nui Island, a totem to the potential for a society to exceed the carrying capacity of its land.
Source: Cliff Wassman.

even though they know such systems are ultimately hugely damaging to the climate they leave their own grandchildren. Architecture schools around the world are sending young professionals out who have no idea of the impacts of the buildings they design on our children's future, and government's laissez faire concerns for the interests of lobbyists over those of their own citizens ensure that if things do not change quickly we all suffer the sooner. Just as with the banking sector, which fouled, and continue to be allowed to foul, their own nests, and ours, on an industrial scale, we can see evidence of the Rapa Nui syndrome all around us in the way we design, procure and build buildings.

Rapa Nui, or Easter Island, is a small (166 km²), inaccessible island in the Pacific Ocean, 2000 miles from the nearest centre of population on Tahiti, where the islanders outgrew their resources and ended up destroying themselves. The available land for agriculture was no longer sufficient to feed the growing population, the islanders cut down all the trees on the island for fuel and to build their great moais, or totem statues, and without the means to build canoes and leave the island, they eventually resorted to war and cannibalism. Many theorists see what happened on Easter Island as a warning to us all. They call it the Rapa Nui syndrome (Figure 16.5).

DESIGNING FOR 3°C OF CLIMATE CHANGE

In order to provide a clear view of the way forward for the built environment we would like to propose that we now focus on designing for three degrees of climate change as follows (Table 16.1).

Table 16.1. Forecasting: a very rough draft of the trends that may be involved in the forecasting of dysfunctional or adaptive (shaded) approaches to temperature increases in the built environment from projected trends, and a range of scenarios

Temperature	Buildings	Communities	Infrastructure	System capacity
Up to 1°C	BAU	BAU	BAU: centralized	BAU: global markets
Denial	Poor form/fabric AC promoted	Inequality rife Ghettoization	Road/air expansion Poor maintenance	Few constraints Unequal access
Low-carbon buildings	Low-carbon buildings Materials development Embedded renewables	Climate change planning Solar/low-carbon cities Transition towns	New public transport Local ESCOs Local water treatment	Local food movement Carbon accounting Community models
Up to 2°C	Dead buildings	Growing civil protest	Roads/bridges fail	Resource scarcity
Dysfunctional	Dark buildings Security issues	Breakdown of society Intergroup conflict	Air travel lessens High-use public transport	Communications poor Unequal access
Sense + science	Zero-carbon buildings Energy water storage Strong, good regulation	Protect vulnerable Invest in communities Reduce exposure	Local grids Local ownership of infrastructure Maintenance priority	Resource planning Resource harvesting Equal access
Up to 3°C	Many abandoned	Weather drives civil unrest	Collapse of systems	Unequal access
Collapse	Insecure districts Inadequate shelter	Government breakdown Regional conflict	Weather damage Unequal access	Resource scarcity Movement of populations
Buildings as generators and stores	Heavy, robust, high mass, Building intergrated renewables Passive cooling, natural ventilation prevails Walkable, shading	Inequality avoided Cool urban micro-climates Walkable cities	Reinforced core infrastructure Distributed Local control	Energy and water stored at building and city level Equal allocations

Source: Sue Roaf. BAU: business as usual; AC: air conditioning; ESCO: energy service company.

1°C: DENIAL

The global mean surface temperature is currently around 1°C warmer than its 1860–1990 average. Even now at 1°C, most designers and decision makers are oblivious to, or in denial about, the need to radically improve building and community development. While many espouse 'sustainable development', they patently still act otherwise. The UK Government and the professions continue to trumpet their sustainable communities and zero-carbon buildings while supporting the interests of developers and manufacturers in applying regulations, policies and strategies for promoting, for instance, cheap buildings and buildings on flood plains. These same statutory and voluntary tools are often actually designed to actively discourage the development of passive, low-energy, naturally ventilated buildings by promoting, for instance, air-conditioned buildings in their stead.[8] The need for urgent action to reduce greenhouse gas emissions, and the apparently sly avoidance of that action (as evidenced also with Heathrow's third runway), provides us with a paradox, the type of paradox that lies at the heart of the failure to effectively regulate the financial markets before 2008 and to avoid the expansion of UK airports at a time of shrinking air travel. Somewhere there is an elephant in the room that no one is talking about. Is it Corruption? Is it Capitalism? Is it Stupidity? Is it heartless Selfishness? Is it Ignorance? Is it Cynicism? The buying and selling of influence at the highest levels of government exposed recently amongst members of the British House of Lords would suggest that all of the above are at work.

Attempts to provide leadership in the field of sustainable development often appear risible. In the UK we have a Code for Sustainable Homes that in its Energy and CO_2 subcategory gives 2.5 points for the 'reduced fabric heat loss parameter', 2.5 points for the inclusion of cycle racks and 2.5 points for energy-efficient external lighting. The fabric of the envelope of the building is the most important single piece of the jigsaw puzzle of low-energy building design. Cycle racks and external lighting are extremely cheap elements for developers to include in the building design costs. In the US Leading in Energy and Environmental Design (LEED) rating system, buildings have to have central air conditioning systems in order to qualify for the efficient-energy systems points in LEED ratings (see p. 231). Table 16.1 sketches the possible characteristics of adaptive or dysfunctional developments as intimated in Figure 16.2. Does it not strike the reader that in the face of the severity of such impacts these paradoxes need to be urgently dealt with? Please note that sustainability is a word that has had little resonance in the contents of this book until now. Interesting that it should arise when we are discussing systematic performance fudges in the system.

Even 'green' individuals, groups and organizations with reputations for being extremely visionary and effective, for some inexplicable reason, have not ventured into the heart of the problems in buildings. We have very high-profile political lobbying against airports and coal-fired power stations but not against energy- or water-profligate buildings. If a new 10MW glass tower block is to be put up in the city no one gets out in the streets to object. We even have the spectacle of the globally lauded eco-warrior Bono proposing to build a huge new glass tower in the centre of Belfast and so-called eco-warrior Ken Livingstone who on the one hand implemented leading-edge policies on transport in London but on the other wanted to fill London up with glass towers. When a financially non-viable, and hugely energy-profligate glass 'Shard' tower is scrapped, and then refinanaced by a Gulf sheikh, despite the absence of any market for new office space in London, no one protests? Why? The people of London will have to face energy shortages and pay to build new transport, water and electricity generation capacity to serve the environmental nightmare of a building just to satisfy the hubris and ambitions of an Arab investor who wants his erection to stand 'greater than all that have gone before'. Such a tower is a much more effective way of putting a spanner in the works of our economy than any bomb on a Soho street could be but no one protests against the Shard!

The message has, for some reason, simply not got through to decision makers, or the general public, that if such dinosaur buildings were never again built, and if every building in Britain consumed minimal energy and water, and harvested and stored a proportion of its own energy, we would not only not need new coal and nuclear power stations or new water reservoirs but we could afford to begin to deal with the demolition and replacement of the least efficient or most dangerous of those that already exist. The real environmental offenders in the built environment are not the terraced homes of the north, which the government suggested demolishing, but the glass towers of the city.[9–11] Who will pay for their demolition in the future? Again the ordinary Londoner no doubt will pay.

The most systematically effective tool devised to date, to provide incontrovertible evidence of building performance, has been the use of actual performance measurements in real buildings through the European Energy Performance of Buildings Directive (EPBD) process.[12,13] This has demonstrated that the Business as Usual obsession with 'efficiency' has led to some very poor 'green' buildings. The genius of the EPBD approach is to look at the performance of the whole building as used. But inevitably the lobbyists have been at work again, and as effective as ever, and even now the EU government is busy watering down the Directive to require only modelled performance to be displayed, to address construction and investment industry concerns.

In the short time we have left to act, the speed and effectiveness with which we can build correct and effective knowledge, understanding and action are crucial. Yet the privatization of the research organizations of the original UK national utilities for water, gas, transport and electricity has been an enormous blow to our fundamental ability to develop real solutions for the future. The loss, in particular, of the UK Building Research Establishment in the 1990s was a hugely retrograde step as it saw the dismantling of one of the finest building research organizations in the world, to be replaced by a privatized research company that works largely on short-term product-related contracts, and no longer funds science fundamental. Many of the real boffins, the blue skies, lifetime scientists were lost in the change. Fortunately some countries, including Australia, have maintained national research bodies, such as the Commonwealth Scientific and Research Organization (CSIRO), which continues world-class research with global as well as urgently needed local benefits.

1°C: GENERATION TRANSITION – MOVEMENTS FOR CHANGE

In spite of the many reactionary forces that have a firm hand on the tiller of developments in the built environment, not least those in the heart of government, there is an emerging generation of people who do 'get it' and are working intelligently to rapidly develop our ability and capacity to adapt across a range of fronts, including those of green building and community design, water efficiency and reuse, energy demand reduction, equipment efficiency, quality of life, transport and urban farming. We owe a particular debt of gratitude to many people working as non-governmental organizations (NGOs), including Friends of the Earth,[14] Greenpeace,[15] the Campaign to Stop Climate Change[16] and not least the WWF (formerly the World Wildlife Fund),[17] building on the important foundations laid by Ralph Rookwood and the Town and Country Planning Association,[18] who have done much to develop and promote low-carbon and sustainable buildings and communities. Really important too is the influence of emerging youth groups like People and Planet[19] who are aiming to radicalize school and university students to become Agents of Change in their own futures. At play here is a whole range of city-level movements such as the Low-Carbon Cities and Kyoto Cities[20] movements and the Solar Cities Movements,[21] but in the UK perhaps the most rapidly growing has been the Transition Towns movement.[22] The scale for successful action seems to be particularly effective at that of the small group, the organization and the city. Individuals often feel powerless when acting alone and top–down politics for the built environment (with parallels perhaps in the financial world) simply does not seem to be primarily concerned about global or local environmental, social or economic impacts, being rather obsessed with the importance of conventional wisdom, promotion of the status quo and an overriding need to perpetuate the benefits of the market-driven economy.

If we were able to put together a single High-Dependability Transition Consortium to plot future paths and programmes for action such transition groups would be at the heart of it.; perhaps, necessarily, to a significantly greater extent than government departments and quangos, which are run on public funds to move markets on, but they only do this by endorsing current government programmes, rating systems and regulations, so merely become agents for the perpetuation of Business as Usual model. Low-key publications, organizations and websites are particularly important in operating under the radar of powerful conventional forces in communicating real debate and wisdom.[23]

2°C: DYSFUNCTIONAL COMMUNITIES

Soaring fuel poverty, resource scarcity, rising costs and poor government are already leading to civil unrest on a growing scale globally as we begin to approach 2°C. On 24th October 2008 the streets of Dublin were filled with thousands of the over-70s who had been informed that they would from now on have to pay for medical care. They marched shoulder to shoulder with the students who now have to pay for their university fees. There is anger from both the young and the old against the failing of conventional capitalism in a city where in the early twentieth century many people died as the foreign authorities battled against the 'rise of Bolshevism' in the starving middle and working classes.

In December 2008 the streets of Athens in Greece erupted in weeks of violence, initially by disaffected youths but later strikes and demonstrations by angry citizens. Demonstrations broke out, in the wake of events in Athens, in cities around Europe amongst a generation of youths who felt alienated from the societies around them. Throughout 2008 civil unrest flared up around the world, in the USA as industries and communities collapsed under pressure from the failing economy, in China amongst toy factory workers thrown out on the streets without work or pay because the US markets had dried up, and in Mumbai by citizens furious at incompetent security services and a government that did not protect them from the carnage inflicted by a handful of terrorists. The list goes on and on, and such events are occurring not only in less developed countries but in the hearts of the capital cities of the heart of the old 'civilized' world. Iceland was the first country to topple its own government in January 2009 as a result of the global economic depression that began in 2008, but others followed. Social inequality will always breed dissent.

Richard Wilkinson, in his book on the *Impact of Inequality*,[24] argued that social inequality has malign effects on public health, and that all societies fall on a continuum of degrees of social inequality.[25] He also argued that one way to cope with a challenge to society is to explicitly reduce the level of social inequality. Therefore, during the Second World War, the government explicitly created and imposed a greater degree of social equality, which made society better able, and more willing, to cope with the challenges that they faced.

Similar examples can be found in Europe. During the Second World War, income differences narrowed dramatically in Britain. This was partly due to the effect of war on the economy, which led to a decline in unemployment and a diminution of earnings differentials among employed people. But it was also a result of a deliberate policy pursued by the government to gain the 'cooperation of the masses' in the war effort.[26] We quote from Richard Titmuss's essay *War and Social Policy*,[27] in which he says that, to that end, 'inequalities had to be reduced and the pyramid of social stratification had to be flattened'. To ensure that the burden of war was seen as fairly shared, taxes on the rich were sharply increased, necessities were subsidized, luxuries were taxed, and a wide range of food and other goods was rationed to ensure a fair distribution. The Beveridge Report of 1941, which set out plans for the post-war development of the welfare state, including the establishment of the National Health Service, had the same purpose: to present a picture of a fairer future and so gain people's support for the war effort. Although the well-known sense of camaraderie during the war came partly from a sense of unity in the face of a common enemy, it was also increased by the greater emphasis on equality and fairness. If people felt the burden of war had fallen disproportionately on the mass of the working population, leaving the rich unaffected, the sense of camaraderie and cooperation would surely have turned to resentment.'

The importance of connecting the different social sectors of a city vertically through the income strata is obviously important, but so too is the horizontal or spatial relationship of the rich and the poor. Where shear lines exist between social extremes they can become flashpoints for popular unrest, as evidenced many histories of civil conflicts. Though much is written about cities less is written on how cities interact with their hinterland, or suburbs with each other. As energy prices increase, the individual and community isolation experienced now is likely to increase, so places that are already remote will seem even more remote, places that are a long commute now will move beyond commuting distance. Access to basic resources will be unequally distributed between social groups on grounds of cost and proximity to a particular resource. For some goods and services urban populations may be better served while for others rural communities may be more fortunate. While it is academically popular to take a city-based approach, policy makers should look to understanding the connections between communities and ways in which critical disparities between them can be reduced. The growth in a 'whole systems' approach to modelling resource flows within the larger ecosystem of a country, region or community offers hope that a more organic and modular society might be developed in the longer term to which the allocation of scarce resources can be achieved fairly.

The speed with which communities can tip over the edge of 'civilized' behaviour was noted above. Such outbursts of anger are often presented as some kind of negative social breakdown. However, protesters seldom kill and where deaths do occur it is typically the law and order forces that do the killing. One person's riot is seen by another as rightful protest and the putting of pressure on those who they perceive to be impediments to change. Through 2008, in the face of huge economic hardships, the American public was comparatively quiet, in contrast to the previous US movements on the streets over issues such as the Vietnam War or Civil Rights. The opportunity for democratic change and the voting in of President Obama may well have provided a legitimate form of protest that was chosen by those hurting from the collapse of the US economic system.

As people lose their jobs, get hungry, thirsty, cold or hot they, or we, will react. Every country must address and deal with the issue of inequality of opportunity in a manner they consider appropriate and proportional to their own problems. The impacts of growing resource constraints, divided societies, poor governance and failing economies will be exacerbated by extreme weather

16.6.
At least one man died during police hemming in of demonstrators during the G20 Summit in London in April 2009, at a time when civil unrest around the world is escalating during a period of global recession.
Source: Reuters.

events and growing fuel and food shortages. The scale of the dangers posed by such confluences of circumstances indicates the urgency of acting quickly to reduce the likelihood of the breakdown of civil society, to protect lives and property at a time of growing scarcity.

Scotland, as an example, has a particular problem with fuel poverty, where a family spends more than 10% of its income on energy. In 2007 some 10% of the 2.5 million homes were deemed to be fuel poor. By mid-2008, in the wake of soaring costs for gas and electricity, this figure had risen to 20% and by the end of 2008 it was reported as having reached 35%. There are simple ways of reducing the fuel costs of heating buildings, including cavity wall insulation, changing to low-energy lighting, installing thermostatic valves on radiators, insulating the loft and installing double or secondary glazed windows and doors (Table 16.2). To put these measures into the average house takes around five days to complete. Scotland has a range of more 'hard to treat' home types such as tenements, and because of the problem of rising levels of fuel poverty the Scottish Government is investing in improvement of this stock in particular.[28]

What would be the cost of taking such measures? Rajat Gupta's study at 2005 prices indicated that to treat the entire UK building stock to achieve over 60% reductions in energy use and emissions would cost the UK economy in the region of £200–£250 billion. The UK economy at its height was worth around £1.7 trillion (£1700 billion) so the cost to the economy of future-proofing every house would be around 1–2% of gross domestic product (GDP), each year for 10 years.

Table 16.2. Benefits of secondary glazing installation programme

Environmental	Improving the energy efficiency
	Reducing carbon emissions
Social	Increasing internal thermal comfort and reducing weather-related mortality rates
	Reducing fuel poverty and enhancing occupant well-being
	Improving occupant health, reducing indoor moisture and mould, lowering related costs
	Sound-proofing homes and thus improving the quality of life for occupants in them
	Providing a visible deterrent/barrier to burglars for exposed and vulnerable people
Economic	Increasing employment/local skills base
	Cycling local cash within the community

Source: Sue Roaf.

Colin Challen, the crusading low-carbon MP, points out that the railway transformation in Britain occurred is a similarly short period. The first passenger railway was built in 1832 and by 1844 'railway mania' had set in. By then there were 240 proposals for new lines before Parliament, worth around £100 million at a time when the UK GDP was worth around that mark per annum. By 1850, around 6000 miles of railway lines had been built. As we have seen today the money can be found if necessary, for instance to bail out the creaking twentieth century car industry with billions of dollars and pounds in loans, on which there are no guarantees that they will ever be paid back if the companies ultimately fail.

While such sums are speedily invested in often obsolete business structures, products and industries, why is strategic new money not being found to invest in future-proofing the ordinary family against climate change? In the process of making every building low energy and low impact, strong local industries and communities would also be developed. The cost of investing in energy efficiency and renewables is often not realistically costed by pundits. For instance, energy generated by photovoltaics (PVs) is typically compared to the cost of baseload energy supplies from coal and nuclear plants (see p. 298), whereas in urban contexts PV electricity typically displaces peak air conditioning loads in commercial buildings. PVs can be effectively used to reduce increasingly unaffordable summer cooling peak loads. Wind energy effectively displaces winter evening peak loads. Costed into the benefits of future-proofing citizens should be the added value of building the low-carbon economy.

The PV market has been growing at an average of over 40% per annum for the last five years. How much more sensible to invest in this sector than in manufacturing capacity producing environmentally disastrous sports utility vehicles (SUVs)? Yet it is the SUV/car industry that gets the enormous injections of government cash to prop up its failed models. In the First and Second World Wars car factories were turned into tank and munitions factories almost overnight. The same could happen again in the dying towns of the rust belt of North America, which could be turned over to producing wind turbines and wave power generators and ensure themselves a viable future. Reinforcing locally economies has huge benefits in terms of paying for the improvement in housing stock and related health, thus resulting in savings on health bills. Finally, one cost that is not factored in to estimates of such investments is the social cost. The protests in Greece in 2009 cost the slowing economy an estimated minimum of 240 billion euro in lost business, damages and insurance payouts. The two weeks of violence saw around 600 shops and more homes destroyed, hurt consumer sentiment and damaged tourism, which represents nearly one-fifth of Greek GDP. A general strike added to the financial costs and from Greece civil distur-bances spread to adjoining countries. Widespread strikes in UK industry in January 2009 over the absence of jobs also caused huge financial damage but that only occurred after the wider economy had gone into massive decline. Far-sighted government is needed to keep communities together at times of rapid change.

2°C: SENSE AND SCIENCE – THE ADAPTIVE APPROACH

The 2°C Sense and Science approach is already promoted by many who espouse the 'techni-cal fix approach', amongst whom Amory Lovins is perhaps the best known. His work on 'Factor Four'[29] reductions in resource use, predicated on doubling production output while halving the resource and the environmental impacts, is seen as a credible foundation on which a low-carbon and resource-efficient economy could be built. How this approach deals with climate change is not developed.

The Sense and Science approach is exemplified by the report by Jake Hacker and Stephen Belcher, *Beating the Heat*,[30] in which a range of building types, including homes, schools and hospitals, is systematically modelled in future climates, modified and remodelled to review the cost and energy benefits of various different adaptational strategies. By looking at heat gains and losses, solar gain, windows, ventilation, temperature, humidity, wind speed, thermal mass, insu-lation, fabric performance and internal gains, buildings proved capable of being sensibly modified to remain habitable in a warmer future. To achieve this the best buildings have an appropriate form, have thermal mass, are naturally ventilated and shaded from the summer sun, and gener-ate much of their own energy. Efficient equipment plays a part in this mix but is not as important as getting the basic architecture of the building design right, learning how buildings provide shel-ter and thermal comfort in reality, and using adaptive standards with which to design truly passive buildings.

The Sense and Science approach is what should be done today, and can be funded through conventional funding routes, by the construction industry, with governments and research coun-cils, and it is what will pave the way for 3°C building- and community-level solutions. Associated with the Sense and Science approach must be the systematic dismantling of the barriers in the built environment to twenty-first century building types developing that were outlined at the end of Chapter 15. Businesses, services, professions, communities and ordinary people will need to 'reorder normality', rearrange the paths they take, and the costs they apportion, to make buildings happen, to plan carefully to future-proof their own lives and businesses.

The Sense and Science approach will take the lessons available from the growing number of books such as this and the decision makers in the built environment will 'get it'. They will begin to design the built environment to cope with climate change, in a post-Peak Oil economy, with a rapidly diminishing resource base and more polluted world. They are perhaps the most important people on this planet today because the quality of their decisions will colour all our lives in the coming decades.

The Sense and Science approach takes a broad and deep look at the risks we face. This is being done by individuals, communities, businesses, organizations and governments who appreciate that many risks may emerge from the cracks in time between the electoral and political planning horizons; boundaries between projects and areas of responsibility. It is increasingly understood that not only must Risk be quantified but responsibility for it must be attributed. If the decision is taken to wait and see because the uncertainty is too great to warrant taking action towards adaptation now, then we have to know who made that decision and they should under law be accountable for its consequences. If there is a lack of acceptance or understanding of risks associated with implementation, then if not doing anything results in negative consequences then the people who made that decision should be accountable if it was taken without due diligence.

The Sense and Science approach does not let people get away with negligence or actions that jeopardize the good of the Global Commons. A core requirement must be increasing the power of the law to combat the unscrupulous, to provide redress against wrongs and to allow open criticism of what is wrong or not working. This means revision of a range of laws including those on accountability for actions taken, for instance on the placing buildings in harm's way on flood plains. So be it if we can sue the local planner or minister who gave planning permission for developments that flood and flood others, as can happen in Sweden and France. So be it if we can sue architects or engineers for failure in their duty of care if their buildings overheat or flood if they can be shown to have been negligent, even through ignorance. High on the agenda for the revision of UK laws are those dealing with libel, where they protect the powerful at the expense of the common good.

THE 3°C SOLUTIONS: STRONG COMMUNITIES

In this book, you have the evidence of the scale of the impacts and trends that have gone before and that shed light on the future. The scale of the adaptation challenge ahead of us is enormous and will require both strong governments and strong communities to succeed. Set out in Tables 16.3 and 16.4 is a range of strategies that must be followed to ensure that we succeed in the endeavour.[31] If we are to achieve a generation of truly low-energy buildings, to manage the retreat of communities from coastal and riverine flood plains, to retool our industry for the low-carbon, fossil fuel-free future, we need strong and visionary government.

We are not talking about just rearranging the deck chairs on the Titanic. We are looking at the need, in the face of growing global populations, increasing resource depletion, and the slowing[32] and possible eventual collapse of the growth economies to change the direction our lives and societies are heading in. This means a reordering of society in such a way that equality of opportunity and access to resources becomes a reality and that the impacts of climate change are not disproportionately loaded onto one sector of society to the benefit of others.

A good place to start looking for ways forward is to go back to where we started, at the beginning of the fossil fuel age, when a lack of mobility meant that communities were inevitably close and dependent to a large extent on that which they could produce around them. If we look at what we have lost socially since then, a good place to start is with the works of Richard Putnam, who wrote of America's declining social capital. In 2000, in *Bowling Alone*,[33] he wrote on the realm of civic engagement and social connectedness and ably demonstrated that over the last three decades of the twentieth century there had been a fundamental shift in:

- **Political and civic engagement**. Voting, political knowledge, political trust and grassroots political activism are all down. Americans sign 30% fewer petitions and are 40% less likely to join a consumer boycott, as compared to just a decade or two ago. The declines are equally visible in non-political community life: membership and activity in all sorts of local clubs and

Table 16.3. Improving community resilience to extreme weather events, from studies done by the Insurance Council of Australia

	General insurance industry actions	Action by governments	Actions by individuals and businesses
1. Community understanding of weather related risks	• Provide industry advice and research to governments and the community regarding the probabilities and costs of extreme weather events	• Develop a concise public education campaign through an appropriate authority regarding specific climate change impacts and changes to extreme weather events for communities on a regional basis • Implement mandatory risk information disclosure and acceptance requirements as part of all State based property transfer regulations for all extant and predicted risks relevant to a property	• Use of the presented education information to make risk appropriate decisions regarding assets and operations as part of an annual risk assessment & management cycle
2. Risk appropriate land use planning and zoning	• Provide industry advice and guidance to governments and the community regarding the risk implications of particular developments and projects under consideration with regard to extreme weather events	• Implement risk appropriate land use planning legislation harmonized across all states to prevent inappropriate development on land subject to inundation, specifically: – no residential or commercial development should occur on land currently subject or predicted to be subject to a 1 in 50yr return period of inland flooding unless mitigation works have been carried out to maintain a 1 in 100yr risk exposure limit. – no residential or commercial development should occur on land currently subject to or predicted to become subject to a 1 in 50yr return period for storm surge unless mitigation works have been carried out to maintain a 1 in 100yr risk exposure limit Implement a southerly expansion of cyclone and wind storm related building codes to counter the predicted southerly expansion of severe cyclones Implement legislation harmonized across all states requiring mandatory disclosure of all known & predicted risk data by state & local governments to property purchasers during property conveyance and title search processes	• Use of the presented education information to make risk appropriate decisions regarding assets and operations as part of an annual risk assessment & management cycle

(Continued)

Table 16.3 Continued

	General insurance industry actions	Action by governments	Actions by individuals and businesses
3. Risk appropriate mitigation measures	• Provide industry advice and research to governments & the community regarding the observed benefits of improved mitigation, e.g. storm water drainage and flood levies • Provide industry data and event observations regarding failed or poorly performing mitigation infrastructure that has caused damage to the community	• Review current funding and approval mechanisms for Disaster Mitigation works, with a view to expansion of the fund to allow for more rapid implementation of mitigation works in high priority areas • Expansion of the current National Disaster Mitigation Program to include upgrades and repairs to critical stormwater and drainage systems	• Implement appropriate mitigation mechanisms on privately owned property in accordance with best practice recommendations from Standards Australia and/or Local Development Guidelines
4. Risk appropriate property protection standards	• Provide best practice guidance to property owners and developers regarding risk adaptation and mitigation steps for property facing extreme weather events & climate change impacts • Analyse and deliver pricing incentives for lower risk development involving risk improved property	• Expansion of the Building Code of Australia to incorporate property protection as a fundamental basis for consideration in building design and construction	• Property owners or developers – undertake a critical analysis of existing property protection measures available and implement measures that are appropriate to the risks predicted over the lifespan of the property

5. Financial risk mitigation in the community	• Develop and implement public education and financial literacy programs regarding personal financial risk mitigation • Undertake ongoing product development to cater to non-insured demographics parallel to any increasing demand • Continue insurance product innovation addressing extreme weather risks and rewarding sustainable or 'greener' behaviour that contributes to climate change reversal • Continue to perform catastrophe modelling and development of capitalization options to maintain a healthy and stable general insurance market • Continue to participate in global management of the insurance market cycle to facilitate availability of competitive & appropriate levels of general insurance in Australia	• Removal of taxes on all general insurance products, thereby encouraging greater adoption of personal financial risk mitigation	• Individuals & businesses in the community implement Business Continuity Planning that incorporates extreme weather initiated damage on essential assets as well as impacts on external resources or markets critically relied upon • Individuals & businesses in the community undertake practical assessment of the risks to assets and seek appropriate cover for those risks
6. Community emergency and recovery planning	• Ensure that the industry's catastrophe coordination arrangements keep pace with community needs and advancements in State recovery capabilities as climate change forces advancements in emergency response	• Continuous best practice review and capability development by Australian emergency response & recovery agencies, as the nature of extreme weather changes and new emergency response and recovery needs emerge	• Individuals & Businesses undertake appropriate disaster preparation and recovery planning before any extreme weather event occurs

Source: Kerrie Kelley, CEO.[31]

Table 16.4. Strategies for risk alleviation against climate change hazards sorted by exposure, vulnerability, strategy and solution theme

	Hazard	Exposure	Vulnerability	Solution	Theme
Sea level Hazard level 1	70 cm to 4/7 m By 2100	Low coastal sites Storm tracks Marine pinch-points	All buildings/settlements Lack warnings/information Restricted evacuation Unregulated developer greed	IERC, MP, MR, SC Strengthen defences Map exposure, IP, PS	Good planning Nationalize/invest Education New laws
Flooding	More intense rainfall	Flood plains	All buildings/settlements	Map exposure, IP, PS	Education
Hazard level 1		Dam, canal, levee shadows Low-lying adjacent area	Restricted evacuation Poor drainage infrastructure Lack warnings/information Civil unrest Unregulated developer greed	IERC, MP, MR, SC, CR Infrastructure investment	Good planning Nationalize/invest New laws
Fire	Escalating intensity	Settlement edges	Low water reserves	Increase water storage	Nationalize/invest
Hazard level 2	Hotter, stronger winds	Low-density settlements	Timber buildings Poor fire-fighting resource Restricted evacuation Lack warnings/information	Building Regulations IERC, MP, MR, SC, Strengthen defences Map Exposure, IP, PS	Decisive government Good planning Nationalize/invest Education
Heat Hazard level 2	2°C to 6°C	Geomorphological location Heat island Location in city/building	Poor buildings; PS Weak communities Poor health services	Building Regulations Reduce heat island Educate construction industry	Decisive government Education Education
		To atypical temp. range	Energy supply failures Response relies on energy Lack warnings/information Civil unrest	Affordable secure energy Reduce energy demand IERC, MP, MR, SC, CR Importable solutions	Nationalize/invest Education Good planning Decisive government

				Map exposure, IP, PS	Education
Storms	More intense lows	Morphing storm tracks	Poor buildings		
Hazard level 2		Geomorphological location Location in city/building	Restricted evacuation	Building Regulations	Decisive government
Freezing	Cold snaps, ice storms	Geomorphological location	Lack warnings/information	IERC, MP, MR, SC, CR	Good planning
			Poor buildings, PS	Building Regulations	Decisive government
Hazard level 2		To atypical temp. range Location in city/building	Remoteness/isolation	Importable solutions	Education
			Poor health services	Educate construction industry	Education
			Energy supply failures	Affordable secure energy	Nationalize/invest
			Response relies on energy	Reduce energy demand	Education
Drought	Multi-year	Lack of water, transient sources	Lack warnings/information Too many people	IERC, MP, MR, SC, CR IERC, MP, MR, SC	Good planning Good planning
Hazard level 3	Melting ice	Reduction, transient sources	Poor water quality	Clean water programme	Nationalize/invest
			Poor water storage capacity	Increase water storage	Nationalize/invest
			Civil unrest	Importable solutions	New laws

Source: Sue Roaf. IERC: increase emergency response capacity; MP: move populations; MR: managed retreat; IP: insurance pricing; PS: paradigm shift building/community type; SC: strong communities; CR: climate refuges.

civic and religious organizations have been falling at an accelerating pace. In the mid-1970s the average American attended some club meeting every month, by 1998 that rate of attendance had been cut by nearly 60%.

- **Informal social ties**. In 1975 the average American entertained friends at home 15 times per year; the equivalent figure (1998) is now barely half that. Virtually all leisure activities that involve doing something with someone else, from playing volleyball to playing chamber music, are declining.
- **Tolerance and trust**. Although Americans are more tolerant of one another than were previous generations, they trust one another less. Survey data provide one measure of the growth of dishonesty and distrust, but there are other indicators. For example, employment opportunities for police, lawyers, and security personnel were stagnant for most of this century; indeed, America had fewer lawyers per capita in 1970 than in 1900. In the last quarter century these occupations boomed, as people have increasingly turned to the courts and the police.

As M.K. Smith points out:[34]

We are not talking here simply about nostalgia for the 1950s. School performance, public health, crime rates, clinical depression, tax compliance, philanthropy, race relations, community development, census returns, teen suicide, economic productivity, campaign finance, even simple human happiness – all are demonstrably affected by how (and whether) we connect with our family and friends and neighbours and co-workers.

This growing disconnect has been highlighted by many writers, from Jane Jacobs[35] to Jonathan Neale.[36] To date, climate change mitigation and adaptation strategies have seldom been associated with the rethinking of social infrastructures, but the economic carnage that started in 2008 and the exposure of the underbelly of capitalism may change this.

The time has come to invest again in our communities. This is not the time to close and sell off our post offices to asset-stripping foreign companies, but rather to build them into the solid financial heart of all communities. This is not the time to sell off our playing fields and village halls, but to invest in them as social hubs from which strong communities can be grown. This is the time to invest in making every building into a decent shelter that can withstand extreme weather, that can harvest and store energy and water and provide us with the safe havens in which we can survive in relative, low-energy, comfort. This is not the time to start pulling the flood sirens out of communities, but rather putting them in.[37] Every community will have to be helped to build resilience, to learn how to live low-carbon lives,[38] to minimize its exposure to the hazards ahead, to protect its vulnerable and build local self-reliance. To achieve this we need to research, relearn, re-educate and rethink our economies, societies and relationship with the environment, and quickly. Two new professions are urgently needed, one that can calculate the capacity of our ecosystems and markets, and the second that can equitably allocate resources among our citizens, just as Aubrey Meyer has done for global CO_2 emissions in his work at the Global Commons Institute.[39] Then, of course, we need a strong, clear and far-sighted government that works for the good of the commons.

CONCLUSIONS

It is the responsibility of our generation to rebuild our world in such a way that our children and children's children can survive decently in a post-fossil fuel future in a rapidly changing climate. The scale of this apparently simple task is exacerbated by the fact that we are increasingly exceeding the capacity of many ecosystems to support human societies in the expectations to which they have become accustomed over the last century. Up until now much has been pretty normal, but from now on everything will be very different. The 'nice' decade, the happy half century, for many in the developed world is over. At the heart of this challenge is the apparently simple task of intelligently preparing our buildings and cities for the changes ahead.

We are through the 1°C warmer stage in the evolution of modern society. Now is the time to put aside the denial and the deniers. We must clean out the regulatory stables of their twentieth century vested interests and thinking. We must persuade all involved in the business of making buildings and cities happen of the urgent need to change our fundamental building paradigms and to draw up a plan to implement change.

The 2°C solutions will involve Sense and Science and low-carbon buildings, technologies, communities, economies and societies. In the built environment this will involve a systematic root and branch review of the form and functioning of our related professions and the policies, guidelines, regulations and standards they use to inform the form of our built environment.

We must begin designing today to put in place the 3°C solutions in time, centred around models of strong communities and resilient low-carbon buildings. To do so involves a reordering of our social structures on a bedrock of equity of opportunity and resource allocation, because without it, no one will be safe in a rapidly changing world. To do so requires us to reduce the exposure and the vulnerability of our populations to the growing climate hazards which in turn will require huge financial investment and difficult decisions on the planned retreat of communities and facilities to safer ground.

We have roughly estimated that this will require the UK Government to spend an estimated £10–15 billion per year over the next 10 years on improving the ageing housing stock in the UK alone. This is not money being poured 'down the drain', as it has been on wars and in banks. This money will be used to employ people in local communities who will, by spending their wages, inject it directly back into the economy, rather than hiding it in offshore tax havens like so many of the large multi-national corporations in the UK. Not least, low-energy buildings, combined with a reduction in private transport, will dramatically cut fossil fuel use, saving billions, reducing reliance on the unstable international fuel markets, extending the lifespan of the existing fossil fuel reserves and enabling us all to make renewable energy supplies sufficient for most of our needs. This is a workable plan for fuel security, unlike that involving the dash to coal or more nuclear generation capacity.

Designing for 3°C of climate change will need serious planning, at every level by all concerned. Planners, architects and engineers will need to work with government and the communities to bring the necessary deep changes about. Professional bodies such as RIBA, CIBSE and RICS will need to reorder their education programmes and run serious training campaigns to ensure that both the Science and the Sense is understood and implemented.[40] Building designers must be rapidly weaned off the current unsustainable design obsessions and building paradigms. Hubris must be left behind.

The efforts and the benefits of preparing and paying for our adaptation to a world with 3°C of climate change must be fairly distributed, and be seen to be so. Only a fair future is a safe future, for any of us.

Ozymandias
  Horace Smith (1779–1849)
In Egypt's sandy silence, all alone,
Stands a gigantic Leg, which far off throws
The only shadow that the desert knows.
'I am great Ozymandias' saith the stone,
'The King of Kings; this mighty city shows
The wonders of my hand.' The city's gone,
Nought but the leg remaining to disclose
The site of that forgotten Babylon.
We wonder, and some hunter may express
Wonder like ours, when through that wilderness
Where London stood, holding the wolf in chase
He meets some fragment huge, and stops to guess
What powerful but unrecorded race
Once dwelt in that annihilated place.

NOTES AND REFERENCES

1 The world population has risen from 1.65 billion in 1900 to 6.08 billion in 2000. The United Nations Population Division predicts that the world population will peak in 2040 at 7.47 billion and then begin to decline. See <http://www.ncpa.org/pi/internat/pd062200f.html>.

2 Per-capita consumption worldwide has increased by 3% per year during the past quarter century (<http://www.iisd.org/susprod/newbackground.htm>) and the rate of increase is rising rapidly with the expansion of the Indian and Chinese economies.

3 For full details of the Ross Garnaut Review see <http://www.garnautreview.org.au/>, 2008.

4 The best of the books is perhaps: P. Newton (Ed.), Transitions: Pathways Towards Sustainable Urban Development in Australia. CSIRO Publishing and Springer, 2008.

5 J. Nicol, S. Roaf, Adaptive thermal comfort and passive buildings. This describes the importance of understanding human behaviour to understand how best to design buildings, in: M. Santamouris (Ed.), Passive Cooling, James & James Science Publishers, 2007.

6 R. Gupta, Investigating the potential for local carbon dioxide emission reductions: developing a GIS-based domestic energy, carbon-counting and carbon-reduction model. Unpublished PhD thesis, Department of Architecture, Oxford, Oxford Brookes University, 2005.

7 The argument for a New Vernacular is put in S. Roaf, M. Fuentes, S. Thomas, Ecohouse: A Design Guide, Architectural Press, 2007. Ways in which we might go about training a new generation of young architects for the New Vernacular are dealt with in S. Meir, S. Roaf, The future of the vernacular: towards new methodologies for the understanding and optimisation of the performance of vernacular buildings, in: L. Asquith, M. Vellinga (Eds.), Vernacular Architecture in the Twenty-First Century: Theory, Education and Practice. Spon, London, 2005. Paul Oliver Feschrift volume.

8 P. Tuohy, For his full paper on this subject see <http://www.nceub.org.uk/index.php?pagename=Research.WindsorConference2008>.

9 S. Roaf, R. Gupta, Safe as solar houses, Chapter 2 in Nuclear Power Unnecessary, Dangerous and Expensive – The Case for a Non-nuclear Energy Strategy in the UK, 2007, this report was

designed by Kste Bryant and produced by Liz Day as the result of evidence presented to an audience at Portcullis House, Westminster, 28 November 2006. <http://www.nuclearpower-nothanks.co.uk>.

10 S. Roaf, R. Gupta, Optimising the value of domestic solar roofs: drivers and barriers in the UK, in: D. Elliot (Ed.), Sustainable Energy: Opportunities and Limitations: An Introductory Review of the Issues and Choices, Palgrave/McMillan, 2007.

11 S. Roaf, Drivers and barriers for water conservation and use in the UK, in: D. Butler, F. Memon (Eds.), Water Conservation and Reuse, Spon, 2005.

12 See <http://www.buildingsplatform.org>.

13 See <http://www.usablebuildingstrust.org> for excellent information on post-occupancy evaluation of buildings.

14 See <http://www.foe.co.uk>.

15 See <http://www.greenpeace.org.uk>.

16 See <http://www.campaigncc.org>.

17 See <http://www.wwf.org.uk>.

18 See <http://www.tcpa.org.uk>.

19 See <http://peopleandplanet.org>.

20 See <http://www.iclei.org> and <http://www.kyotousa.org>.

21 S. Roaf, M. Fuentes, R. Gupta, Solar cities: the Oxford solar initiative, see also the excellent work being done by Elaine Morrison in the Dundee Solar Cities organization on <http://www.dundeesuncity.org.uk>, in: M. Jenks (Ed.), Future Form and Design of Sustainable Cities, Architectural Press, 2005, pp. 355–371.

22 See <http://www.transitiontowns.org>.

23 See the journals Building for a Future (<http://www.buildingforafuture.co.uk>) and Environmental Building News (<http://www.buildinggreen.com>), the website of the Society of Building Science Educators (<http://www.sbse.org>) and Ed Mazria's great website: <http://www.architecture2030.org>.

24 R. Wilkinson, The Impact of Inequality: How to Make Sick Societies Healthier, Routledge, London, 2006.

25 The authors would particularly like to thank Peter Reid of Dunfirmline for his thoughtful contributions to the text on social equality and the importance of hinterland connections.

26 R.M. Titmuss, Essays on the Welfare State, Allen and Unwin, London, 1958.

27 See also R.M. Titmuss, Problems of Social Policy. HMSO, London, 1950. See <http://www.ibiblio.org/hyperwar/UN/UK/UK-Civil-Social/index.html>. This publication was one in the History of the Second World War, United Kingdom Series, edited by W.K. Hancock.

28 S. Roaf, K. Baker, A. Peacock, Evidence on Tackling Hard to Treat Properties, a study conducted for the Scottish Government, August 2008. See <http://www.scotland.gov.uk/Publications/2008/10/17095821/0>.

29 E. Von Weizacker, A. Lovins, L.H. Lovins, Facto Four: Doubling Wealth, Halving Resource Use, Allen and Unwin, Sydney, 1997.

30 J. Hacker, Beating the Heat, <http://www.arup.com/_assets/_download/download396.pdf>, 2005.

31 Insurance Council of Australia, Improving Community Resilience to Climate Change, For full report see <http://www.insurancecouncil.com.au/Portals/24/Issues/Community%20 Resilience%20Policy%20150408.pdf>, 2008, This table was shown by Kerry Kelly, CEO of the Insurance Council of Australia, at her talk at the Sustainable Building Conference 08 in Melbourne, Australia, in the first session on Adapting Buildings and Cities for Climate Change. For a podcast of the session see <http://www.sbo8.org>.

32 T. Trainer, Transitioning to a simpler way, in: P. Newton (Ed.), Transitions: Pathways towards Sustainable Urban Development in Australia, CSIRO Publications and Springer, Australia, 2008, pp. 667–674.

33 See R.D. Putnam, Bowling alone: America's declining social capital. J. of Democracy, 6(1) (1995) 65–78.

34 M.K. Smith, Robert Putnam. in: The Encyclopaedia of Informal Education, <http://www.infed. org/thinkers/putnam.htm>. See also <http://www.bowlingalone.com/media.php3>, 2001, 2007.

35 J. Jacobs, The Death and Life of Great American Cities, Random, New York, 1961.

36 J. Neale, Stop Global Warming – Change the World, Bookmarks Publications, London, 2008.

37 In January 2009 the Environment Agency and the police began the process of removing the 57 sirens from the coastal communities of Norfolk that are vulnerable to coastal flooding and in which many died during the floods of 1953, to the concern of many local communities. They decided that a better warning mechanism was by telephone. See Caroline Davies in the Observer, 1 February 2009, p. 23.

38 See <http://www.gci.org.uk/>.

39 For good guides to low-carbon living see <http://www.lowcarbonlife.net> and <http://www. carbondetox.org>.

40 See the Report on Green Jobs: Towards Decent Work in a Sustainable, Low-Carbon World from the International Labour Organization on: <http://www.ilo.org/global/What_we_do/Publications/ Newreleases/lang-en/docName-WCMS_098503/index.htm>. It concludes that the global market for environmental products and services is projected to double from US$1370 billion per year at present to US$2740 billion by 2020, according to a study cited in the report: Half of this market is in energy efficiency; clean technologies are already the third largest sector for venture capital and renewable energy generates more jobs than employment in fossil fuels. Projected investments of US$630 billion by 2030 would translate into at least 20 million additional jobs in the renewable energy sector.

41 For a great book on buildings and cities as part of our ecosystems see P. Newman, I. Jennings, Cities as Sustainable Ecosystems: Principles and Practices. Island Press, Washington, 2008.

LIST OF ABBREVIATIONS

ABI:	Association of British Insurers
AGCM:	atmospheric general circulation model
ANSI:	American National Standards Institute
API:	American Petroleum Institute
AR4:	Fourth Assessment Report
ARB:	Architect's Registration Board
ASHRAE:	American Society of Heating, Refrigeration and Air conditioning Engineers
BGS:	British Geological Survey
BKCC:	Building Knowledge for a Changing Climate
BMS:	building management system
BRE:	Building Research Establishment
CABE:	Commission for Architecture and the Built Environment
CDM:	Construction Design and Management
CEBE:	Centre for Education in the Built Environment
CEN:	Comité Européen de Normalisation (European Committee for Standardisation)
CFC:	chlorofluorocarbon
CHP:	combined heat and power
CIBSE:	Chartered Institution of Building Services Engineers
CII:	Chartered Insurance Institute
CO$_2$:	carbon dioxide
COP-1:	First Conference of the Parties
CRED:	Center for Research in the Epidemiology of Disasters
DEC:	Display Energy Certificate
DEFRA:	Department of the Environment, Food and Rural Affairs
DFID:	Department of Food and International Development
DTI:	Department for Trade and Industry
DU:	Dobson Unit
EA:	Environment Agency
EC:	European Commission
EPBD:	Energy Performance of Buildings Directive
EPC:	Energy Performance Certificate
ESCO:	energy service company

ETS:	emissions trading scheme
EU:	European Union
GCM:	general circulation model
GDP:	gross domestic product
GWP:	Global Warming Potential
HC:	hydrocarbon
HFC:	hydrofluorocarbon
HSE:	Health and Safety Executive
HVAC:	heating, ventilation and air conditioning
ICE:	Institution of Civil Engineers
IEA:	International Energy Agency
IMF:	International Monetary Fund
IMO:	International Maritime Organization
IPCC:	Intergovernmental Panel on Climate Change
ISO:	International Organization for Standardization
ITPOES:	Industry Taskforce on Peak Oil & Energy Security
IUCN:	International Union of Conservationists
LEED:	Leading in Energy and Environmental Design
LNG:	liquid natural gas
MPGL:	master power generating licence
NC:	National Certification
NDA:	Nuclear Decommissioning Authority
NGO:	non-governmental organization
PCB:	polychlorinated biphenyl
PFC:	perfluorocarbon
PFI:	Private Finance Initiative
PLEA:	passive low-energy architecture
PMV:	predicted mean vote
PPG:	planning policy guideline
PV:	photovoltaic
RCEP:	Royal Commission Report on Environmental Pollution
RIBA:	Royal Institute of British Architects
RPZ:	registered power zone
SBSE:	Society of Building Science Educators
SBSTA:	Subsidiary Body for Scientific and Technological Advice
SCEP:	Study of Critical Environmental Problems
SEPA:	Scottish Environment Protection Agency
SET:	standard effective temperature
SMIC:	*Study of Man's Impact on the Climate*
SSMI:	Special Sensor Microwave Imager
STP:	standard temperature and pressure
SUDS:	sustainable drainage system
TUC:	Trades Union Congress
UKCIP:	UK Climate Impacts Programme
UNESCO:	United Nations Educational, Scientific, and Cultural Organization

UNEP:	United Nations Environment Program
UNFCCC:	United Nations Framework Convention on Climate Change
UNHCR:	United Nations High Commissioner for Refugees
UPS:	uninterruptible power supply
USGBC:	US Green Building Council
UV:	ultraviolet
WHO:	World Health Organization

INDEX